Emerging AI, Governance, and Digital Innovations for Sustainable Organizations

Muhammad Anshari
Universiti Brunei Darussalam, Brunei

Patricia Ordóñez de Pablos
The University of Oviedo, Spain

Mohammad Nabil Almunawar
https://orcid.org/0000-0001-5296-2576
Universiti Brunei Darussalam, Brunei

IGI Global
Scientific Publishing
Publishing Tomorrow's Research Today

Vice President of Editorial	Melissa Wagner
Director of Acquisitions	Mikaela Felty
Director of Book Development	Jocelynn Hessler
Production Manager	Mike Brehm
Cover Design	Jose Rosado

Published in the United States of America by
IGI Global Scientific Publishing
701 East Chocolate Avenue
Hershey, PA, 17033, USA
Tel: 717-533-8845 | Fax: 717-533-7115
Website: https://www.igi-global.com E-mail: cust@igi-global.com

Library of Congress Cataloging-in-Publication Data

ames: Anshari, Muhammad, 1977- editor | Ordóñez de Pablos, Patricia, 1975- editor | Almunawar, Mohammad Nabil, 1960- editor

Title: Emerging AI, Governance, and Digital Innovations for Sustainable Organizations / edited by Muhammad Anshari, Patricia Ordóñez de Pablos, Mohammad Nabil Almunawar.

Description: Hershey, PA: IGI Global Scientific Publishing, [2026] | Includes bibliographical references. | Summary: "This book explores how AI, robotics, and human-robot collaboration are transforming organizational structures, workforce dynamics, and governance. Blending research, case studies, and practical insights, it offers a multidisciplinary guide to building sustainable, ethical, and innovative organizations in an era of intelligent automation"-- Provided by publisher.

Identifiers: LCCN 2026002987 (print) | LCCN 2026002988 (ebook) | ISBN 9798337386072 (hardcover) | ISBN 9798337386089 (paperback) | ISBN 9798337386096 (ebook)

Subjects: LCSH: Artificial intelligence--Business applications | LCGFT: Essays

Classification: LCC HD45 . E3643 2026 (print) | LCC HD45 (ebook)

LC record available at https://lccn.loc.gov/2026002987

LC ebook record available at https://lccn.loc.gov/2026002988

British Cataloguing in Publication Data
A Cataloguing in Publication record for this book is available from the British Library.

Editorial Advisory Board and List of Reviewers

Editorial Advisory Board

List of Reviewers

Table of Contents

Detailed Table of Contents

AI integration in keeps to transform the nature of governance as AI's capacity to process big data, pattern detection, simulations, predictive analysis, enables evidence-based decision-making to foster inclusivity and responsiveness. AI helps policymakers to design public engagement mechanism, policy interventions that are responsive, transparent, support participatory approaches. AI adoption in policy discourse raises ethical concerns regarding data privacy, fairness, transparency, accountability needs to frame robust regulatory mechanism for interdisciplinary collaboration. The study focuses on AI inclusion transforms policy discourse, makes process inclusive, responsive by identifying AI tools enhance informed decisions, and citizen role in policymaking. Findings depict, AI significant role mends capacity of policymakers, leads to citizen-centric governance. AI benefits in policymaking demand to address key ethical concerns to uphold digital equity

The use of Artificial Intelligence (AI) to support work processes has become a common practice in various organizations. With the increasing adoption of AI in various organizational functions, the interaction between human capabilities and AI systems has become a central issue in achieving optimal performance. Employee-AI Collaboration is increasingly becoming a critical factor in enhancing organizational productivity in the digital era. This study conceptually explores how Employee-AI Collaboration can contribute to Organizational Productivity through the mediating roles of Employee Performance, Knowledge Sharing, and Decision-Making Effectiveness. The synergy between humans and AI is expected to improve operational efficiency, accelerate the flow of knowledge, and support more accurate and timely decision-making processes. Understanding the mediation mechanism provides strategic insights for organizations in effectively integrating AI to promote productivity through human and technological collaboration.

Artificial intelligence (AI) is rapidly becoming central to governance, raising concerns about accountability, fairness, and long-term social impact. Brunei Darussalam, guided by the national philosophy of Melayu Islam Beraja (MIB), offers a distinctive case for reflection through its prohibition-oriented approach to drug use and trade. The study found that prohibition reflects taw īd and the maqā id al-sharīʿah, particularly the preservation of life (if al-nafs) and intellect (if al-ʿaql), yet also revealed persistent recidivism, limited shūrā (consultation and coordination), and reintegration processes that require further strengthening in the face of stigma and employment barriers. To interpret these dynamics, the chapter applies Basma Abdelgafar's (2018) Public Policy in Islam (PPI) framework, which emphasises taw īd, maqā id, shūrā, and i lā . It argues that insights from Brunei's drug governance can inform AI regulation by framing technology as "governed infrastructure," highlighting both opportunities for support and risks of bias or exclusion.

Artificial intelligence (AI) is increasingly seen as a crucial instrument for tackling the most serious difficulties confronting modern industry, including the quest of sustainability. The usage of AI is assisting businesses in navigating corporate sustainability difficulties, but present research lacks a thorough examination of how firms employ AI to improve sustainability. Finally, this paper provides an integrated paradigm for sustainability-oriented AI adoption, emphasizing the need of connecting AI activities with organizational sustainability goals in order to preserve a competitive edge and drive development. As a result, it emphasizes the importance of strong data management, system integration, and continuous performance monitoring in order to eliminate opposition to AI adoption and fully realize AI's promise in the quest of sustainability.

The rapid growth of digital technology has transformed marketing, particularly in social commerce, where AI-driven personalization enhances customer experience and efficiency. This study uses a systematic literature review (SLR) to analyze its impact, benefits, and challenges for SMEs in developing countries. AI enables real-time data analysis, personalized recommendations, and automated customer service, boosting engagement and conversion rates while reducing costs. However, SMEs face financial constraints, low digital literacy, and data privacy concerns, alongside competition from large platforms. Despite these barriers, AI-driven personalization remains crucial for sustainable growth. Future research should explore AI adoption models, policy frameworks, and strategies to overcome challenges, providing valuable insights for SMEs seeking competitive advantage.

As organizations navigate the Fourth Industrial Revolution, the use of AI and robotics in core business functions is essential. This research analyzes Human-Robotic Collaboration (HRC) as a driver for augmented organizations combining human and machine intelligence to boost productivity, agility, and innovation. It highlights key requirements for AI empowerment, such as data infrastructure, ethical governance,

Preface

The accelerating convergence of artificial intelligence (AI), robotics, and expert systems is reshaping the foundations of modern organizations. Across both public and private sectors, we are witnessing a profound transformation in how work is conceived, structured, and executed. As robots and intelligent systems become increasingly embedded in organizational processes, Human–Robot Collaboration (HRC) is emerging not as a distant possibility, but as a defining feature of contemporary organizational life.

The content that follows in this volume "*Emerging AI, Governance, and Digital Innovations for Sustainable Organizations*" captures this pivotal moment. Organizations across industries are deploying advanced technologies alongside human talent to enhance productivity, streamline operations, and expand the boundaries of innovation. These developments offer extraordinary opportunities to reimagine business models and address complex societal and operational challenges.

Yet, the integration of HRC also presents new and pressing questions. How do organizations prepare their workforces for collaboration with autonomous systems? What ethical and governance frameworks are needed to ensure responsible and equitable deployment? How will organizational cultures, structures, and strategies adapt in response to intelligent machines becoming part of everyday workflows? This edited book addresses these questions by examining the multifaceted dynamics of HRC and its implications for organizational design, change management, and operational strategy.

Our primary aims in curating this volume are to:

- Investigate the opportunities and challenges posed by HRC in organizational contexts.
- Analyze how HRC influences business processes, organizational models, and workforce dynamics.
- Highlight practical implementations of robots, AI, and expert systems alongside human teams.

- Provide insights into the future of work in organizations embracing HRC.

The chapters that follow bring together research, case studies, and theoretical perspectives from a diverse range of sectors including manufacturing, healthcare, public administration, and service industries. Through these contributions, we hope to illuminate the evolving relationship between humans and robotic systems, offering readers both depth of understanding and actionable insights.

This volume is designed for academic researchers, students, practitioners, policymakers, and organizational leaders who seek to engage with the rapid technological shifts redefining work and organizational sustainability. Whether you are analyzing the societal impacts of automation, designing new governance frameworks, or implementing HRC initiatives in practice, we hope this book serves as a valuable resource and a catalyst for further inquiry.

As editors, we extend our gratitude to the contributing authors for their rigorous scholarship and to the readers who continue to explore and shape the future of human–machine collaboration. We invite you to engage deeply with the ideas presented here and to join the ongoing conversation on how emerging AI and digital innovations can empower sustainable, resilient, and human-centered organizations.

ORGANIZATION OF THE BOOK

Chapter 1: AI Integration Enhancing Inclusivity and Responsiveness in Public Policy Development

The opening chapter examines how artificial intelligence is reshaping the governance landscape, particularly through its powerful capacities for data processing, pattern detection, simulation, and predictive analytics. These capabilities enable more evidence-based, inclusive, and responsive policymaking by supporting tailored public engagement mechanisms and transparent decision-making processes. At the same time, the chapter underscores that AI's growing influence introduces critical ethical considerations surrounding data privacy, fairness, transparency, and accountability. Through an exploration of contemporary tools and citizen-centered applications, the authors argue that AI can strengthen policymakers' capabilities and foster more participatory governance. Yet they emphasize that these benefits are contingent upon robust regulatory frameworks and interdisciplinary collaboration that safeguard digital equity and ensure responsible use.

Chapter 2: Employee-AI Collaboration and Organizational Productivity

This chapter provides a conceptual exploration of how collaboration between employees and AI systems can enhance organizational productivity. With AI increasingly embedded across sectors, understanding the interplay between human capabilities and intelligent technologies has become essential. The authors highlight employee performance, knowledge sharing, and decision-making effectiveness as key mediating mechanisms that shape the impact of Employee–AI Collaboration on productivity. By accelerating information flows, improving operational efficiency, and enhancing the precision of decisions, the synergy between humans and machines emerges as a strategic pathway for digital-era competitiveness. The chapter offers organizations practical insights into designing AI integration efforts that empower employees rather than displace them, ultimately fostering more resilient and productive workplaces.

Chapter 3: Islamic Governance and AI: Insights from Brunei Darussalam

Drawing from Brunei Darussalam's governance of illicit drug use and trade, this chapter offers a unique lens through which to examine AI's role in moral and ethical governance frameworks. Rooted in the national philosophy of Melayu Islam Beraja (MIB), Brunei's prohibition-oriented approach is interpreted through foundational Islamic principles, particularly those relating to the preservation of life and intellect. The analysis reveals both strengths and ongoing challenges such as limited consultation mechanisms and reintegration barriers that complicate policy effectiveness. By applying Basma Abdelgafar's Public Policy in Islam (PPI) framework, the authors propose a broader perspective on AI as "governed infrastructure," capable of supporting inclusive policy goals while also posing risks of bias, exclusion, and weakened accountability. Through this case, the chapter provides valuable insights for developing AI governance models that are ethically grounded and socially attuned.

Chapter 4: AI-Driven Robotics for Organizational Change Toward Sustainability

Chapter 4 explores the emerging role of AI-driven robotics as a catalyst for organizational transformation toward sustainability. While AI has become central to tackling complex ecological and operational challenges, the authors highlight a persistent gap in understanding how organizations strategically deploy AI to achieve sustainability outcomes. Their integrated paradigm emphasizes aligning AI initiatives with broader sustainability goals, supported by strong data governance, robust system integration, and ongoing performance assessment. The chapter argues that overcoming internal resistance and ensuring cohesive digital strategies are vital to realizing AI's full potential in driving sustainable innovation. Ultimately, it positions AI-driven robotics as a powerful enabler of competitive advantage and long-term organizational resilience.

Chapter 5: AI-Driven Personalization in Social Commerce for SME Sustainability in Developing Countries

In the context of rapidly expanding digital markets, this chapter examines how AI-powered personalization is transforming social commerce and shaping the sustainability of small and medium enterprises (SMEs) in developing nations. Through a systematic literature review, the authors demonstrate how real-time analytics, tailored recommendations, and automated customer support systems can boost engagement, improve customer satisfaction, and expand revenue opportunities. Nevertheless, SMEs often face substantial barriers including limited financial resources, inadequate digital literacy, and mounting data privacy concerns that hinder effective AI adoption. Despite these challenges, the chapter affirms AI-driven personalization as an essential driver of competitive advantage and long-term viability. It concludes with a call for future research on adoption strategies, regulatory frameworks, and capacity-building initiatives that can help SMEs fully leverage AI-enabled social commerce.

Chapter 6: Building the Foundations of Augmented Organizations through AI Empowerment

This chapter investigates how AI and robotics serve as foundational drivers in the emergence of augmented organizations enterprises that combine human and machine intelligence to achieve superior agility, innovation, and productivity. Highlighting the requirements for successful AI empowerment, including robust data infrastructure, ethical governance, and widespread digital literacy, the authors examine how AI alters workforce structures, job designs, and decision-making processes. Drawing on real-world examples across industries, they illustrate AI's potential to improve safety, elevate employee satisfaction, and enhance organizational performance. The chapter also addresses critical challenges, such as resistance to change, skill shortages, and algorithmic bias, emphasizing the importance of human-centered design principles. It concludes by advocating for trust-based ecosystems where continuous learning and collaboration underpin the evolution of augmented organizations.

Chapter 7: Blockchain-Enabled KPI Systems for Flexible Work Arrangements

Focusing on the growing shift toward flexible work models, this chapter presents an insightful study on organizational readiness for blockchain-based key performance indicator (KPI) systems in Brunei Darussalam. With flexible working arrangements such as Work from Anywhere and Flextime becoming increasingly prevalent, the chapter proposes a blockchain-enabled performance measurement framework supported by 5G infrastructure. Using mixed methods, including surveys, sentiment analysis, and forecasting tools, the authors reveal strong organizational interest in transparent, accountable, and technologically supported performance tracking. Their findings suggest that with adequate policy backing and digital infrastructure, blockchain-integrated KPI systems can significantly enhance trust, productivity, and fairness in remote work environments. The chapter positions blockchain not merely as a technological upgrade but as a fundamental enabler of future-ready workforce management.

Chapter 8: Autonomous Systems in Agriculture—An Innovation Framework

This chapter delves into the transformative impact of autonomous systems on agriculture, emphasizing how AI, robotics, and data analytics are reshaping global food production. The authors propose a comprehensive innovation framework that integrates technological, economic, institutional, environmental, and social dimensions to guide the sustainable deployment of autonomous agricultural technologies. Through historical reflections, case studies, and policy analyses, the chapter identifies key enablers such as infrastructure development and digital competence alongside persistent barriers, including regulatory gaps and disparities in access to innovation. A core argument centers on the need for ethical and inclusive innovation strategies to ensure that smallholders benefit from technological advancements and that agricultural systems remain ecologically resilient. This framework provides a strategic tool for aligning digital transformation with global sustainability objectives, particularly those articulated in the UN Sustainable Development Goals.

Chapter 9: Navigating Organizational Culture Shifts in the Modern Business Landscape

The final chapter explores the pivotal role of organizational culture in navigating the rapid technological and demographic shifts shaping contemporary business environments. By integrating theoretical models including Schein's organizational culture framework and Hofstede's cultural dimensions with real-world case studies, the authors provide a nuanced account of how organizations adapt to digitalization, AI integration, hybrid work arrangements, and increased demands for diversity and inclusion. The chapter highlights the centrality of employee engagement, leadership behavior, and structured change management practices in fostering sustainable cultural transformation. It concludes by emphasizing the importance of cultural agility and ethical leadership as organizations confront the evolving challenges of the future of work, underscoring culture as both a strategic asset and a catalyst for long-term resilience.

CONCLUSION

As we bring this volume to a close, we reflect on the breadth and depth of insights presented across its chapters' insights that collectively illuminate a transformative moment in organizational life. The integration of AI, robotics, autonomous systems, and digital innovations is no longer a distant prospect but a defining force shaping governance, industry, and society at large. Through research grounded in diverse contexts from public policy and Islamic governance to social commerce, agriculture, and organizational culture this book demonstrates that technological change is multifaceted, deeply contextual, and fundamentally human in its implications.

A common thread running through these contributions is the recognition that technology's value is realized not merely through adoption, but through thoughtful integration that centers ethics, inclusivity, and sustainability. Whether examining flexible work arrangements supported by blockchain, citizen-centric policymaking empowered by AI, or augmented organizations built on human–machine collaboration, the chapters highlight a shared imperative: organizations must align digital innovation with their broader mission, values, and societal responsibilities.

At the same time, the volume underscores that the journey toward AI-enabled and sustainable organizations is complex. It requires robust governance frameworks, interdisciplinary collaboration, digitally literate workforces, and leadership capable of navigating uncertainty with vision and integrity. As editors, we are encouraged by the growing global commitment to responsible innovation and by the practical, actionable frameworks our contributors offer for advancing this commitment.

This book aims not only to capture the present state of emerging technologies but also to stimulate further inquiry and dialogue. We hope it serves as both a scholarly resource and a catalyst for practitioners, policymakers, and researchers seeking to shape the future of work and governance in ways that are equitable, transparent, and human-centered. The ongoing evolution of AI and digital systems presents unprecedented opportunities to build more resilient, responsive, and sustainable organizations and it is our collective responsibility to ensure that these opportunities are realized for the benefit of all.

Muhammad Anshari
Patricia Ordóñez de Pablos
Mohammad Nabil Almunawar
Editors

Introduction

THE AI TRANSFORMATION

The rapid evolution of artificial intelligence (AI) and its derivative technologies (machine learning, deep learning, generative models, and autonomous systems) is fundamentally reshaping organizational practices, public policy, and societal structures. No longer a futuristic vision, AI is now embedded in decision-making processes across business, government, and civil society.

Its extraordinary capacities for large-scale data processing, pattern recognition, simulation, and predictive analytics offer unprecedented opportunities to build more efficient, inclusive, and sustainable organizations. However, these very same capabilities also expand risks including algorithmic bias, social exclusion, loss of human agency, environmental harm, and the erosion of public trust when deployed without strong and purposeful governance.

The Governance Imperative

This edited volume argues that AI's transformative potential can only be fully and responsibly realized through robust, value-driven governance frameworks that purposefully align people, processes, and technology. Effective AI governance must guide developers, AI providers, corporations, programmers, and policymakers in designing, deploying, and monitoring algorithms that are fair, transparent, auditable, and deliberately free from harmful bias.

Fairness is not merely a technical criterion. It is a prerequisite for genuine inclusivity, ensuring that AI systems do not perpetuate historical inequalities based on gender, race, ethnicity, socioeconomic status, disability, or geography.

AI and Environmental Sustainability

The sustainability imperative demands that AI itself becomes a positive force for the planet and its inhabitants. From energy-intensive training of large language models to the lifecycle carbon footprint of data centers, AI's environmental costs are significant and growing.

Beyond mitigation, AI must actively support the United Nations Sustainable Development Goals (SDGs) and the broader agenda of sustainable organizations. This includes:

- Optimizing resource use in supply chains
- Enabling precision agriculture
- Improving healthcare equity
- Enhancing circular economies
- Informing climate-resilient urban planning

Transforming Public Services

In public services, AI is redefining the governance landscape. Advanced analytics and real-time data flows empower evidence-based policymaking, predictive resource allocation, personalized citizen services, and more participatory forms of democracy through digital deliberation platforms and sentiment analysis of public feedback.

Nevertheless, these advances raise profound ethical and legal questions:

- Who owns the data that trains public-sector AI?
- How do we prevent algorithmic discrimination in welfare distribution, criminal justice, or hiring?
- How can citizens hold opaque "black-box" systems accountable?

The answers lie in regulatory frameworks that embed universal values (human dignity, justice, solidarity, and stewardship of the common good) into every layer of the AI lifecycle, from conception and training to deployment.

Values at the Core

This book contends that AI and its derivative technologies cannot be treated as value-neutral tools. Every line of code, every training dataset, and every objective function encodes choices that reflect particular worldviews and power relations.

Consequently, universal values must serve as the governing compass for AI applications in both private and public sectors, across all industries. Only by proactively embedding these values can we ensure that digital innovations serve the successful of people rather than their exploitation.

Muhammad Anshari
Patricia Ordóñez de Pablos
Mohammad Nabil Almunawar
Editors

Chapter 1
AI Integration Enhancing Inclusivity and Responsiveness in Public Policy Development

Muhammad Asfand yar
https://orcid.org/0000-0002-1598-5629
Universiti Brunei Darussalam, Brunei

Mahani Hamdan
https://orcid.org/0000-0003-3859-4433
Universiti Brunei Darussalam, Brunei

Muhammad Anshari
https://orcid.org/0000-0002-8160-6682
Universiti Brunei Darussalam, Brunei

ABSTRACT

AI integration in keeps to transform the nature of governance as AI's capacity to process big data, pattern detection, simulations, predictive analysis, enables evidence-based decision-making to foster inclusivity and responsiveness. AI helps policymakers to design public engagement mechanism, policy interventions that are responsive, transparent, support participatory approaches. AI adoption in policy discourse raises ethical concerns regarding data privacy, fairness, transparency, accountability needs to frame robust regulatory mechanism for interdisciplinary collaboration. The study focuses on AI inclusion transforms policy discourse, makes process inclusive, responsive by identifying AI tools enhance informed decisions,

DOI: 10.4018/979-8-3373-8607-2.ch001

and citizen role in policymaking. Findings depict, AI significant role mends capacity of policymakers, leads to citizen-centric governance. AI benefits in policymaking demand to address key ethical concerns to uphold digital equity

1. INTRODUCTION

AI integration in public policy development process keeps to transform the nature of e-governance because of AI's capacity to process big and diverse data, pattern detection, policy simulations, and support predictive analysis, enables evidence-based decision-making in policy process that foster inclusivity and responsiveness and adaptability. AI-driven tools and models helps policymakers to design public engagement mechanism and develop policy interventions that are responsive, transparent, and support participatory approaches for diverse social needs and equitable governance. AI adoption in policy development discourse raises ethical concerns and AI regulations challenges regarding data privacy, fairness, transparency, and accountability and needs to frame robust regulatory mechanism consists of interdisciplinary collaboration among AI, data, policy, and governance experts. This synthetic study focuses on how AI inclusion transforms public policy discourse and makes process more inclusive and responsive by identifying AI-driven tools (data analytics, predictive modelling, natural language processing) enhance informed decisions, evidence-based, and citizen role in policymaking and governance. The findings of this study depict, AI significant role in improving decision-making capacity of policymakers by automation of policy tasks, thus leads towards citizen-centric governance for community diverse needs and tailored services. However, the benefits of AI inception policymaking demand to address key ethical concerns such as algorithmic bias, data privacy, and digital divides to uphold the digital equity. The study proposes solutions such as robust regulations, stakeholder's engagement mechanism, and systematic evaluation that guarantee AI services to the public interest. The results enable to policymakers and researchers to leverage responsible, equitable, and adaptive use of AI responsibly for more fair, inclusive, responsive, transparent, and smart policy outcomes.

The era of AI advent is recognised as a revolution that has made profound transformations across different sectors such as urban planning, smart cities, shows promising and significant progress. AI innovation improves effectiveness, efficiency, responsiveness, and adaptive governance model that supports better decision-making, improve public services based on data process, and accurate analysis (Elsyra, 2023). AI leverage in public policy development is poised to nuanced tools of data analytics, facilitate stakeholder's participation, provide predictive analysis, and support real-time policy interventions that enables the policymakers to transcend from outdated mode to evidence-based decision-making to address public policy issues and social problems in more adaptive and responsive way. AI applications in public policy cycle offers informed decisions based on pattern detection, predictive modelling, data insights, policy simulations, sentiment analysis, thus provides a revamp to policy cycle and move towards data-driven by making efficient, inclusive and responsive governance. A study discussed technological innovation in public policy cycle and data-driven policymaking, highlights the pitfalls of AI-driven policymaking and emphasised on regulations and regulatory process in the AI-based public policymaking (Buttow, 2025).

AI-driven systems (tools, models, and techniques) can generate, connect, in-depth analysis, and interpretate big data with great precision enables policy scientists (makers, researches, and analysts) to develop, formulate, design, and evaluate public policies grounded in empirical and verified data as evidence to deal multifaceted policy challenges. These AI potentials allow policymakers to apply evidence-based approaches by understanding deeper insights of complex policy dynamics. Precise, accurate and inclusive analytical capabilities of AI provide strength to design relevant, equitable and effective policies over time by mitigating biases practiced in traditional policy structure (Chy & Buadi, 2024).

Furthermore, AI-driven platforms such as Chatbots and intelligent assistant systems, for example, enable 24/7 citizen interaction and tailored services, improves public participation in processing policy feedback loop from diverse demographics, synthesize public preferences into actionable insights (Wolniak & Stecuła, 2024). This fosters an improved policy responsive system, uninterruptedly refine policies based on real-time data input, moves towards inclusive and responsive government that leaves no one behind. AI integration in public decision-making enhance efficiency, transparency, accountability, public service delivery and trust (Caiza et al., 2024). AI technological integration able to break the governance inertia and accelerate the iterative policy cycle by development of continuous responsive loops for informed decisions. The growing trend to adopt AI in policy sciences (public policy, public administration, governance) enhance transparency, optimise resource allocations and encourage public participation in policy decisions in diverse socio-economic landscape (Sieber et al., 2025). AI systems can inadvertently reinforce existing biases if trained on flawed data, and they raise novel privacy and ethical concerns (Dwivedi et al., 2021). Moreover, many policymakers lack the technical skills and infrastructure needed to deploy AI effectively. Addressing these issues is crucial: without safeguards, AI could widen social gaps rather than bridge them. Table 1 (a & b) illustrates the key potentials and limitation of AI inclusion in policy discourse.

Table 1. (a) Key opportunities for AI in public policy

Evidence-based analysis	**Automating large-scale data analysis enables more accurate forecasting and impact assessment of policies.**
Process automation	AI (e.g. RPA, chatbots) can handle routine administrative tasks, reducing workloads and freeing staff for higher-value work
Personalized citizen services	Intelligent assistants and tailored communication improve accessibility of government services to individual needs
Predictive modelling and simulation	AI-powered simulations allow policymakers to model policy scenarios and anticipate outcomes before implementation

Table 2. (b)Key challenges identified include

Algorithmic bias and fairness	**Risk of discriminatory outputs**
Privacy and security	Protecting citizen data
Resource and skill gaps	lack of funding, infrastructure and expertise
Regulatory uncertainty	Insufficient laws or standards governing AI use

In light of these potentials and pitfalls, this study investigates the mechanism of AI-driven tools that enhance inclusivity (broader citizen participation and equity) and responsiveness (timely, adaptive action) by examining recent studies and case examples to understand what works, what risks remain, and what governance measures are needed. To address these obstacles requires coordinated strategies involving policymakers, technologists, and civil society.

1.1 Problem Statement

Although AI applications in public policymaking have promising and effective impacts such as automated decisions, predictive insights, data analytics, and resource allocation that enhance inclusive and responsiveness. However, there is a need to address unresolved ethical challenges include data privacy, and algorithmic bias along with technical lacking, institutional barriers, and infrastructural inefficiencies to unlock AI full potential in fostering inclusivity and responsive public policy framework. This gap demand to highlight careful attention to consider AI challenges to improve inclusivity and responsive in public policy development.

1.2 Aim

This study aims to highlight the specific mechanisms that AI enhance inclusivity and responsiveness in public policy development for equitable governance while addressing ethical challenges in parallel.

1.3 Objectives

The key objective of this study is to explore the mechanisms that support inclusivity and responsiveness in public policy development structure keeping ethical implications for greater public participation and tailored public services.

1.4 Question

The study is designed to address the following questions.

1. How AI-driven platforms ensures inclusivity and responsiveness in public policy development?
2. What are the mechanisms that enhance inclusivity and responsiveness in public policy development?

1.5 Scope

The study encompasses a comprehensive analysis of how AI enhance the inclusivity and responsiveness in public policy development focusing best practices and mechanisms that improves public engagement, data-driven insights, informed decisions and foster adaptive governance. The study also assesses the ethical implications of AI inclusion in public policy development process.

1.6 Significance

The study contributes to provide a comprehensive knowledge of AI transformative potential that can foster inclusivity and responsiveness in development of public policy discourse that can equip the policy scientists with quantifiable insights to develop ethical outline for effective deployment of citizen-centric AI policy, administration, and governance.

2. LITERATURE REVIEW

The available literature on AI and public policy intersection highlights both transformative potential and inherent risks with key focus on inclusivity and responsiveness. A fundamental knowledge and critical lens are necessary for the policymakers to navigate the potentials and complexities of AI integration in public policy and to evaluate the overstated claims of AI solutions examining both strengthens and weaknesses. The evaluation mechanism should include the prevalent discussion on inherent AI intricacies, ethical challenges of AI deployment in public policy, data governance, regulatory framework, transparency, robust accountability, and fairness in making intelligent based decisions that ensure inclusivity and responsiveness (Yuan & Chen, 2025).

On positive side, researchers consensus that AI's data-processing capabilities can make policymaking more efficient and effective (Mikhaylov et al., 2018). AI-driven policy simulations have key impact to design policy instruments and drivers for policy interventions to promote inclusivity, adapt rapid changes, and minimise unplanned consequences and unforeseen crisis (Zuiderwijk et al., 2021). AI-driven literacy enables the policymakers to accept AI-based solution by recognising the AI's potentials and limitations in policy discourse (discussions and decisions). This in-depth understanding of AI knowledge is pivotal for inclusivity, responsiveness, and effectiveness in AI based policymaking and governance that allows more nuanced in policy discourse. The AI integration in policy cycle shifts governance from consultive to predictive mode based on data-driven insights to update proactive policy interventions rather than reactive policy responses and enables policy decisionmakers to design real time solutions and maintain public trust (Vatamanu & Tofan, 2025).

On the negative side, the AI-driven intelligent systems can exacerbate the existing social inequalities and generate biased decisions and discriminatory outcomes that poses a significant risk to public trust (Lloyd, 2018). The challenges of AI inclusion in policy domain raises the ethical concerns like algorithmic bias, privacy intrusions and cybersecurity risks despite the admitted fact that AI improves the public governance (Cheong, 2024). Moreover, compound difficulties include fragmented approaches, unclear gaols, inadequate trainings, resistance to change, limited knowledge of AI adoption, and overreliance on technology without understanding the reparations in the policy discourse increase the sensitivity of AI applications (Sun & Medaglia, 2019). These challenges demand to adopt a strategic mechanism, multi-stakeholder engagement, interdisciplinary collaborations, data guidelines, capacity building, and public private partnership that can design, develop, and implement ethical framework of AI use in public policy to fully harness the potentials based on inclusivity and responsiveness. The ethical framework carefully develops to address the key concerns of AI-driven intelligent systems and ensures the principles of fairness, transparency and accountability in making informed decisions under autonomous system (Cheong, 2024). Furthermore, the establishment of data collection standards, quality assurance protocols, and algorithmic guidelines are also important in designing ethical use of AI in public policy to gain public trust and response.

A study used the DEEP-MAX scoring system that can continuously monitor and evaluate the performance of AI systems (Dwivedi et al., 2021). Data is the raw material and AI the tool to create targeted, cost-conscious policies that improve lives and by rapidly sifting through big data, AI can detect needs during crises (e.g. pandemics or disasters) and guide evidence-based program design (Levy et al., 2021). Public-sector studies likewise suggest that predictive analytics can forecast service demand and identify at-risk populations, thereby enabling proactive governance (Sigfrids et al., 2023). In sum, AI can extend the reach of human decision-makers, it processes information at scale and generates analytical insights that support more nuanced policy choices (Levy et al., 2021).

Several researchers warn that AI systems inherit and amplify societal biases in the training content. Unchecked, algorithmic decisions such as in employment, law-enforcement or welfare distribution) may perpetuate inequalities (Novelli & Sandri, 2024). Privacy is another concern, governments must implement robust safeguards against the leakage of citizens' private data, or court distrust from the population. Relatedly, there is the threat of a digital divide, not all citizens have equal access or digital literacy to benefit from AI-based services. Without inclusive design, advanced technologies have the potential to exclude vulnerable groups. Public distrust is another concern highly discussed, studies report worries over government AI projects' unfairness and lack of accountability (Yuan & Chen, 2025).

Implementation barriers are widely noted by many public organizations lack the necessary talent and infrastructure to adopt AI at scale. Developing countries often face unreliable internet, limited computing power, and scarce high-quality data for training models. This creates uneven capabilities, while wealthy cities experiment with smart urban governance, smaller municipalities struggle with basic data integration (Xu et al., 2024). Significant investment in hardware (sensors, servers) and training programs is required for AI readiness.

Evidence driven policymaking hinges on interdisciplinary approach, technological integration, robust ethical framework, and active mechanism of public engagement to confirm that AI best serves as a tool for inclusivity and responsiveness in policy decisions. These ingredients allow iterative policymaking cycle to adopt AI-driven systems for continual improvement in reaction to emergent social challenges and public feedback. The black-box problem of some AI systems poses serious challenges to develop public trust, and to counter this, design of public engagement method based on social values is curial to align with technological systems for the legitimacy of AI-driven solutions in balancing the pace of rapid AI evolution and social needs (Starke & Lünich, 2020). The skewed predictions and unfair outcomes due to historical biased training data demands to devise rigorous data validation protocols with the ability to detect data biasness in designing intelligent system solutions. For this, policymakers can actively collaborate with AI experts and data scientists to define the optimise parameters of policy objectives that reflect the needs of policy audience and mitigate the risk of unintended outcomes.

Governance frameworks are considered essential, as recommend by studies ethical guidelines and multi-stakeholder oversight to mitigate risks. The literature repeatedly emphasizes the need for transparency and accountability in AI (Loi & Spielkamp, 2021). A study focuses on responsible AI principles, fairness, human oversight, transparency, and accountability to prevent harms and identifies a robust ethical framework and continuous evaluation as critical factors for AI in governance (Visave, 2025). Table 2 summarizes the main opportunities and challenges discussed in the literature.

Table 3. Strengths and limitations of AI in policy cycle

Aspect	Potential Benefits	Associated Challenges
Evidence-based Planning	Enables analysis of large datasets for data-driven, targeted policy decisions	Requires high-quality, unbiased data; may entrench existing biases if uncorrected
Citizen Engagement	AI platforms (e.g. chatbots, surveys) can gather diverse feedback and personalize services	Digital literacy and access gaps can exclude some populations; trust concerns may limit participation
Operational Efficiency	Automates routine tasks and processes, freeing staff for complex work	Upfront investment in technology and training; resistance from workers or unions
Predictive Analytics	Forecasts trends (e.g. demand, risks) allowing proactive interventions	Complexity of social issues may limit model accuracy; requires interdisciplinary input
Ethical & Governance	Can enhance transparency (e.g. explainable AI), continuous monitoring of outcomes	Algorithmic opacity, accountability gaps; need for robust regulation and oversight

3. METHODOLOGY

This research employs a qualitative systematic review approach, by conducting a systematic literature review following PRISMA framework of recent scholarly articles, reports, and policy guidelines on AI in public policy, public administration, and governance focusing on inclusivity and responsiveness. In parallel, examine **illustrative case studies** from various levels of government where AI tools have been deployed (e.g. local e-governance projects, national policy labs). Sources include 110 peer-reviewed journals, policy documents, and international originations reports from Scopus, Web of Science, Google scholar published between 2018 to 2025. 45 records exclude due to irrelevance, lack of empirical analysis, and out of scope, and 20 sources are in final inclusion for detailed analysis. The figure 1 shows PRISMA statement of this study is presented.

Figure 1. PRISMA 2020 flow diagram of the current study on inclusivity and responsiveness of AI in policymaking

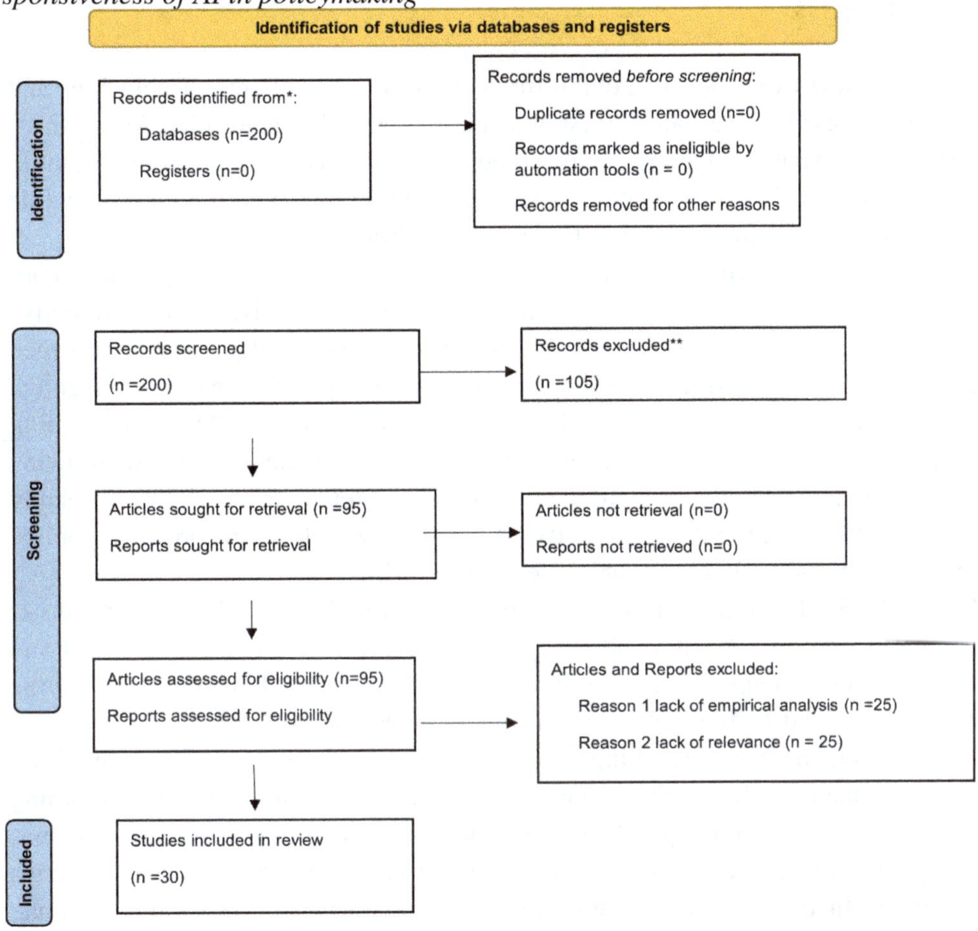

**Records identified from Scoups database.*
*** Records excluded due to reasons mentioned in the text.*

The methodological framework facilities to synthesise the findings from the sources of empirical studies on AI in public policy, public administration, and governance identify common themes, evidence of outcomes, and challenges relates to inclusivity and responsiveness. The methodology employs to analyse the literature review on AI's impact on policy processes and to explore the best mechanism, frameworks, principles, practices, and guidelines that foster policy inclusivity and responsiveness.

4. RESULTS

The review reveals several notable trends regarding AI's effects on inclusivity and responsiveness in governance. First, when implemented thoughtfully, AI enhances analytical capacity and evidence use in policymaking. However, it is important to consider the challenges of data privacy, algorithmic bias, and digital risks while acknowledging the potential benefits of AI in public policy.

The primary findings show that deliberate adoption of AI keeping ethical considering and stakeholder's engagement mechanism, the analytical and predictive capacity of public policy enhances significantly and leads to data-driven, informed decisions, effective and equitable policy outcomes. AI systems can examine through vast data to uncover insights that human analysts might miss. Machine-learning models have been used to predict urban traffic flows and energy demand, allowing planners to allocate resources more efficiently (Di Stefano et al., 2023). The study finds multiple cases where predictive algorithms enable more proactive policy measures in optimizing renewable energy grids, flood early-warning systems (Al-Raeei, 2025). These advances suggest that AI can make the policy process faster and more rigorous. As BCG observes, AI can complement human judgment and lead to a more comprehensive policy development process. In essence, data is the raw material and AI the tool for generating targeted solutions.

However, these benefits hinge on responsible implementation. The literature indicates that gains in efficiency and responsiveness are contingent on overcoming issues of data and model quality. For instance, many studies stress that unless bias and privacy are actively managed, AI-driven decisions may fail to serve all groups equitably. In practice, this means policies recommended by AI require human oversight and frequent review. Therefore, successful AI integration often involves establishing clear protocols for monitoring algorithmic outcomes and intervening when necessary (for example, by adjusting models or providing alternative services to disadvantaged communities). The successful policy solutions based on AI-driven systems demands a rigours framework that have the ability to monitor and evaluate the performance of AI systems and ensure the intended objectives of policy inclusivity and responsiveness.

Second, stakeholder involvement emerges as crucial. Multiple cases highlight that involving citizens and relevant stakeholders input while designing an AI system enhances acceptance and relevance and provides the legitimacy to AI solutions. Active stakeholder's participation fosters the public trust and ensures AI as a catalyst that reflects according to social values and community needs for collective welfare (Chen et al., 2023). Governments are experimenting with interactive platforms that use AI to aggregate public feedback, for instance, chatbots that engage users in multiple languages or sentiment analysis of social media on policy topics. Such tools can broaden participation by reaching citizens who might not attend traditional consultations. For example, Singapore's 24/7 AI chatbots have increased citizen satisfaction by tailoring information to individual needs. These examples illustrate how technology can lower barriers to engagement. Consistently, experts recommend treating AI projects as collaborative, iterative pilots and soliciting user feedback to refine systems. Such practices enable public participation in data-driven and AI-based solutions enhances the legitimacy, inclusivity, and responsiveness of a public policy.

Third, in sectoral domains such as urban planning and climate policy, AI shows promise for improving sustainability and resilience. The application of AI in different public policy domains offers optimise resource allocation, predictive data insights, and evidence-based decisions for e-governance, climate mitigation and adaptation strategies, air, water, and environmental quality, early warning systems, foster urban planning, smart and resilient cities, green infrastructures, public transport networks, efficient and renewables systems. The AI-driven policy simulations pose the significant positive impacts on different policy interventions for targeted and effective policy response. The United Nations reports that AI-driven tools help identify emission hotspots, optimize traffic routing, and plan resilient infrastructure by integrating satellite and sensor data. In developing countries, AI-enabled early-warning systems are being deployed to anticipate extreme weather, allowing governments to mobilize resources more effectively. These applications demonstrate how AI can extend government capability in complex, multidisciplinary problems.

Yet, this analysis also confirms major constraints, many municipalities lack reliable data and technical capacity to implement such solutions. Without investment in data collection and governance, even powerful AI models cannot reach their potential. The UNFCCC emphasizes that to harness AI for climate action, governments must invest in digital infrastructure and inclusive data practices (Lainjo, 2024). In summary, the current analytical evidence suggests that AI can improve the inclusivity and responsiveness of public policy, but only when supported by appropriate safeguards and social infrastructure. It accelerates analysis and citizen engagement, but its effectiveness depends on stakeholder trust, data quality, and equitable access.

5. DISCUSSION

There is significant progress in AI deployment in policy process that enhances inclusivity and responsiveness, however, the ethical implications remain a critical concern that needs to frame and implement an ethical mechanism and regulations to ensure the principles of fairness, transparency, accountability, and equity (Machado et al., 2025). In addition to this, public discourse mechanism in the policy decisions is also important to address the ethical challenges and to harness the full benefits of AI deployment in public policy and to promote equitable AI-driven solutions keeping the social values and needs (Kinder et al., 2023). AI integration facilities participatory governance by providing AI platforms to citizens to contribute in policymaking and analyse their feedback in the form of sentiment, opinions, and preferences and enables a bottom to top model in public policy development process. Policy scientist used sentiment analysis by employing NLP and ML models on AI-driven platforms and extract key insights in the form of trends and patterns by analysing public sentiments foster more inclusive, responsive, and adaptive policymaking (Kramer et al., 2024). AI inclusion in policymaking process justifies the policy choices, support policy execution, and analyse policy effects and evaluation. AI also facilitates the performance of predictive models for more accurate, precise, and reliable forecasting for long-term policy impacts and enables more proactive and responsive governance.

This discussion integrates the insights above and explores strategies for enhanced inclusive and responsive in responsible AI adoption in public policy with ethical governance is essential. A unanimous cautionary thought prevails in academia that AI is not a risk-free option. Algorithms trained on historical data can perpetuate discrimination as seen in past cases like automated exam grading or credit scoring. Therefore, any AI-driven deployment in public services should have governed by regulatory frameworks (Misra et al., 2020). The literature calls for embedding fairness, accountability, and transparency at every step. Governments are urged to mandate impact assessments for automated systems and to maintain human oversight (human plus AI) in critical decision-making (Nay & Daily, 2022). One study discussed that during policy identification and evaluation, fairness and social impact principles should be explicitly applied.

Table 4. Strategies to harness the benefits while mitigating risks

Develop robust ethical and regulatory frameworks	Governments should enact standards for AI (analogous to data protection laws) that enshrine fairness and accountability. This includes requirements for explainable algorithms and regular auditing of AI systems
Invest in skills and infrastructure	Public agencies need access to AI talent and computing resources. Training programs for civil servants and partnerships with academia or the private sector can fill expertise gaps. Governments should also upgrade digital infrastructure (broadband, cloud systems) to support AI applications, especially in underserved regions
Engage citizens in the process	Government should be open and inclusive in order to win over the hearts of the people. Governments must engage stakeholders by performing consultations and pilot projects. Pilot projects with citizen oversight (like used in the "AI Challenge" program of Finland) help to harmonize AI solutions and community value. Public education campaigns help give awareness of AI's promise and limitations to dispel fears and misconceptions
Implement AI incrementally with continuous evaluation	Not a generic rollout, AI systems need to be installed incrementally (starting with pilots) and rigorously tested. Regular outcome measurement allows refinement and learning throughout. For instance, the Canadian government demands extensive repeated testing of every automatic decision system in order to guarantee that they make fair decisions

Applying these guiding principles, governments can mitigate the policy tension, and tip the balance toward AI-informed policy interventions independently producing outcomes which are inclusive as opposed to adverse externalities. Policymakers, technical experts, and civil society multi-stakeholder consultation is key to success of all mechanism. Through such multi-stakeholder processes alone, the study suggests, a new era of public trust wherein AI facilitates governments to respond and act fairly.

6. CONCLUSION

In conclusion, integrating AI into public policy holds immense potential to make governance more inclusive and responsive. AI's ability to analyse big data and model complex scenarios can enable evidence-based decision-making and anticipate citizen needs in real time. Such capabilities allow policymakers to craft highly tailored interventions and democratize access to services. By processing diverse inputs (e.g. social media, surveys), AI tools can amplify marginalized voices and help ensure that policies address the concerns of all population segments.

However, realizing this potential is not automatic. AI-driven policy must be pursued with vigilance to ethics and fairness. Without robust safeguards, biases in algorithms could entrench inequality, and privacy breaches could undermine public trust. The literature indicates that the transformative promise of AI will only be fulfilled if it is coupled with strong governance clear regulations, transparent processes, and continuous oversight. Interdisciplinary collaboration is also essential:

technologists, social scientists, and community representatives must work together to guide AI applications.

Overall, AI can be a powerful enabler of more equitable and adaptive governance, but intentional design and governance frameworks are required. Governments should embrace AI as a tool for democratic innovation, while taking care to ensure that its benefits are distributed fairly. With thoughtful implementation, AI has the promise not only to enhance policy effectiveness but also to strengthen public trust by making government more transparent, accountable, and responsive.

REFERENCES

Al-Raeei, M. (2025). The smart future for sustainable development: Artificial intelligence solutions for sustainable urbanization. *Sustainable Development (Bradford), 33*(1), 508–517. DOI: 10.1002/sd.3131

Buttow, C. V. (2025). Data-Driven Policy Making and Its Impacts on Regulation: A Study of the OECD Vision in the Light of Data Critical Studies. *European Journal of Risk Regulation, 16*(1), 114–132. DOI: 10.1017/err.2024.73

Caiza, G., Sanguña, V., Tusa, N., Masaquiza, V., Ortiz, A., & Garcia, M. V. (2024). Navigating governmental choices: A comprehensive review of artificial Intelligence's impact on decision-making. *Informatics (MDPI), 11*(3), 64. DOI: 10.3390/informatics11030064

Chen, Y.-C., Ahn, M. J., & Wang, Y.-F. (2023). Artificial intelligence and public values: Value impacts and governance in the public sector. *Sustainability (Basel), 15*(6), 4796. DOI: 10.3390/su15064796

Cheong, B. C. (2024). Transparency and accountability in AI systems: Safeguarding wellbeing in the age of algorithmic decision-making. *Frontiers in Human Dynamics, 6*, 1421273. DOI: 10.3389/fhumd.2024.1421273

Chy, M. K. H., & Buadi, O. N. (2024). Role of machine learning in policy making and evaluation. *International Journal of Innovative Science and Research Technology (IJISRT), 0 [].*DOI: 10.38124/ijisrt/IJISRT24OCT687

Di Stefano, A. G., Ruta, M., & Masera, G. (2023). Advanced digital tools for data-informed and performance-driven design: A review of building energy consumption forecasting models based on machine learning. *Applied Sciences (Basel, Switzerland), 13*(24), 12981. DOI: 10.3390/app132412981

Dwivedi, Y. K., Hughes, L., Ismagilova, E., Aarts, G., Coombs, C., Crick, T., Duan, Y., Dwivedi, R., Edwards, J., Eirug, A., Galanos, V., Ilavarasan, P. V., Janssen, M., Jones, P., Kar, A. K., Kizgin, H., Kronemann, B., Lal, B., Lucini, B., & Williams, M. D. (2021). Artificial Intelligence (AI): Multidisciplinary perspectives on emerging challenges, opportunities, and agenda for research, practice and policy. *International Journal of Information Management, 57*, 101994. DOI: 10.1016/j.ijinfomgt.2019.08.002

Elsyra, N. (2023). The role of artificial intelligence in government services: a systematic literature review. *Open access indonesia journal of social sciences, 6*(3), 998-1003.

Kinder, T., Stenvall, J., Koskimies, E., Webb, H., & Janenova, S. (2023). Local public services and the ethical deployment of artificial intelligence. *Government Information Quarterly*, *40*(4), 101865. DOI: 10.1016/j.giq.2023.101865

Kramer, M. A., Leavens, A., & Scarlat, A. (2024). Harnessing AI for efficient analysis of complex policy documents: a case study of Executive Order 14110. *arXiv preprint arXiv:2406.06657.*

Lainjo, B. (2024). The role of artificial intelligence in achieving the United Nations sustainable development goals. *Journal of Sustainable Development*, *17*(5), 1–30. DOI: 10.5539/jsd.v17n5p30

Levy, K., Chasalow, K. E., & Riley, S. (2021). Algorithms and decision-making in the public sector. *Annual Review of Law and Social Science*, *17*(1), 309–334. DOI: 10.1146/annurev-lawsocsci-041221-023808

Lloyd, K. (2018). Bias amplification in artificial intelligence systems. *arXiv preprint arXiv:1809.07842.*

Loi, M., & Spielkamp, M. (2021). Towards accountability in the use of artificial intelligence for public administrations. Proceedings of the 2021 AAAI/ACM Conference on AI, Ethics, and Society DOI: 10.1145/3461702.3462631

Machado, H., Silva, S., & Neiva, L. (2025). Publics' views on ethical challenges of artificial intelligence: A scoping review. *AI and Ethics*, *5*(1), 139–167. DOI: 10.1007/s43681-023-00387-1

Mikhaylov, S. J., Esteve, M., & Campion, A. (2018). Artificial intelligence for the public sector: Opportunities and challenges of cross-sector collaboration. *Philosophical Transactions. Series A, Mathematical, Physical, and Engineering Sciences*, *376*(2128), 20170357. DOI: 10.1098/rsta.2017.0357 PMID: 30082303

Misra, S. K., Das, S., Gupta, S., & Sharma, S. K. (2020). Public policy and regulatory challenges of artificial intelligence (AI). *International Working Conference on Transfer and Diffusion of IT* DOI: 10.1007/978-3-030-64849-7_10

Nay, J., & Daily, J. (2022). Aligning Artificial Intelligence with Humans through Public Policy. *arXiv preprint arXiv:2207.01497.*

Novelli, C., & Sandri, G. (2024). Digital democracy in the age of artificial intelligence. *arXiv preprint arXiv:2412.07791.*

Sieber, R., Brandusescu, A., Sangiambut, S., & Adu-Daako, A. (2025). What is civic participation in artificial intelligence? *Environment and Planning. B, Urban Analytics and City Science*, *52*(6), 1388–1406. DOI: 10.1177/23998083241296200

Sigfrids, A., Leikas, J., Salo-Pöntinen, H., & Koskimies, E. (2023). Human-centricity in AI governance: A systemic approach. *Frontiers in Artificial Intelligence*, *6*, 976887. DOI: 10.3389/frai.2023.976887 PMID: 36872934

Starke, C., & Lünich, M. (2020). Artificial intelligence for political decision-making in the European Union: Effects on citizens' perceptions of input, throughput, and output legitimacy. *Data & Policy*, *2*, e16. DOI: 10.1017/dap.2020.19

Sun, T. Q., & Medaglia, R. (2019). Mapping the challenges of Artificial Intelligence in the public sector: Evidence from public healthcare. *Government Information Quarterly*, *36*(2), 368–383. DOI: 10.1016/j.giq.2018.09.008

Vatamanu, A. F., & Tofan, M. (2025). Integrating artificial intelligence into public administration: Challenges and vulnerabilities. *Administrative Sciences*, *15*(4), 149. DOI: 10.3390/admsci15040149

Visave, J. (2025). Transparency in AI for emergency management: Building trust and accountability. *AI and Ethics*, *5*(4), 1–14. DOI: 10.1007/s43681-025-00692-x

Wolniak, R., & Stecuła, K. (2024). Artificial intelligence in smart cities—applications, barriers, and future directions: a review. *Smart cities, 7*(3), 1346-1389.

Xu, H., Omitaomu, F., Sabri, S., Li, X., & Song, Y. (2024). Leveraging generative ai for smart city digital twins: A survey on the autonomous generation of data, scenarios, 3d city models, and urban designs. *arXiv e-prints*, arXiv: 2405.19464.

Yuan, Q., & Chen, T. (2025). Holding AI-based systems accountable in the public sector: A systematic review. *Public Performance & Management Review*, *48*(6), 1–34. DOI: 10.1080/15309576.2025.2469784

Zuiderwijk, A., Chen, Y.-C., & Salem, F. (2021). Implications of the use of artificial intelligence in public governance: A systematic literature review and a research agenda. *Government Information Quarterly*, *38*(3), 101577. DOI: 10.1016/j.giq.2021.101577

Chapter 2

Employee-AI Collaboration and Organizational Productivity:

Mediating Effects of Employee Performance, Knowledge Sharing, and Decision-Making Effective

Sofyan Ashari Nur
Universitas Tidar, Indonesia

Muafi Muafi
https://orcid.org/0000-0002-5078-4670
Universitas Islam Indonesia, Indonesia

ABSTRACT

The use of Artificial Intelligence (AI) to support work processes has become a common practice in various organizations. With the increasing adoption of AI in various organizational functions, the interaction between human capabilities and AI systems has become a central issue in achieving optimal performance. Employee-AI Collaboration is increasingly becoming a critical factor in enhancing organizational productivity in the digital era. This study conceptually explores how Employee-AI Collaboration can contribute to Organizational Productivity through the mediating roles of Employee Performance, Knowledge Sharing, and Decision-Making Effectiveness. The synergy between humans and AI is expected to improve operational efficiency, accelerate the flow of knowledge, and support more accurate

DOI: 10.4018/979-8-3373-8607-2.ch002

and timely decision-making processes. Understanding the mediation mechanism provides strategic insights for organizations in effectively integrating AI to promote productivity through human and technological collaboration.

INTRODUCTION

The development of artificial intelligence (AI) has revolutionized the way organizations operate in various sectors. AI is now not only a tool for automation assistance but also a strategic partner in supporting decision-making, improving efficiency, and accelerating the flow of information within organizations (Necula et al., 2024; AG et al., 2023). In this context, collaboration between employees and AI (employee-AI collaboration) has become an increasingly important approach for enhancing organizational productivity in the digital era. The implementation of AI in work management software such as Asana and Microsoft Teams has proven to increase productivity by 30% and 35%, respectively, demonstrating the tangible impact of the synergy between humans and technology (El Hammoumi et al., 2024).

Theoretically, the relationship between AI and productivity can be explained through the Knowledge-Based View (KBV) approach, which places AI as an extension of the cognitive capacity of employees. AI allows employees to focus on high-value tasks by transferring administrative workloads to machines (Yin et al., 2024). Furthermore, from the perspective of organizational change theory, the adoption of AI can promote structural innovation that accelerates work efficiency. However, the effectiveness of human-AI collaboration heavily depends on individual readiness and leadership support in creating an adaptive work environment (Bankins et al., 2024). AI also plays a significant role in the objective evaluation of employee performance, including assessing soft skills that were previously difficult to quantify (Gafni et al., 2024).

Despite literature showing a positive relationship between AI and productivity enhancement, the mechanism by which human-AI collaboration affects organizational productivity is not fully understood. Previous research has focused more on the direct relationship between AI and organizational outcomes, without delving deeper into the mediating role of aspects of employee behavior. However, some studies have emphasized that AI can improve work efficiency, employee engagement, and job satisfaction, which in turn affect productivity (Malik et al., 2023; Kassa & Worku, 2025; Dutta et al., 2023; Liang et al., 2024). Therefore, it is important to further investigate the role of mediating variables such as employee performance, decision-making efficiency, and knowledge sharing in explaining this relationship.

Employee performance has been proven to be a significant factor in bridging the positive impact of AI on organizational productivity. When AI is used to support daily work, employees can complete tasks more effectively and efficiently (Vrontis et al., 2023). Malik (2024) highlights that the implementation of AI in human resource processes enhances employee engagement and performance, which in turn affects organizational productivity. On the other hand, the study by Kassa and Worku (2025) on Ethio Telecom found that the positive effects of AI usage on productivity are significantly mediated by the improvement in employee performance. Therefore, employee performance is an important pathway that needs to be considered in the analysis of employee-AI collaboration and organizational productivity.

In addition, decision-making efficiency also becomes an important channel for increasing productivity through employee collaboration and AI. AI is capable of improving information quality, managing ethical issues, and accelerating the decision-making process, thereby enhancing the overall effectiveness of the organization (Baabdullah, 2024; Neiroukh et al., 2024). This collaboration creates synergy, where AI handles data analysis and repetitive tasks, while humans focus on the strategic aspects of decisions (Tummalapalli et al., 2024). Rulandari and Silalahi (2025) emphasize that the adaptability of AI to organizational environmental changes allows the decision-making process to become more responsive and contextual. The study by Dutta et al. (2023) also supports this by showing how AI chatbots increase engagement and efficiency in organizations.

The last important mediating variable is knowledge sharing. Sharing knowledge between employees and teams is a crucial foundation for optimizing the use of AI. Without a culture of knowledge sharing, the potential of AI cannot be fully utilized (Masih et al., 2018). AI enables collective learning processes and the development of innovative solutions through access to broader data and insights (Kong et al., 2023; Asefa et al., 2023). The study by Shaikh et al. (2023) shows that knowledge sharing significantly mediates the impact of AI on employee productivity. Gazi et al. (2024) also emphasize the importance of a culture of knowledge sharing in strengthening the relationship between AI and sustainable organizational performance. In this context, knowledge sharing becomes a crucial link between technology and the innovative capacity of organizations (Olan et al., 2022).

LITERATURE REVIEW AND CONCEPTUAL PROPOSITION

Employee–AI Collaboration and Organizational Productivity

Artificial Intelligence (AI) has become a key factor in increasing employee productivity by automating repetitive tasks, providing personalized recommendations, and supporting more efficient decision-making (Necula et al., 2024; AG et al., 2023). In the context of organizations, AI serves not only as an operational aid but also as a change agent that enables efficiency in communication, collaboration, and task management. For example, the use of AI in work management software such as Asana and Microsoft Teams has been proven to increase productivity by 30% and 35% respectively (El Hammoumi et al., 2024). This indicates that AI plays a strategic role in optimizing individual and team performance by reducing manual workload and increasing flexibility in work.

From a theoretical perspective, the impact of AI on productivity can be explained through the knowledge-based view (KBV) theory, where AI acts as an extension of the cognitive capacity of employees, allowing them to focus on higher-value tasks. Moreover, organizational change theory states that the implementation of AI can promote structural adaptation that accelerates innovation and work efficiency (Yin et al., 2024). However, the effectiveness of AI in increasing productivity greatly depends on leadership supporting change and employees' readiness to adapt to new technology (Bankins et al., 2024). Other studies also show that AI can improve performance evaluation objectively, especially in assessing the soft skills of employees that were previously difficult to quantify (Gafni et al., 2024). Thus, the relationship between AI and productivity is not only direct through automation but also indirect through changes in human resource management and organizational culture.

Based on this literature review, it can be proposed that: "The application of AI in the work environment has a positive impact on employee productivity through task automation, increased collaboration, and changes in the performance evaluation system". This hypothesis is supported by findings from various studies showing a significant relationship between AI and the improvement of work efficiency (Malik et al., 2023; Bankins et al., 2024). Moreover, the role of leadership in supporting the implementation of AI also becomes a moderating factor that can strengthen the impact of AI on productivity (Yin et al., 2024). Therefore, further research is needed to explore how organizational and leadership factors can optimize the benefits of AI in increasing employee productivity.

P1: Employee – AI Collaboration can improve organizational productivity

Mediation Role of Employee Performance in the Effect of Employee–AI Collaboration on Organizational Productivity

Employee-AI collaboration is a strategic approach in the modern workplace that combines human capabilities with technology to enhance organizational performance. This collaboration encompasses the use of AI technology to support employees' work in various aspects, ranging from simplifying administrative processes to making faster and more accurate decisions (Vrontis et al., 2023). In this context, employee performance refers to how effectively and efficiently an employee completes their tasks and responsibilities in the work environment. Organizational productivity is the ultimate outcome expected from this collaboration, reflecting the organization's ability to achieve its goals by using resources optimally (Kassa & Worku, 2025).

Effective collaboration between employees and AI can enhance employee performance through increased efficiency, accuracy, and reduced workload (Malik, 2024). When AI is used to simplify work processes and support decision-making, employees can focus more on high-value strategic tasks. With the improvement of employee performance, the productivity of the organization also increases. In this relationship, employee performance plays a mediating role that bridges the positive impact of AI collaboration on organizational productivity. This means that although AI has a direct effect on productivity, most of its influence is channeled through the improvement of employee performance. Therefore, organizations need not only adopt AI technology but also ensure that the technology is designed to enhance the experience and effectiveness of employee work (Kong et al., 2023).

A number of empirical studies support this logical framework. Kassa and Worku (2025) show that the use of AI in Ethio Telecom has a positive impact on organizational productivity, and this effect is significantly mediated by the improvement in employee performance. Malik (2024) also found that the implementation of AI in HR processes can enhance employee engagement and performance, which in turn increases productivity. Moreover, the research by Liang et al. (2024; Dutta et al. 2023) indicates that human-AI collaboration, both in the context of manufacturing and services, can improve work efficiency and employee satisfaction.

P2: Employee performance mediates the positive effect of employee–AI collaboration on organizational productivity.

Mediation Role of Decission Making Efficiency in the Effect of Employee–AI Collaboration on Organizational Productivity

Collaboration between employees and artificial intelligence (AI) is an increasingly recognized strategic approach in the context of modern organizational management. Within this framework, the efficiency of decision-making (decision-making efficiency) is positioned as a mediating variable bridging the relationship between employee-AI collaboration and organizational productivity. AI has the capability to enhance information quality, support the search for novelty, and manage ethical issues in the decision-making process (Baabdullah, 2024). As a consequence, decision-making quality and speed improve, significantly contributing to innovation performance and organizational productivity (Neiroukh et al., 2024). Therefore, decision-making efficiency can be conceptualized as an important mechanism for maximizing the value of human-AI collaboration.

Logically, collaboration between employees and AI enables more efficient task distribution: AI takes over repetitive and analytical tasks, while employees focus on strategic and contextual decisions. This approach creates synergy that accelerates the decision-making process and improves the accuracy of strategic decisions (Tummalapalli et al., 2024). In this context, decision-making efficiency becomes a crucial pathway for transforming the benefits of AI-employee collaboration into increased organizational productivity. AI not only speeds up the decision-making process but also adapts decisions to the dynamic organizational environment (Rulandari & Silalahi, 2025). Therefore, the higher the efficiency in decision-making mediated by AI, the greater the increase in organizational productivity that can be achieved.

A number of previous studies support this logic. Neiroukh et al. (2024) show that AI capabilities significantly accelerate and improve the quality of organizational decisions, which in turn has a positive impact on productivity. Meanwhile, a study by Dutta et al. (2023) focuses on the role of AI-based chatbots in increasing employee voice and engagement, which also contributes to efficiency and productivity. This statement emphasizes the importance of technology-based approaches in enhancing organizational effectiveness in the disruptive digital era.

P3: Decision-making efficiency mediates the positive effect of employee–AI collaboration on organizational productivity.

Mediation Role of Knowledge Sharing in the Effect of Employee–AI Collaboration on Organizational Productivity

Collaboration between employees and artificial intelligence (employee-AI collaboration) is a strategic approach that allows the use of AI capabilities to enhance organizational productivity. AI plays a role in automating routine tasks and providing data-based support for decision-making, thereby enabling employees to focus on high-value activities such as innovation and creativity (Kong et al., 2023; Asefa et al., 2023). In this context, knowledge sharing (sharing knowledge) is positioned as a significant mediating variable. The knowledge shared between individuals and teams can enhance the organization's ability to optimally absorb and utilize AI technology to promote productivity and innovation (Shaikh et al., 2023; Gazi et al., 2024).

Logically, when collaboration between employees and AI occurs without support from a knowledge-sharing culture, the potential of AI will not be maximally utilized. Knowledge sharing enables the transfer of skills, understanding of AI functions, and the development of more innovative and adaptive solutions (Masih et al., 2018). Therefore, knowledge sharing becomes a key element in connecting the use of AI by employees with the increase in organizational productivity. This collaboration accelerates organizational learning and promotes the formation of higher collective intelligence (Olan et al., 2022). Thus, the efficiency of AI utilization in the work process depends on how far the organization can build a work environment that actively supports knowledge sharing.

Several studies support the role of knowledge sharing mediation in this context. For example, Shaikh et al. (2023) show that knowledge sharing positively mediates the impact of AI on employee productivity. Gazi et al. (2024) add that a culture of sharing knowledge can strengthen the relationship between AI capabilities and organizational sustainable performance. Olan et al. (2022) also found that the success of AI implementation in organizations is greatly influenced by the effectiveness of the knowledge sharing process.

P4: Knowledge sharing mediates the positive effect of employee–AI collaboration on organizational productivity.

Figure 1. Research Framework

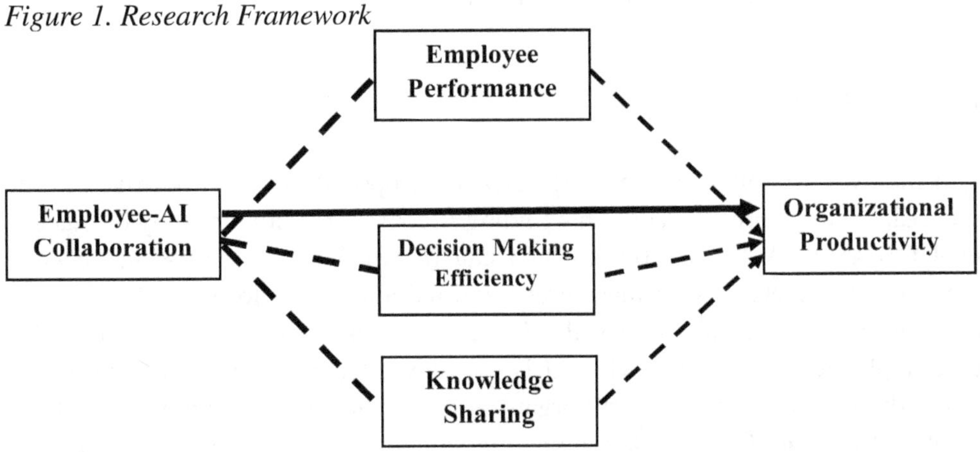

RESEARCH METHODS

This study is a conceptual exploration based on a literature review to examine the relationship between Employee-AI Collaboration and Organizational Productivity, with a focus on the mediating roles of Employee Performance, Knowledge Sharing, and Decision-Making Effectiveness. The methodology used in this study includes a comprehensive theoretical review and synthesis of the conceptual framework, as well as empirical studies from various disciplines of science, including human resource management, information technology, and organizational behavior.

By critically analyzing and integrating various scholarly sources, this research aims to build a solid conceptual framework that describes how collaboration between humans and AI can enhance organizational productivity through improved individual performance, more effective knowledge flow, and higher-quality decision-making.

The proposals developed in this research originate from a deep exploration of the main concepts and theories that have been established in previous literature, while also identifying gaps in current understanding and offering new perspectives on the integration of technology in human work processes.

This research methodology does not involve the collection of primary data or empirical testing, but instead relies entirely on secondary data and relevant literature to provide a theoretical foundation for the relationship between the variables studied. This conceptual approach provides an initial foundation for empirical research in the future, as well as a guide for academics and practitioners in understanding the practical implications of employee-AI collaboration on organizational productivity through the proposed mediation mechanism.

DISCUSSION

Employee-AI collaboration is significantly proposed to have a positive impact on organizational productivity. This finding is consistent with the study by Necula et al. (2024) and AG et al. (2023), which state that the integration of AI in the work environment accelerates business processes and allows employees to focus more on high-value tasks. This empirical evidence strengthens the first proposition (P1) that employee collaboration with AI is not only a technological trend but also a major driver in enhancing overall organizational efficiency and output. AI acts as a catalyst in simplifying work complexity, managing information, and promoting faster execution.

The recommended implementation for companies in this context is to build an AI adoption strategy that is not only technical but also human-centric. Companies should provide comprehensive training on the relevant use of AI for each work unit. Moreover, the integration of AI into work processes needs to be planned with a co-creation approach between employees and system developers, ensuring that the technology truly supports, rather than replaces, the role of employees.

Furthermore, research findings indicate that employee performance mediates the impact of employee-AI collaboration on organizational productivity, supporting proposal two (P2). When AI is used to assist with daily tasks, employees tend to show significant performance improvements due to the reduction in administrative burden and an increase in strategic thinking space (Malik, 2024; Vrontis et al., 2023). On the other hand, the study by Kassa and Worku (2025) also emphasizes that the increase in organizational productivity is greatly influenced by the more optimal individual performance due to AI support.

Recommendations for companies are to ensure that AI adoption is always accompanied by measurement and feedback on employee performance. Performance management systems need to be adjusted to reflect the work contributions generated through AI assistance, not just manual output. Moreover, organizations should provide incentives to employees who successfully leverage AI productively, as part of a strategy to increase adoption and work motivation.

The subsequent results support proposal three (P3), which is that decision-making efficiency mediates the positive relationship between AI-collaboration and organizational productivity. This reinforces the role of AI as a support in making faster, more accurate, and data-based decisions (Baabdullah, 2024; Neiroukh et al., 2024). In practice, AI can be used to develop business scenarios, project outcomes of decisions, and even provide algorithm-based recommendations for each strategic policy. This is highly relevant in dynamic environments that require quick responses.

For decision-making recommendations, companies can develop a dashboard that combines AI and predictive analysis. This system can be used by managers to make real-time data-based decisions. Moreover, training on data literacy and understanding of AI outputs should be provided to key stakeholders to ensure that decision-making efficiency is not only supported by AI but also comprehended by the human users.

The final findings support the fourth proposal (P4), which is that knowledge sharing mediates the relationship between employee collaboration with AI and organizational productivity. AI indirectly promotes knowledge sharing by providing access to information, automated documentation, and collaborative learning experiences (Shaikh et al., 2023; Gazi et al., 2024). However, without an organizational culture that supports openness and collaboration, the benefits of AI in enhancing knowledge sharing will not be optimized (Masih et al., 2018; Olan et al., 2022).

Practical recommendations for companies include building an AI-based knowledge sharing platform that can be used by all employees across functions. For example, by integrating AI systems into a knowledge management system (KMS) that encourages knowledge documentation, open discussions, and community-based learning. Organizations should also establish policies that promote knowledge contribution, such as rewards for employees who actively share insights and work findings.

Overall, this research emphasizes that the impact of human-AI collaboration on productivity is not linear, but rather mediated by various behavioral and structural factors within the organization. This shows that the implementation of AI must be holistic—not just focusing on the technological aspect, but also considering individual performance, decision-making processes, and knowledge-sharing mechanisms that support organizational learning. Therefore, effective AI adoption must be based on the synergy between humans, processes, and technology.

CONCLUSION

In general, achieving organizational productivity in the era of digital transformation can be significantly supported by fostering effective employee–AI collaboration. When organizations integrate AI into their operations while enabling employees to actively engage with such technologies, the synergy will enhance employee performance, accelerate decision-making processes, and promote knowledge sharing within the organization. These mediating factors collectively contribute to increased productivity across various organizational levels.

The adoption of AI not only automates routine tasks but also reshapes organizational culture and work dynamics, allowing employees to focus on strategic and high-value activities. As more organizations embrace AI technologies, a cascading effect is likely to emerge where collaborative AI adoption becomes a new standard of productivity and innovation. Consequently, broader organizational ecosystems—across industries and sectors—will experience measurable improvements in performance and agility.

Strengthening the role of employee–AI collaboration opens up new avenues for organizations to meet the demands of competitiveness and innovation in the digital economy. Future research should prioritize cross-sectoral collaboration between scholars, AI developers, and industry leaders to ensure ethical, inclusive, and effective AI integration. Longitudinal studies are also essential to assess the sustained impact of AI adoption on organizational outcomes, including changes in employee behavior and organizational culture.

LIMITATION

Implementing employee–AI collaboration in the workplace requires significant organizational readiness and investment in digital infrastructure. The successful adoption of AI depends on the availability of skilled employees, continuous training, and leadership commitment to change management. Moreover, disparities in digital literacy among employees may hinder the full realization of AI's benefits.

Additionally, AI integration often demands adjustments to existing workflows, data systems, and performance evaluation mechanisms, which may initially disrupt routine operations. Hence, organizations must ensure strong alignment between technological upgrades and human capital development. Commitment from top management, supported by robust policies and inclusive strategies, is crucial to ensuring that the transformation leads to sustainable productivity improvements across all organizational levels.

REFERENCES

AG. A. G., Su, H. K., & Kuo, W. K. (2023, June). Unleashing Potential of Employees through Artificial Intelligence. In *2023 IEEE 5th Eurasia Conference on Biomedical Engineering, Healthcare and Sustainability (ECBIOS)* (pp. 204-206). IEEE.

Asefa, K., Kant, D. S., & Debela, K. L. (2023, November). Effect of Transformational Leadership on Organizational Performance: The Mediating Role of Employee Commitment and Expert Systems (AI) Inclusion in Ethiopia. In *2023 International Conference on Communication, Security and Artificial Intelligence (ICCSAI)* (pp. 305–310). IEEE. DOI: 10.1109/ICCSAI59793.2023.10421269

Baabdullah, A. M. (2024). Generative conversational AI agent for managerial practices: The role of IQ dimensions, novelty seeking and ethical concerns. *Technological Forecasting and Social Change*, *198*, 122951. DOI: 10.1016/j.techfore.2023.122951

Bankins, S., Ocampo, A. C., Marrone, M., Restubog, S. L. D., & Woo, S. E. (2024). A multilevel review of artificial intelligence in organizations: Implications for organizational behavior research and practice. *Journal of Organizational Behavior*, *45*(2), 159–182. DOI: 10.1002/job.2735

Dutta, D., Mishra, S. K., & Tyagi, D. (2023). Augmented employee voice and employee engagement using artificial intelligence-enabled chatbots: A field study. *International Journal of Human Resource Management*, *34*(12), 2451–2480. DOI: 10.1080/09585192.2022.2085525

El Hammoumi, A., Seghyar, N., El Hammoumi, A. M., & El Ouali, A. (2024, December). The Impact of Artificial Intelligence on Employee Adaptability to Remote Work. In *2024 3rd International Conference on Embedded Systems and Artificial Intelligence (ESAI)* (pp. 1-5). IEEE. DOI: 10.1109/ESAI62891.2024.10913897

Gafni, R., Aviv, I., Kantsepolsky, B., Sherman, S., Rika, H., Itzkovich, Y., & Barger, A. (2024). Objectivity by design: The impact of AI-driven approach on employees' soft skills evaluation. *Information and Software Technology*, *170*, 107430. DOI: 10.1016/j.infsof.2024.107430

Gazi, M. A. I., Rahman, M. K. H., Masud, A. A., Amin, M. B., Chaity, N. S., Senathirajah, A. R. B. S., & Abdullah, M. (2024). AI capability and sustainable performance: Unveiling the mediating effects of organizational creativity and green innovation with knowledge sharing culture as a moderator. *Sustainability (Basel)*, *16*(17), 7466. DOI: 10.3390/su16177466

Kassa, B. Y., & Worku, E. K. (2025). The impact of artificial intelligence on organizational performance: The mediating role of employee productivity. *Journal of Open Innovation, 11*(1), 100474. DOI: 10.1016/j.joitmc.2025.100474

Kong, H., Yin, Z., Baruch, Y., & Yuan, Y. (2023). The impact of trust in AI on career sustainability: The role of employee–AI collaboration and protean career orientation. *Journal of Vocational Behavior, 146*, 103928. DOI: 10.1016/j.jvb.2023.103928

Liang, X., Rasheed, U., Cai, J., Wibranek, B., & Awolusi, I. (2024). Impacts of collaborative robots on construction work performance and worker perception: Experimental analysis of human–robot collaborative wood assembly. *Journal of Construction Engineering and Management, 150*(8), 04024087. DOI: 10.1061/JCEMD4.COENG-14390

Malik, A. (2024). A study on the relationship of artificial intelligence applications in HR processes for assessing employee engagement, performance, and job security. *International Review of Management and Marketing, 14*(5), 216–221. DOI: 10.32479/irmm.16838

Malik, A., Budhwar, P., & Kazmi, B. A. (2023). Artificial intelligence (AI)-assisted HRM: Towards an extended strategic framework. *Human Resource Management Review, 33*(1), 100940. DOI: 10.1016/j.hrmr.2022.100940

Masih, N., Sriratanaviriyakul, N., El-Den, J., & Azam, S. (2018, June). The role of knowledge sharing on employees' innovation initiatives. In *Proceedings of the 8th International Workshop on Computer Science and Engineering*, Bangkok, Thailand (pp. 28–30). DOI: 10.2139/ssrn.3212950

Necula, S. C., Fotache, D., & Rieder, E. (2024). Assessing the impact of artificial intelligence tools on employee productivity: Insights from a comprehensive survey analysis. *Electronics (Basel), 13*(18), 3758. DOI: 10.3390/electronics13183758

Neiroukh, S., Emeagwali, O. L., & Aljuhmani, H. Y. (2024). Artificial intelligence capability and organizational performance: Unraveling the mediating mechanisms of decision-making processes. *Management Decision*. Advance online publication. DOI: 10.1108/MD-10-2023-1547

Olan, F., Arakpogun, E. O., Suklan, J., Nakpodia, F., Damij, N., & Jayawickrama, U. (2022). Artificial intelligence and knowledge sharing: Contributing factors to organizational performance. *Journal of Business Research, 145*, 605–615. DOI: 10.1016/j.jbusres.2022.03.008

Rulandari, N., & Silalahi, A. D. K. (2025). *Human-AI collaboration for efficiency and employee job satisfaction in public administration: insights from a resource-based perspective. Transforming Government: People*. Process and Policy., DOI: 10.1108/TG-09-2024-0149

Shaikh, F., Afshan, G., Anwar, R. S., Abbas, Z., & Chana, K. A. (2023). Analyzing the impact of artificial intelligence on employee productivity: The mediating effect of knowledge sharing and well-being. *Asia Pacific Journal of Human Resources, 61*(4), 794–820. DOI: 10.1111/1744-7941.12385

Tummalapalli, H. K., Rao, A. N., Kamal, G., Kumari, N., & Kumar, J. R. S. (2024). Exploring AI-Driven Management: Impact on Organizational Performance, Decision Making, Efficiency, and Employee Engagement. *Journal of Management Research and Analysis*. (Dalam proses publikasi).

Vrontis, D., Christofi, M., Pereira, V., Tarba, S., Makrides, A., & Trichina, E. (2023). Artificial intelligence, robotics, advanced technologies and human resource management: A systematic review. *Artificial Intelligence and International HRM*, 172–201.

Yin, Z., Kong, H., Baruch, Y., Decosta, P. L. E., & Yuan, Y. (2024). Interactive effects of AI awareness and change-oriented leadership on employee-AI collaboration: The role of approach and avoidance motivation. *Tourism Management, 105*, 104966. DOI: 10.1016/j.tourman.2024.104966

Chapter 3
Islamic Governance and AI:
Insights From Brunei Darussalam's Governance of Illicit Drug Use and Trade

Nurezzya Abdullah
https://orcid.org/0009-0005-8499-3023
Universiti Brunei Darussalam, Brunei

Mahani Hamdan
https://orcid.org/0000-0003-3859-4433
Universiti Brunei Darussalam, Brunei

Asiyah Kumpoh
https://orcid.org/0000-0003-0439-8944
Universiti Brunei Darussalam, Brunei

ABSTRACT

Artificial intelligence (AI) is rapidly becoming central to governance, raising concerns about accountability, fairness, and long-term social impact. Brunei Darussalam, guided by the national philosophy of Melayu Islam Beraja (MIB), offers a distinctive case for reflection through its prohibition-oriented approach to drug use and trade. The study found that prohibition reflects taw īd and the maqā id al-sharī ah, particularly the preservation of life (if al-nafs) and intellect (if al- aql), yet also revealed persistent recidivism, limited shūrā (consultation and coordination), and reintegration processes that require further strengthening in the face of stigma and employment barriers. To interpret these dynamics, the chapter applies Basma Abdelgafar's (2018) Public Policy in Islam (PPI) framework, which emphasises

DOI: 10.4018/979-8-3373-8607-2.ch003

taw īd, maqā id, shūrā, and i lā . It argues that insights from Brunei's drug governance can inform AI regulation by framing technology as "governed infrastructure," highlighting both opportunities for support and risks of bias or exclusion.

INTRODUCTION

In recent years, artificial intelligence has moved from the periphery of technological research to the heart of governance practice. Machine learning algorithms predict criminal behaviour, allocate welfare benefits, optimise traffic flows, and even inform judicial sentencing. International organisations and national governments alike are racing to harness AI's potential, while at the same time grappling with the risks of bias, opacity, and surveillance (Jobin et al., 2019; Cath, 2018).

For Muslim-majority societies, these debates intersect with a rich tradition of ethical and legal reasoning. Islamic governance refers to a system of rule grounded in the Qur'an and Sunnah, exemplified in the Prophetic Madinan polity and further developed during the era of the Khulafāʾ al-Rāshidūn as models of justice and consultation (Kamali, 2009). Guided by the maqā id al-sharīʿah which are the preservation of faith, life, intellect, progeny, and wealth (Auda, 2008). Governance is directed toward the protection of essential values and the promotion of societal well-being.

Brunei's national philosophy of Melayu Islam Beraja (MIB) integrates Malay identity, Islamic values, and the monarchy, and functions as the guiding framework for national identity and governance (Setyadi, 2024). The philosophy ensures that public policy reflects religious and ethical considerations, making the application of an Islamic governance lens especially pertinent. At the core of Brunei's drug governance is the Misuse of Drugs Act (MDA), Chapter 27, enforced by the Narcotics Control Bureau (NCB), established in 1988 under the Prime Minister's Office. The NCB has sought to integrate religious principles into its anti-drug strategies, balancing the moral imperative to prohibit intoxicants with the public health need to rehabilitate offenders.

Situated within this governance context, Basma Abdelgafar's (2018) Public Policy in Islam (PPI) framework offers a useful analytical tool for linking traditional Islamic values to contemporary governance challenges. Brunei's experience thus creates a rich case study for considering how Artificial Intelligence (AI) might be applied responsibly.

AI tools are already being used to predict recidivism risk and guide judicial decision-making, though studies highlight both their potential (Kleinberg et al., 2018) and their risks of bias (Angwin et al., 2016). These tensions echo concerns in global AI ethics frameworks (OECD, 2019; UNESCO, 2021). These applications raise questions highly relevant to Brunei's drug policy experience: Can predictive analytics genuinely help reduce recidivism, or do they risk amplifying stigma and bias? Can AI facilitate *shūrā* by analysing public sentiment and supporting more inclusive consultation? And can AI contribute to reintegration efforts, for example by assisting with employment matching, or will it instead intensify surveillance and exclusion?

The Public Policy in Islam (PPI) framework with its emphasis on *taw īd*, *maqā id*, *shūrā*, and *i lā* offers a lens for approaching these questions . By applying this framework as an analytical tool with normative implications, the chapter explores how AI can function as governed infrastructure: not a neutral instrument, but a technology that must be embedded within ethical and societal commitments (UNESCO, 2021; ICESCO, 2024; Elmahjub, 2023).

PROHIBITION, HARM REDUCTION, AND THE ISLAMIC GOVERNANCE LENS

Brunei Darussalam's drug policy cannot be fully understood without situating it in two broader intellectual currents: the global evolution of drug governance, particularly the tension between prohibition and harm reduction, and the Islamic theory of governance embodied in the Public Policy in Islam (PPI) framework. This section examines these foundations in detail, establishing the conceptual anchors that inform both Brunei's policy orientation and this study's analytical framework.

The Dominance of Prohibition

Zero tolerance policy, or the prohibitionist approach, was established by the 1961 Single Convention on Narcotic Drugs as the method of prohibiting certain substances and suppressing their production, distribution, and abuse for the good of the general public (Bewley-Taylor & Jelsma, 2016) . It was the most opted method in dealing with illicit drugs worldwide, and became known as the "war on drugs," politically supported by the image of politicians who are "tough on crime" (Boettke, 2013). Policymakers of drug prohibition assert that the strict banning of substances can lessen and eliminate the illegal drug market through the demand and supply chain. Through prohibition, the perceived hassle and fear of fines, prison time, and the cost of eluding enforcement agencies were expected to deter both demand and supply factors .

Today, the "war on drugs" and zero-tolerance policies are being challenged on multiple fronts. In recent times, an increasing number of people from different levels of society have openly criticised punitive and extreme drug prohibition, arguing that such policies are expensive yet ineffective, violate rights, and worsen health outcomes. Several countries, such as Portugal, New Zealand, and Switzerland, have moved away from the "war on drugs" approach, shifting toward legalisation, decriminalisation, and harm reduction strategies (Csete et al., 2016; Global Commission on Drug Policy, 2021).

The Rise of Harm Reduction

Harm reduction is a set of policies and practices intended to reduce the negative effects of drug and alcohol use. The main feature of harm reduction is that drug users are not expected to abstain from drugs all at once but emphasise practical goals such as safe use and consequence reduction instead of the idealised goal of drug use elimination (Harm Reduction International [HRI], 2023). It covers illicit drugs and legal drugs and is grounded in the field of public health and advocacy movements (Csete et al., 2016).

The practices and policies of harm reduction put public health and well-being at the forefront, which has been evident over the years during international drug policy debates. The overall framework is no longer based on drug policy objectives, but rather on human rights as the entry point. In March 2019, a meeting between leading human rights experts with United Nations Member States and United Nations entities led to the establishment of The International Guidelines on Human Rights and Drug Policy (World Health Organization [WHO], 2021).The International Guidelines provides recommendations on several things to highlight the human-rights aspect of drug policy, including recommendations on discriminatory policing practices, decriminalisation of drugs for personal use, and ending the death penalty for drug-related breaches of the law.

The global shift towards harm reduction reflects a recognition that prohibition cannot eliminate demand. Instead, governance must adapt, integrating public health perspectives into law enforcement strategies.

The contrast between prohibition and harm reduction highlights the need for governance approaches that are not only pragmatic but also value-driven. In Muslim contexts, this conversation is framed within the broader paradigm of Islamic governance.

Islamic Governance

Islamic governance is distinctive in that it embeds moral, spiritual, and legal dimensions within statecraft. The Qur'an and Sunnah provide the foundational principles, and scholars have historically framed governance in terms of the higher objectives of Islamic law (*maqā id al-sharī ah*). These objectives preservation of religion (if al-dīn), life (if al-nafs), intellect (if al-ʿaql), lineage (if al-nasl), and property/wealth (if al-māl) serve as normative benchmarks for evaluating policy (Auda, 2008).

Islamic jurisprudence also recognises human fallibility and insists on i lā (reform), ensuring that governance combines the clarity of prohibition with pathways for repentance and rehabilitation. This dual emphasis reflects the ethical depth of Islamic governance: protection and preservation of the community alongside compassion for individuals (Auda, 2008; Kamali, 2009; Chapra, 2019).

To apply these values in a structured way to modern policy analysis, a coherent framework is required. Basma Abdelgafar's Public Policy in Islam (PPI) provides such a framework, offering four interlinked pillars that operationalise these concepts in the field of governance and public policy.

Public Policy in Islam

Basma Abdelgafar's framework for Public Policy in Islam (PPI) consists of four main components: (1) Unification (taqwa and tawhid), (2) Justification (Maqasid al-Shari'ah), (3) Collective decision-making (Shura), and (4) Reform (Islah). The primary aim of the PPI framework was to advance the scholarly study and practical application of Islamic principles to governance, public policy and related matters. Unification under creation helps to establish boundaries in policy making that protects people and other living things. Justification, or purposefulness, in policy making ensures that all policies are aimed towards accomplishing divine purpose. Collective decision making takes into account multiple stakeholders and public consensus, and reform means that policies must result in improvement (Abdelgafar, 2018).

Therefore, Basma Abdelgafar's Public Policy in Islam (PPI) framework is employed as the analytical lens to interpret findings from Brunei's governance of illicit drug use and trade and to extend these insights to the governance of artificial intelligence (AI). The PPI framework is selected for three main reasons. First, its four components are broadly aligned with conventional good governance principles, making the framework both familiar and adaptable for policy assessment. Second, the model is dynamic, enabling the analysis of existing policies while also offering a structured way to evaluate future governance choices. Third, it incorporates the very principles central to Islamic governance justice, consultation, and reform which are also at the heart of debates on AI ethics and regulation (OECD, 2019; UNESCO, 2021; ICESCO, 2024).

LINKING DRUG GOVERNANCE TO AI ETHICS

The conceptual parallels between drug governance and AI governance are striking. Both involve domains with potential for profound social harm but also legitimate uses, creating dilemmas for regulators (Csete et al., 2016; Babor et al., 2018). Both face global pressures for harmonisation, whether through United Nations conventions on narcotics or emerging frameworks for AI governance such as the OECD Principles (2019) and UNESCO's *Recommendation on the Ethics of AI* (2021). In each case, policymakers struggle to balance prohibition with pragmatic harm reduction.

Prohibitionist approaches to AI, such as calls to ban facial recognition technologies or lethal autonomous weapons, echo Brunei's strict drug laws sending a strong moral signal but risking enforcement challenges and the creation of "black markets" (Cath, 2018; UNESCO, 2021). By contrast, harm-reduction approaches in AI including algorithmic audits, bias-mitigation strategies, and stakeholder consultation parallel Brunei's efforts to integrate rehabilitation and religious education into drug policy (Jobin et al., 2019; OECD, 2019). The Public Policy in Islam (PPI) framework provides a useful bridge between these domains: *taw īd* aligns with the principle of human dignity, *maqā id* with human rights and well-being, *shūrā* with participatory governance, and *i lā* with adaptive and continuous reform (Abdelgafar, 2018; Auda, 2008).

This chapter therefore argues that the PPI lens offers a robust normative foundation not only for interpreting Brunei's approach to drug governance but also for guiding global debates on how to ethically govern transformative technologies such as artificial intelligence.

Findings from Brunei's drug policy

Brunei Darussalam's experience with drug governance illustrates the complexities of sustaining an approach rooted in prohibition while engaging with broader social and ethical considerations. Prohibition remains a strong moral stance consistent with taw īd and the objectives of the maqā id al-sharīʿah, particularly the preservation of life (if al-nafs) and intellect (if al-ʿaql) . Anchored in the *Misuse of Drugs Act* (1978), this approach reflects the Islamic prohibition of intoxicants. At the same time, the empirical evidence indicates that effectiveness is uneven, particularly when judged against long-term outcomes in deterrence, rehabilitation, and reintegration .

The findings showed that enforcement dominates Brunei's approach, while preventive education and rehabilitation are present but less emphasised . Quantitative data between 2012 and 2024 illustrate this imbalance. Drug-related arrests consistently ranged from 453 to 851 cases annually, peaking in 2020 before declining during COVID-19 restrictions (531 cases in 2021), and rising again to 777 in 2024. This enforcement-centred orientation contrasts with the more limited attention to shūrā (consultation) and to long-term rehabilitation and reintegration, which remain areas requiring greater strengthening (Narcotics Control Bureau,personal communication, 2024). Together, these patterns highlight governance tensions that resonate with contemporary debates on artificial intelligence (AI), where policymakers likewise weigh the risks of restrictive control against the need for innovation, transparency, and dignity (Elmahjub, 2023; UNESCO, 2021).

The following subsections outline three major dynamics identified in Brunei's case and consider how they parallel emerging debates in AI governance:

(a) persistent recidivism and relapse,
(b) limited shūrā and inter-agency coordination, and
(c) reintegration processes where stigma and employment remain ongoing concerns.

Persistent Recidivism and the Limits of Deterrence

Repeat arrests accounted for just over half of all drug-related arrests in 2022 and rose further to 60.9% in 2023, highlighting persistent challenges with deterrence (Biro Kawalan Narkotik, 2024, 2025). By contrast, relapse among former Pusat Al-Islah residents under supervision has steadily declined, from 22–29% between 2018 and 2022 to 15% in 2023 and only 5% in 2024. This suggests that individuals who complete structured rehabilitation programmes may have a better chance of sustaining long-term recovery and avoiding relapse, even as enforcement data show that cycles of re-arrest remain common in the wider offender population. This dual pattern mirrors international experience, where punitive enforcement without strong aftercare often leads to revolving cycles of drug use and re-offending (Csete et al., 2016; UNODC, 2022).

From a governance perspective, these figures highlight the importance of coupling deterrence with sustainable support structures. For Brunei, the persistence of recidivism demonstrates the need to reinforce i lā (reform) by ensuring long-term social and economic support. The tension between short-term deterrence and long-term behavioural change in Brunei's drug policy echoes wider AI governance debates. Globally, governments and institutions wrestle with whether to pursue prohibitionist strategies such as bans on high-risk applications like facial recognition or lethal autonomous weapons (Cath, 2018; ICESCO, 2024) or to design regulatory mechanisms that promote safety, transparency, and fairness without stifling innovation (OECD, 2019; UNESCO, 2021). As scholars note, an exclusive focus on immediate control can entrench bias and hinder reform, while continuous oversight and iterative improvement are essential for sustainable governance of AI (Kleinberg et al., 2018; Dressel & Farid, 2018; NIST, 2023).

Shūrā and Coordination Challenges

The study noted that Shura in Brunei is limited, often taking the form of meetings rather than structured consultation . While the NCB integrates enforcement, rehabilitation, and preventive education under one roof, coordination with other agencies and community stakeholders remains inconsistent . Policymakers themselves acknowledged the need for stronger collaboration with families, religious leaders, and civil society partners.

This partial implementation of shūrā reflects broader governance gaps in inclusivity. In Islamic governance, shūrā is a moral and procedural obligation, designed to capture diverse perspectives and ensure that policies reflect both expert and community input (Auda, 2008; Kamali, 2009). When consultation is limited or formalistic, affected communities may feel excluded, thereby undermining legitimacy. International evidence similarly underscores that drug policy responses which neglect community engagement often struggle to achieve long-term legitimacy and effectiveness (Babor et al., 2018; UNODC, 2018; UNESCO, 2021). This suggests that while centralisation can deliver coherence, inclusivity may remain constrained without structured participatory mechanisms.

The governance gap in shūrā parallels debates in AI governance. Globally, AI ethics frameworks including UNESCO's *Recommendation on the Ethics of AI* (2021) emphasise inclusivity and stakeholder participation to avoid reinforcing structural inequalities. If consultation remains limited, whether in drug policy or AI, governance risks becoming top-down, potentially overlooking key concerns from communities most affected.

Rehabilitation and Reintegration

Brunei has invested in rehabilitation through Pusat Al-Islah, where programmes combine vocational training, religious education, counselling, and afercare though supervision . This reflects recognition of the importance of *i lā* and aligns with international best practice (WHO, 2021; UNODC, 2018). However, employment among supervisees stood at 53.5% in 2023 but declined sharply to 33% in the provisional 2024 data, which only cover admissions up to June 2024 (NCB, 2025). While the 2024 figures are not final, the downward trend highlights persistent barriers to reintegration, including stigma, limited labour market absorption, and the difficulties faced by former offenders in securing long-term employment.

These barriers are closely linked to relapse risk. International experience shows that employment is one of the strongest predictors of sustained recovery (Csete et al., 2016). In Brunei, where the labour market is small and tightly regulated, former offenders may find it particularly difficult to secure stable jobs, reinforcing cycles of marginalisation. The persistence of stigma both social and institutional compounds these obstacles.

From the perspective of Islamic governance, these outcomes point to an under-realisation of *i lā* . Rehabilitation must extend beyond spiritual and vocational training to address social acceptance and structural barriers. Without stronger reintegration pathways, prohibition risks undermining the maqā id objectives of protecting life, intellect, and dignity.

The challenge of reintegration resonates with AI governance debates. Just as drug policy cannot end with detention and treatment, AI governance cannot end with the adoption of technical fixes like audits. Long-term oversight, continuous monitoring, and mechanisms for redress are required to ensure technologies serve society without reinforcing exclusion.

Taken together, these dynamics show that Brunei's drug governance combines the moral clarity of prohibition with ongoing difficulties in sustaining long-term outcomes. While prohibition reflects Islamic values of protecting life and intellect, the findings point to the need for stronger emphasis on long-term rehabilitation, employment-based reintegration, and more structured shūrā processes . These patterns are not unique to Brunei; international studies note that prohibitionist regimes often experience similar cycles of detection, punishment, and relapse (Csete et al., 2016; Eastwood, Fox, & Rosmarin, 2016).

Brunei is distinctive in its grounding of Islamic values through the national philosophy of Melayu Islam Beraja (MIB). The findings highlight prohibition as a strong moral stance, consistent with Islamic principles of taw īd and the maqā id al-sharīʿah, while also pointing to areas including the application of shūrā (consultation) and the sustainability of reintegration (i lā) where further strengthening is needed . These insights are not only relevant for understanding Brunei's domestic governance but also provide a vantage point for reflecting on wider global challenges.

The analysis suggests that the dilemmas observed in Brunei balancing deterrence with rehabilitation, ensuring meaningful consultation, and supporting reintegration amid social stigma parallel the questions now being raised about emerging technologies such as artificial intelligence. In this sense, Brunei's policy experience becomes a useful case for considering how an Islamic governance lens, particularly the PPI framework, might guide the design of ethical and effective AI governance. Section 4 therefore examines these intersections, asking how AI could both strengthen governance in such areas and potentially complicate them.

APPLYING THE FINDINGS TO AI GOVERNANCE: OPPORTUNITIES AND RISKS

The findings identified in Brunei's drug policy persistent recidivism and relapse, limited consultation (shūrā) and coordination, and reintegration challenges related to stigma and employment resonate closely with emerging debates in artificial intelligence (AI) governance.

Each reveals how AI could be harnessed to strengthen policy effectiveness, but also how poorly governed systems may worsen the very challenges they are meant to resolve. This section examines these intersections, highlighting both opportunities and risks, and situating them within the Public Policy in Islam (PPI) framework.

Persistent Recidivism and the Limits of Deterrence

The patterns suggest that prohibition produces strong short-term deterrence but does not guarantee long-term behavioural change and that recidivism has remained consistently high, with repeat arrests forming the majority of cases in recent years. AI could contribute to addressing recidivism by supporting tailored rehabilitation and aftercare. Machine learning tools can analyse attendance records, health indicators, and social factors to predict relapse risks, enabling earlier interventions. Digital health platforms and AI-driven counselling tools could extend the reach of limited staff, providing 24/7 support for those undergoing recovery (WHO, 2021). In other contexts, predictive analytics have been used to identify low-risk offenders who can benefit from community-based sentences, with evidence from the U.S. showing that such approaches can lower reoffending when combined with judicial oversight (Kleinberg et al., 2018).

Yet the risks are equally clear. If predictive relapse scores are shared with enforcement rather than health services, AI could transform supportive monitoring into punitive surveillance, reinforcing stigma and perpetuating cycles of criminalisation. International experience warns that algorithmic risk assessment systems can encode historical biases, producing disproportionate burdens on already marginalised groups (Angwin et al., 2016; Dressel & Farid, 2018).

From the PPI perspective, *i lā* (reform) requires that AI be used to support rehabilitation rather than punishment. The *maqā id* imperative of protecting life and intellect also demands that interventions respect dignity and avoid unjustified harm . Thus, AI has potential to strengthen rehabilitation in Brunei but only if governed as a tool of compassion and reform, not as an extension of punitive control.

Shūrā and Coordination

The study noted that Shura in Brunei is limited, often taking the form of meetings rather than structured consultation, and that coordination with other agencies and communities remains inconsistent. This reflects the broader challenge of ensuring that governance is not only centralised and coherent, but also inclusive and participatory.

AI technologies offer opportunities to address this gap. Natural language processing can process thousands of citizen inputs in multiple languages Malay, English, Arabic and summarise them for policymakers. Sentiment analysis can reveal the priorities of different groups, while clustering algorithms can map where communities converge or diverge on policy options. AI-assisted platforms could also generate "You said → We did/Why not" summaries, ensuring that citizens see how their contributions shape outcomes, thereby strengthening legitimacy (UNESCO, 2021).

However, there are risks. Automated summarisation may erase minority voices, privilege dominant groups, or distort inputs depending on training data. In AI governance, critics warn that participation tools can create an illusion of consultation without genuine responsiveness (Jobin et al., 2019). As the study emphasised, the absence of structured consultation in Brunei's drug policy risks leaving affected communities excluded, a pattern that could easily be replicated if AI platforms are not governed transparently.

From the PPI lens, *shūrā* is not optional but an obligation. Consultation must be authentic, inclusive, and transparent . AI can help expand participation, but it must be designed with safeguards to preserve minority perspectives, document data sources, and allow for community feedback on summaries. In this way, AI can complement but not replace human-led deliberation.

Rehabilitation and Reintegration

Rehabilitation in Brunei is centred at Pusat Al-Islah, where programmes combine vocational training, religious education, and counselling, whereas supervision of former offenders is administered separately by the aftercare section of the same institutional framework. These programmes reflect Brunei's recognition of i lā and align with international best practice (UNODC, 2018; WHO, 2021). However, employment among supervisees has shown an ongoing downward trend in recent years, with available data indicating a steady decline during the post-rehabilitation period.

AI could play a supportive role here by linking services across agencies and matching individuals with employment opportunities. Privacy-preserving data integration techniques such as federated learning could connect health, education, and labour market information without compromising confidentiality. AI-based job-matching platforms could translate vocational training from PAI into real-world employment opportunities, while bias-auditing tools ensure that past convictions do not unfairly exclude individuals.

However, the misuse of AI in this space could reinforce stigma. If reintegration data are used for surveillance, former offenders may be perpetually labelled as "high risk," undermining dignity (*karāmah*) and discouraging rehabilitation. The findings highlighted that stigma and limited employment are strongly linked to relapse, making this a particularly sensitive area.

From a PPI perspective, *i lā* requires that reintegration be strengthened through compassion and social support, while *maqā id* emphasises protecting life and intellect. Islamic ethical concepts such as *ma la ah* (public interest) and Data Waqf (treating data as a trust for social good) can serve as governance models for ensuring that AI data systems are managed responsibly (Elmahjub, 2023; ICESCO, 2024).

Across these three dynamics, AI emerges as both a potential solution and a source of risk. Brunei's drug governance demonstrates the moral clarity of prohibition but also the ongoing challenges of sustaining rehabilitation, consultation, and reintegration. AI systems, if governed responsibly, could enhance rehabilitation, broaden consultation, and integrate reintegration services. Yet if poorly managed, they risk reproducing stigma, bias, and exclusion.

The PPI framework offers a pathway to navigate these dilemmas. *Taw īd* ensures coherence of purpose, *maqā id* provide ethical justification, *shūrā* grounds participation, and *i lā* embeds reform. These principles resonate with global AI ethics frameworks (OECD, 2019; UNESCO, 2021; ICESCO, 2024) but also provide a distinctive moral and theological grounding.

While Section 4 has outlined how Brunei's findings resonate with AI governance debates, the next step is to consider what this means in practice. Section 5 therefore turns to the wider implications for policymakers in Brunei and beyond, identifying how AI can be harnessed to strengthen rehabilitation, consultation, and reintegration and what safeguards are needed to ensure alignment with Islamic governance principles.

IMPLICATIONS FOR POLICY AND RESEARCH

The findings from Brunei's drug policy analysis, when extended to the governance of artificial intelligence, suggest significant implications at three interrelated levels: national policy, global ethical frameworks, and the future trajectory of interdisciplinary research.

Policy Implications for Brunei

For Brunei, the adoption of AI technologies in sensitive domains such as drug governance offers considerable promise, but only under carefully constructed safeguards. Predictive analytics could support relapse prevention by allowing rehabilitation programmes to be tailored to individual risks and needs. However, as global evidence demonstrates (Angwin et al., 2016; Kleinberg et al., 2018), risk prediction without dignity-preserving safeguards risks amplifying bias, reinforcing stigma, and undermining rehabilitation. Thus, AI in Brunei must be embedded within governance arrangements that prioritise *karāmah* (dignity) and *urmah* (privacy), consistent with the maqā id's emphasis on the preservation of life (*if al-nafs*) and intellect (*if al- aql*).

Equally, AI-enabled platforms could be mobilised to institutionalise *shūrā*. Current policymaking processes in Brunei often rely on top-down consultation that is formal rather than substantive. Natural language processing and multilingual AI tools could expand participation by synthesising inputs from diverse communities, enabling consultation that is more inclusive, representative, and transparent. Yet, the risk of "participation-washing" where algorithms simulate inclusivity while privileging majority voices requires clear audit mechanisms, echoing UNESCO's (2021) call for participatory and accountable AI governance.

Finally, reintegration support could be significantly enhanced by AI. Brunei's data indicate that employment outcomes for supervisees have been on a downward trend in recent years, suggesting that structural and social barriers particularly stigma and limited access to stable work continue to undermine reintegration efforts. AI-powered labour market platforms could bridge this gap by matching rehabilitated individuals to appropriate opportunities, monitoring outcomes in real time, and identifying structural barriers. Nonetheless, unless designed to counteract discrimination, such systems could entrench exclusion by embedding historical patterns of bias. Thus, the adoption of AI in this domain must be explicitly aligned with i lā (reform), positioning technology not as a punitive extension of enforcement, but as a tool to restore dignity and facilitate social acceptance.

Implications for Global AI Governance

Beyond Brunei, this case study illustrates the broader value of Islamic governance principles for global debates on AI ethics. The four pillars of the PPI framework *taw īd*, *maqā id*, *shūrā*, and *i lā* —resonate strongly with international frameworks but also provide distinctive normative grounding. The OECD Principles on AI (2019) stress transparency, accountability, and human-centred values; UNESCO's Recommendation on the Ethics of AI (2021) foregrounds fairness, inclusivity, and human rights; and the ICESCO Riyadh Charter (2024) integrates Islamic values such as justice and mercy. The PPI framework, grounded in the classical maqā id al-sharīʿah the preservation of religion (dīn), life (nafs), intellect (ʿaql), progeny (nasl), and property (māl) (Auda, 2008; Kamali, 2009) emphasises broader values such as justice (ʿadl), dignity (karāmah), and social welfare, which contemporary scholars highlight as central to Islamic governance (Chapra, 2019).

This Islamic governance perspective challenges the assumption that AI can be governed purely through secular regulatory instruments. Instead, it reframes AI as a governed infrastructure not a neutral technology, but a tool embedded within moral, cultural, and theological commitments. This is particularly relevant in Muslim-majority societies, where public legitimacy often rests on alignment with Islamic values. By foregrounding maqā id, shūrā, and i lā , the PPI framework shows how AI governance can be contextualised within traditions of justice and consultation, rather than reduced to technocratic efficiency.

Research Implications

From a research perspective, the Brunei case underscores the need for interdisciplinary inquiry that bridges Islamic governance, technology ethics, and empirical policy analysis. Three areas emerge as priorities.

First, there is a need to operationalise maqā id-based benchmarks for AI governance. Just as impact assessments are required in environmental policy, AI systems in sensitive domains could be evaluated against benchmarks that test their capacity to preserve life, intellect, and dignity. Developing such tools would make Islamic values measurable within governance processes.

Second, Islamic models of data governance such as *Data Waqf* (Nashwan, 2025) merit further exploration. Treating sensitive data as a trust for the benefit of the community offers an ethical alternative to models that commodify or over-surveil personal information.

Third, empirical research is required to assess whether AI interventions genuinely improve outcomes in contexts such as rehabilitation and reintegration. Pilot projects should be designed to test whether AI reduces relapse rates, enhances inclusivity in consultation, or improves employment outcomes for rehabilitated offenders. Crucially, such studies must not only measure efficiency but also test for alignment with dignity and justice.

Taken together, these implications show that Brunei's governance experience provides lessons not only for national policymakers but also for global regulators and researchers. The PPI framework demonstrates how Islamic governance principles can complement international AI ethics frameworks by embedding justice, consultation, and reform at the heart of technological governance. By translating abstract values into concrete applications relapse prevention, inclusive consultation, and reintegration support, the analysis highlights both the promise of AI and the risks of its misuse. The research agenda that follows calls for operationalising Islamic governance principles as practical benchmarks for AI, ensuring that technology remains accountable not only to governments and corporate actors but also to enduring moral and spiritual commitments.

In this sense, the adoption of AI in Brunei's drug governance is not just a technical question but a test of governance coherence: whether technological innovation can be harnessed in ways that serve the unity of purpose, preserve higher objectives, institutionalise consultation, and sustain reform.

CONCLUSION

This chapter has shown through insights from Brunei Darussalam's governance of illicit drug use and trade provide a valuable lens for thinking about the governance of artificial intelligence (AI). Prohibition in Brunei reflects taw īd and the maqā id al-sharīʿah, but its governance experience also demonstrates the limits of deterrence when not matched with sustained i lā and structured shūrā . These dynamics echo broader questions in AI governance, where policymakers must balance restriction with innovation, central authority with inclusive participation, and immediate control with long-term sustainability.

The application of the Public Policy in Islam (PPI) framework shows how Islamic governance principles can address these dilemmas. *Taw īd* provides coherence of purpose, *maqā id* supply ethical thresholds, *shūrā* grounds legitimacy in consultation, and *i lā* demands continuous reform. Taken together, these principles demonstrate that AI, like drug policy, cannot be left as a neutral or purely technical matter; it must be governed as infrastructure embedded within enduring values of justice and human dignity (OECD, 2019; UNESCO, 2021; ICESCO, 2024; Elmahjub, 2023).

Conceptually, this chapter contributes by extending the PPI framework into the field of AI governance, showing how an Islamic normative model can complement and deepen global ethics frameworks. Practically, it illustrates that Muslim-majority societies often perceived as peripheral in technology debates can instead offer distinctive insights rooted in long-standing traditions of justice, consultation, and reform.

In closing, the lesson is that both drug governance and AI governance face the temptation of prohibition as the simplest solution. Yet enduring success depends on embedding consultation, protection, and reform within governance structures. Anchored in *taw īd*, *maqā id*, *shūrā*, and *i lā* , AI can be steered not as an opaque force beyond control but as infrastructure accountable to ethical and societal commitments. Brunei's experience shows that Islamic governance is not a constraint on innovation but a necessary contributor to building ethical, transparent, and just digital futures.

REFERENCES

Abdelgafar, B. (2018). *Public policy: Beyond traditional jurisprudence: A Maqasid approach*. International Institute of Islamic Thought. DOI: 10.2307/j.ctvkc6778

Angwin, J., Larson, J., Mattu, S., & Kirchner, L. (2016). Machine bias: There's software used across the country to predict future criminals. And it's biased against Blacks. *ProPublica*. https://www.propublica.org/article/machine-bias-risk-assessments-in-criminal-sentencing

Auda, J. (2008). *Maqasid al-Shariah as philosophy of Islamic law: A systems approach*. International Institute of Islamic Thought. DOI: 10.2307/j.ctvkc67tg

Auda, J. (2008). *Maqasid al-Shariah: A beginner's guide*. International Institute of Islamic Thought. DOI: 10.2307/j.ctvkc67c6

Babor, T., Caulkins, J., Edwards, G., Fischer, B., Foxcroft, D., Humphreys, K., & Strang, J. (2018). *Drug policy and the public good* (2nd ed.). Oxford University Press. DOI: 10.1093/oso/9780198818014.001.0001

Bewley-Taylor, D., & Jelsma, M. (2016). Regime change: Re-visiting the 1961 Single Convention on Narcotic Drugs. *The International Journal on Drug Policy*, *23*(1), 72–81. DOI: 10.1016/j.drugpo.2011.08.003

Boettke, P., Coyne, C., & Hall, A. (2013). Keep Off the Grass: The Economics of Prohibition and U.S. Drug Policy. *Oregon Law Review*, *91*(4), 1075–1077.

Cath, C. (2018). Governing artificial intelligence: Ethical, legal and technical opportunities and challenges. *Philosophical Transactions. Series A, Mathematical, Physical, and Engineering Sciences*, *376*(2133), 20180080. DOI: 10.1098/rsta.2018.0080

Chapra, M. U. (2019). *The future of economics: An Islamic perspective* (New ed.). The Islamic Foundation.

Csete, J., Kamarulzaman, A., Kazatchkine, M., Altice, F., Balicki, M., Buxton, J., & Wolfe, D. (2016). Public health and international drug policy. *Lancet*, *387*(10026), 1427–1480. DOI: 10.1016/S0140-6736(16)00619-X

Dressel, J., & Farid, H. (2018). The accuracy, fairness, and limits of predicting recidivism. *Science Advances*, *4*(1), eaao5580. Advance online publication. DOI: 10.1126/sciadv.aao5580

Eastwood, N., Fox, E., & Rosmarin, A. (2016). *A quiet revolution: Drug decriminalisation across the globe*. Release. https://www.release.org.uk/publications/quiet-revolution-drug-decriminalisation-across-globe

Elmahjub, E. (2023). Artificial Intelligence (AI) in Islamic Ethics: Towards pluralist ethical benchmarking for AI. *Philosophy & Technology*, *36*(4), 1–24. DOI: 10.1007/s13347-023-00668-x

Global Commission on Drug Policy. (2021). *Time to end prohibition. Geneva: Global Commission on Drug Policy*. https://www.globalcommissionondrugs.org/reports/time-to-end-prohibition

Harm Reduction International. (2023). *The global state of harm reduction 2023*. Harm Reduction International.

Islamic World Educational, Scientific and Cultural Organization. (2024). *Riyadh charter on ethics of artificial intelligence*. ICESCO.

Jobin, A., Ienca, M., & Vayena, E. (2019). The global landscape of AI ethics guidelines. *Nature Machine Intelligence*, *1*(9), 389–399. DOI: 10.1038/s42256-019-0088-2

Kamali, M. H. (2009). *Shari'ah law: An introduction*. Oneworld Publications.

Kleinberg, J., Lakkaraju, H., Leskovec, J., Ludwig, J., & Mullainathan, S. (2018). Human decisions and machine predictions. *The Quarterly Journal of Economics*, *133*(1), 237–293. DOI: 10.1093/qje/qjx032

Nashwan, A. J. (2025). Data endowment as a digital waqf: An Islamic ethical framework for AI development. *Philosophy & Technology*, *38*(2), 74. Advance online publication. DOI: 10.1007/s13347-025-00905-5

National Institute of Standards and Technology. (2023). *AI risk management framework (AI RMF 1.0)*. U.S. Department of Commerce., DOI: 10.6028/NIST.AI.100-1

Organisation for Economic Co-operation and Development. (2019). *OECD principles on artificial intelligence*. OECD Publishing. https://oecd.ai/en/ai-principles

Setyadi, M. H. (2024). Melayu Islam Beraja: Identitas nasional Brunei Darussalam. *CARITA: Jurnal Sejarah dan Budaya*, 2(2), 109–118. DOI: 10.35905/carita.v2i2.7406

United Nations Educational, Scientific and Cultural Organization. (2021). *Recommendation on the ethics of artificial intelligence*. UNESCO. https://unesdoc.un.org/ark:/48223/pf0000380455

United Nations Office on Drugs and Crime. (2018). *International standards on drug use prevention*. UNODC.

United Nations Office on Drugs and Crime. (2022). [UNODC.]. *World Drug Report*, •••, 2022.

World Health Organization. (2021). *Ethics and governance of artificial intelligence for health: WHO guidance*. World Health Organization.

KEY TERMS AND DEFINITIONS

AI Governance: The frameworks, policies, and ethical principles that guide how AI is designed, deployed, and monitored to ensure accountability, fairness, and public trust

Harm Reduction: A set of practical strategies intended to minimize the negative health, social, and legal impacts associated with drug use without necessarily reducing drug consumption.

Islamic Governance: Governance system guided by Islamic principles and ethics derived from the Qur'an, Sunnah, and scholarly consensus (Ijma).

Prohibition Policy: Drug policies characterized by stringent law enforcement and punitive measures aimed at eliminating illicit drug production, distribution, and consumption.

Public Policy in Islam (PPI): A Islamic Governance framework developed by Basma Abdelgafar that incorporates Tawhid, Taqwa, Maqasid al-Shari'ah, Shura, and Islah into the policy-making process to ensure ethical and effective governance.

Chapter 4

AI-Driven Robotics for Enabling Organizational Change Towards Sustainability

Leena Jenefa
https://orcid.org/0000-0002-1324-7083
Hindustan Institute of Technology and Science, Chennai, India

M. Jayakumar
https://orcid.org/0009-0006-4569-495X
Vel Tech Rangarajan Dr. Sagunthala R&D Institute of Science and Technology, Chennai, India

R. M. Dilip Charaan
https://orcid.org/0009-0002-1332-4592
Vel Tech Rangarajan Dr. Sagunthala R&D Institute of Science and Technology, Chennai, India

P. R. Therasa
https://orcid.org/0000-0002-5172-0791
R.M.K. Engineering College, India

F. George
St. Joseph College of Engineering, Chennai, India

D. Amutha
St.Mary's College, Thoothukudi, India

ABSTRACT

Artificial intelligence (AI) is increasingly seen as a crucial instrument for tackling the most serious difficulties confronting modern industry, including the quest of sustainability. The usage of AI is assisting businesses in navigating corporate sustainability difficulties, but present research lacks a thorough examination of how firms employ AI to improve sustainability. Finally, this paper provides an integrated paradigm for sustainability-oriented AI adoption, emphasizing the need of connecting AI ac-

DOI: 10.4018/979-8-3373-8607-2.ch004

tivities with organizational sustainability goals in order to preserve a competitive edge and drive development. As a result, it emphasizes the importance of strong data management, system integration, and continuous performance monitoring in order to eliminate opposition to AI adoption and fully realize AI's promise in the quest of sustainability.

INTRODUCTION

Enabling organizational transformation for sustainability necessitates a multi-faceted strategy that includes leadership commitment, effective communication, stakeholder participation, and a focus on creating a sustainable culture. As more firms prioritize sustainability, the obstacles involved with carrying out these operations have increased (Di Vaio et al., 2020). It entails identifying change drivers, overcoming possible roadblocks, and encouraging organizational innovation.

Empowering people is another critical component of generating long-term transformation. Change does not occur in isolation or from the top down; rather, it occurs when everyone throughout the business feel motivated and capable of making a contribution. Artificial intelligence has emerged as a major factor affecting the global commercial environment. In this digital age, AI technologies have emerged as critical tools for improving operational efficiency, decision-making, and creativity throughout the world. Artificial intelligence covers many technologies, including machine learning, robotics, natural language processing, and artificial neural networks.

Companies should invest in training and tools to assist staff understand sustainability concepts and how to apply them to their unique responsibilities. A manufacturing line worker, for example, may learn about waste reduction measures, whilst a marketing team could promote the company's environmentally friendly products.

Organizations may utilize their workforce's creativity and enthusiasm for sustainability by providing chances for workers to offer ideas and lead projects (Domisch et al., 2019). AI technologies in supply chain management include artificial neural networks, agent-based systems, and genetic algorithms. Artificial neural networks are software-based AI systems that mimic the structure of the human brain, consisting of numerous linked neurons in which information is stored.

Its indirect consequences are larger and less evident, and include enhanced decision-making, and increased public consciousness (Gupta et al., 2021).

Artificial intellect is gradually seen as a crucial instrument for tackling the most serious difficulties confronting modern industry, including the quest of sustainability. Artificial intelligence (AI) is increasingly acknowledged as a crucial tool for tackling modern industry' most urgent concerns, including the quest of sustainability (Haefner et al., 2021). The usage of AI is assisting trades in steering business sustainability difficulties, nonetheless current investigate lacks a complete exploration of how organizations employ AI to promote sustainability (Haftor et al., 2021). New AI-related technologies present chances for operations to enhance production efficiency, cut costs, and bring value to customers. Smart factories may employ real-time data and artificial intelligence to operate independently and flexibly. Smart factories may use AI to adapt and support various production situations, as well as handle varying production configurations, demand quantities, and manufacturing technologies (Qu & Kim, 2024).

This study elicits insights from sustainability practitioners who play critical roles in operationalizing strategy goals and performance reporting by studying practices in exemplary multinational corporations.

Over the last century, technological innovation has played a critical role in the growth of commercial efficiency and global sustainability initiatives. Artificial intelligence (AI) has emerged as a highly transformational technology, dubbed the "revolution of the century". Recent advances in AI, particularly generative AI, have transformed communication and data analysis across a wide range of businesses, well beyond the technology industry (Rantala et al., 2023).

AI improves transparency by evaluating large amounts of data from diverse sources in real time, allowing for more actual monitoring and ensuring conformity to human rights and ecological norms (Russell & Norvig, 2003).

AI-powered robotics is a fast expanding discipline that is altering a wide range of businesses, engineering, agriculture, and building (Schwaeke et al., 2024). AI may not only improve efficiency but also serve as a catalyst for sustainability in IB. It may play an important role in accomplishing the United Nations Sustainable Development Goals by improving sustainability behaviors like as carbon footprint reduction and responsible consumerism. AI technology can handle difficult global concerns such as climate change, poverty, and food insecurity.

The constant quest of intelligent robotic systems has resulted in a symbiotic partnership between human ingenuity and AI, with AI-powered independent automobiles, drones, and robots revolutionizing conveyance, health care, and survey.

It provides litheness and education capabilities, revolutionizing how machines interact with people. This trend represents a paradigm shift in personnel management and overall corporate performance, harnessing the revolutionary potential of AI technology. In the worldwide fight for top talent, when traditional recruitment approaches struggle to keep up with competitive expectations, it is clear that businesses must utilize innovative recruiting technologies

The combination of AI and automation ushers in a new age in which robots become friends and reasoning extensions of humanoid competences (Jenefa et al., 2024a). Notably, AI dramatically improves day-to-day HR processes, notably in recruiting, leading to increased recruiter efficiency.

Robotics has the potential to assist our society in addressing many present and anticipated difficulties, as outlined in the United Nations' Sustainable Development Goals project. Prior research has examined the influence of Artificial Intelligence (AI) on the SDGs using a rigorous consensus-based expert elicitation method (Jenefa & Jayakumar, 2025; Haidegger et al., 2023; Boesl & Liepert, 2016).

Moving on to the employment level, entire job functions are beginning to be replaced with AI technology. Notably, the introduction of virtual assistant software redefining customer service by providing 24/7 help, which is especially useful for IBs aiming to reach international markets without the requirement for a physical present.

Robots often need a considerable investment and provide money for capital owners as well as, in certain cases, high-skilled personnel who are difficult to replace with robots. Other people, often less skilled or undereducated, who are already at the bottom of the national income distribution, may see their salaries fall or perhaps become unemployed. A tax on robot workers is frequently discussed as a potential approach to close the skilled-unskilled pay gap (Torelli et al., 2020). Leveraging smart technology, artificial intelligence, robotics, and algorithms (STARA) skills, as well as green innovation for sustainable development, provides competences for green innovative proof. Green organisational innovative evidence may help to attract prospective investors interested in evolving the United Nations' SDG program for environmental sustainability.

REVIEW OF LITERATURE

Technology has grown significantly in recent years, changing the basic ways that organizations operate and produce value. In recent years, AI's considerable effect on both society and technology has emerged as something having the ability to determine the future growth of the global economy (Torelli et al., 2020). AI applications can handle environmental collapse, uncertainty, and social upheaval by providing first insights for management education and commercial enterprises in the midst of fast social and technical transition. Advances in artificial intelligence (AI) have transformed the area of robotics, resulting in the creation of AI-powered robots with greater skills and intelligence.

However, the integration of AI and robots raises ethical questions about social ramifications, employment displacement, and the need for ethical norms in the design and operation of these technologies. The rising monetary impact of AI may lead to increased inequality as educational and computer resources are unevenly distributed throughout the world (Jenefa et al., 2024b).

They have generally focused on particular uses or theoretical implications of artificial intelligence for business sustainability efforts. AI use case for green technology start-ups that deviates from typical methodologies. However, there is a critical paucity of research that completely and systematically addresses how businesses might apply and grow AI to achieve their sustainability objectives (Bolukbasi et al., 2016).

This rise poses both obstacles and opportunity for AI applications in a variety of sectors. AI applications in public administration systems have grown more important in the workout of state influence and public inspiration.

To be pertinent in sustainability administration, AI's influence must be measurable. Managers should put in place processes to analyze and assess how AI technologies help to sustainability goals. Data-driven impact measurement enables managers to make more informed decisions, enhance AI systems, and communicate real changes to stakeholders (Jenefa et al., n.d.).

As robotics, automation, and artificial intelligence (AI) become more prevalent in human life, an informed discussion about their influence on society becomes increasingly important. To facilitate such an interchange among all impacted parties, the authors believe it is critical to provide accessible and intelligible information regarding the structure of different technologies (Khamis et al., 2021).

Robotics technology alters sectors by driving long-term development, enhancing healthcare delivery, reducing inequality, and supporting economic growth. Robotics promotes inclusion and efficiency by innovating and automating, enabling marginalized areas while addressing global concerns in accordance with the United Nations' sustainable development goals. Despite substantial study on the impact of robotics on sustainable development goals (SDGs), there has been little attention paid to how these technologies affect healthcare, innovation, inequality, and economic growth, particularly in poor countries (Jayakumar et al., 2024a).

AI-powered automation boosts economic development and productivity while also improving the labor market and employment picture. Despite good contributions in industries such as manufacturing, the advancement of AI-powered robotics is not without obstacles (Priyatharsini et al., 2025).

Incorporating artificial intelligence into production is regarded separate from digitalization and technology integration (Charaan et al., 2025).

AI is an umbrella word that refers to a wide range of techniques and approaches, and it has evolved as a prominent topic in computer science. Almost all AI algorithms are designed to do a particular job, hence the term artificial narrow intelligence would be more appropriate than AI (RM et al., 2024).

Figure 1. AI application in Manufacturing Unit

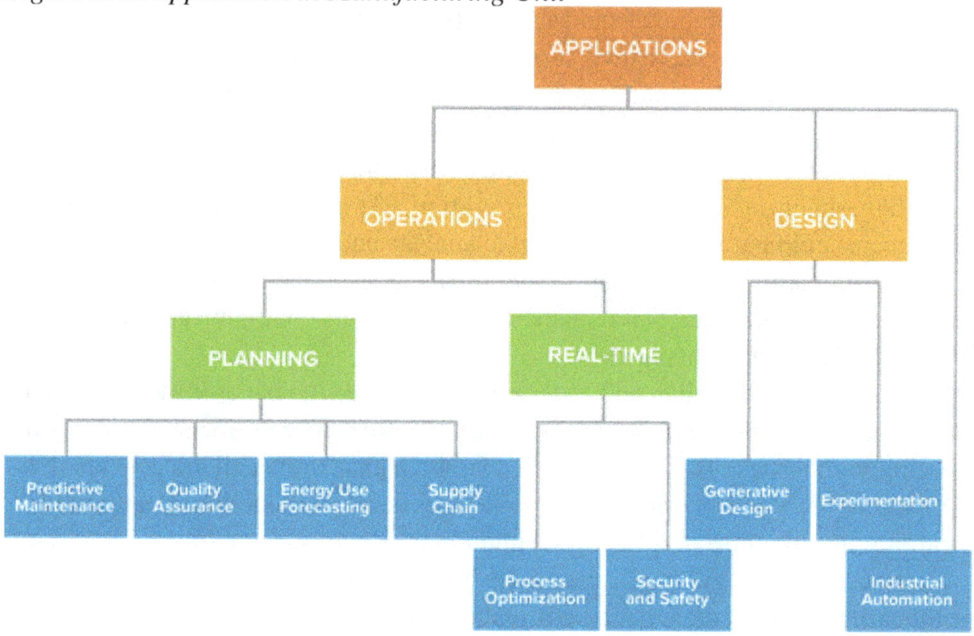

Predictive maintenance is studying sensor data from equipment to predict possible problems and development keep routines to avoid unneeded downtime. It is one of the most prevalent uses for AI/ML in industrial industries, such as aerospace, chemicals, electronics, and consumer products production (Jayakumar et al., 2024b).

Quality assurance is critical for consumer health and safety. Preventing quality failures may increase customer satisfaction while lowering expenses and waste. AI/ML models have showed potential in improving quality control in a variety of manufacturing industries. Recent research has demonstrated that CNNs can match, and in some cases surpass, existing approaches for detecting flaws in produced products (Sheffi, 2024). This is especially relevant in additive manufacturing, where characteristics like density and porosity may have a substantial impact on the end product's mechanical qualities.

Supply chain management is one of the most important and difficult aspects of industrial operations, as supply networks can span many nations and continents. AI/ML may be utilized in applications that help and improve supply chains by using predictive analytics and real-time data analysis to manage inventory and production planning.

ENABLING CORPORATE SUSTAINABILITY THROUGH AI

The emergence of artificial intelligence (AI) heralds a transformational era in a variety of fields, including management methods. AI-driven management represents a significant shift in how businesses employ technology to improve decision-making processes, operational efficiency, and overall performance. Given that highly qualified knowledge workers will dominate operations, MNE executives must reevaluate their cultures, provide additional employee engagement possibilities, and address employee concerns about privacy, excessive corporate control, and dehumanization.

Corporate sustainability is the strategy firms take to guarantee they meet their commitments to both present and future stakeholders (Eklof et al., 2024). The translation of artificial intellect and machine knowledge from concept to real-world skills is a critical facilitator of the quarter engineering rebellion as it combines AI/ML with other emerging technologies to alter industry (Jagatheesaperumal et al., 2021).

Corporate sustainability is a complicated, multifaceted notion that is always evolving. As a result, firms face a substantial problem in maintaining a high degree of corporate sustainability throughout time (Ahdadou et al., 2024; Dyllick & Hockerts, 2002).

IoT adoption has resulted in the widespread creation of smart and connected devices, as well as cheaper and more efficient operations. This one will change. Individuals' global lifestyles and lives evolve, as do thriving businesses that develop new inventions. This projection by the claims that in the next years, a global corporation that has dispersed lots of keen gadgets would support monetary growing value many times more across almost every economic industry. The deployment of the Internet is nothing more than a large-scale, wide system, and the essential notion underpinning Internet access is that it will reveal facts about devices interconnected through a network, as well as the movement of data, and we may assume that it will affect individuals (Baumgartner & Ebner, 2010).

The incorporation of Artificial Intellect into business sectors has ushered in a new era of sustainability practices, changing environmental and social governance (ESG) approaches. This extensive survey investigates the multiple effects of AI on business sustainability, looking at both the potential benefits and concerns. Companies may improve their sustainability efforts by integrating various AI technologies such as machine learning, natural language processing, and robots, resulting in more efficiency, less waste, and inventive solutions to challenging environmental challenges (Appannan et al., 2023). However, the adoption of AI poses substantial problems, including energy usage, ethical issues, and the socioeconomic repercussions of automation.

Industry 4.0 and high-tech markets offer unique opportunities for optimizing corporate accounting and reporting due to high demand for quality and advanced automation tools. Advanced technologies, like AI and datasets, offer several potential to enhance management information systems' efficacy. However, the issue comes with the current method of managing product quality in industry 4.0 (Geissbauer et al., 2017).

The combination between sustainability and innovation is crucial in tackling these issues. Corporate sustainability innovation is to create new goods, processes, or business models that balance environmental and social goals with economic success. Integrating sustainability into supply chains may give strategic benefits like as innovation, competitiveness, and long-term economic viability (Krishnan, 2022). This strategy ensures regulatory compliance, decreases environmental impact, and promotes innovation through sustainable corporate practices. Sustainable supply chain management improves operational effectiveness and meets the needs of environmentally conscientious customers.

ROBOTIC TECHNOLOGY ADOPTION IN ORGANIZATIONS

Figure 2 illustrates how the revolutionary integration of AI in robotic systems has altered a variety of industries, including healthcare, manufacturing, and transportation. Industrial robots are already an essential component of modern industry. Incorporating AI into current industrial robots has the potential to significantly improve human-robot interaction (Koren et al., 2024).

It might enable robots to swiftly adapt to changing human behavior while maintaining safety and efficiency. Researchers, traders, and labor economists debate the impact of technology adoption on productivity and automation, including robots and AI, on employment. The literature suggests that the rate of job loss due to new productivity technologies may outrun the rate of finding new employment opportunities. AI-powered robots demonstrate greater flexibility and learning capabilities, allowing them to complete tasks with accuracy and agility.

Figure 2. Robotic Application

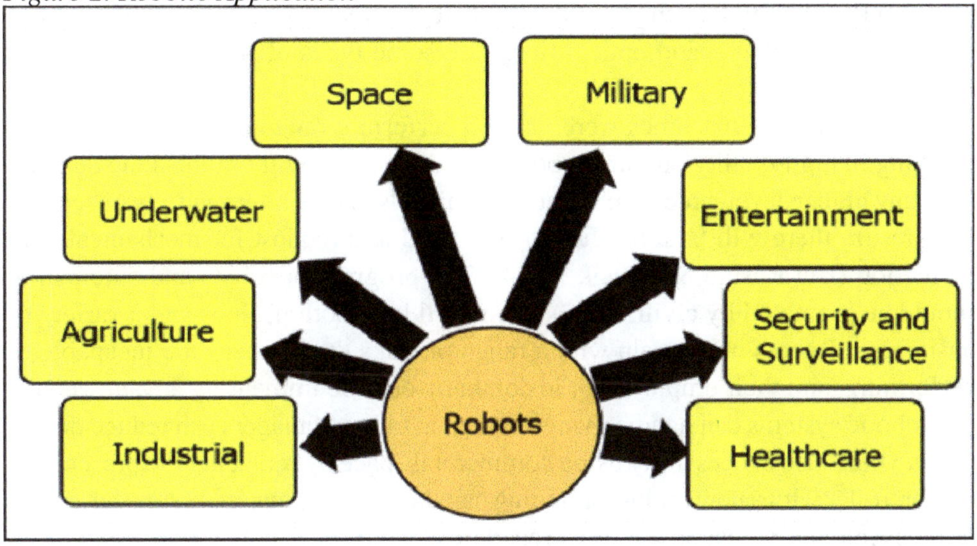

The ethical concerns of AI-driven robots are significant, addressing social repercussions, employment market dynamics, and equal access to modern technologies (Marichamy et al., 2024; Yugendran et al., 2025). Robots are widely used in industries to load and unload machinery and parts, replacing manual labor and mechanical techniques. Robots can duplicate intended duties, execute correctly, and work with adjacent equipment. Consider using industrial robots in work environments that are dangerous, unhealthy, hazardous, uncomfortable, or unpleasant for people (Singla et al., 2025). This automaton support takes a significant investment, but it also yields significant returns. Automated machines are thus beneficial investments since they improve productivity in manufacturing (Essays, 2022).

Furthermore, the introduction of AI-powered robotics has changed the employment market by increasing productivity and offering new possibilities in industries like manufacturing.

These robots can carry out complex sequences of jobs. Production robotics may perform a number of functions, including as assembling and enabling. These are certainly designed to do a range of assembly jobs while reducing the time necessary to generate them. In reality, artificial intelligence and machine learning algorithms have been integrated into robotic arms to assist manufacturers in responding to important circumstances (Kragic et al., 1970). Numerous studies show that industrial robots improve productivity and lead to changes in the labor market. New technology often has disruptive effects during adoption and development, and its real worth may not be immediately apparent.

Robotic arms were meant to do repetitive, specialized tasks. Typically, the part or item that the robot will change is already existent in place. Logical method contacts valves, photo eyeballs, and optical fibers are some types of senses (Jayakumar et al., 2024c).

Many industrial machines were used to perform a range of repetitive actions, resulting in high-quality output. Robotics advancements will diminish the demand for many higher-level, precision vocations while also benefiting a variety of sectors. As a result, there will be a balance of true need and request for mechanical help on the job (Bin Rashid & Kausik, 2024). The progress of robots and automation should be promoted by civilization since it will help both persons and a variety of businesses. Robots might help with a range of tasks that humans are incapable of performing, and their employment in combat would be immensely advantageous.

Robotic systems can handle many projects at once. Managers can reduce device layout while also successfully using commercial space by replacing the present microcontroller with a new multi-computing capability. Food manufacturers have used robotics into their meat processing procedures (Wu et al., 2023). These gadgets use AI, imaging technology, or cameras to perform a range of tasks. Anything may be cut, measured, packaged, and palletized by them. Companies with a large number of sensors would monitor equipment and manufacturing methods to prevent unusual products and solutions.

However, ethical and legal issues exist, needing a deliberate strategy to navigate the complicated environment of AI and robotics integration.

AI AND SUSTAINABILITY

When we investigated the use of AI with a focus on environmental sustainability, we discovered data that distinguishes between its direct and indirect effects on sustainability initiatives. The rise of artificial intellect and deep knowledge skills has marked a watershed moment in several industries, notably sustainability. These novel technologies have shown amazing promise for supporting sustainable habits, particularly in the areas of renewable energy and environmental health.

AI is used to handle city transportation using self-driving vehicles, as well as deploy robots for restaurant service and infrastructure maintenance (Martínez et al., 2020). Advanced AI platforms, known as metropolitan Intelligent Platforms, can manage traffic, safety, and air quality in metropolitan areas.

Effective corporate governance, including independent directors and strategic supervision, may boost innovation and sustainability results (Al-Ansi et al., 2024). Research shows that corporate governance has a favorable influence on sustainable growth, with innovation efficiency functioning as a moderating element. Software robots are increasingly taking on roles as coworkers, teammates, and bosses, transforming traditional teams into hybrid systems. Independent directors play a crucial role in promoting research and development, emphasizing the need for strong governance structures to drive long-term innovation.

Direct implications refer to AI's direct and observable influence on environmental sustainability. AI applications help to decrease environmental damage and optimize resource use (Vasudevan et al., 2024). Corporate sustainability efforts for gender equality emphasize the need of inclusivity in promoting sustainable business practices. Promoting gender equality in organizations improves both social sustainability and performance, driving innovation. These efforts show how diversity management may be integrated into business sustainability plans (Abdul-Khalil et al., 2023).

CONCLUSION

Modern technology should enhance, not replace, people's daily lives and jobs. Innovative technology and IT solutions should foster creativity and enable intellect, sensitivity, and empathy.

As industries grow, AI will play an increasingly crucial role in securing technical supremacy. Businesses may successfully manage the complexity of incorporating AI into their sustainability plans by prioritizing sustainability, encouraging adaptation, and aligning AI projects with their organizational goals.

Automation and robots are having an influence on several industries. Manufacturing processes are becoming more complex and diverse as a result of digitalization and the increased use of cutting-edge computer technologies such as artificial intelligence (AI). Industrial automation solutions are increasingly being used to both optimize and automate processes.

Increased mechanization is necessary in this modern, more difficult operational environment. In the future, traditional employment will be replaced with robotically optimized work. It is debatable how far advanced robots will finally displace industry workers. AI-powered robots offer enormous promise across businesses and sectors. However, the integration of AI and robots poses ethical concerns regarding society, labor markets, and technological democratization.

The fast advancement of AI/ML technology has created an unparalleled potential to change the industrial business. This assessment addressed a wide range of manufacturing applications, highlighting AI/ML's potential to enhance production safety, efficiency, productivity, and sustainability. However, there are still ethical concerns, legalities, and societal preparedness for AI-driven robotics research and implementation. To leverage the promise of AI-powered robotics while reducing hazards, ethical governance and responsible innovation are required.

Robots have the potential to improve the total work force by generating opportunities that need a diverse set of skills.

To support the long-term growth of robotics, the robotics community would benefit immensely from initiatives to raise awareness, provide tools, and share expertise.

REFERENCES

Abdul-Khalil, S., Abdul-Rahman, S., Mutalib, S., Kamarudin, S. I., & Kamaruddin, S. S. (2023). A review on object detection forautonomous mobile robot. *IAES International Journal of Artificial Intelligence*, *12*(3), 1033–1043. DOI: 10.11591/ijai.v12.i3.pp1033-1043

Ahdadou, M., Aajly, A., & Tahrouch, M. (2024). Enhancing corporate governance through AI: A systematic literature review. *Technology Analysis and Strategic Management*, ●●●, 1–14.

Al-Ansi, A., Al-Ansi, A. M., Muthanna, A., & Koucheryavy, A. (2024). Blockchain technology integration in service migration to 6Gcommunication networks: A comprehensive review. *Indonesian Journal of Electrical Engineering and Computer Science*, *34*(3), 1654–1664. DOI: 10.11591/ijeecs.v34.i3.pp1654-1664

Appannan, J. S., Mohd Said, R., Ong, T. S., & Senik, R. (2023). Promoting sustainable development through strategies, environmental management accounting and environmental performance. *Business Strategy and the Environment*, *32*(4), 1914–1930. DOI: 10.1002/bse.3227

Baumgartner, R. J., & Ebner, D. (2010). Corporate sustainability strategies: Sustainability profiles and maturity levels. *Sustainable Development (Bradford)*, *18*(2), 76–89. DOI: 10.1002/sd.447

Bin Rashid, A., & Kausik, M. A. K. (2024, December). AI revolutionizing industries worldwide: A comprehensive overview of its diverseapplications. *Hybrid Advances*, *7*, 100277. DOI: 10.1016/j.hybadv.2024.100277

Boesl, D. B., & Liepert, B. (2016, October). 4 Robotic Revolutions-Proposing a holistic phase model describing future disruptions in the evolution of robotics and automation and the rise of a new Generation 'R'of Robotic Natives. In *2016 IEEE/RSJ International Conference on Intelligent Robots and Systems (IROS)* (pp. 1262-1267). IEEE. DOI: 10.1109/IROS.2016.7759209

Bolukbasi, T., Chang, K.-W., Zou, J., Saligrama, V., & Kalai, A. (2016). Man is to computer programmer as woman is to homemaker? Debiasing word embeddings. *Advances in Neural Information Processing Systems*, *29*, 4349–4357.

Charaan, R. D., Mallad, A., Maram, B., Mamodiya, U., & Nidhya, M. S. (2025). 3D Modelling and Printing in Smart Transportation System. In *Driving Green Transportation System Through Artificial Intelligence and Automation: Approaches, Technologies and Applications* (pp. 411–422). Springer Nature Switzerland. DOI: 10.1007/978-3-031-72617-0_22

Di Vaio, A., Palladino, R., Hassan, R., & Escobar, O. (2020). Artificial intelligence and business models in thesustainable development goals perspective: A systematic literature review. *Journal of Business Research*, *121*, 283–314. DOI: 10.1016/j.jbusres.2020.08.019

Domisch, S., Kakouei, K., Martínez-López, J., Bagstad, K. J., Magrach, A., Balbi, S., Villa, F., Funk, A., Hein, T., Borg-wardt, F., Hermoso, V., Jähnig, S. C., & Langhans, S. D. (2019). Social equity shapes zone-selection: Balancing aquatic biodiversity conservation and ecosystem services delivery in the transboundary DanubeRiver Basin. *The Science of the Total Environment*, *656*, 797–807. DOI: 10.1016/j.scitotenv.2018.11.348

Dyllick, T., & Hockerts, K. (2002). Beyond the business case for corporate sustainability. *Business Strategy and the Environment*, *11*(2), 130–141. DOI: 10.1002/bse.323

Eklof, J., Snis, U., Hamelryck, T., Grima, A., & Ronning, O. (2024). AI Implementation and Capability Development in Manufacturing: An Action Research Case.

Essays, A. A. (2022, July 29). A problem statement of Robotics Technologies Information Technology Essay. UK Essay.

Geissbauer, R., Schrauf, S., Berttram, P., & Cheraghi, F. (2017). Digital Factories 2020: Shaping the future of manufacturing. *URL: https://www.*

Gupta, S., Langhans, S. D., Domisch, S., Fuso-Nerini, F., Felländer, A., Battaglini, M., Tegmark, M., & Vinuesa, R. (2021). *Assessing whether artificial intelligence is an enabler or an inhibitor of sustainability at indicator level.* Transp Eng. DOI: 10.1016/j.treng.2021.100064

Haefner, N., Wincent, J., Parida, V., & Gassmann, O. (2021). Artificial intelligence and innovation management:A review, framework. *Technological Forecasting and Social Change*, *162*, 120392. DOI: 10.1016/j.techfore.2020.120392

Haftor, D. M., Costa Climent, R., & Lundström, J. E. (2021). How machine learning activates data network effects in business models: Theory advancement through an industrial case of promoting ecological sustain-ability. *Journal ofBusiness Research*, *131*, 196–205. DOI: 10.1016/j.jbusres.2021.04.015

Haidegger, T., Mai, V., Mörch, C. M., Boesl, D. O., Jacobs, A., Khamis, A., & Vanderborght, B. (2023). Robotics: Enabler and inhibitor of the sustainable development goals. *Sustainable Production and Consumption*, *43*, 422–434. DOI: 10.1016/j.spc.2023.11.011

Jagatheesaperumal, S. K., Rahouti, M., Ahmad, K., Al-Fuqaha, A., & Guizani, M. (2021). The duo of artificial intelligence and big data for industry 4.0: Applications, techniques, challenges, and future research directions. *IEEE Internet of Things Journal*, *9*(15), 12861–12885. DOI: 10.1109/JIOT.2021.3139827

Jayakumar, M., Jenefa, L., Badrinarayanan, M. K., Sarah, K. S., Kumar, A., & Kumar, R. M. (2024, December). Exploring Organizational Adoption of Innovative Technologies in Consumer Online Purchase. In *2024 International Conference on Emerging Research in Computational Science (ICERCS)* (pp. 1-6). IEEE. DOI: 10.1109/ICERCS63125.2024.10895563

Jayakumar, M., Jenefa, L., Mishra, N., Kumar, A., & Sumitha, S. (2024, December). Artificial Intelligence In Digital Marketing Platform: Impact In Consumer Buying Behaviour. In *2024 International Conference on Emerging Research in Computational Science (ICERCS)* (pp. 1-6). IEEE.

Jayakumar, M., Kumar, A., Ganesh, K. S., & Jenefa, L. (2024, December). Impact of AI for Online Shopping through Enhancing Personalised Recommendations. In *2024 International Conference on Emerging Research in Computational Science (ICERCS)* (pp. 1-6). IEEE. DOI: 10.1109/ICERCS63125.2024.10894946

Jenefa, L., & Jayakumar, M. (2025). Digital Transformation Challenges: Adaptation to AI Technologies in Service Marketing. In *Strategic Workforce Reskilling in Service Marketing* (pp. 111-132). IGI Global Scientific Publishing.

Jenefa, L., Jayakumar, M., Catherine, S., Kumar, S. A., Tripathi, R., & Jeevitha, M. The Application of Artificial Intelligence and Robotics in Healthcare Services. In *Revolutionizing Healthcare Services* (pp. 27–45). CRC Press. DOI: 10.1201/9781003531272-3

Jenefa, L., Kanchana, K., Jayakumar, M., & Kumar, A. (2024, December). The Impact of Artificial Intelligence for Developing Supply Chain Collaboration Performance: An Empirical Investigation. In *2024 International Conference on Emerging Research in Computational Science (ICERCS)* (pp. 1-4). IEEE. DOI: 10.1109/ICERCS63125.2024.10894938

Jenefa, L., Kumar, A., Yiong, B. L. C., Jayakumar, M., & Sakthivel, M. (2024, November). The Implementation of Artificial Intelligence Tools In Retail Sector Among Consumers-A New Evolution Traditional to Morden. In *2024 International Conference on Electronic Systems and Intelligent Computing (ICESIC)* (pp. 220-223). IEEE. DOI: 10.1109/ICESIC61777.2024.10846326

Khamis, A., Meng, J., Wang, J., Azar, A. T., Prestes, E., Takács, Á., & Haidegger, T. (2021). Robotics and intelligent systems against a pandemic. *Acta Polytechnica Hungarica, 18*(5), 13–35. DOI: 10.12700/APH.18.5.2021.5.3

Koren, I., Jarke, M., Michael, J., Heithoff, M., Tacke Genannt Unterberg, L., Stachon, M., & van der Aalst, W. M. (2024, May). Navigating the Data Model Divide in Smart Manufacturing: An Empirical Investigation for Enhanced AI Integration. In *International Conference on Business Process Modeling, Development and Support* (pp. 275-290). Cham: Springer Nature Switzerland. DOI: 10.1007/978-3-031-61007-3_21

Kragic, D., Gustafson, J., Karaoguz, H., Jensfelt, P., & Krug, R. (1970, January 1). Interactive, collaborative robots: Challenges and opportunities. *IJCAI (United States).*

Krishnan, L. R. K. (2022). Impact of Using AI in Manufacturing Industries. *Journal of the International Academy for Case Studies, 28.*

Marichamy, D., Sankar, M., Sivaprakash, P., Chithambaramani, R., Charaan, R. D., & Ithayan, J. V. (2024, August). Machine Learning Based Abnormal Human Behaviour Detection. In *2024 Second International Conference on Intelligent Cyber Physical Systems and Internet of Things (ICoICI)* (pp. 1155-1159). IEEE. DOI: 10.1109/ICoICI62503.2024.10696376

Priyatharsini, G. S., Bhimaavarapu, K., Charaan, R. D., Konakalla, J. P., & Chandralekha, E. (2025, March). Design and Analysis of Smart Health Care Predictions Using Machine Learning. In *2025 International Conference on Machine Learning and Autonomous Systems (ICMLAS)* (pp. 389-395). IEEE.

Qu, C., & Kim, E. (2024). Reviewing the roles of AI-integrated technologies in sustainable supply chain man-agement: Research propositions and a framework for future directions. *Sustainability (Basel), 16*(14), 6186. DOI: 10.3390/su16146186

Rantala, T., Ukko, J., Nasiri, M., & Saunila, M. (2023). Shifting focus of value creation through industrial digital twins—From internal application to ecosystem-level utilization. *Technovation, 125*, 102795. DOI: 10.1016/j.technovation.2023.102795

RM., D. C., Chithambaramani, R., & Marichamy, D. (2024, September). Historical Strategies Flow Detection for Organizations using Machine Learning. In *2024 International Conference on Integration of Emerging Technologies for the Digital World (ICIETDW)* (pp. 1-6). IEEE.

Russell, S. J., & Norvig, P. (2003). Artificial Intelligence A Modern Approach; Pearson Education [1] S.J. Russell and P. Norvig, Artificial Intelligence A Modern Approach; Pearson Education. 2003.on. In Pearson.

Schwaeke, J., Peters, A., Kanbach, D. K., Kraus, S., & Jones, P. (2024). The new normal: The status quo of AI adoption in SMEs. *Journal of Small Business Management*.

Sheffi, Y. (2024). Technology is not enough: Potential job displacement in an AI-driven future. *Journal of Supply Chain Management. Logistics and Procurement*, *6*(4), 338–351. DOI: 10.69554/FAVX7910

Singla, B., Shalender, K., & Singh, N. (Eds.). (2025). Navigating Data Science: Unleashing the Creative Potential of Artificial Intelligence.

Torelli, R., Balluchi, F., & Furlotti, K. (2020). The materiality assessment and stakeholder engagement: A content analysis of sustainability reports. *Corporate Social Responsibility and Environmental Management*, *27*(2), 470–484. DOI: 10.1002/csr.1813

Vasudevan, I., Nasurudeen, M. M., Kumar, M. S., Charaan, R. D., Kumar, S. A., & Jenefa, L. (2024, November). Hierarchical Model for Email Fraud Detection Using Naïve Bayes and SVM. In *2024 First International Conference for Women in Computing (InCoWoCo)* (pp. 1-6). IEEE. DOI: 10.1109/InCoWoCo64194.2024.10863458

Wu, Y.-C., Liu, Y.-C., Tsao, C., & Huang, R.-Y. (2023, March). Micro expression recognition robot. *IAES International Journal of Robotics and Automation*, *12*(1), 20–28.

Yahya, R., Jailani, R., Hanapiah, F. A., & Zakaria, N. K. (2024). A scoping review of artificial intelligence-based robot therapy for children with disabilities. *Indonesian Journal of Electrical Engineering and Computer Science*, *33*(3), 1855–1865. DOI: 10.11591/ijeecs.v33.i3.pp1855-1865

Yugendran, V., Jenefa, L., Jayakumar, M., & Sakthivel, M. (2025, March). Ethics of AI Technology Interruption and Discomfort on Employee Turnover. In *2025 International Conference on Data Science, Agents & Artificial Intelligence (ICDSAAI)* (pp. 1-6). IEEE.

Chapter 5
AI-Driven Personalization in Social Commerce for SME Sustainability in Developing Countries

Yoga Religia
https://orcid.org/0000-0002-7496-0819
Universitas Pembangunan Nasional Veteran Yogyakarta, Indonesia

Yussi Ramawati
Atma Jaya Catholic University of Indonesia, Indonesia

Muafi Muafi
https://orcid.org/0000-0002-5078-4670
Islamic University of Indonesia, Indonesia

ABSTRACT

The rapid growth of digital technology has transformed marketing, particularly in social commerce, where AI-driven personalization enhances customer experience and efficiency. This study uses a systematic literature review (SLR) to analyze its impact, benefits, and challenges for SMEs in developing countries. AI enables real-time data analysis, personalized recommendations, and automated customer service, boosting engagement and conversion rates while reducing costs. However, SMEs face financial constraints, low digital literacy, and data privacy concerns, alongside competition from large platforms. Despite these barriers, AI-driven personalization remains crucial for sustainable growth. Future research should explore AI adoption models, policy frameworks, and strategies to overcome challenges, providing valuable insights for SMEs seeking competitive advantage.

DOI: 10.4018/979-8-3373-8607-2.ch005

1. INTRODUCTION

The advancement of digital technology has driven transformation in marketing strategies and business interactions, particularly within the social commerce ecosystem. Social commerce is not merely a transaction platform but also enhances the shopping experience through the integration of artificial intelligence (AI) (Leong et al., 2024). AI enables real-time customer data analysis, which is leveraged to develop personalized marketing strategies. By understanding customer preferences, businesses can offer more relevant products and services, increase engagement, and strengthen consumer loyalty (Rane, 2023). For SMEs, AI-driven personalization presents a strategic opportunity to compete in an increasingly competitive market without relying on large investments in traditional marketing (Khan, 2024). Therefore, adopting AI-driven personalization is a key element in enhancing the effectiveness of social commerce and fostering stronger relationships between SMEs and their customers. This integration has been shown to create more dynamic and adaptive business models that resonate with modern consumer expectations.

In the context of SMEs in developing countries, AI-driven personalization serves as a catalyst for enhancing competitiveness and business sustainability (Kurrahman et al., 2025). Given the constraints in resources and operational capacity, SMEs often struggle to provide services on par with larger corporations. AI enables SMEs to automate various business aspects, such as data-driven product recommendations, customer service via chatbots, and dynamic pricing strategies tailored to buyer behavior (Okeke et al., 2024). By leveraging these capabilities, SMEs can offer a more personalized and responsive shopping experience without relying on a large workforce. Beyond improving customer satisfaction, AI-driven personalization helps SMEs optimize operational efficiency, reduce ineffective marketing costs, and accelerate the sales conversion process (Michael, 2025). These capabilities are particularly critical in developing economies where resource efficiency is paramount for survival and growth. Simply put, AI is not only a tool for enhancing customer interactions but also a crucial driver of long-term SME business sustainability.

A recent survey conducted by Salesforce in early 2025 highlights the crucial role of artificial intelligence (AI) in supporting the sustainability of SMEs in Indonesia, a developing country whose economy heavily relies on this sector (BisnisKUMKM, 2025). Survey data shows that the adoption of AI among Indonesian MSMEs has reached an impressive level, with 77% of business leaders reporting they have either used or experimented with the technology. Furthermore, 97% of respondents stated that the implementation of AI directly contributed to an increase in their business revenue, a strong indicator of the technology's effectiveness. The perceived benefits include improved operational efficiency, expanded market reach, and optimized customer service. The most widely implemented AI use cases in Indonesia are text-based search engines, marketing campaign optimization, and automated customer recommendation systems. Although the benefits are evident, the survey also revealed challenges faced by MSMEs, such as the increasing complexity of technology and concerns related to data security and the ethical use of AI. However, the fact that 92% of MSMEs acknowledge that improved data quality is directly proportional to an increase in revenue, indicates a growing awareness of the importance of a strong data foundation for optimal AI utilization. By adopting AI, MSMEs are not only boosting productivity but also have great potential to compete and thrive in the digital economy era.

Based on data from Techbehemoths (2025), the use of AI among SMEs has reached a substantial and diverse level of adoption. This global survey, which involved 698 SMEs across 53 countries, indicates that AI adoption is no longer a marginal phenomenon but an integral part of modern business strategy. Strikingly, more than three-quarters (77.87%) of all respondents reported using AI, either moderately (45.16%) or extensively (32.71%). This data provides strong evidence that SMEs globally are recognizing AI's significant potential to drive growth and efficiency. The application of AI also varies, with Sales and Marketing departments being the most dominant at 80.2% usage, followed by product development and research. This reflects the focus of SMEs on improving customer interaction, acquisition, and the efficient creation of content, which was reported as the primary purpose of AI use (70%). Furthermore, the most frequently utilized types of AI are Natural Language Processing, Machine Learning, and Predictive Analytics, which collectively enable the automation of repetitive tasks (66%) and in-depth data analysis (57%). These statistics underscore a paradigm shift where AI is no longer the exclusive domain of large corporations but an essential tool for SMEs to enhance their competitiveness and sustainability in the global market.

Despite its numerous benefits, the implementation of AI-driven personalization by SMEs in developing countries still faces significant challenges. One of the primary obstacles is limited capital and investment in advanced technology, which makes it difficult for many SMEs to adopt AI-based systems (Bhalerao et al., 2022; Iyelolu et al., 2024). Additionally, low digital literacy among SME owners and operators poses a barrier to effectively understanding and managing AI technology (Bhalerao et al., 2022). Another major concern is data privacy and customer data protection, which remain critical issues in AI-driven personalization strategies. Data protection regulations in some developing countries are still underdeveloped (Ramadhan & Wijaya, 2022), requiring SMEs to navigate legal uncertainties when utilizing AI. Furthermore, SMEs must compete with large e-commerce platforms that have already integrated AI into their operations, compelling them to be more innovative in leveraging AI to remain relevant in the digital market. Therefore, navigating these complex hurdles requires not only financial investment but also strategic planning and ongoing education.

This study aims to explore the role of AI-driven personalization in enhancing the competitiveness and sustainability of SMEs in developing countries through social commerce. By examining its benefits, challenges, and effective implementation strategies, this research seeks to provide strategic insights for SMEs on optimizing AI technology for business growth. Additionally, this study highlights how AI can support SMEs in developing more adaptive and data-driven business strategies. By analyzing various relevant studies, this research offers practical guidance for SMEs on utilizing AI to enhance customer engagement, optimize operations, and drive continuous innovation. Thus, this study not only contributes to academic literature but also provides concrete solutions for SMEs in navigating the dynamics of the digital market. Ultimately, this research serves as a valuable resource for policymakers, business leaders, and academics seeking to understand and promote the adoption of AI for sustainable SME development.

2. THEORETICAL FOUNDATION

2.1. SME Sustainability in Developing Countries

The sustainability of SMEs in developing countries presents a significant challenge amid global competition and the evolving digital economy. SMEs often face various obstacles, including limited access to technology, a shortage of skilled human resources, and business regulations that do not fully support digital innovation (Omowole et al., 2024). Additionally, low digital literacy among SME owners frequently hampers the optimization of technology-based marketing strategies, thereby reducing their competitiveness in an increasingly dynamic digital ecosystem (Rialti & Zollo, 2023). One of the key factors influencing SME sustainability is the adoption of technology in their business operations (Prasanna et al., 2019). Digital technology, particularly AI and social commerce, enables SMEs to overcome capital constraints by offering more efficient automation solutions (Păuceanu et al., 2023). For instance, AI can assist in inventory management, customer service, and market analysis, allowing SMEs to allocate their resources more optimally. By leveraging these technologies, SMEs have a greater opportunity to grow and compete in the digital marketplace, even with limited resources.

Beyond technology, SME sustainability is also influenced by shifting consumer preferences toward more environmentally friendly and ethical products (Ebrahimi et al., 2021). Modern consumers increasingly demand transparency in production processes and prioritize businesses that uphold sustainability values (Deshmukh &

Tare, 2024). Consequently, SMEs must adapt to these trends by integrating more sustainable business practices, such as utilizing eco-friendly raw materials or adopting marketing strategies that support the circular economy. Sustainability-oriented strategies not only help SMEs meet consumer expectations but also create opportunities for long-term brand loyalty and differentiation in the market. Consumers today are more inclined to support businesses that align with their ethical values, meaning that SMEs adopting green business practices may experience increased customer retention and positive brand perception.

The integration of AI in social commerce can further enhance SME sustainability by optimizing customer engagement strategies. AI-driven tools such as personalized marketing, chatbots, and automated recommendation systems help SMEs provide better consumer experiences, fostering stronger relationships with their customers. These digital tools allow SMEs to analyze customer behavior patterns and deliver targeted content, making their marketing efforts more efficient and impactful. Additionally, AI-powered analytics assist SMEs in optimizing their advertising budgets, ensuring that their resources are allocated to the most effective channels.

By embracing both technology-driven and sustainability-oriented strategies, SMEs can enhance their competitiveness and ensure long-term business growth. Collaboration with stakeholders, such as digital platforms and AI solution providers, can also accelerate SME adoption of AI-driven personalization. By integrating AI-driven personalization into their business models, SMEs can improve customer engagement, streamline marketing efforts, and enhance operational efficiency. Ultimately, this strategic alignment helps them navigate market complexities and build a resilient foundation for the future.

Ensuring SME sustainability in developing countries requires a strategic approach that includes technological adoption and sustainability-driven initiatives. While SMEs face numerous challenges, leveraging AI-driven personalization and aligning with global consumer trends toward sustainability can significantly improve their long-term viability. By proactively integrating digital tools and data-driven personalization strategies, SMEs can enhance operational efficiency, build stronger relationships with customers, and thrive in an increasingly competitive digital economy. This dual focus on technology and ethical practices is key to unlocking new growth opportunities and achieving a competitive advantage.

2.2. Social Commerce and SME Growth

The advancement of digital technology has driven a shift from traditional e-commerce to social commerce (Attar et al., 2022), which has gained popularity among businesses, including SMEs. Social commerce integrates interactive features of social media with commercial activities, allowing transactions to occur directly on platforms such as Facebook, Instagram, and TikTok (Griffin, 2024). Beyond serving as a promotional tool, social commerce enables businesses to build closer relationships with customers through direct interactions, such as live shopping, customer reviews, and recommendation-sharing features. With a more personalized and community-based approach, social commerce creates a more engaging shopping experience compared to conventional e-commerce (Attar et al., 2022).

For SMEs, social commerce presents a significant opportunity to reach a broader market with lower marketing costs than traditional marketing strategies. Features such as live streaming and user-generated content enable SMEs to enhance product visibility without requiring substantial investment in physical infrastructure (Zhang & Erturk, 2022). Furthermore, social commerce platforms often provide analytical tools that help businesses understand customer preferences and optimize their marketing strategies more effectively (Liao et al., 2021). By leveraging customer behavior data, SMEs can tailor their product and service offerings to better meet consumer needs.

One of the key advantages of social commerce for SMEs is its ability to facilitate seamless engagement with customers. Unlike traditional e-commerce, where interactions are often transactional, social commerce fosters two-way communication between businesses and consumers. Through comments, direct messages, and interactive features such as polls or Q&A sessions, SMEs can gather real-time feedback from their audience. This continuous engagement not only strengthens customer relationships but also allows businesses to make quick adjustments to their marketing strategies based on consumer responses.

However, despite the significant growth opportunities that social commerce offers, SMEs also face several challenges, such as increasing competition in the digital marketplace and changes in social media platform algorithms that can affect product visibility (Kedi et al., 2024b). As more businesses enter the social commerce space, SMEs must find innovative ways to differentiate themselves from competitors. One effective approach is leveraging AI-driven personalization, which allows SMEs to provide more customized shopping experiences by analyzing user data and preferences. AI-powered recommendation engines can suggest products tailored to individual customers, increasing conversion rates and customer satisfaction.

Additionally, building customer trust in online transactions is a crucial factor in the success of social commerce (Al-kfairy et al., 2024). Since social commerce transactions often occur outside of traditional e-commerce platforms, concerns about payment security, product authenticity, and customer service reliability can impact consumer confidence. SMEs must adopt transparent business practices, such as offering clear return policies, using secure payment gateways, and actively engaging with customers to address their concerns. Positive customer reviews and testimonials also play a vital role in building credibility and attracting new buyers.

Moreover, the effectiveness of social commerce is heavily influenced by content quality and engagement levels. SMEs need to invest in high-quality visual content, such as professional product images and engaging videos, to capture consumer interest. Live streaming has emerged as a powerful tool in social commerce, allowing businesses to showcase their products in real time, answer customer inquiries instantly, and create an immersive shopping experience. AI-driven tools, such as automated captioning and sentiment analysis, can further enhance live shopping sessions by providing insights into customer reactions and optimizing content delivery.

Therefore, the integration of artificial intelligence (AI) has become an increasingly essential strategy for SMEs to enhance the effectiveness of social commerce, particularly in delivering a more personalized and data-driven shopping experience. AI-powered chatbots, for example, can assist SMEs in handling customer inquiries efficiently, providing instant responses to frequently asked questions and guiding customers through the purchasing process. Automated chat systems not only improve customer service but also free up time for SMEs to focus on other critical business operations. Additionally, AI-driven analytics tools can help SMEs identify trends, measure campaign performance, and adjust marketing efforts accordingly. This synergistic relationship between AI and social commerce allows SMEs to operate with the agility and intelligence of larger enterprises.

Ultimately, social commerce presents a valuable opportunity for SMEs to expand their market reach, engage with customers more effectively, and optimize their marketing strategies through data-driven insights. However, to maximize the benefits of social commerce, SMEs must address challenges such as intense competition, algorithm changes, and trust-building. By leveraging AI-driven personalization, maintaining transparent business practices, and utilizing interactive content, SMEs can create a more engaging and successful social commerce presence. As digital technology continues to evolve, SMEs that adapt to these changes and embrace innovation will be better positioned to sustain long-term growth in the social commerce ecosystem. The ability to harness these new technologies will be a key differentiator for SMEs aiming for long-term viability and competitiveness.

2.3. AI-Driven Personalization

The advancement of AI technology has enabled higher levels of personalization in business-customer interactions, particularly within the social commerce ecosystem. AI-driven personalization refers to the use of artificial intelligence algorithms to understand customer preferences and tailor shopping experiences in real time (Bhuiyan, 2024). This technology encompasses various mechanisms, such as Natural Language Processing (NLP)-based chatbots, product recommendation systems, and dynamic pricing models adjusted according to customer purchasing patterns

(Behare et al., 2025). By continuously analyzing data, AI can identify individual customer needs and provide more relevant recommendations, thereby enhancing satisfaction and loyalty.

One of the key implementations of AI-driven personalization is chatbots, which enable SMEs to provide automated customer service 24/7 (Patil, 2024). NLP-based chatbots can understand and respond to customer inquiries more naturally, offer suitable product suggestions, and guide customers through the purchasing process. Additionally, AI-based recommendation systems play a crucial role in increasing sales conversion rates by displaying the most relevant products in customers' feeds based on transaction history and browsing behavior (Kushwah, 2024). These technologies have been widely adopted by social commerce platforms to enhance the effectiveness of digital marketing.

Another major advantage of AI-driven personalization is its ability to segment customers based on behavioral patterns. Traditional marketing strategies often rely on broad demographic data, which may not accurately reflect individual preferences. AI, on the other hand, can process vast amounts of data to categorize customers into micro-segments based on their interests, purchase history, and engagement levels. This allows SMEs to craft highly targeted marketing campaigns, increasing the likelihood of customer interaction and conversion.

Beyond chatbots and recommendation systems, AI is also utilized in dynamic pricing, where product prices are adjusted based on factors such as market demand, inventory levels, and customer profiles (Karunakaran et al., 2024). This approach helps SMEs optimize their pricing strategies, improve competitiveness, and maximize profitability. For example, AI-driven pricing models can analyze competitor pricing in real time and suggest optimal pricing adjustments to maintain a competitive edge. This not only ensures that SMEs remain relevant in the market but also helps them maximize revenue without compromising affordability for customers.

Furthermore, AI-driven personalization enhances customer retention by delivering individualized promotions and loyalty rewards. Instead of generic discount campaigns, AI enables SMEs to offer personalized incentives based on a customer's purchasing behavior. For instance, frequent buyers may receive exclusive discounts on their favorite products, while first-time customers may be given special offers to encourage repeat purchases. This level of personalization strengthens brand loyalty and encourages long-term customer relationships.

Given these benefits, AI-driven personalization has become an invaluable tool in social commerce, enabling SMEs to create more personalized, efficient, and data-driven shopping experiences. However, successful implementation of AI-driven personalization requires SMEs to collect and analyze high-quality data. Many small businesses struggle with fragmented or incomplete customer data, limiting AI's ability to generate accurate insights. To overcome this challenge, SMEs must invest in data collection strategies that integrate multiple touchpoints, such as social media interactions, website visits, and past purchase records.

Moreover, AI-driven personalization must be balanced with ethical considerations, particularly concerning data privacy and customer trust. As AI systems gather vast amounts of personal data, SMEs must ensure compliance with data protection regulations and be transparent about how customer information is used. Building trust through responsible AI practices, such as offering customers control over their data preferences and implementing secure data storage measures, is crucial for sustaining long-term engagement.

It is safe to say that AI-based personalization is transforming the way SMEs interact with customers in the social commerce landscape. By leveraging AI-powered chatbots, recommendation systems, dynamic pricing, and customer segmentation, SMEs can provide more relevant and engaging shopping experiences. However, to fully realize the benefits of AI-driven personalization, SMEs must address challenges related to data quality, ethical concerns, and customer trust. With the right strategies in place, AI can serve as a powerful tool for SMEs to enhance competitiveness, optimize operations, and foster lasting customer relationships in the evolving digital economy.

2.4. The Role of AI in Enhancing SME Competitiveness

Amid increasingly intense business competition, AI has emerged as a strategic tool that helps SMEs overcome resource constraints and enhance their competitiveness (Iyelolu et al., 2024). One of AI's primary benefits is its ability to analyze customer data quickly and accurately, allowing SMEs to make data-driven decisions in their marketing and operational strategies (Magableh et al., 2024). By understanding customer purchasing patterns, SMEs can target the right audience, reduce inefficient marketing costs, and improve the effectiveness of their digital campaigns. AI-driven marketing automation enables SMEs to optimize their advertising efforts by delivering highly personalized content to the right customers at the right time. AI can analyze browsing history, purchase behavior, and engagement metrics to refine ad targeting, ensuring that marketing budgets are spent efficiently and yield higher conversion rates.

Beyond marketing, AI also contributes to operational efficiency by automating tasks that previously required manual labor. AI-powered chatbots can handle customer service without human intervention, while AI-driven inventory management systems can predict market demand and optimize stock levels (Kedi et al., 2024a). For instance, AI-powered predictive analytics can help SMEs anticipate sales trends, allowing them to manage inventory more effectively and reduce the risk of overstocking or stockouts. This predictive capability is especially beneficial for SMEs with limited storage capacity and working capital, as it minimizes financial losses due to unsold products or supply chain disruptions.

By automating these aspects, SMEs can allocate resources to more strategic business areas, enhance operational efficiency, and accelerate business growth. Additionally, AI-powered automation tools help streamline order processing, logistics coordination, and payment handling, reducing the likelihood of human errors and improving overall business productivity. Through these improvements, SMEs can provide faster service, leading to enhanced customer satisfaction and stronger brand loyalty.

Furthermore, AI opens new opportunities for SMEs to create more personalized and interactive customer experiences (Iyelolu et al., 2024). With technologies such as AI-based recommendations and social media sentiment analysis, SMEs can better understand customer needs and adjust their products or services in real time (Bhuiyan, 2024). Sentiment analysis tools allow businesses to track customer opinions across social media and review platforms, helping them respond proactively to feedback and improve their offerings. This real-time responsiveness strengthens brand reputation and demonstrates a commitment to customer satisfaction.

Another crucial aspect of AI in enhancing SME competitiveness is its role in customer retention and engagement. AI-driven loyalty programs can analyze customer behavior and tailor rewards based on individual shopping habits. For example, an AI-powered system can identify frequent buyers and offer them exclusive discounts or personalized recommendations, increasing the likelihood of repeat purchases. Such targeted incentives create a more engaging shopping experience and foster long-term customer relationships. Moreover, AI assists SMEs in making more informed strategic decisions by providing real-time insights into market conditions, competitor activities, and consumer trends. AI-driven business intelligence tools aggregate data from multiple sources, enabling SMEs to identify emerging opportunities and threats. This data-driven approach reduces reliance on intuition-based decision-making and enhances overall business agility, allowing SMEs to pivot quickly in response to market changes.

These innovations not only foster customer loyalty but also help SMEs build sustainable competitive advantages in an increasingly dynamic market. As AI technology continues to evolve, its applications in SME competitiveness will become even more sophisticated. Future developments in AI, such as generative AI for automated content creation, AI-powered visual search for e-commerce, and blockchain-integrated AI for secure transactions, will further revolutionize how SMEs operate in the digital economy.

It can be said that AI is a powerful enabler of SME competitiveness, offering benefits ranging from data-driven marketing optimization and operational automation to customer engagement and strategic decision-making. SMEs that embrace

AI-driven solutions can improve efficiency, enhance customer relationships, and stay ahead in an increasingly competitive landscape. However, successful AI adoption requires SMEs to continuously invest in digital skills, data infrastructure, and ethical AI practices to ensure sustainable and responsible implementation. By leveraging AI effectively, SMEs can not only survive but thrive in the evolving digital economy.

2.5. Gap and Novelty

Although existing literature has extensively discussed the role of AI and social commerce in the growth of SMEs in general, there remains a significant gap that has not been fully explored, particularly in the specific context of SMEs in developing countries. Most prior studies have focused on technology adoption in advanced markets, where digital infrastructure, technological literacy, and regulatory support are more mature. Previous research, as highlighted in several articles, tends to emphasize the benefits of AI such as automation and personalization, but pays less attention to the unique challenges faced by SMEs in developing countries, such as limited capital, uneven internet access, and the lack of a supporting ecosystem. For example, studies on AI in Indonesia (BisnisKUMKM, 2025) provide positive adoption data but only scratch the surface of deeper issues such as data readiness and consumer trust in AI within environments that are inherently different from Western markets. Furthermore, the aspects of AI ethics and data privacy within the cultural and regulatory context of developing countries remain underexplored. This gap creates an urgent need for research that directly addresses these issues.

This study aims to bridge that gap by offering a unique and relevant novelty. First, the study specifically targets the context of SMEs in developing countries, rather than merely adopting theories from advanced markets. The focus on AI-driven personalization in the context of social commerce for SME sustainability is a combination that has rarely been explored holistically. We will analyze how AI not only helps SMEs improve efficiency and sales but also directly contributes to long-term sustainability by building customer loyalty and optimizing resource utilization. Unlike previous studies that often view AI as a purely operational tool, we position it as a strategic relationship builder between SMEs and their consumers, which is key to sustainability. The second novelty lies in our mixed-methods approach—both qualitative and quantitative—that will identify not only the benefits but also the specific barriers faced by SMEs in developing countries, such as challenges in managing data quality and building trust among privacy-concerned customers. We will provide practical and in-depth insights on how SMEs can overcome these obstacles with strategies tailored to their operational realities. Thus, this study will not only enrich the academic literature but also provide practical and concrete guidance for SME practitioners, policymakers, and technology solution providers.

3. RESEARCH METHODOLOGY

This study adopts a Systematic Literature Review (SLR) approach to analyze the impact of AI-driven personalization in social commerce for SMEs. The decision to employ the SLR method is considered highly appropriate given the scope and nature of the research objectives, as it allows the researchers to synthesize a wide range of scholarly works in a structured and transparent manner. The use of SLR is particularly relevant in addressing the identified research gap, where the existing body of literature has not yet provided a comprehensive and holistic understanding of how AI and social commerce intersect, especially within the specific context of SMEs operating in developing countries. Previous studies have often concentrated on advanced economies where digital infrastructure, regulatory frameworks, and consumer readiness are already well established, leaving limited insights into the unique challenges faced by SMEs in less developed contexts. By adopting the SLR approach, this research not only seeks to map existing findings but also to critically evaluate and integrate them to build a broader and deeper perspective. The synthesis of diverse studies enables the identification of recurring patterns, emerging themes, and critical contradictions that may not be visible in individual works. This process provides a more nuanced understanding of the benefits of AI, such as efficiency gains, enhanced customer engagement, and improved resource utilization, while also highlighting the barriers and risks, including data privacy concerns, technological readiness, and financial constraints. Furthermore, the SLR approach makes it possible to reveal underexplored dimensions of AI application, such as its role in long-term sustainability and relationship-building between SMEs and their customers. Ultimately, the adoption of this methodology strengthens the contribution of the study by ensuring that its insights are not only grounded in empirical evidence but also situated within the broader academic discourse on AI and social commerce.

Data collection was carried out through a systematic literature search across several leading academic databases, including Scopus, Web of Science, and Google Scholar. The search strategy followed the PRISMA (Preferred Reporting Items for Systematic Reviews and Meta-Analyses) guidelines to ensure transparency and replicability of the research process. Keywords used in the search included various combinations of terms such as "AI-driven personalization," "social commerce," "SMEs," "artificial intelligence," "customer engagement," and "digital transformation for small businesses." These keywords were selected to cover multiple aspects of AI utilization in SMEs within social commerce. The included articles were selected based on strict inclusion and exclusion criteria. The inclusion criteria required that articles be peer-reviewed, specifically address AI-driven personalization in social commerce for SMEs, and be published between 2021 and 2025. Conversely, articles focusing on large enterprises without emphasis on SMEs, those not written in English, or those lacking a clear research methodology were excluded from the analysis. From an initial pool of 178 articles, 14 were deemed most relevant and selected for further analysis after the screening process.

Data analysis was conducted using a thematic analysis approach, which enabled the categorization of the selected studies into several key dimensions to capture both the breadth and depth of existing research. Each article was examined carefully in relation to its research objectives, study context, methodological choices, variables of interest, and primary findings. This multi-layered categorization allowed for the identification of overarching patterns across studies as well as the recognition of context-specific nuances that are often overlooked in fragmented analyses. To present these insights more systematically, the findings were organized into a comprehensive literature review table, which serves as both a summary and a comparative tool for evaluating the current state of knowledge.

In order to strengthen the validity and reliability of the review, the literature analysis was conducted in a manner that strictly adhered to established standards of systematic research. Particular attention was given to ensuring transparency in reporting, reproducibility of the review process, and clarity in how themes and categories were derived from the evidence base. The analysis also sought to reach thematic saturation, meaning that new studies no longer contributed substantially different insights to the existing categories. This saturation point is crucial, as it indicates the robustness of the patterns identified and minimizes the likelihood of overlooking significant themes. Moreover, the systematic and structured approach of this study provides a strong foundation for generating both theoretical and practical contributions. From an academic perspective, the study highlights critical gaps in the literature, while from a practical standpoint, it offers actionable insights that SMEs, policymakers, and technology providers can use to optimize AI-driven personalization strategies within social commerce. By doubling as both an academic synthesis and a practical guideline, the findings of this analysis are positioned to make a meaningful contribution to advancing knowledge and informing real-world practices in the SME context.

4. RESULTS

4.1. The Impact of AI-Driven Personalization on Social Commerce

AI-driven personalization has significantly transformed the social commerce ecosystem (Mubdir et al., 2025), particularly in enhancing customer experience and operational efficiency for SMEs. Various studies indicate that AI-based personalization enables businesses to better understand customer preferences through transaction data analysis, search behavior, and customer interactions on digital platforms (Bhuiyan, 2024). Technologies such as NLP-based chatbots and product recommendation systems allow AI to create a more interactive shopping experience tailored to individual needs (Behare et al., 2025). Additionally, AI enables more accurate predictions of consumption trends, assisting SMEs in developing more effective and data-driven marketing strategies (Kedi et al., 2024a).

The enhancement of customer experience through AI is not limited to facilitating product recommendations but also extends to the responsiveness of customer service (Patil, 2024). For instance, AI-powered chatbots provide instant customer support without time constraints, expediting purchasing decisions. Furthermore, AI-driven dynamic pricing helps SMEs adjust product prices based on market demand, consumer trends, and competition levels, ultimately improving their competitiveness in social commerce (Okeke et al., 2024). AI also enables personalized promotions and discounts, allowing each customer to receive tailored offers based on their shopping history and preferences (Bhuiyan, 2024). By implementing these strategies, SMEs can increase conversion rates and strengthen customer loyalty to their brands (Rane, 2023).

From an efficiency perspective, AI helps SMEs automate various business processes, including inventory management, market trend analysis, and more targeted digital marketing campaign planning (Ikpe, 2024). By reducing reliance on human labor for repetitive tasks, SMEs can allocate resources more effectively for innovation and product development. Data from a Salesforce survey highlights this, revealing that 97% of Indonesian SMEs acknowledge the significant benefits of AI, with 77% already experimenting with or using AI in their businesses (BisnisKUMKM, 2025). The top three AI use cases in Indonesia include text-based search engines, marketing campaign optimization, and automated customer recommendations. Additionally, AI-powered systems can identify potential customers through big data analysis, enabling SMEs to target more relevant audiences in their marketing strategies (Bhalerao et al., 2022). Enhanced operational efficiency allows SMEs not only to cut costs but also to improve the quality of services they offer.

Furthermore, AI-driven personalization impacts SMEs in social commerce by increasing customer trust in brands (Iyelolu et al., 2024). With a structured, predictive, and preference-based shopping experience, customers are more likely to develop stronger relationships with businesses they trust. AI also assists SMEs in building a better digital reputation through more responsive customer service features and data-driven marketing strategies tailored to target audiences (Telukdarie et al., 2024). Therefore, AI-driven personalization not only enhances customer experience but also strengthens SMEs' competitiveness in an increasingly digital market.

Based on previous studies, the impact of AI-driven personalization in social commerce for SMEs can be categorized into four stages, each playing a crucial role in optimizing business performance and enhancing customer engagement. These stages include data input, AI analysis, personalization services, and their overall impact on SMEs. By understanding and effectively implementing each stage, SMEs can maximize the benefits of AI-driven personalization, ensuring they remain competitive in the digital marketplace.

- First Stage: **Data Input**

The first stage of AI-driven personalization begins with the collection of customer-related data, which forms the foundation for AI algorithms to generate meaningful insights. The data collected includes transaction history, search behavior, social media interactions, and demographic details. Social commerce platforms such as Facebook, Instagram, and TikTok provide SMEs with vast amounts of real-time customer data, enabling them to build a more detailed understanding of consumer behavior.

For SMEs, effective data collection is critical to ensuring accurate AI-driven personalization. Businesses must implement structured mechanisms to gather high-quality data, such as integrating customer relationship management (CRM) systems, using tracking pixels on their websites, and encouraging customers to engage with personalized surveys. Additionally, leveraging first-party data—information collected directly from customer interactions—helps SMEs create a more comprehensive customer profile while maintaining data privacy compliance.

However, data collection presents challenges, particularly for SMEs with limited technological infrastructure. Many SMEs struggle to capture and store large volumes of customer data efficiently. To address this issue, SMEs can utilize cloud-based AI platforms that offer scalable storage and analytics solutions. These platforms allow SMEs to streamline data input while minimizing operational costs. Moreover, businesses should ensure transparency in their data collection practices to build customer trust and comply with evolving data privacy regulations.

- Second Stage: **AI Analysis**

Once data is collected, the next stage involves AI processing and analysis, where advanced machine learning models, natural language processing (NLP), and big data analytics come into play. The AI system evaluates consumer behavior patterns, identifies trends, and determines the most relevant personalization strategies.

In social commerce, AI analysis is crucial for predicting customer needs and preferences. By utilizing machine learning algorithms, SMEs can detect recurring buying patterns, identify seasonal trends, and even anticipate emerging product demands. For example, if AI detects that a particular customer frequently purchases skincare products, it can predict future buying behavior and suggest complementary products such as facial masks or serums.

Sentiment analysis, another key AI-powered tool, enables SMEs to assess customer feedback from product reviews and social media comments. By analyzing customer sentiment, SMEs can gain deeper insights into consumer satisfaction levels, identify areas for improvement, and proactively address potential concerns before they escalate.

Additionally, AI-powered segmentation allows SMEs to group customers based on shared behaviors and preferences. Rather than adopting a one-size-fits-all approach, businesses can divide their customer base into micro-segments, ensuring that marketing campaigns and promotions are highly targeted and relevant.

- Third Stage: **Personalization Services**

Following AI analysis, the next step involves applying AI-driven insights to enhance customer experience through various personalization services. SMEs can leverage AI-based recommendations, automated customer interactions, and dynamic pricing strategies to optimize social commerce engagement.

One of the most effective AI-driven personalization services is AI-powered product recommendations. AI dynamically suggests products tailored to each user's preferences by analyzing browsing history, previous purchases, and in-session behaviors. Personalized recommendations improve user experience, increase conversion rates, and drive higher sales.

AI-powered chatbots further enhance the shopping experience by offering 24/7 automated customer support. These chatbots provide real-time assistance, answer customer queries, and guide shoppers through the purchasing process. More advanced chatbots, powered by NLP, can simulate human-like interactions, ensuring seamless and engaging communication with customers.

Dynamic pricing is another powerful AI-driven personalization service that allows SMEs to adjust product prices in real time based on factors such as demand, competition, and customer purchasing power. For instance, if AI detects high demand for a specific product, the pricing model can increase its price slightly to maximize revenue. Conversely, when demand declines, the system can automatically lower the price to attract more buyers. This data-driven approach helps SMEs optimize profitability while maintaining market competitiveness.

Furthermore, personalized promotions based on AI-driven insights enable SMEs to create targeted discount offers. By analyzing customer loyalty and purchasing history, AI can generate exclusive discounts for repeat buyers, first-time customers, or users who abandon their shopping carts. This strategic approach encourages higher engagement and customer retention.

- Final Stage: **Impact on SMEs**

The final stage highlights the overall benefits AI-driven personalization provides to SMEs. By implementing AI-based strategies effectively, SMEs can enhance their competitiveness, strengthen customer relationships, and optimize operational efficiency.

A global survey of 698 SMEs in 53 countries revealed that 45.16% use AI moderately, while 32.71% use it extensively (Techbehemoths, 2025). The most common applications are in sales and marketing (80.2%), where AI is primarily used for content creation (70%), task automation (66%), and data analysis (57%). This demonstrates that SMEs are actively leveraging AI as a strategic tool for growth.

AI-driven personalization significantly improves customer satisfaction by ensuring that consumers receive relevant recommendations, timely support, and seamless shopping experiences. Enhanced personalization leads to higher engagement, increased brand loyalty, and repeat purchases.

From an operational standpoint, AI-driven automation reduces the workload on SME employees, allowing businesses to focus on innovation and strategic growth. With AI handling customer interactions, inventory management, and pricing optimization, SMEs can allocate their human resources more effectively toward business development and expansion efforts.

Additionally, AI-driven personalization enhances SMEs' marketing effectiveness by providing data-backed insights. Rather than relying on intuition, SMEs can make informed decisions on product offerings, promotional campaigns, and customer engagement strategies. This results in reduced marketing expenditures and higher returns on investment.

AI also plays a critical role in strengthening SMEs' digital presence by helping them build a strong online reputation. Through AI-driven sentiment analysis, SMEs can monitor customer perceptions and address negative feedback promptly, ensuring they maintain a positive brand image in the digital marketplace.

As AI technology continues to advance, SMEs that integrate AI-driven personalization into their business models will be better positioned to compete in the ever-evolving social commerce landscape. The ability to adapt to changing consumer expectations and market trends through AI-powered solutions will ensure long-term sustainability and growth for SMEs in developing economies.

By effectively implementing AI-driven personalization through data input, AI analysis, personalization services, and impact assessment, SMEs can unlock new opportunities for growth and success in social commerce. Each stage plays a vital role in optimizing business performance, strengthening customer relationships, and enhancing overall competitiveness. With continuous advancements in AI technology, SMEs must remain proactive in adopting innovative AI solutions to stay ahead in the digital economy. Simply put, the four stages of AI-driven personalization in social commerce for SMEs are illustrated in Figure 1.

Figure 1. The Four Stages of AI-Driven Personalization in Social Commerce

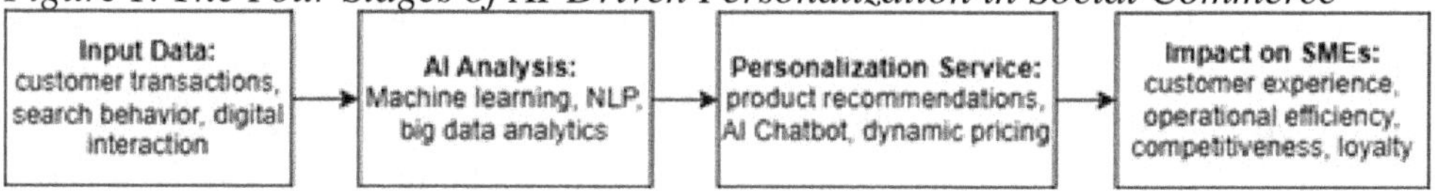

Source: figure prepared by the authors.

4.2. Benefits of AI-Driven Personalization for SMEs

The adoption of AI-driven personalization in social commerce offers various advantages for SMEs, particularly in enhancing customer engagement, loyalty, and operational efficiency (Iyelolu et al., 2024; Okeke et al., 2024). With AI's ability to analyze customer data in depth, SMEs can deliver more relevant content, including personalized product recommendations, targeted promotions, and interactive communication through chatbots (Patil, 2024). This leads to higher customer engagement, as shoppers receive a more tailored shopping experience that aligns with their preferences and needs. AI-driven personalization allows SMEs to interact with customers on a more personal level, making them feel valued and understood. By analyzing previous purchases, browsing behavior, and engagement history, AI can help SMEs create hyper-personalized shopping journeys that enhance the overall customer experience.

Beyond improving customer engagement, AI also plays a crucial role in fostering customer loyalty toward SMEs (Patil, 2024; Rane, 2023). By offering faster, more accurate, and personalized services, customers are more likely to have positive experiences that encourage repeat purchases. AI-driven recommendation systems, for instance, not only suggest products based on individual preferences but also provide incentives such as exclusive discounts for frequent buyers (Liao et al., 2021). For example, AI can identify customers who frequently purchase skincare products and offer them a special loyalty reward, such as a discount on their next purchase or early access to new product launches. This targeted approach helps SMEs retain customers and encourage long-term brand loyalty. Another significant benefit of AI-driven personalization is its ability to reduce cart abandonment rates. Many online shoppers abandon their carts before completing a purchase, often due to distractions, pricing concerns, or lack of urgency. AI-powered retargeting strategies can help SMEs re-engage these customers by sending personalized follow-up emails, offering limited-time discounts, or displaying reminder notifications. These efforts can significantly increase conversion rates and recover potential lost sales.

From an operational efficiency perspective, AI enables SMEs to automate various business functions that previously required human intervention (Kurrahman et al., 2025). AI-powered chatbots can reduce the workload of customer service teams, while AI algorithms optimize inventory management by predicting product demand based on historical data (Kedi et al., 2024b). For example, instead of manually tracking inventory levels, SMEs can use AI-driven inventory management systems to forecast demand trends and automatically restock popular products. This minimizes the risk of stockouts and overstocking, ensuring smoother supply chain operations. By streamlining business processes, SMEs can reduce operational costs and improve profitability. AI-driven automation also enhances order fulfillment processes by predicting peak demand periods and optimizing warehouse logistics. With AI analyzing sales data, SMEs can anticipate which products will be in high demand and prepare their supply chains accordingly. This leads to faster order processing, reduced shipping delays, and improved customer satisfaction. Additionally, AI-driven personalization helps SMEs make smarter marketing investments. Instead of spending resources on broad, untargeted advertising campaigns, SMEs can use AI to allocate their marketing budgets more effectively. AI analyzes customer data to determine which advertising channels and promotional strategies yield the highest return on investment (ROI). By focusing on high-performing campaigns, SMEs can reduce wasted ad spend and maximize their revenue potential.

Despite these significant benefits, the implementation of AI-driven personalization is not without its challenges and risks, especially for SMEs in developing countries. One of the primary obstacles is the high cost of AI technology and the lack of a robust technological infrastructure (Bhalerao et al., 2022; Iyelolu et al., 2024). Many SMEs have limited capital to invest in advanced AI systems and may struggle with inadequate internet connectivity and data storage capabilities. Furthermore, low digital literacy among SME owners and employees poses a significant barrier to effectively adopting and managing AI solutions. They may lack the technical skills to interpret AI-generated data or to troubleshoot system issues, which can hinder the successful integration of these technologies into their business models.

Another major concern is related to data privacy and security. AI-driven personalization relies heavily on collecting and analyzing vast amounts of customer data, which raises serious ethical and legal questions. In many developing countries, data protection regulations are still evolving (Ramadhan & Wijaya, 2022), leaving SMEs to navigate an uncertain legal landscape. Customers may also be hesitant to share personal information with businesses, particularly smaller ones, due to concerns about misuse of their data. Building and maintaining customer trust in a digitally driven environment is a critical challenge that SMEs must overcome. Finally, there is the risk of over-reliance on AI, where businesses may lose the ability to apply human judgment and creativity in their operations. While AI can automate tasks and provide data-driven insights, the human touch remains essential for building genuine customer relationships and adapting to unforeseen market changes. Therefore, a balanced approach is needed, where SMEs leverage the power of AI while also investing in human skills and ethical data practices to ensure long-term sustainability.

Therefore, AI-driven personalization benefits not only marketing efforts but also overall business management. The integration of AI enables SMEs to operate more efficiently, improve customer relationships, and stay ahead in the competitive digital marketplace. As AI technology continues to advance, its role in SME sustainability will become even more significant, helping businesses adapt to evolving consumer expectations and market trends. By embracing AI-driven personalization, SMEs can create highly tailored shopping experiences, increase customer retention, and drive long-term growth in the social commerce landscape. See Figure 4.2.

Figure 2. The Benefits of AI-Driven Personalization for SMEs

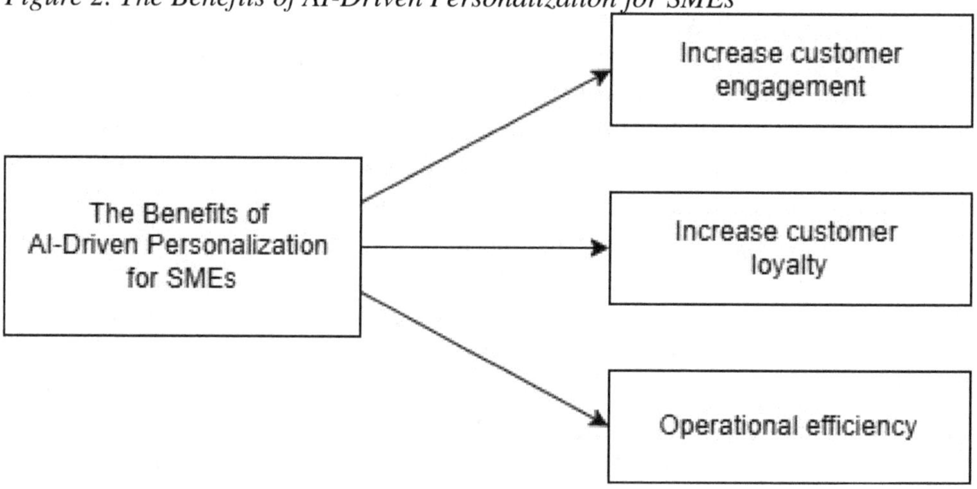

Source: figure prepared by the authors.

4.3. Challenges and Future Directions

While AI-driven personalization offers various benefits for SMEs in social commerce, its implementation still faces several challenges that need to be addressed. One of the primary challenges is the availability and quality of customer data. AI requires accurate and extensive data to generate effective personalization. However, SMEs often struggle to systematically collect, store, and analyze customer data, especially if they lack the necessary digital infrastructure (Bhuiyan, 2024). Additionally, AI adoption is still limited by resource constraints and technical expertise.

Many SMEs lack employees with the necessary skills to manage and optimize AI technology within their operations (Ikpe, 2024). Implementing AI often requires a significant initial investment in software, hardware, and workforce training, which can be a barrier for SMEs with limited capital (Kedi et al., 2024b). Another challenge is customer trust and acceptance of AI-driven personalization. While AI-based personalization can enhance customer experiences, concerns regarding data privacy and the security of personal information persist. Some customers may feel uncomfortable with their data being used for personalization, making it crucial for SMEs to adopt transparent and ethical strategies in managing customer data (Telukdarie et al., 2024).

Beyond these general challenges, the use of AI in social commerce for SMEs introduces specific ethical and regulatory complexities. The issue of data privacy and protection is paramount. As AI systems collect vast amounts of personal data, SMEs must navigate a complex landscape of data protection regulations, which are often underdeveloped in developing countries (Ramadhan & Wijaya, 2022). A single data breach or misuse could severely damage customer trust and brand reputation, as evidenced by numerous cases where large companies faced public backlash and legal action over data mishandling. Additionally, there is the risk of algorithmic bias. AI models trained on skewed or incomplete data can perpetuate and even amplify existing biases, leading to discriminatory outcomes. For example, a recommendation system might favor products for a specific demographic, inadvertently excluding others. This can limit market reach and alienate potential customers. A case in point is when a company's hiring algorithm was found to be biased against female candidates because it was trained on historical data from male-dominated roles, a potential pitfall that SMEs must be aware of when using AI for any form of automated decision-making.

Table 1. Challenges and Potential Solutions in the Implementation of Ai-Driven Personalization for SMEs

Main challenge	Potential solution
Data Limitations & Low Quality	Implement scalable and user-friendly CRM systems for data collection; leverage built-in analytics features of social commerce platforms; focus on first-party data.
Cost and Lack of Technical Expertise	Adopt cloud-based AI solutions with a subscription model (*pay-as-you-go*); partner with AI service providers; invest in digital training for employees.
Customer Privacy and Trust Issues	Implement transparent data privacy policies; use data anonymization; provide customers with options to manage their data; educate customers on the benefits of personalization.
Algorithmic Bias	Conduct regular audits of AI algorithms to identify and correct biases; use diverse and representative datasets for AI model training; combine AI-based decisions with human oversight.

Looking ahead, research and development in AI-driven personalization should focus on several key aspects. First, developing more accessible and cost-effective AI solutions for SMEs. Innovations such as cloud-based AI platforms and no-code AI solutions can help SMEs adopt this technology without requiring significant investments in infrastructure or technical expertise. Second, enhancing AI integration within SMEs' business strategies. AI can be applied beyond marketing and customer service to areas such as supply chain management, inventory optimization, and deeper market trend analysis. By leveraging AI more comprehensively, SMEs can strengthen their overall competitiveness in the rapidly evolving digital ecosystem. Finally, emphasizing transparency and educating customers about the benefits of AI-driven personalization. By fostering trust through open communication about how customer data is used to enhance their shopping experience, SMEs can increase adoption rates and improve the effectiveness of AI-driven strategies. By addressing these challenges and continuously developing innovative strategies, AI-driven personalization can become an increasingly powerful tool for helping SMEs thrive in the digital era and enhance their competitiveness in social commerce. Table 4.1 presents the key challenges faced by SMEs in implementing AI-driven personalization, along with potential solutions identified from the literature.

5. CONCLUSION AND RECOMMENDATIONS

This study highlights the pivotal role of AI-driven personalization in bolstering the competitiveness of SMEs within the social commerce ecosystem in developing countries. Based on the literature review, AI has been found to significantly contribute to increased customer engagement, loyalty, and data-driven operational efficiency. The integration of AI-driven personalization in social commerce enables SMEs to understand customer preferences more accurately through the analysis of transaction data and digital interactions. Technologies such as NLP-powered chatbots, product recommendation systems, and dynamic pricing allow SMEs to offer more personalized and interactive services, leading to higher conversion rates and stronger customer loyalty. Additionally, AI optimizes inventory management and marketing strategies, helping SMEs respond to market trends more quickly and efficiently. From a business perspective, AI-driven personalization not only enhances customer engagement but also strengthens customer loyalty and operational efficiency. By enabling SMEs to offer more relevant promotions and automate various business processes—including stock management and customer service—AI helps SMEs allocate resources more effectively, reduce operational costs, and improve profitability.

However, the implementation of AI-driven personalization also faces challenges, such as limited technological resources, low levels of digital literacy, and difficulties in data integration. Furthermore, the need for transparency and ethical considerations in handling customer data remains a critical concern for SMEs adopting AI. Therefore, a more inclusive approach is required for AI adoption, including digital training programs for SME operators and the development of more affordable and user-friendly AI solutions. Overall, this study provides strategic insights for SMEs on optimizing AI to strengthen their competitive advantage in the digital era. With more effective AI utilization, SMEs can not only improve customer satisfaction and operational efficiency but also sustain and grow within the increasingly competitive social commerce landscape.

5.1. Managerial and Policy Implications

The findings of this study carry significant implications for both SME managers and policymakers. For managers, the key takeaway is the need to shift from traditional, intuition-based decision-making to a data-driven approach. Managers must prioritize investing in foundational digital infrastructure to collect high-quality data, as AI's effectiveness is directly proportional to data quality. This involves implementing systems like Customer Relationship Management (CRM) and utilizing analytics features on social commerce platforms. Furthermore, managers must invest in training their workforce to build digital literacy, which will enable them to effectively manage and optimize AI technologies and overcome the barrier of a lack of technical expertise. This is not just about using AI, but about integrating it as a strategic tool to enhance customer relationships and operational processes.

For policymakers, the implications are equally crucial. Governments must recognize the vital role of SMEs in the economy and create a supportive ecosystem for their technological adoption. This includes formulating clear data protection and privacy regulations, which are currently underdeveloped in many developing countries. The absence of a strong legal framework can hinder AI adoption due to concerns over data security and customer trust. Furthermore, governments should consider providing incentives such as subsidies or tax breaks for SMEs that invest in AI solutions. They should also initiate and fund digital literacy programs to bridge the skills gap, making AI more accessible and easier to implement for a wider range of SMEs.

5.2. Strategic Recommendations

Based on the benefits and challenges identified, this study offers strategic recommendations tailored for different stakeholders.

- For SMEs: Start with simple, cost-effective, cloud-based AI solutions. Rather than a large-scale overhaul, begin by adopting one or two key tools, such as AI-powered chatbots for customer service or product recommendation plugins for social commerce platforms. Prioritize the collection of first-party data to build a comprehensive customer profile. Focus on building customer trust through transparency in data collection practices. This can be achieved by clearly communicating how customer data is used to enhance their shopping experience.
- For Government and Regulators: The government's role should be facilitative and protective. They must establish clear and consistent data governance policies to build consumer confidence and mitigate legal uncertainties for SMEs. Collaboration with private tech companies and educational institutions to develop affordable and user-friendly AI solutions tailored for the specific needs of SMEs is also highly recommended.
- For Researchers: There is a need for more empirical research on the implementation of AI for SMEs in developing countries. Future studies should move beyond a general discussion of benefits and explore how AI can address specific challenges in these regions, such as uneven internet access and limited capital.

5.3. Future Research Directions

As AI technology evolves, several avenues for future research emerge. First, there is a need to explore the potential of Generative AI for SMEs. This includes its application in automated content creation, such as generating product descriptions, social media posts, and personalized marketing visuals. Researchers could investigate how these tools can reduce marketing costs and enable SMEs to scale their content efforts with minimal resources.

Second, the field of Emotional AI presents an intriguing research direction. Future studies could examine how AI can be used to analyze customer emotions from their interactions (e.g., through sentiment analysis of comments or video reactions) to create more empathetic and emotionally resonant marketing campaigns and customer service experiences. This could be a powerful way for SMEs to build deeper, more meaningful connections with their audience.

Finally, the ethical dimension of AI, particularly AI ethics and algorithmic bias, requires more attention within the context of SMEs in developing countries. As AI models become more sophisticated, it is crucial to understand and mitigate potential biases that could lead to unfair or discriminatory outcomes. Research should focus on developing frameworks and practical guidelines for SMEs to implement AI responsibly, ensuring data privacy and maintaining customer trust in an increasingly digital world. These research directions will not only enrich the academic literature but also provide concrete solutions to help SMEs thrive sustainably in the future.

REFERENCES

Al-kfairy, M., Shuhaiber, A., Al-khatib, A. W., Alrabaee, S., & Khaddaj, S. (2024). Understanding Trust Drivers of S-commerce. *Heliyon, 10*(1), e23332. DOI: 10.1016/j.heliyon.2023.e23332 PMID: 38163094

Attar, R. W., Almusharraf, A., Alfawaz, A., & Hajli, N. (2022). New Trends in E-Commerce Research: Linking Social Commerce and Sharing Commerce: A Systematic Literature Review. *Sustainability (Basel), 14*(23), 16024. DOI: 10.3390/su142316024

Behare, N., Lakhani, D. Y., Vasmatkar, A., Waghulkar, S., Sayankar, V. N., Naik, A., . . . Behare, S. N. (2025). AI-Powered Personalization: Revolutionizing Mobile Commerce for Enhanced Customer Experiences. In *Leveraging AI for Effective Digital Relationship Marketing* (pp. 163-198). IGI Global. DOI: 10.4018/979-8-3693-5340-0.ch006

Bhalerao, K., Kumar, A., Kumar, A., & Pujari, P. (2022). A study of barriers and benefits of artificial intelligence adoption in small and medium enterprise. *Academy of Marketing Studies Journal, 26*(1), 1–6.

Bhuiyan, M. S. (2024). The role of AI-enhanced personalization in customer experiences. *Journal of Computer Science and Technology Studies, 6*(1), 162–169. DOI: 10.32996/jcsts.2024.6.1.17

Bisnis, K. U. M. K. M. (2025). *Survei Ungkap 97% UMKM di Indonesia Rasakan Manfaat AI untuk Bisnis*. 2025. Retrieved July from https://bisniskumkm.com/survei-ungkap-97-umkm-di-indonesia-rasakan-manfaat-ai-untuk-bisnis

Deshmukh, P., & Tare, H. (2024). Green marketing and corporate social responsibility: A review of business practices. *Multidisciplinary Reviews, 7*(3), 2024059–2024059. DOI: 10.31893/multirev.2024059

Ebrahimi, P., Khajeheian, D., & Fekete-Farkas, M. (2021). A SEM-NCA Approach towards Social Networks Marketing: Evaluating Consumers' Sustainable Purchase Behavior with the Moderating Role of Eco-Friendly Attitude. *International Journal of Environmental Research and Public Health, 18*(24), 13276. DOI: 10.3390/ijerph182413276 PMID: 34948884

Griffin, L. (2024). The power of social content: Transforming digital commerce. *Journal of Digital & Social Media Marketing, 12*(2), 129–140. DOI: 10.69554/LSZN9443

Ikpe, E. O. (2024). Adoption and implementation of artificial intelligence in small businesses in selected developing countries. *Journal of Health, Applied Sciences & Management, 8*(1), 26–34-26–34. DOI: 10.4314/johasam.v8i1.3

Iyelolu, T. V., Agu, E. E., Idemudia, C., & Ijomah, T. I. (2024). Driving SME innovation with AI solutions: overcoming adoption barriers and future growth opportunities. *International Journal of Science Technology Research Archive, 7*(1), 036-054. DOI: 10.53771/ijstra.2024.7.1.0055

Karunakaran, S., Hemasundari, M., Suguna, R., & Thandauthapani, A. (2024). Integrating AI and ML for dynamic pricing strategies: Innovations in marketing analytics and revenue management. *2024 International Conference on Power, Energy, Control and Transmission Systems (ICPECTS)*, Chennai, India. DOI: 10.1109/ICPECTS62210.2024.10780375

Kedi, W. E., Ejimuda, C., Idemudia, C., & Ijomah, T. I. (2024a). AI Chatbot integration in SME marketing platforms: Improving customer interaction and service efficiency. *International Journal of Management & Entrepreneurship Research, 6*(7), 2332–2341. DOI: 10.51594/ijmer.v6i7.1327

Kedi, W. E., Ejimuda, C., Idemudia, C., & Ijomah, T. I. (2024b). Machine learning software for optimizing SME social media marketing campaigns. *Computer Science & IT Research Journal, 5*(7), 1634–1647. DOI: 10.51594/csitrj.v5i7.1349

Khan, M. A. (2024). Understanding the Impact of Artificial Intelligence (AI) on Traditional Businesses in Indonesia. *Journal of Management Studies Development, 3*(02), 146–158. DOI: 10.56741/jmsd.v3i02.584

Kurrahman, T., Ming, T. F., K., L. M., Kanchana, S., & and Tseng, M.-L. (2025). Generative AI capabilities for green supply chain management improvement: extended dynamic capabilities view. *International Journal of Logistics Research and Applications*, 1–28. DOI: 10.1080/13675567.2025.2479006

Kushwah, U. (2024). The role of artificial intelligence in personalizing consumer experiences: A study on predictive analytics in the e-commerce sector. *Vidhyayana - An International Multidisciplinary Peer-Reviewed E-Journal, 10*(1), 298-320. https://j.vidhyayanaejournal.org/index.php/journal/article/view/1961

Leong, L.-Y., Hew, T. S., Ooi, K.-B., Hajli, N., & Tan, G. W.-H. (2024). Revisiting the social commerce paradigm: The social commerce (SC) framework and a research agenda. *Internet Research, 34*(4), 1346–1393. DOI: 10.1108/INTR-08-2022-0657

Liao, S.-H., Widowati, R., & Hsieh, Y.-C. (2021). Investigating online social media users' behaviors for social commerce recommendations. *Technology in Society, 66*, 101655. DOI: 10.1016/j.techsoc.2021.101655

Magableh, I. K., Mahrouq, M. H., Ta'Amnha, M. A., & Riyadh, H. A. (2024). The Role of Marketing Artificial Intelligence in Enhancing Sustainable Financial Performance of Medium-Sized Enterprises Through Customer Engagement and Data-Driven Decision-Making. *Sustainability (Basel), 16*(24), 11279. DOI: 10.3390/su162411279

Michael, O. (2025). Maximising the Potentials of Small and Medium Scale Business Enterprises in Developing Nations Through the Use of Artificial Intelligence: AI Adoption by SMEs in the Developing Nations. In *The Future of Small Business in Industry 5.0* (pp. 215-246). IGI Global Scientific Publishing. DOI: 10.4018/979-8-3693-7362-0.ch009

Mubdir, G. A., Hashim, S., Ayob, A. H., & Rosli, N. (2025). Exploring Customer Engagement in Social Commerce: A Literature Review of Frameworks, Pathways, and Emerging Trends. *Engineering, Technology &. Applied Scientific Research, 15*(2), 20601–20608. DOI: 10.48084/etasr.9452

Okeke, N. I., Alabi, O. A., Igwe, A. N., Ofodile, O. C., & Ewim, C. P.-M.Nnenna Ijeoma OkekeOlufunke Anne AlabiAbbey Ngochindo IgweOnyeka Chrisanctus OfodileChikezie Paul-Mikki Ewim. (2024). AI-driven personalization framework for SMES: Revolutionizing customer engagement and retention. *World Journal of Advanced Research and Reviews, 24*(1), 2019–2035. DOI: 10.30574/wjarr.2024.24.1.3208

Omowole, B. M., Olufemi-Philips, A., Ofadile, O., Eyo-Udo, N. L., & Ewim, S. E. (2024). Barriers and drivers of digital transformation in SMEs: A conceptual analysis. *International Journal of Frontline Research in Multidisciplinary Studies, 5*(2), 019-036. DOI: 10.56781/ijsrst.2024.5.2.0037

Patil, D. (2024). Artificial Intelligence-Driven Customer Service: Enhancing Personalization, Loyalty, And Customer Satisfaction. *Loyalty. Customer Satisfaction, 5057432*. Advance online publication. DOI: 10.2139/ssrn.5057432

Păuceanu, A. M., Văduva, S., & Nedelcu , A. C. (2023). Social Commerce in Europe: A Literature Review and Implications for Researchers, Practitioners, and Policymakers. *Journal of Theoretical and Applied Electronic Commerce Research, 18*(3), 1283–1300. DOI: 10.3390/jtaer18030065

Prasanna, R., Jayasundara, J., Naradda Gamage, S. K., Ekanayake, E. M. S., Rajapakshe, P. S. K., & Abeyrathne, G. (2019). Sustainability of SMEs in the Competition: A Systemic Review on Technological Challenges and SME Performance. *Journal of Open Innovation*, *5*(4), 100. DOI: 10.3390/joitmc5040100

Ramadhan, K. R., & Wijaya, C. (2022). The Challenges of Personal Data Protection Policy in Indonesia: Lesson learned from the European Union, Singapore, and Malaysia. *Technium Social Sciences Journal*, *36*(1), 18–28. DOI: 10.47577/tssj.v36i1.7442

Rane, N. (2023). Enhancing customer loyalty through Artificial Intelligence (AI), Internet of Things (IoT), and Big Data technologies: improving customer satisfaction, engagement, relationship, and experience. *SSRN*, 4616051. DOI: 10.2139/ssrn.4616051

Rialti, R., & Zollo, L. (2023). *Digital Transformation of SME Marketing Strategies*. Palgrave Macmillan Cham., DOI: 10.1007/978-3-031-33646-1

Techbehemoths. (2025). *How SMEs Use Artificial Intelligence in 2024 - Survey Results*. Tech Behemoths. Retrieved July from https://techbehemoths.com/blog/how-smes-use-ai

Telukdarie, A., Dube, T., Munsamy, M., Murulane, K., & Mongwe, R. (2024). Navigating Digital Challenges for SMEs: A Two-Tier Approach to Risks Mitigation and Sustainability. *Sustainability (Basel)*, *16*(14), 5857. DOI: 10.3390/su16145857

Zhang, L., & Erturk, E. (2022). Potential lessons from Chinese businesses and platforms for online networking and marketing: An exploratory study. *Social Sciences & Humanities Open*, *6*(1), 100274. DOI: 10.1016/j.ssaho.2022.100274

Chapter 6
Building the Foundations of Augmented Organizations Through AI Empowerment

R. N. Ravikumar
https://orcid.org/0009-0009-3705-1681
Marwadi University, Rajkot, India

S. Aarthi
https://orcid.org/0009-0006-9064-2091
Marwadi University, Rajkot, India

Zokir Mamadiyarov
Termez University of Economics and Service, Termez, Uzbekistan

ABSTRACT

As organizations navigate the Fourth Industrial Revolution, the use of AI and robotics in core business functions is essential. This research analyzes Human-Robotic Collaboration (HRC) as a driver for augmented organizations combining human and machine intelligence to boost productivity, agility, and innovation. It highlights key requirements for AI empowerment, such as data infrastructure, ethical governance, digital literacy, and co-created ecosystems. The impact of AI in reshaping jobs, workflows, and decision-making is explored, with examples from various industries showcasing AI's positive effect on productivity, safety, and employee satisfaction. Challenges like resistance to change, skill gaps, algorithmic bias, and governance

DOI: 10.4018/979-8-3373-8607-2.ch006

needs are also discussed. The chapter emphasizes a human-centered design, where AI collaborates rather than replaces, enabling organizations to succeed through trust, adaptability, and continuous learning.

1. INTRODUCTION

The organisations that are operating in such a dynamic environment in the present times have indeed been put to a staggering challenge and opportunity of how they will define and redefine operating procedures, generation of ideas and competition. What has made the automation in such supporting systems possible is that it has been the revolutionizing factor of virtually anything and everything that an organization would require to achieve; be it in the making of decisions, strategy execution it would transform the very pillars that successful organizations are built on. An augmented organization is a technological innovation, not only that but also a junction where intelligent systems add, not take away, functions. Therefore, artificial intelligence is giving organizations structures, cultures, and systems that allow organizations to work hand in hand with humans and be flexible and introduce novelties in every risk that an organization strives to make the most of all its functions to achieve sustainable growth (Abraham, 2023). These would be the basics which the present book or research on principles, strategies and structures would be focusing on in setting its foundation. The reason is the most essential focus areas are captured and as organizations move towards the structuring of their data infrastructure, ethical AI, talent development, organization culture and leadership agility, the areas of focus must be strategized. It also shows examples of such companies that are currently undertaking their AI to streamline their processes and provide more action and best practices.

1.1 Overview of the Fourth Industrial Revolution and Its Challenges

It is the synthesis of the whole aspect of the media and the actual environment. The other standard abandoned by this industrial revolution is a new standard. It is increasing very fast, by its place, more than the rest, as though this figure could be calculated by it. Not alone is this latest industrial revolution technologically superior but there is a speed, a scale and a systemic effect that cuts across industries and societies which the last one, its predecessor, did not. The latest technologies such as AI-robotic blockchain, IoT, bio-technology, and the development of materials are changing the functions of the organizations, their interaction with the customers, and the methods of value provision. However, nothing is achieved without difficulty. An agile, data-driven, ethical, and resilient organization is needed to survive and thrive in such a changing environment (Anjorin et al., 2024). They have to devise ways of responding to emerging and multifaceted dilemmas such as cyber threats, AI ethical concerns, labour dislocation, growing labour skills disparity, regulatory confusion and remaining innovative. The fourth industrial revolution needs higher adaptability, centricity of data, ethical responsibility and robustness to not just survive but also flourish in the turbulent environment. The Figure 1 explains the main technologies behind the Fourth Industrial Revolution, which are AI-Robotics, Industry 4.0, IIoT, Blockchain, Biotechnology, and Advanced Materials. These interrelated fields are changing the industries via innovation and digital combination.

Figure 1. Fourth Industrial Revolution

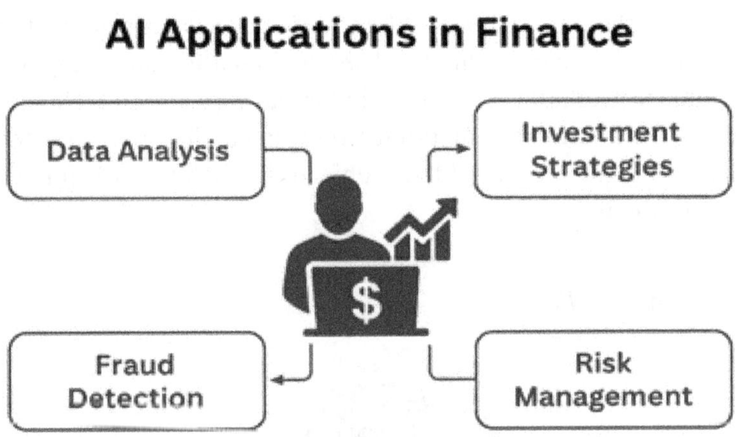

1.2 Role of AI and Robots in Transformation of Organizations

The drivers of reformation are AI and robotics, and as such, the future of work and business is in AI. They are opening their eyes to organizations to make superior choices-by personalizing the customer experience and predicting the market trends to streamline operations and may even develop new business patterns. All those innovative ways will provide sufficient chances on efficiency in performance and consequently rethink the process of introducing innovations. Some of the AI divisions which open unimaginable possibilities of propelling productivity and innovation include machine learning, natural language processing, and computer vision-are just a few (Balasubramaniam et al., 2020). Robotics revolutionizes industries, including the manufacturing and the health care industries. Robots are no longer limited to do repeated manual tasks but they are increasingly being incorporated with AI to do complex cognitive work, to work with humans (robots), and work independently in dynamic and unstructured contexts.

With AI and robotics, productivity-enhancing, human-capacity augmentation, and redefining the traditional roles, processes, and structures, along with the roles in organizations will emerge. They are at the core of what can be termed as the augmented organization. Enabling intelligent systems to assist and not to replace people in the procedure of performing tasks of higher-order, triggering creativity, and introducing beneficial change is the priority. Companies, which will not be surpassed by the Fourth Industrial Revolution, will not be those whose lead must be set in terms of introducing AI and robotics. They are the ones that will be thoughtful enough to consider the integration of AI and robotics as a human-centered, more effective, and intelligent partner in establishing a smarter future. Figure 2 shows the most prominent results of the Fourth Industrial Revolution technological development in the field of improving productivity, expanding human potential, and building flexible organizations. All these objectives push towards innovation and transformation of the industry.

Figure 2. Role of AI and Robot

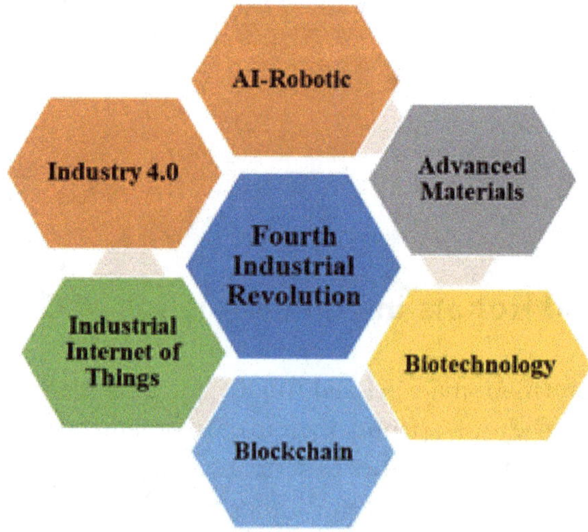

1.3 Objective of the Chapter

The chapter is focused on discovering how organizations can take the opportunities of Artificial Intelligence (AI), robotics, and the recent digital technologies and be augmented organizations. It will research on how AI has provided a clear cut in the working process, decision making and a human to machine interaction. The chapter is concerned with the key stone of the AI empowerment, which is ethical governance, digital literacy and creation of intelligent cases. The chapter has expounded the ways AI can be useful in enhancing productivity, innovation, and resilience on the premises of an analysis of practical examples in the field. Finally, it also gives the narrow attention on how AI can empower the potential of humans in order to create resilient businesses in adaptation, ethical, and future-oriented.

2. THE CONCEPT OF AUGMENTED ORGANIZATIONS

The companies that use high-tech solutions, i.e., artificial intelligence, robotics, Internet of Things (IoT), and data analytics to improve their efficiency, decision-making and flexibility of their work, are referred to as augmented organizations. Augmented organizations, in contrast to traditional versions, allow combining human intelligence and abilities of machines, which will allow organizations to be smarter and more dynamic in an extremely complex world. These companies are not merely automating jobs, but they are incubating intelligent systems, which can help in the supplement of the human functions to enable things to be innovative, nimble and tough. The real-time and predictive insights and automation analysis enhance the organisations to react to the change in the market quickly, enhance the customer experience, or retain the control over the internal processes (Brock and von Wangenheim, 2019). They establish culture of learning and flexibility in which there is system and employee collaboration. This in-between style transforms the industries as well as makes the organisations competitive.

The future of sustainable and intelligent model of business enterprises is potentially in augmented organizations as it is an intelligent model of business in the digitally disrupted world where businesses can act and react to the greater complexity and interconnectivity of the world. Therefore, an augmented organization is highly positioned in the future. The current method these organizations are training to thrive in this new AI age is by eliminating the race against machines as well as devising systems where human ability and machine smartness can be used to provide futures that are constantly clever, more robust and innovative. Table 1 presents the main characteristics of augmented organizations with major focus on human-AI cooperation, flexibility, ethical innovation. These features allow flexibility of adaptation, evidence-based management and lifelong learning of the workforce.

Table 1. Key Features of Augmented Organizations

Feature	Description
Human-AI Collaboration	Combines human empathy/creativity with AI's speed/analytical power.
Agile Adaptive Structures	Fluid designs that evolve quickly with technological advances.
Data-Driven Culture	Decisions based on continuous data collection, analysis, and action.
Ethical Innovation	AI systems built with fairness, transparency, and social impact in mind.
Continuous Learning	Workforce upskilled to collaborate with AI and adapt to new roles.

2.1 Definition of Augmented Organizations

An augmented organization plans to use AI and other advanced digital technologies with a purposeful goal of enhancing human capacity, better decision-making, and innovation in all areas of operation. Rather than fully substituting human workers, augmented organizations regard the technology in the shop as collaborative intelligence, which amplifies human creativity and expression, boosts productivity and effectiveness, and enables more informed, flexible and effective actions. With the so-called augmented organizations, data analysis, automation, pattern recognition, and predictive modelling are skills that intelligent systems unfold to human abilities of critical thinking, emotional intelligence, and creativity. All these complement each other and contribute to the creation of a new organizational structure that is highly adaptive and resilient, ethically-based, and even successful even in a rapidly changing environment of the Fourth Industrial Revolution.

2.2 Explanation of Human-Robotic Collaboration (HRC) as a Key Enabler

Human-Robotic Collaboration (HRC) is a harmonious group of interactions between people and robots where the two collaborate to complete a task that either of them would not feel comfortable working on independently. Unlike the conventional approach to automation where robots are isolated, HRC emphasizes personal contact, work areas, and real-time collaboration between humans and smart devices. HRC is one of the most important enablers in augmented organizations because it enables organizations to leverage the capabilities of human adaptability, creativity, and judgment with precision, endurance, and comprehensive analysis of robotics

(Brunnbauer, 2023). Instead of replacing humans, collaborative robots will assist humans in performing the repetitive or unsafe tasks and, instead, the humans can focus their time on other activities that are more valuable to them: problem-solving, innovation, and strategic thinking. HRC establishes a collaborative setting that enables companies to the purpose of augmented organizations issues production growth and efficiency increase concurrently with a corresponding enhancement in occupational safety and ergonomic workplace conditions. They promote speed of innovation and adaptation, which assists companies to respond to emerging demands. In addition, they facilitate the loose and immeasurable activities, which can experience discontinuities without disruption.

2.3 Convergence of Human Intelligence and Machine Intelligence

The combination of the human and machine intelligence is a groundbreaking moment in the performance and innovations of organisations. The machine intelligence that can provide the best speed, accuracy, and computing power of a machine must be introduced in line with the capability of human intelligence to be creative, comprehend feelings and moral judgment. Using this synergy, organizations can better solve complicated tasks, develop informed decisions within less time and also generate adaptive solutions to the dynamic environment. Artificial Intelligence Artificial Intelligence in augmented organizations the manner in which individuals with intelligent systems work within augmented organizations is such that, the human puts in context, moral judgment, and the machine performs the data processing, pattern recognition, and automation (Chen & Biswas, 2021). This collaboration is not only enhancing the functionality of activities but also functions as a data of innovation since it enables an instinctive mentality and information-driven logic. To explain the instance, the artificial intelligence devices support the specialists working in the sphere of medicine, finance, and engineering and leave human beings to give the field-related interpretation of the results and make the needed steps according to the forecasts. The more this convergence is attained, the more will be the age of intelligent enterprise and there will the human-machine partnerships produce the new form of productivity, the new form of the creative process and new form of strategic businesses.

3. KEY REQUIREMENTS FOR AI EMPOWERMENT IN ORGANIZATIONS

In order to be successful in AI implementation, organizations ought to effectively connect their implementation activities on four pillars, such as People, Process, Culture, and Governance. It is well equipped with data infrastructure and AI thrives on quality, secure and real time data. Investments on data collection, data management and data processing ensure the effective training of models and operation. The AI strategy must be concisely explained and its value linked with AI, using the way in which it may help to resolve the problems, the place where it may add value, and the way it supplements human talents regarding functions (Edilia and Larasati, 2023). The leadership commitment is paramount-leaders are supposed to be in the fore-front in adopting AI, resource mobilization, and improving an innovation-based environment. Cooperation across the functions is essential, and AI is not something that exists independently and only exists in IT; but the data team, business unit, human resource and compliance should be part of it to ensure it will respond to the actual needs of the organization. The upskilling of talents is as important as well, and in this case, the employees should undergo training in AI, data-oriented thinking, and others operating in the system. Ethical and responsible AI practices; that is, transparency, fairness, and accountability should inform the implementation. Lastly, agile culture and scalable technology eco-system like cloud computing and cybersecurity make it possible to adopt fast and scale securely.

3.1 Data Infrastructure: Robust Systems for Collection, Storage & Analysis

The era of AI has changed the meaning of data to the meaning of new oil that is the resource that cannot be overestimated as it drives intelligent systems. Nonetheless, artificial intelligence models are prone to being supplied with low-quality data, which may be raw and/or unstructured and will result in a poor decision-making situation. It requires an excellent data infrastructure that is comprised of three factors. First of all, there is data capture, which implies one of the aggregations of structured and unstructured (e.g., social media feedback) information in low-stability media such as IoT devices, CRM software, and ERP (Farayola et al., 2023). Second, the data storage can and must support secure, scalable and cost-effective solutions, typically data warehouses or data lakes constructed on an on-demand cloud. Lastly, full-fledged analytics and AI based data processing is applied to search patterns, create predictions and deliver data in real-time as the tool of real- time decision-making. The Amazon recommendation engine is one of those cases, and the efficient data infrastructure is needed to address the interactions of millions of users (a day) with the system so that they could be offered a recommendation.

3.2 Ethical AI Governance: Responsible and Fair Uses of AI

It is essential to integrate ethics into AI systems during the entire lifecycle at the time when they will have an increasing degree of autonomy and power in impacting organizations. Ethical AI governance is supposed to make AI creation and deployment responsible and equitable. These entail a number of major tenets. In bias management, the data that contains biased and unfair predictions and results is avoided by using a variety and representative of data. Transparency will involve explaining and understanding the process of AI decision-making, no longer relying on the dark-side shadows of the so-called black-box models. Accountability will mean that there is a transparent responsibility to the actions driven by AI but there is still human decision-making and control (Garbuio & Lin, 2019). Privacy protection addresses the secure processing of personal and sensitive information with regard to the regulations like GDPR. One such remarkable instance is the so-called Responsible AI framework implemented by Microsoft that relies on the following principles of ethical AI design: fairness, reliability, privacy, inclusiveness, and transparency. Such frameworks are necessary to create a sense of trust and guarantee that AI will run in the greater interest of the society.

3.3 Digital Literacy: Empowering AI & Tech Skills

The success of any AI systems in an organization is directly associated with the level of the digital literacy of the workforce. All the high-tech AI tools will be practically useless in case employees are not prepared to deploy them in an appropriate manner. There are some main elements of digital literacy. To begin with, employees should know the basics of AI, that is, its possible capabilities and limitations. Second, critical thinking is essential- the employees must be taught that recommendations by an AI-based system should not be taken blindly. Third, cooperation means practical, training methods to work with AI assistants, chatbots, decision-support systems, and, of course, platforms of data visualization (Giri et al., 2019). Finally, creation of a culture of lifelong learning will perpetuate the evolution of the workforce by keeping up with the changing technology. A good example that demonstrates the practicality of such practice is Accenture that regularly hosts AI boot camps and reskilling programs among its consultants, allowing them to remain competitive and collaborate effectively with intelligent systems. These initiatives allow employees to lead the way to the success of AI in the organization.

3.4 Co-Created Ecosystems: Human-AI-System Collaboration

Real empowerment of AI, instead, comes through the disconnection of human and machine work but through a truly collaborative work where both parties add value to the other. The co-created ecosystems put the design of AI to the forefront of human-centered inputs in which a focus is directed at building systems that complement the human ability but do not substitute. The method makes sure that AI contributes to decision-making, creativity, and strategic control. The feedback loops are essential here with the possibility of adjusting the AI continuously and enhancing its performance as more people add information to it. Along with them, interconnected systems have been designed to seamlessly apply AI to the entire business functionality, IoT equipment, cloud, and robotics, forming a single and smart network in business operations (Gomes et al., 2022). Adaptive collaboration also increases productivity-machines do complex calculations and repeat the tasks; human beings do emotional intelligence, strategic direction and judgment. An example is in the production factories of BMW where the robots do heavy lifting jobs and people direct the processes, adjust or coordinate it. Such synergy explains the efficiency of collaborative ecosystems.

4. IMPACT OF AI ON JOBS, WORKFLOWS, AND DECISION MAKING

Artificial Intelligence (AI) is essentially transforming the organizational processes, affecting the job profiles, working flows and decision-making approaches. Instead of destroying jobs, the essence of AI is to revamp them, and that is to automate those processes which are by their nature routine and repetitive, such as data entry work, basic customer service, and bookkeeping. Meanwhile, the number of requests with the need of creativity, emotional intelligence, and strategic thinking is increasing (Gudigantala et al., 2023). New jobs like AI trainers, bias auditors, and prompt engineers are appearing, and the importance of reskilling and AI literacy lies in them. When it comes to workflows, AI has automated such routine tasks as scheduling and verification of documents, thus letting the employees work on the tasks of more importance. Artificial intelligence-based supply chain optimization is a possibility since intelligent workflows are enabled by real-time data and predictive analytics, which make it possible to be adaptive. AI will also increase the fusion between man and machine making the employees decision-makers and the AI-assisted machine controllers. AI helps in data-driven insights when it comes to decision-making because it will speed up the process and increase accuracy based on predictive modelling and scenario calculations. The tools are now provided to the leaders who can evaluate risk and also predict the outcomes in a better way. As an example, AI in healthcare helps in the preliminary diagnosis, and the final decision is left to physicians. This human judgment and machine intelligence synergy is creating more intelligent, quicker and more strategic organizational decisions.

4.1 Reconceptualizing Conventional Jobs and Workflows

AI is changing the status quo on yesterday jobs and redesigning the way workflow is performed in any industry. Work design is fundamentally changing because of AI, as opposed to simply undertaking automation. There is the emergence of cross-hybrid roles; the roles of being a professional in a certain field by having extensive knowledge and at the same time being able to communicate with AI tools. As an example, financial analysts can use more time to analyze the information generated by AI and apply these insights to making strategic decisions because they do not waste time to compile the information (John et al., 2023). Relocation of tasks is also quite evident where, an AI system is assigned repetition and rule-based task whereas human beings are assigned tactical, creative and people operations. The workflows are more dynamic and data driven and are continuously being updated real time AI inputs making them more receptive and malleable. In addition, the workplace is evolving and turning into a co-working space since it is increasingly a place where human and AI work in unison, AI is no longer only a tool, but a partner who thinks, alerts of dangers, and proposes further steps of actions. Reconceptualization is not only shaving off a bit of efficiency but it is also reconsidering the role of human beings in the AI-enhanced ecosystems. The table 2 describes the effects of AI on employment and labor process, which includes the automation of routine processes and the emergence of new AI-based jobs. It highlights the aspect of smart workflows that facilitate real-time flexibility and tactical human engagement.

Table 2. AI's Impact on Jobs and Workflows

Aspect	Impact
Job Transformation	Routine tasks automated; demand rises for creativity/strategic skills.
New Roles	Emergence of AI trainers, bias auditors, and collaboration managers.
Workflow Automation	AI handles scheduling, invoicing, and data entry; humans focus on strategy.
Intelligent Workflows	Dynamic processes adapt in real-time (e.g., AI-driven supply chain

4.2 How AI Amplifies Human Judgment and Decision-Making Processes

Artificial Intelligence can contribute significantly more to human decision-making enterprise and provide new information, increased objectivity, and forecasting qualities. Among the numerous advantages, it is possible to mention the enhancement of the situation awareness because of the processing of great volumes of data and narrowing the information to the most crucial one to provide the decision-makers with a better perception of the situation of the moment (Lee et al., 2019). The ability to predict the trends, detect the anomalies and predict the situations, AI can provide the information, which would not be easy to access in purely human resources. AI can also help in the removal of cognitive bias because it does not communicate subjectively as it presents information in data and reveals less of an inclination to influence the individual subject to emotion or judgement provided it is properly designed. During the intricate solving of problems, AI grants the human being the power to assess the number of variables at the same time allowing the much more assured decision making. One of the most real examples is retail because AI systems examine the live buying habit to anticipate customer preferences, thus enabling companies to position products in a much better manner and generate a higher profit. Finally, AI becomes a strong enhancement of human judgment.

4.3 Boost Efficiency, Create Innovation, and Release New Value

The implementation of AI in the organization has transparent advantages in terms of efforts of efficiency, innovation, and value creation. Automation helps to increase efficiency as it prevents errors, promotes faster communication, and efficient time-wasting processes. As an example, AI-driven chatbots use customer queries at the rate of thousands of queries at a time, improving the quality of service, and letting human operators attend to complicated problems. AI also assists creativity and innovation, offers shopping patterns, recommends new product ideas and increases research, like pharmaceuticals where AI can speed drug scientific research (Oyekunle & Boohene, 2024). Also, AI creates new sources of value-some companies have broken open AI insights into paid services such as predictive maintenance or customer-specific customer experiences. Some employ AI to access different markets or provide hyper-personalized products or services. Netflix, Spotify, or other companies show it with their efficient customization engines based on AI and their use to enhance user activity, loyalty, and revenues to an impressive extent. In short, AI enables organizations to become smarter in their operation, innovate at faster rates, and create a new realm of business value.

5. INDUSTRY EXAMPLES AND CASE STUDIES

AI is changing industries by implementing real-world solutions and being able to measure the results. IBM Watson Health is helping oncologists deliver the insight of diagnosis and treatment advice in the healthcare field. In production, BMW employs robots powered by AI in assembly belts, which increases the level of precision and effectiveness. AIs are applied to detect fraud and execute trading at financial firms, whereas retail leaders, such as Amazon and Netflix, employ an AI to make personal recommendations and manage inventory (Radhakrishnan & Gupta, 2020). In farming, drones with AI and analysis technology maximize yield and reduce wastage. The case studies have provided an opportunity to illustrate the role of AI in boosting productivity, investments, and decision-making in various industries, in which previously existing traditional routines are being replaced by smarter, data-driven processes.

5.1 Healthcare Industry

The world of healthcare is not an exception, and Artificial Intelligence (AI) possesses a revolutionary character to perfect the administrative processes and clinical decision-making. Using AI solutions, frequent routine intelligent tools are created, which are automated in terms of an appointment booking, billing, and Electronic Health Record (EHR) management, which offers a relief of an administrative burden on a health worker. More to the point, AI is also being used in the field of healthcare diagnostics, particularly when reviewing medical imagery, including X-rays, MRIs, and CT scans and assist the doctors in their task by giving faster and more precise interpretation. The case of the IBM Watson Health can be discussed as one of the shining lights; an AI application that aids oncologists in diagnosing their patients, as well as helping them develop a treatment plan to the latter. Watson processes giant volumes of clinical data, research and history of patients to prescribe evidence-based treatment systems (Aikenberg and van den Hoven, 2020). It possesses a life-long learning ability that enhances the decision-making of the physicians such that no two patients get similar treatment and quality medical care. The implications of AI to healthcare are complicated. It is achieved through reducing the amount of time devoted to processing lab results and medical records to make it high-efficiency. The novelty of the advanced AI technology capable of processing rather difficult biomedical information contributes to the innovation, as the drugs are discovered much faster (Ali et al., 2023). In addition to this, AI will yield to novel values of providing personal health findings, prevention rules, and wellness. Altogether, AI gives the healthcare systems the ability to serve smarter, faster, and patient-centered care. The figure 3 shows some significant uses of Artificial Intelligence in the healthcare sector. In the middle, AI is symbolized as a cooperative power between robots and the work of medical personnel. Eight application areas surround the center, namely Diagnostics, Drug Discovery, Personalized Care, Remote Monitoring, Preventive Advice, Administrative Tasks, and Patient Monitoring. Every area is presenting the ways in which AI is assisting clinical decisions, improving patient care, automating administrative tasks, and helping to innovate and become more efficient in healthcare systems.

Figure 3. AI Applications in Healthcare

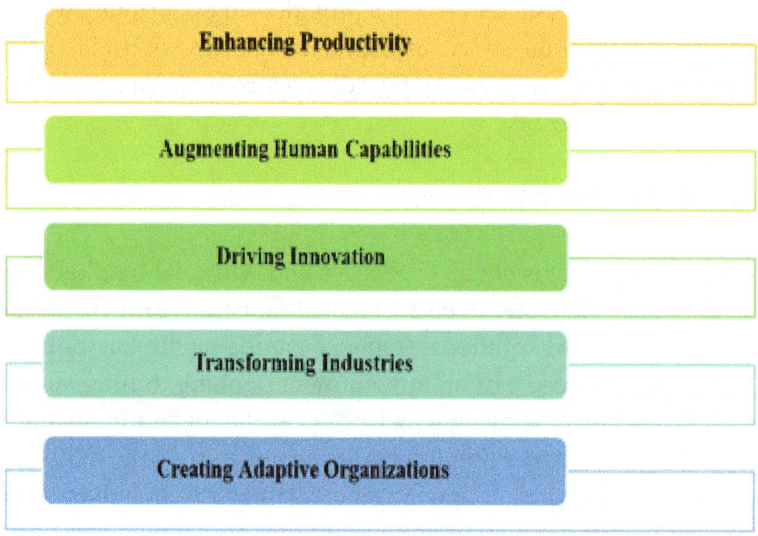

5.2 Manufacturing Industry

Artificial intelligence is assuming a center stage to change careers and processes of the manufacturing sector by facilitating automation, precision, and predictive intelligence. That can be predictive maintenance, quality assurance, or robotization with AI, but it is making processes more efficient, less expensive due to downtime, and more productive (Breidbach & Maglio, 2020). As AI takes the weight of the monotonous and physically exhausting routine, human workers will be able to devote their efforts to other activities of a higher level: process optimization, strategic planning, and continuous improvement. One of the most interesting examples is the Human-Robot Collaboration (HRC) model of BMW. Robots in BMW assembly lines are AI-based that could cooperate with human workers in a more-human working environment. These robots take care of high-lifting and repetitive tasks but human workforce does quality tests and fine-tuning. Such synergy enhances accuracy, as well as eliminates physical pressure on employees, and accelerates the production process. The influence of AI in the industry is quite considerable. With predictive maintenance, efficiency is enhanced since the amount of unpredicted equipment damage is lowered and the machines are accessible more. The innovation will be achieved through centered innovation of flexible and smart manufacturing systems that will enable it to adjust to changes in demand or the design of a product (Dignum et al., 2018). Artificial intelligence is also playing another role where it is enabling new value to be added through quality improvement of a product, enabling flexibility of an operation and improvement of overall profitability. The transformation will help enable a smarter, safer and agile manufacturing ecosystem. The figure 4 demonstrates how Artificial Intelligence is integrated in the manufacturing industry. The Human-Robot Collaboration is illustrated by a human worker and robotic arm in the middle of the picture, and there are four major applications of AI, including Predictive Maintenance, Quality Assurance, Robotics Automation, and Process Optimization. All of the components are graphically connected with the directional arrows and demonstrate how AI is used to make manufacturers more productive, enhance the quality and facilitate the innovative process of strategic processes, which will lead to a smarter, safer and more agile manufacturing environment.

Figure 4. AI Applications in Manufacturing

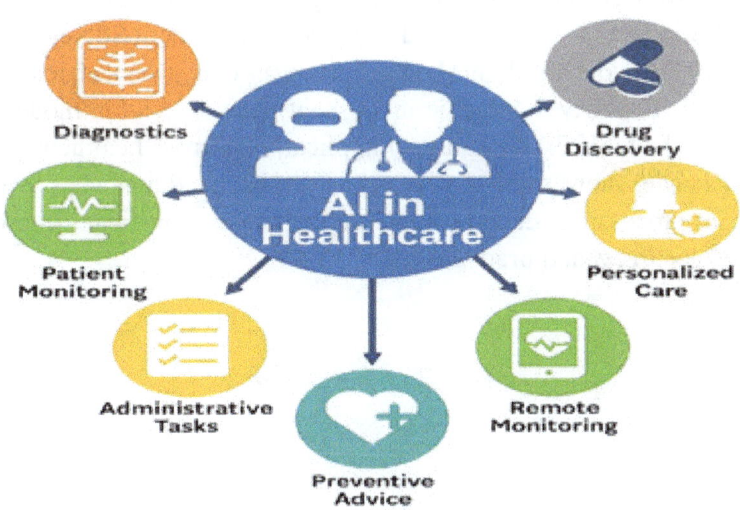

5.3 Finance Industry

AI is revolutionizing the financial sector by increasing efficiency, precision, and strategic decision-making in most areas of the business. Among many other uses, AI plays a major role in the data analyses, fraud detection, risk management, and development of investment strategy (Greene et al., 2019). Market clearing using AI tools is a new possibility where financial professional can predict the market and make maximized investment portfolios and give individual customer services which lead to great productivity of operations and customer satisfaction. Another good example is the COiN platform by JPMorgan Chase that is made to automate the process of reviewing complex legal documents that used to require hours, but with AI, can be done within a matter of minutes. Besides, JPMorgan also uses AI in predictive analytics in other wealth management deals where it uses data to make settlement decisions. The role of AI in the financial sector is massive. Automation increases efficiency during compliance and transaction monitoring tasks. Innovation is an art of accurately predicting the behavior in the market using AI models and recommend the market on the right investments they must make (Jobin et al., 2019). Moreover, the introduction of AI is associated with another kind of value, the democratization of financial services, and robo-advisors allow delivering personalized wealth management services to more clients at an affordable price, providing them with high-quality financial planning. In general, AI is transforming finance by allowing more intelligent choices, minimizing risks, and improving customer interaction. The figure 5 illustrates key applications of Artificial Intelligence in the financial sector. At the center, a human figure using a laptop with a dollar symbol signifies AI-driven financial decision-making. Four connected boxes represent core applications: Data Analysis, Fraud Detection, Investment Strategies, and Risk Management. The layout highlights how AI enhances operational efficiency, reduces financial risk, and drives strategic investment planning within modern finance environments. The table 3 highlights AI applications across healthcare, manufacturing, and finance, showcasing real-world use cases like diagnostics, automation, and document processing. Each example demonstrates significant improvements in efficiency, accuracy, and productivity.

Figure 5. AI Applications in Finance

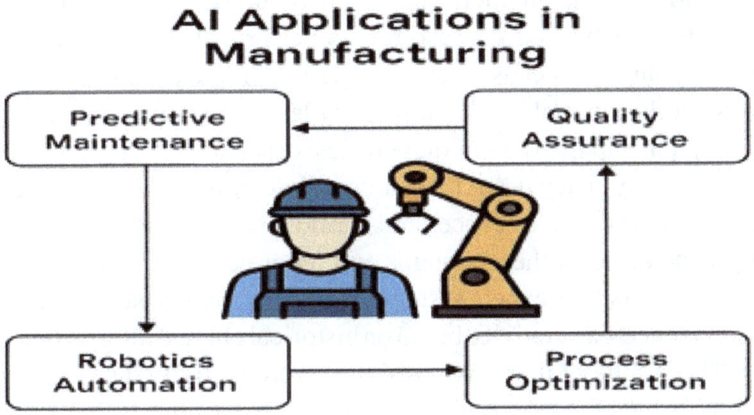

Table 3. Case Studies of AI Integration

Industry	Example	AI Application	Outcome
Healthcare	IBM Watson Health	Diagnostic aid and treatment planning.	Faster processing, personalized care.
Manufacturing	BMW's HRC	Robots handle heavy tasks; humans oversee quality.	Increased productivity and safety.
Finance	JPMorgan Chase's COiN	Automates legal document review.	Reduced processing time from hours to minutes.

5.4 AI, Robotics & Expert Systems In Human Collaboration

Artificial intelligence, robotics, and the expert system are greatly improving human cooperation in industries such as manufacturing and health care (automating menial (task) or facilitating complex decision-making). The production line at Tesla is a bright example of the use of AI-powered robots, the use of the machine learning models that assist with quality control, and predictive maintenance systems in the manufacturing industry (Josimovski et al., 2023). Tesla uses robots to carry out repetitive and manual work (whether it is welding, painting, and assembling), whereas human employees take on problem-solving, quality, and adjustment of the manufacturing process. AI also helps to track the health of machinery and pre-assess possible failures so that maintenance may be carried out beforehand and production planning timely. The synergy has given birth to huge productivity returns where the plant is able to manufacture more vehicles without losing its quality. The safety of workers has been enhanced because robots perform the dangerous duties and staff satisfaction is higher because they can carry out more capable and interesting tasks which boost their morale and competency levels. Siemens Healthineers uses AI and expert systems in the field of diagnostics, especially in medical imaging, in the healthcare industry. They use AI to study radiology images in order to identify the early-stage diseases such as cancer and cardiovascular conditions.

Normalcy is detected in these systems and reported as abnormal to be further checked by the doctors. An expert system also helps a physician in that they will come up with evidence-based advice based on historical clinical information (Olatoye et al., 2024). The results of it are substantial- the productivity increases, since the diagnosis is performed quicker, which means that even more patients are able to be treated within shorter periods of time. This increases safety since the critically diagnosed patients are detected early and accurately thus lowering the chances of being misdiagnosed. The level of job satisfaction of healthcare professionals has also increased since AI helps to take care of administrative tasks and enables such professionals to pay more attention to their patients and make complicated medical decisions. Put together, these examples show that AI, robotics, and expert systems do not substitute human labour but augment it, making them more efficient, secure, and satisfying and allowing them to innovate and make wiser decisions in various fields.

5.5 Positive Outcomes of AI, Robotics, and Expert Systems Integration

Revenue and profit margins have grown tremendously due to the introduction of AI, robotics and expert systems into the business that has resulted in increased productivity as a result of automation of the routine and the repetitive tasks (Ruggeri et al., 2022). This enables the human labour to specialize in activities involving high-value addition and hence accelerates the accomplishment of tasks, exploitation of resources, and growth in general in business. Here, safety has also been tremendously enhanced nowadays with AI and robotics able to do the dangerous jobs with heavy machinery, use of chemical substances that are hazardous or skilful surgery with little chance of damaging a human worker. With this move, not only is it protecting its employees, but also improving the reliability of its operations. Further, the satisfaction of the workers has also risen with AI replacing the monotonous or body intensive tasks thus leaving the workers to undertake more creative and judgmental duties which need or require emotional intelligence. This change will lead to a more inspiring workplace and an increase in morale with constant desire to grow as a professional (Stone et al., 2020). All these advantages go to show the extent to which smart technologies are transforming the workplace to a more effective, protective and satisfying place.

6. CHALLENGES IN IMPLEMENTING AI AND ROBOTICS

Implementing AI and robotics in the real world pose challenges of integration into existing systems or workflows. Many organizations operate with legacy infrastructures that are not compatible for modern AI solution implementation and incur enormous costs and delays during transitions (Agnihotri et al., 2023). Interoperability can also be hindered, limiting the potential of AI, due to a lack of standardized data formats and protocols across departments or industries. Employees resisting changes, fearing that the shift towards an AI solution will cost them their jobs, or feeling that they do not have the required technical training to support such efforts slow the acceptance and effectiveness of AI initiatives.

Another essential challenge remains to be the ethical, secure, and transparent use of AI and robotics. Privacy of the data, algorithmic bias, and accountability issues can erode trust and confidence in these technologies. For instance, an AI system could amplify inequalities by producing biased outcomes while a lack of transparency in how decisions are made would cause an auditing nightmare or at least make it impossible to explain the outcomes to stakeholders (Raju & Sumallika, 2023). Hence, ensuring legal compliance, cybersecurity, and ethical governance frameworks remain extremely complex tasks, and removing these barriers will require a balanced approach that not only combines technological innovation with insightful policy-making, but also provides opportunities for inclusive stakeholder engagement. The table 4 outlines key challenges in AI adoption, including outdated legacy systems, employee resistance, and ethical risks. It also highlights the difficulty organizations face in ensuring regulatory compliance with evolving data protection laws.

Table 4. Challenges in AI Implementation

Challenge	Description
Legacy Systems	Incompatibility with modern AI solutions, requiring costly transitions.
Employee Resistance	Fear of job loss or lack of technical readiness slows adoption.
Ethical Concerns	Risks of bias, privacy violations, and lack of transparency in AI decisions.
Regulatory Compliance	Complexity in adhering to GDPR and industry-specific regulations.

7. HUMAN-CENTERED AI: COLLABORATION AND TRUST

It is in fact a design towards human-and machine-centricity as opposed to its replacing itself that would make available collaborative technology at the workplace. These systems are built as supplements of human ability, wherein a designated human individual can devote more time to creative, strategic areas, and empathetic areas of his/her job (Roberts et al., 2021). It requires the complete knowledge of human resources to collaborate following the mechanisms of feedback including humans in the non-competitive but complementary environments. This philosophy will be based on the establishment of a trusting relationship between human employees and AI systems at the core. Trust is built based on the transparency, predictability, and comprehensiveness of how and why AI systems take decisions. They are more empowered than they are displaced because they are involved in the implementation and design of the systems. Also, empathy in design, capturing human values, feelings, experiences, etc., will make sure that AI solutions not only do not, but enhance the quality of the workplace in general (Shrestha et al., 2019). This is why such human-centered approach will be relevant in ensuring that AI application in industries becomes sustainable and ethical to enhance effectiveness.

7.1 Transparency and Accountability in Human-Centered AI

The trust in human-based systems of AI is supported by clarity and responsibility. The employees and stakeholders should understand how AI systems work through data, insights, and conclusions. The explainable outputs will also decrease the black box perception of AI and allow human workers to either correct or correct AI recommendations. Responsibility involves setting boundaries of responsibilities such that human beings are the final decision-makers with AI being a support system. This alignment will guarantee ethical and compliant operations to avoid making use of sensitive data and biased results (Raju & Sumallika, 2023). Organizations can build trust in AI by promoting open dialogue and sharing algorithmic policies and engaging different teams in design. With trust, the workers put AI processes in a different perspective, believing that it is not their replacement but rather a trusted and dependable partner that uses their judgment and ingenuity to supplement it.

7.2 Empathy and Human Values in AI Collaboration

Besides technical reliability, the functional human-centered AI must include humanity and human values. This entails developing AI systems, which detect and react to emotional, social, and cultural elements of work. A possible example of empathy-based design is the adaptive AI assistants that modulate their speech style or employment of workload balance based on the degree of stress of the user. Sustainability of the collaboration meaning fairness and psychological safety are key elements of sustainable collaboration and are provided by the inclusion of human values. Such understanding systems can also be used and make the level of work satisfaction great as employees feel represented and not controlled or cast out. Moreover, the process can be optimized continuously and as per the requirements of human beings by implementing user feedback loops into the AI applications (Raju and Sumallika, 2023). Empathy and values become first, AI proves to be not only a technological appliance, but a partner of productive, healthy and desirable working conditions where innovation has learned to thrive and human dignity is not disregarded.

8. STRATEGIES FOR ORGANIZATIONAL TRANSFORMATION THROUGH AI ADOPTION

Housing AI within an organization means more than just employing such technology as well as changes in strategic direction, cultural redirection and leadership. Such transformation ensures that AI adoption conforms with organizations' objectives, enables productivity enhancement besides benefiting employees and other stakeholders. Hence, following are key strategies for AI adoption in the organization (Tambe et al., 2019). The table 5 presents essential strategies for successful AI adoption, emphasizing strong leadership, continuous upskilling, and ethical governance. It also highlights the importance of cross-functional collaboration to ensure smooth and effective AI integration.

Table 5. Strategies for AI Adoption

Strategy	Action
Leadership Commitment	Communicate vision, address fears, and lead by example.
Continuous Learning	Implement AI-powered training platforms for upskilling.
Ethical Frameworks	Ensure transparency, fairness, and accountability in AI systems.
Cross-Functional Teams	Collaborate across IT, HR, and business units for seamless integration.

8.1 Leadership: Steer Organizations Towards AI Adoption

Successful integration of artificial intelligence into organizations will depend on powerful and visionary leadership that will lead groups through technical and cultural transformation (Bhatt, 2022). AI introduces lots of changes into workplaces, decision-making, and job description, and such changes may cause resistance on the part of employees. The fear of being replaced or losing control of work is one of the main issues as most employees are afraid that AI will cause their positions to become unnecessary or that their choices will be taken away and ignored. Also, a clear vision of the leadership may be missing, which can negatively affect the process of adoption since the teams could not comprehend how AI will improve their work or resonate with the organizational objectives. Leaders should explain a powerful vision of AI to address such challenges and specify how this technology can increase productivity, promotion of innovation, and a better working environment (Cascella et al., 2024). This vision must be in tune with the rest of the objectives of the organization and must emphasize the short-term victories and the long-term benefits. There is also need to find empathy and engagement in order to not ignore the importance of listening to the employees in order to approach to those concerns and inform them that AI will not replace human labour but will be able to assist them. It is highly important to be an example. The presence of leaders in the use of AI by the decision-making process and learning within the organization is an indication of the organizational commitment to transgression and broad acceptance. It is even more crucial that the initiatives of reskilling and upskilling be spearheaded by the leadership in order to ensure that employees feel confident utilizing AI tools and processes. By doing so, leaders will be able to foster trust, remove the fear, and introduce the culture of innovation and flexibility which is an indispensable condition to do AI integration on a sustainable basis.

8.2 Technological Support: AI for Continuous Learning

The AI is a groundbreaking approach to instilling the learning culture of organizations in the long term, which makes organizations flexible and easy to innovate. When AI is integrated into the Learning and Development (L&D) processes, companies will be capable of developing a culture of development, the development of capabilities and flexibility to change within the DNA. However, realizing the vision has some serious problems (Chaibi and Zaiem, 2022). The legacy training systems also tend to be difficult to integrate with AI interfaces and the traditional systems may not be capable to support AI learning experiences. Also, several organizations are facing the constraints of data, where they do not have the facility to capture and interpret the data concerning learning behavior required in customized AI-based training.

AI-driven learning systems provide step-by-step customized content, the freedom to take time and immediate feedback overcoming such barriers. Such websites assist in keeping the staff well informed about the novel technologies and consistent with AI projects at the company. Furthermore, with data-driven knowledge, AI would be able to assess employee performance, detect skill deficiencies and suggest personalized learning journeys that maintain the constant growth (Ghani et al., 2022). The implementation of AI in the regular workflow procedures permits the moment of data-driven choices to be faster and to decrease the number of repeated sub-tasks, thus, contributing to instant learning and operational effectiveness. Notably, in this regard, organizations should also instil the growth mindset in their workers that are to regard AI as being more of an opportunity to improve their careers than as a threat. The emerging tools for learning in the flow of work include AI-powered chatbots and digital assistants that can be used by the workers to become more adaptable without reducing their productivity rate. The practice of accepting the alternative will make AI an agent of a smarter, robust, and a workforce ready to take the future head on.

8.3 Policy Recommendations: Ethical & Inclusive AI Deployment

They're also needing to be made quite effective AI models; yet, they have to be proofed against all points of mischief- bias, ambiguity, discrimination even at the first steps. Ethics through and strong rallying policies must prevail regarding most important application areas of AI in the organization so that no potential disastrous effects such as bias, discrimination, and job displacement-occur (Huang et al., 2024). The problem of AI bias is that, systems can actually sustain or aggravate bias if trained on data that have been marred by negative bias, that is, the training data could be discriminatory. There is more havoc created by organizations which do not have clear and well-defined guidelines on adopting AI technologies because the absence of such ethics provides room for harmful practices. Finally, exclusivity gaps are formed due to the aspect that there are users who are not taken into account in the design of AI systems or do not belong to some of the under-represented groups.

In order to address these issues, organizations need to express AI principles that are ethical in spirit fairness, transparency, and accountability. The data sets should also be varied and not biased and access as well as audits should be imposed equally to ensure that there is fairness. The design of the AI solutions must be inclusive to ensure a large proportion of potential uses among a large pool of end-users who are employees and customers. It must take into account the availability to people with disabilities and attempt to remove further algorithmic biases (Siuly et al., 2018). Audits are to be conducted in cadence to assist in making sure that by the course of time no AI systems turn biased or discriminating and that the stakeholder engagement and accountability are taken care of, which will serve in making decisions with employees, customers, and ethicists. Observing the regulatory laws including GDPR and special industry laws will be important. The general culture and strategy that are backed by top management, IT policy, and ethics are critical towards an effective transformation of organizations that make use of AI in constructing conscientious and inclusive solutions that align with societal principles and guarantee how AI can be used as a driver of success without disintegrating moral standards.

9. CONCLUSION

The necessity to adapt AI and robotics as the foundation of the organizational operating strategy is gaining critical force, and new concerns and opportunities arise with industrialization of the world. This chapter is devoted to the key elements of AI, trying to prepare the organization to be augmented businesses. HRC is the primary change agent in this transformation whereby human intelligence is integrated with that of machine management in order to achieve improved productivity, agility, and innovation. The only way that full change will happen is when organizations will come up with strict methodologies of adhering to minimum requirements of AI empowerment. Second, there is data infrastructure which is equally important and which focuses on how the data collection, storage and processing systems of the organizations are built.

AI systems use data to make decisions on the way to enhance organizational performance. As well as data infrastructure, AI governance must be also ethically oriented, to ensure that AI technologies are used in a responsible way. The digital literacy programs should be established in order to provide various employees with skills to use AI tools. That is what facilitates a workforce that will be flexible to the new normal types of technology and will use the opportunities and benefits of AI. The development of ecosystems to co-create human, AI, and other systems is also a fundamental need to assist in lifelong learning and responsive flexibility of AI systems. AI influences decision-making, restructures work and remodels it, gives titles to jobs and roles. It complements the human judgment and decision making and opens up the prospects of efficiencies and innovations that bring about growth prospects among all industries.

Thus, AI must be regarded as an equal workmate to human workers rather than inherently a substitute to human workers. These are the actual applications of industries with economic efficiency, such as the productivity and safety improvement of a worker, quite significantly the fulfillment of the worker due to AI. Nevertheless, such empowerment with the help of AI does not come easy. The best obstacle to organizations is resistance to change. The workers would not want to change the now quite familiar working system since they will either lose their jobs or fail to adapt to working faster in a more technologically advanced set up. The key to overcoming such a challenge is visibly strong leadership that provides the guidance the introduction of AI with assistance of continuous reskilling and upskilling programmes to ensure that the employees survive the transition. The second of the barriers is the absence of skills: the companies lack the personnel capable of conceptualizing, developing, implementing and maintaining AI-based systems.

Training and education are the keys to proper utilization of AI benefits to organizations. The second bullying issue that should be addressed during the design and implementation of AI is algorithmic bias. It involves open and ethical development of AI systems which are transparent and accountable and non-discriminatory. It should establish mechanisms of governance of AI-focused decision making that would oversee the AI-based systems that are not biased or discriminatory. Companies adopting a human-centered design would therefore be able to make sure that AI supplements and not substitutes the human ability. Effective human-centered design encourages cooperation and relationship with machine and human staff, creating a practical and resourceful workplace. To organizations that are really transformed, the step begins with embracing AI as an AI that can help to complement the potential of humanity, but not an AI that can substitute it. The chapter will offer recommendations to organizational leaders and decision-makers on the ethical, inclusive, and responsible use of AI applications in organizations. The ability to successfully integrate human beings and machines to achieve innovation will bring value and create endless learning. With the development of AI and robots, organizations that are willing to expand themselves can thrive in such an environment.

REFERENCES

Abraham, S. (2023). *The future of fashion is here: Integration of AI in marketing practices of leading fashion retail businesses*. In Toronto Metropolitan University.

Agnihotri, A., Pavitra, K. H., Balusamy, B., Maurya, A., & Bibhakar, P. (2023). Artificial intelligence shaping talent intelligence and talent acquisition for smart employee management. EAI Endorsed Trans. Internet Things, 10.

Ali, S., Kumar, V., & Breazeal, C. (2023). AI Audit: A card game to reflect on everyday AI systems. *Proceedings of the AAAI Conference on Artificial Intelligence*, *37*(13), 15981–15989. DOI: 10.1609/aaai.v37i13.26897

Anjorin, K. F., Raji, M. A., Olodo, H. B., & Oyeyemi, O. P. (2024). Harnessing artificial intelligence to develop strategic marketing goals. Int. j. *Manag. Entrep. Res*, *6*(5), 1625–1650.

Balasubramaniam, N., Kauppinen, M., & Kujala Sari and Hiekkanen, K. (2020). Ethical guidelines for solving ethical issues and developing AI systems. In Product-Focused Software Process Improvement (pp. 331–346). Springer International Publishing.

Bhatt, P. (2022). AI adoption in the hiring process – important criteria and extent of AI adoption. Foresight, ahead-of-print(ahead-of-print).

Breidbach, C. F., & Maglio, P. (2020). Accountable algorithms? The ethical implications of data-driven business models. *Journal of Service Management*, *31*(2), 163–185. DOI: 10.1108/JOSM-03-2019-0073

Brock, J. K.-U., & von Wangenheim, F. (2019). Demystifying AI: What digital transformation leaders can teach you about realistic artificial intelligence. *California Management Review*, *61*(4), 110–134. DOI: 10.1177/1536504219865226

Brunnbauer, M. (2023). How top-down AI introduction leads to incremental business improvement. *Proceedings of the Annual Hawaii International Conference on System Sciences*. DOI: 10.24251/HICSS.2023.745

Cascella, M., Guerra, C., De Feo, R., Cerrone, V., & Farah, S. (2024). Cross-sectional study on medical attitude towards artificial intelligence use in fibromyalgia: Insights from the annual thinking lab on fibromyalgia syndrome (ATLAS 2024). *Translational Medicine @ UniSa*, *26*(2), 153–163. DOI: 10.37825/2239-9747.1066

Chaibi, A., & Zaiem, I. (2022). Doctor resistance of artificial intelligence in healthcare. *International Journal of Healthcare Information Systems and Informatics*, *17*(1), 1–13. DOI: 10.4018/IJHISI.315618

Chen, Y., & Biswas, M. I. (2021). Turning crisis into opportunities: How a firm can enrich its business operations using artificial intelligence and big data during COVID-19. *Sustainability (Basel)*, *13*(22), 12656. DOI: 10.3390/su132212656

Dignum, V., Baldoni, M., Baroglio, C., Caon, M., Chatila, R., Dennis, L., Génova, G., Haim, G., Kließ, M. S., Lopez-Sanchez, M., Micalizio, R., Pavón, J., Slavkovik, M., Smakman, M., van Steenbergen, M., Tedeschi, S., van der Toree, L., Villata, S., & de Wildt, T. (2018, December). Ethics by design. Proceedings of the 2018 AAAI/ACM Conference on AI, Ethics, and Society. DOI: 10.1145/3278721.3278745

Edilia, S., & Larasati, N. D. (2023). Innovative approaches in business development strategies through artificial intelligence technology. *Itsdi*, *5*(1), 84–90. DOI: 10.34306/itsdi.v5i1.612

Farayola, O. A., Abdul, A. A., Irabor, B. O., & Okeleke, E. C. (2023). Innovative Business Models driven by Ai technologies: A review. Comput. Sci. IT Res. j., 4(2), 85–110.

Garbuio, M., & Lin, N. (2019). Artificial intelligence as a growth engine for health care startups: Emerging business models. *California Management Review*, *61*(2), 59–83. DOI: 10.1177/0008125618811931

Ghani, E. K., Ariffin, N., & Sukmadilaga, C. (2022). Factors influencing artificial intelligence adoption in publicly listed manufacturing companies: A technology, organisation, and environment approach. International Journal of Applied Economics. *Finance And*, *14*(2), 108–117.

Giri, C., Jain, S., Zeng, X., & Bruniaux, P. (2019). A detailed review of artificial intelligence applied in the fashion and apparel industry. *IEEE Access : Practical Innovations, Open Solutions*, *7*, 95376–95396. DOI: 10.1109/ACCESS.2019.2928979

Gomes, P., Verçosa, L., Melo, F., Silva, V., Filho, C. B., & Bezerra, B. (2022). Artificial intelligence-based methods for business processes: A systematic literature review. *Applied Sciences (Basel, Switzerland)*, *12*(5), 2314. DOI: 10.3390/app12052314

Greene, D., Hoffmann, A. L., & Stark, L. (2019). Better, nicer, clearer, fairer: A critical assessment of the movement for ethical artificial intelligence and machine learning. *Proceedings of the 52nd Hawaii International Conference on System Sciences*. DOI: 10.24251/HICSS.2019.258

Gudigantala, N., Madhavaram, S., & Bicen, P. (2023). An AI decision-making framework for business value maximization. *AI Magazine*, *44*(1), 67–84. DOI: 10.1002/aaai.12076

Huang, Z., Lim, H. Y.-F., Ow, J. T., Sun, S. H.-L., & Chow, A. (2024). Doctors' perception on the ethical use of AI-enabled clinical decision support systems for antibiotic prescribing recommendations in Singapore. *Frontiers in Public Health*, *12*, 1420032. DOI: 10.3389/fpubh.2024.1420032

Jobin, A., Ienca, M., & Vayena, E. (2019). The global landscape of AI ethics guidelines. *Nature Machine Intelligence*, *1*(9), 389–399. DOI: 10.1038/s42256-019-0088-2

John, M. M., Olsson, H. H., & Bosch, J. (2023). Towards an AI-driven business development framework: A multi-case study. *Journal of Software (Malden, MA)*, *35*(6), e2432. DOI: 10.1002/smr.2432

Josimovski, S., Ivanovska, L. P., & Dodevski, D. (2023). Understanding the consumer dynamics of AI in north Macedonian E-business. *Econ. Cult.*, *20*(2), 64–75. DOI: 10.2478/jec-2023-0016

Lee, J., Suh, T., Roy, D., & Baucus, M. (2019). Emerging technology and business model innovation: The case of artificial intelligence. *Journal of Open Innovation*, *5*(3), 44. DOI: 10.3390/joitmc5030044

Olatoye, F. O., Awonuga, K. F., Mhlongo, N. Z., Ibeh, C. V., Elufioye, O. A., & Ndubuisi, N. L.Funmilola Olatundun OlatoyeKehinde Feranmi AwonugaNoluthando Zamanjomane MhlongoChidera Victoria IbehOluwafunmi Adijat ElufioyeNdubuisi Leonard Ndubuisi. (2024). AI and ethics in business: A comprehensive review of responsible AI practices and corporate responsibility. *Int. J. Sci. Res. Arch.*, *11*(1), 1433–1443. DOI: 10.30574/ijsra.2024.11.1.0235

Oyekunle, D., & Boohene, D. (2024). Digital transformation potential: The role of Artificial Intelligence in business. *Int. J. Prof. Bus. Rev.*, *9*(3), e04499. DOI: 10.26668/businessreview/2024.v9i3.4499

Radhakrishnan, J., & Gupta, S. (2020). Artificial intelligence in practice – real-world examples and emerging business models. In *IFIP Advances in Information and Communication Technology* (pp. 77–88). Springer International Publishing.

Raju, P. V. M., & Sumallika, T. (2023). The impact of AI in the global economy and its implications in Industry 4.0 era. *Information Technology, Education and Society*, *18*(2), 53–62. DOI: 10.7459/ites/18.2.05

Roberts, H., Cowls, J., Hine, E., Mazzi, F., Tsamados, A., Taddeo, M., & Floridi, L. (2021). Achieving a "Good AI Society": Comparing the aims and progress of the EU and the US. *Science and Engineering Ethics*, *27*(6), 68. DOI: 10.1007/s11948-021-00340-7

Ruggeri, F., Lagioia, F., Lippi, M., & Torroni, P. (2022). Detecting and explaining unfairness in consumer contracts through memory networks. *Artificial Intelligence and Law*, *30*(1), 59–92. DOI: 10.1007/s10506-021-09288-2

Shrestha, Y. R., Ben-Menahem, S. M., & von Krogh, G. (2019). Organizational decision-making structures in the age of artificial intelligence. *California Management Review*, *61*(4), 66–83. DOI: 10.1177/0008125619862257

Siuly, S., Huang, R., & Daneshmand, M. (2018). Guest editorial: Special issue on "Artificial Intelligence in Health and Medicine". *Health Information Science and Systems*, *6*(1), 2. DOI: 10.1007/s13755-017-0040-y

Stone, M., Aravopoulou, E., Ekinci, Y., Evans, G., Hobbs, M., Labib, A., Laughlin, P., Machtynger, J., & Machtynger, L. (2020). Artificial intelligence (AI) in strategic marketing decision-making: A research agenda. *The Bottom Line (New York, N.Y.)*, *33*(2), 183–200. DOI: 10.1108/BL-03-2020-0022

Tambe, P., Cappelli, P., & Yakubovich, V. (2019). Artificial intelligence in human resources management: Challenges and a path forward. *California Management Review*, *61*(4), 15–42. DOI: 10.1177/0008125619867910

KEY TERMS AND DEFINITIONS

Augmented Organizations: Organizations that merge human intelligence with advanced technologies such as AI, robotics, IoT, and data analytics to enhance decision-making, efficiency, and adaptability in complex environments.

Human-Robotic Collaboration (HRC): A cooperative interaction where humans and robots work together in real time, combining human creativity and judgment with robotic precision and endurance.

Artificial Intelligence (AI): A branch of computer science focused on creating systems capable of learning, reasoning, and decision-making, often applied to optimize workflows, predictions, and innovation in organizations.

Digital Literacy: The ability of employees to understand, use, and critically engage with digital tools and AI systems, ensuring effective deployment and collaboration with technology.

Ethical AI Governance: A framework of policies and practices that ensure AI systems operate transparently, fairly, and responsibly, safeguarding against bias, privacy violations, and unethical outcomes.

Data Infrastructure: The systems and processes used to collect, store, secure, and analyze structured and unstructured data to support AI-driven decision-making and operations.

Co-Created Ecosystems: Collaborative networks where humans, AI systems, and machines interact seamlessly, ensuring continuous learning, adaptability, and productivity across business functions.

Human-Centered AI: An approach to AI design and implementation that prioritizes human empowerment, trust, empathy, and inclusivity, ensuring AI augments rather than replaces human abilities.

Explainability: The degree to which AI models and their decision-making processes can be understood, interpreted, and trusted by human users.

Algorithmic Bias: The systematic and unfair outcomes produced by AI systems due to biased training data, flawed models, or unrepresentative inputs, which can perpetuate inequality.

Chapter 7
Harnessing Blockchain for Human-Centric Transformation:
Enhancing KPI Outcomes in Flexible Work Models During Recovery Phases

Heru Susanto
https://orcid.org/0000-0002-1823-357X
The Indonesian Institute of Sciences, Indonesia

Desi Setiana
https://orcid.org/0000-0001-9732-2986
University Technology Brunei, Brunei

Alifya Kayla Shafa Susanto
Universiti Teknologi Brunei, Brunei

Andri Saputra
BRIN, Brunei

Syafiq Rowii
Universiti Teknologi Brunei, Brunei

Taufik Yuniantoro
BRIN, Brunei

ABSTRACT

This research study focuses on determining whether an organisation is ready to integrate blockchain technology into its KPI system for measuring employee performance during endemics (post-Covid-19), including the Flexible Working Arrangements (FWA) itself, Work from Anywhere (WFA), Flexible Working Hours (Flextime), and 5G Services (5GS). Consequently, creating and building the proposed concept system (Blockchain KPI System) can aid in better understanding this research topic hypothetically. The objective of this research study was to seek the readiness to embrace the Flexible Working Arrangements (FWAs) during endemic phase with the help of the proposed concept system (Blockchain KPI System) and the

DOI: 10.4018/979-8-3373-8607-2.ch007

5G Network-Edge as support on what kind of jobs scopes that can apply this concept where this could affect employees' performances. People from Brunei Darussalam currently employed in the public or private sectors will make up the majority of the sample population for this study. Decentralisation, security, timestamps, and the cryptographic hash function benefit from integrating blockchain technology into the KPI system. The research methodology focuses on three methods: (i) Primary data collection will come through questionnaires, which will be analysed and yield analysis results using a variety of statistical analysis techniques using IBM SPSS software, (ii) Data crawling will also be conducted – sentiment analysis, and (iii) Forecasting on Flexible Working Arrangement in the future that was based on the dataset from primary data via RapidMiner software. Work from Anywhere, Flextime and 5G Services were considered independent variables. On the other hand, the proposed Blockchain KPI system is the dependent variable. The results indicate that during the endemic phase or new normal, Work from Anywhere, Flextime, and 5G Services have a positive relationship with the proposed concept system. Hence, from the analysis and the results, it can be affirmed that FWA can be implemented in Brunei Darussalam based on the demands, technology, and strong policies to support embracing flexible working arrangements – work from anywhere or flextime.

1. INTRODUCTION

1.1. Introduction

Pandemic Covid-19 is a mysterious outbreak of pneumonia character (Wu, Chen, & Chan, 2020) which causes respiratory problems and infection due to the emergence of the new coronavirus SARS-CoV-2 which was initially founded in Wuhan, China ((WHO), 2020). The pandemic is still here in the world and still affecting many people, businesses, economies, and the national healthcare system, affecting employee performance.

During Covid-19, lots of countries-imposed lockdowns, which significantly affected the organisation. Because the lockdown caused by this Covid-19 disrupted the usual way of working into flexible working mode especially working from home, the need to abide by policies imposed by the government and organisation (Xiao, Becerik-Gerber, Lucas, & Roll, 2021), because the lockdown and Covid-19, it is hard for employees to travel to work in the offices and at the same time reduce more spreading of the virus, which leads to working from home (WFH) (Vyas & Butakhieo, The impact of working from home during COVID-19 on work and life domains: an exploratory study on Hong Kong, 2021). The Covid-19 virus has affected our world for two years, and many things have happened concerning many matters. As well as Organisations were also affected by it and had to do emergency policies to ensure the organisation may run accordingly, even having to work from home. Most countries have initiated the endemic phase, affecting organisations' operations. Some may work at 100% capacity, some or not and possibly extend if working from home. The future of working due to the crisis of Covid-19 probably needs attention as most of the employees may have the comfortableness of WFH in which they may decide to work flexibly even during this endemic or new norm.

Flexible working arrangements (FWA) have been used significantly during Covid-19. This is part of the initiatives that the organisation did to ensure organisation operations remain stable. According to Rahman, Kistyanto & Surjanti (2020), Covid-19 has caused an upsetting problem for organisations in general or Human Resources (HR) specifically, to act faster in the working environment change from the traditional way of work to WFA concerning

implementing the strategy accordingly. According to the authors, there is a positive relationship between WFA and employees' performance.

In every organisation, the critical asset that they have is employees. Employees' performance must work according to and aligned with the organisation's goals and objectives. A key Performance Indicator (KPI) is a tool to measure employees' performance and whether they achieved the set benchmark. Some organisations hold formal meetings and reviews by HR officers to assess employee KPIs. The problem is that if working remotely, it's hard for supervisors or head department, or HR officers to supervise or monitor whether the employees are doing their work or otherwise.

WFH or working remotely can be done through the proposed system. The digitalisation of work systems has increased rapidly and, with the support of blockchain technology, can be a crucial help for organisations (De, Pandey, & Pal, 2020). The starting point of massive WFH was due to the COVID-19 pandemic. But as endemic times have begun, some organisations still implement or maintain WFH policies even post-COVID-19 during endemic. Many systems have been developed due to Covid-19 but having a blockchain KPI system can be a solution for the organisation to monitor and track employees' performance during the endemic. Thus, designing and developing Blockchain KPI System will be completed for this research study to support the research topic.

1.2. Background Study

Brunei Darussalam was not excluded from facing the COVID-19 pandemic. According to (Ministry of Health, Brunei Darussalam, 2020) during the press conference on 9th March 2020, the Minister of Health stated that one positive case has been detected in the country. Due to detecting positive cases, the nations have put on quick action to cope with the pandemic – banning citizens and residents to enter or leave the country as a lockdown has been implemented (Hayat, 2021). The pandemic did not stop there as the second wave came to strike again the nations. The government's action was to tighten the control measures the government has ordered all non-essential employees to work from home (Wong, 2021). As working from home is not a common way of a working environment in Brunei, the government has issued work-from-home guidelines which should be included in any organization's Business Continuity Plan (BCP) (Han, COVID-19: Gov't issues guidelines on working from home,

2021). There is a need in preparing for future pandemics and respond according to (World Health Organization, 2022) stated that the pathogens have the capacity to create epidemics and pandemics of sickness, devastation, and mortality of a magnitude comparable to or larger than SARS-CoV-2 will continue to originate and reappear. Hence, Brunei Darussalam has come up with a National COVID-19 Recovery Plan framework which provides a guideline for Bruneians to prepare to enter the endemic phase with a whole-of-nation approach (Faisal, 2021) with three distinctive endemic phases which include; 1) Containment Phase, 2) Preparation Phase, 3) Transition Phase and 4) Endemic Phase (Prime Minister Office, Brunei Darussalam, 2021) (Han, COVID-19: Brunei unveils lockdown exit plan, 2021). Furthermore, as the 'Early Endemic Phase' has been prolonged a few times, at last, it ended on 31st May 2022 Bruneian will enter a 'new normal' way of life in which the government will lift more restrictions (Borneo Bulletin, 2022) – this will also affect the working environment, as well as more employees, will start to work in the office.

COVID-19 still strikes the world today, but most governments nowadays have tried to move on to the endemic stage. Due to the lockdown during COVID-19, we can see that organisations have been really affected by it and have also implemented a WFH policy. Because of WFH at that time, monitoring and tracking employees become a problem as an organisation might see WFH as challenging to assess employees' performances. To the extent of organisations wondering if their workers are working during WFH. The question is, what if the WFH policy is still imposed and running during endemics?

The workplace is evolving in numerous ways because of advancements in globalization and digital technologies. The emergence of telecommuting has led to new work arrangements that enable employees to work from any location at any time, whether from several office locations, hotels (Narayanan, Menon, Plaisent, & Bernard, 2017), café, libraries or in vehicles (Stiles & Smart, 2021). According to Gifford (2022), the COVID-19 pandemic has taught firms to adapt to new working conditions, particularly during lockdowns to safeguard employee safety, which has resulted in the widespread use of working from home globally.

The world has been experiencing a work environment transition phase from the traditional way of working to working at home. Eventually, there will be flexibility implemented in the organisation during endemics or post-Covid-19. WFA was implemented before Covid-19 to cope with stress-work issues, decrease CO2 pollution and reduce

commuting hours. Using FWA can and will increase employees' performance and productivity depending on the business size. Referring to Gartner 2021 Digital Worker Experience Survey, 43% of participants reported that having flexible work schedules helped them be more productive, while 30% of participants said that spending less or no time commuting helped them be more productive at work (Castrillon, 2022). The permanency of FWAs is still a mystery, but surveys that OECD conducted show that WFAs might continually increase (Bienstock, LaPerla, & Seaman, 2020). According to OECD (2020), flexible work arrangements were popular even before the Covid-19 crisis – this can be seen from the statistics of the use of telework around the globe (Figure 1).

Figure 1. Percentage of using telework around the globe in 2015/2016. (Source: OECD, Productivity gains from teleworking in the post-COVID-19 era: How can public policies make it happen?)

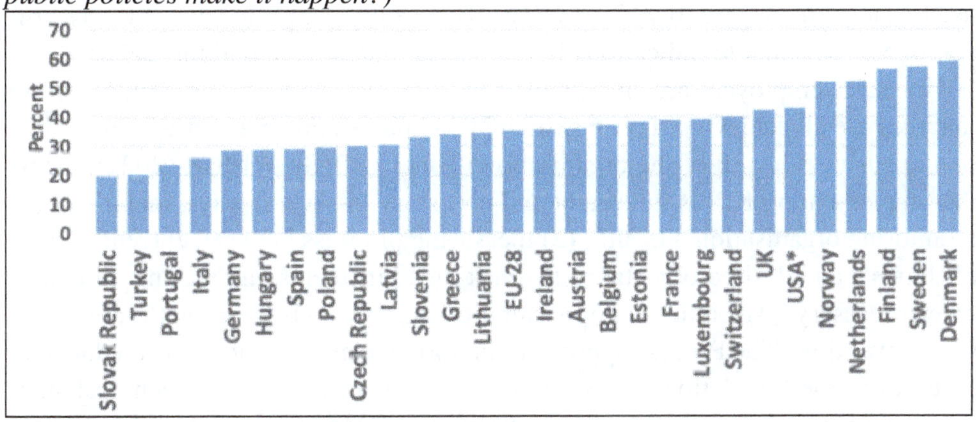

Although FWAs can be convenient for some people, they can be difficult for others too. According to WFH Survey Report from BruCERT (2021), 30% of its respondents prefer to be having their work and school at home – due to internet connectivity which is the main challenge that affects employees and students, work devices and other challenges which will refer to employees and students' wellbeing and mentality as a whole.

FWAs can have both positive and negative impacts towards individual performance, and from those impacts, there is a need for why employee performance must be measured. To some people, FWAs can give them a better work-life balance and reduce their stress level, but to some people, these FWAs can give them a hard time as well. Organisational dedication, passion, vitality, and contentment are elements brought into play by the interaction between

employee wellness, work-life balance, and performance. The results confirm the hunch that employees' well-being will increase as they become more adept at integrating work and personal life. Through enhanced levels of motivation and desire, employees, in a way, "payback" their organisation, which indirectly impacts performance. Thus, the performance can be the quantity base or quality of work. This can be seen from Cranfield University, School of Management research on Flexible Working Performance (2008); there was a positive impact towards the quantity of work and quality of work as the basis of evaluating employees' performances.

According to (Bhatti, Awan, & Razaq, 2014), to be better off compared to other organisations and to gain a competitive advantage, the organisation's objectives must be achieved and by that, there is a need for a performance review which can be done through the performance management system. A key Performance Indicator (KPI) can be described as a financial and non-financial system of measurement that organisations use to achieve the organisation's goals and objectives. KPIs can be described as quantifiable metrics that businesses, institutions, and organisations use to gauge the degree to which their goals have not yet been achieved – it's crucial to choose suitable indications in the measurement (Jamaluddin, Taher, & Yi, 2019). Since employees are an organisation's greatest asset, it is prudent to ensure that they are all achieving their maximum potential, as this may reflect favourably on the business health of the organisation (Timely, 2018). Wishart (2022) asserts that implementing KPI is important and necessary in several ways, including: (1) monitoring organisational health; (2) measuring progress between current accomplishments and desired objectives; (3) making adjustments and staying on course when necessary; (4) looking for opportunities and solving issues; and (5) observing trends over time. The Process approach's importance may be shown by the fact that it serves as the foundation for two modern management systems: technical standardisation through Quality Management systems (QMS) and strategic management through Balanced scorecards (BSC) (Velimirović, Velimirović, & Stanković, 2011). Once the KPI has been set, the employees must complete it to support long- term organisational goals and objectives. An organisation monitoring its regular operations and assessing whether the goal is accomplished can also be referred to as a KPI. It has many tools to measure performance, and most use the Balance Scorecard (BSC) (Asih, Purba, & Sitorus, 2020). In this period, technology has evolved at a rapid pace. Information systems have been a trend towards ensuring everything is online and digitised. Information systems (IS) are an integrated environment of people, hardware, and software that primarily gather and process data for helpful insights by applying procedures to data collection. Information is derived from data by IS procedures, distinguishing between data and information. Raw materials are the basis for the data, which comprises processed data. A database (DB) is essential for storing both current and future data, offering a solid foundation for any decision-making process when the information is required at specific periods (Hasan, 2018). This can be seen as the use to develop the proposed concept system, the Blockchain KPI system.

Blockchain technology (BC) is part of Industry 4.0 which BC features, including improving security, privacy and data transparency, the foremost importance. BC can be defined as s decentralised – where multiple devices can access each node created in the system. It also builds trust in the transaction ecosystem and distribution of ledgers with the help of smart contracts. It can provide traceability in record keeping and other business applications (Javaid, Haleem, Singh, Khan, & Suman, 2021). A blockchain can be connected to a distributed database structured as a set of sequentially ordered blocks with immutable committed blocks. As a component of BC, smart contracts (SC) play a significant role in interactions and agreements between parties, helping to create a new paradigm with nearly endless application possibilities. Three generations of blockchain can be distinguished when Blockchain 1.0 enables applications of digital cryptocurrency transactions; Blockchain 2.0 is applied in SC and is broader than just cryptocurrency. Blockchain 3.0 is the extension of the past two versions. In addition, Blockchain enables decentralised peer-to-peer networks, even when untrustworthy individuals can connect verifiably without needing a trusted authority (Casino, Dasaklis, & Patsakis, 2019). One of the examples that can be used is a research study conducted by Chen (2020); through analysis of KPIs, the communication efficiency between a port-based and a transportation company-based system is greater than that of a typical model system. This is so because both systems depend on having a solid consensus mechanism. The blockchain- based technology can speed up communication between port and transportation businesses and decrease the time containers must wait at ports. Additionally, it can increase the usage of those resources, better distribute transportation resources among numerous businesses, and improve automotive utilisation. Hence, from the above example of the use of Blockchain technology in terms of communication, this can be seen as how an organisation monitors its performance directly and its employees indirectly.

Blockchain technology has been trending and popular for the past few years (Gad, Mosa, Abualigah, & Abohany, 2022). According to (Insider Intelligence, 2022), global

spending on blockchain technology is forecast to reach nearly $17.9 billion in 2024. Currently, there were several industries that have implemented blockchain technology such as banking, healthcare, the government sector, and many more (CB INSIGHTS, 2022). Blockchain technology has evolved over the years; perhaps its market size and revenue also flourished. According to (Gilbert, 2022) findings, it shows that blockchain was anticipated to increase to

$39.7 billion by 2025 and corroborates experts' predictions that blockchain would raise the world's GDP by $1.76 trillion by 2030.

As the statistics show above, it looks like more organizations have interested and implement blockchain technology into their organizations. This is because of the advantages that can be gained from blockchain technology itself. In general, the advantages of blockchain technology are that it can act as a tracking system where it recorded every single piece of data and information which is unchangeable and transparent. Hence why, data and information can be considered valuable, and perhaps that organizations want the exact transactions to be recorded and not tamper with them. Secondly, ease of data access and transfer especially when it involves numerous parties involved and in real-time. Thirdly, authentication with parties' identification allows verifications, authorizations and others and other advantages (Eliaçık, 2022). To understand more about how blockchain technology work, in general, can refer to the diagram below:

Figure 2. How blockchain work. (Source: Blockchain for dummies).

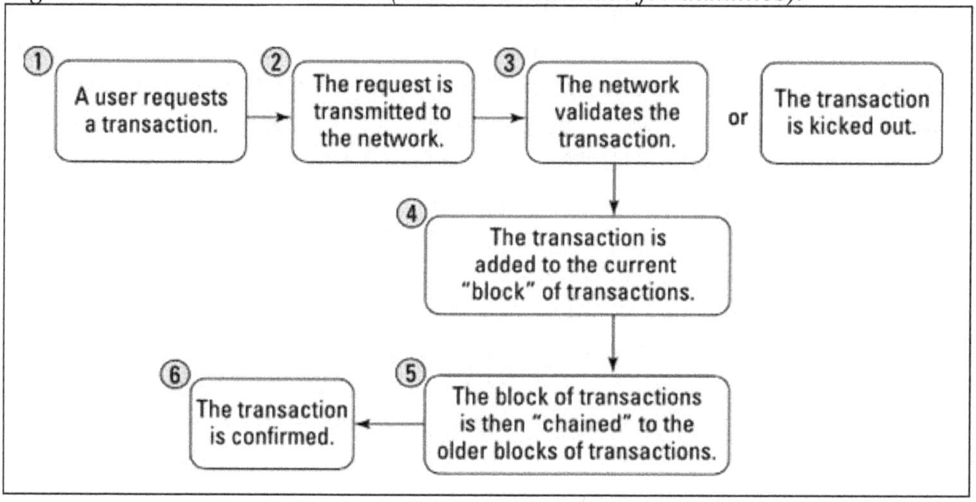

Based on the advantages above, the proposed blockchain KPI system comes into the context. Leveraging blockchain technology in the organization, especially in the human resource area, can be a way for HR officers can get data to analyze to understand their employees' behaviour and patterns.

The most valuable asset in an organization would be its human capital. Any activities that take place within the organization may have an impact on people's psychology and motivations, either positively or negatively, which could indirectly affect people's or employees' performance and the organization's performance (Kaya & Kesen, 2014). Henceforth, having a KPI System in the organization can help to understand employees better by exploiting the data and information from the system.

Nowadays the majority of organizations have utilized HR services through technology and web-based applications. in addition, HR is evolving towards a technology-based profession due to streamlining HR processes, reducing costs, access towards employees' data, real-time metrics and many more (Johnson & Gueutal, 2011). As the HR system integrated with technology was coming even before Blockchain technology come into existence, this already shows high advantages that can be exploited. Moreover, utilizing Blockchain technology in the KPI System will give extra benefits such as tracking, real-time logs recorded, decentralisation, enhanced securities, avoiding tampering data and information, smart contract features, cryptographic features and others.

International Labour Organization (ILO) have analysed that there is a working condition between digitalization and employment in which this theme has been a rise during COVID-19 which creates new job scopes such as casual work and non-traditional job arrangements. Through the introduction of e-formality were able to solve partial labour fair problems – employee relationships, skills, and quality (Charles, Xia, & Coutts, 2022). Hence, proper monitoring for these kinds of jobs is required.

This research study aims to identify the requirements for employee performance, particularly those that connect with the information system and enable information to become digital while working from home. This platform for facilitating remote work for employees integrates blockchain and information systems. Employers can learn when and what their staff work on once the system has been implemented within the company. However, it will provide

workers with a targeted performance so they may qualify for year-end incentives. This approach will make it easier for employers and employees to profit from each other. Nonetheless, the study focuses on the flexibility of working from home and the office or anywhere, especially during post-Covid-19 or endemic. Implementing this proposed KPI blockchain system can still help track and monitor employees working performance.

Note that despite the proposed design KPI system being referenced in the research topic as it relates to HR views, the recommended designs for KPI systems with blockchain and Human Resource Management Systems (HRMS) were noticeably different. The systems and procedures at the point where information technology and human resource management (HRM) interact are referred to as human resource management systems (HRMS). In contrast to how the programming of data processing systems grew into standardized procedures and packages of enterprise resource planning software, it combines HRM as a discipline and in particular its fundamental HR processes and actions with the information technology area (Singh & Bakshi, 2018). The HRMS primarily consists of six modules: personnel management, organizational management, recruitment management, training management, salary management, and system management. These modules integrate enterprise information and implement functions for simple access and simple information database query (Wang, Li, & Li, 2021). Hence, the proposed design system provides a platform for employers to monitor their employees while working flexibly or flextime by submitting their work on the proposed concept system so that it proves they are working and check-in for attendance. Furthermore, the proposed concept system will be not part of HRMS.

1.3. Problem Statement

Pandemic Covid-9 has forced the organisation to transform into a flexible way of working. Lockdown has encouraged WFH, and employees were working from home. These days, WFH is characterised as the ability of employees to work from their homes and not in the designated office, allowing employees to work in their suitability (Hart, 2019). According to Davidescu, Apostu, Paul, & Casuneanu (2020), for future work challenges, human resource management must be redesigned to cope with future challenges. According to Davidescu et al. (2020), in Romania, there is a policy of telework that transformed labour working flexibility that directly affects employees' performance and personal growth performance and indirectly affects organisational performance. Aczel, Kovacs, Lippe, & Szaszi (2021), they have

conducted a survey that consisted of 704 participants of academic positions resulted with due to WFH, significantly during pandemic lockdown decreased work efficiency for almost half of the researchers; according to Aczel et al. (2021), that part of the challenges of WFH is increasing in teleworks fear where it can limit the opportunities for career growth, rewards and acknowledgement and most important how to review performance employees. The performance management system has been badly disturbed due to COVID-19, which led the organisation to go into survival mode by downgrading and altogether abandoning the traditional performance evaluation method (Aguinis & Burgi-Tian, 2021), especially since WFH was initiated. Consequently, the question has been raised of how employers measure employees' performance when work flexibility is imposed during the endemic period.

Employees' performance is very crucial for organisational performance and growth. During pandemics and endemics, flexible working arrangements have been a trend which affects the organisation and employees as the leading player. Studies demonstrate that WFH techniques are widely used in the United States, where 35.2% of workers worked from home in May 2020. WFH is doing a trial in the city due to the outbreak; for many, this will be their first time working remotely, and for the most part, it is working. WFH has a substantial impact as one of the future working models for such a highly inhabited metropolis. The period following the pandemic may be the best time to focus on the working decision that organisations will make. For instance, 9GAG, a well-known online platform with a base in Hong Kong, appears to be the first business in the area to switch permanently to WFH. According to the report, participants in research conducted after the second wave of transmission anticipate having WFH for at least one day per week throughout the endemic. (Vyas & Butakhieo, 2021). So, the employees expect a change in working design in the future where flexible working is still intact even after Covid-19. So, what is the possibility of having the proposed KPI system in the organisation if there is a possibility of 100% transforming to flexible working and maybe the readiness for the organisation and employees if future diseases affect the working environment?

The endemic phase has been discussed globally. According to Galanti, et al., (2021) as per experience during the pandemic COVID-19 with lockdown, the work environment has been in a dynamic adjustment where work from home has been initiated – mainly for FWA. But with entering the endemic phase, more FWA has been rising, such as work from anywhere

or remotely at any location, and flextime working conditions. Monitoring has been raised on whether employees were working or not if flexibility was given as according to Zainal et al., (2022) that the disadvantage of FWA would be monitoring employees' performances. That is why there was needed to understand the characteristics of blockchain technology that can be integrated when developing the proposed concept system (Leible et al., 2019).

The use of FWA was starting to become a trend even before and during the pandemic COVID-19 OECD (2020). There is a point that might need to be considered when implementing FWA – it does not apply to all types of job scopes. This can be seen from Brunei Darussalam's working situation during the pandemic COVID-19, ccording to Wong (2021), the Brunei Darussalam government has ordered all non-essential employees to work from home. Hence, this, shows that only non-essential employees were able to apply FWA as compared to essential workers. An instant example is those employees that are required to be in the location to operate the business such as caregiving, running machines, operating laboratory equipment, and processing consumer transactions in retail establishments and others. On the other hand, tasks like data coding and processing, communication with others, teaching, and counselling might hypothetically be performed remotely (Lund, Madgavkar, Manyika, & Smit, 2020).

Blockchain technologies can be considered an innovative technology that offers several important features. Technology is also evolving such as 5G Network services. How logically is 5G Network can help Blockchain technology, especially for this research study? According to Rahmadika, et. al. (2021), a 5G network can offer protection of traffic network that can be applied flexibly according to the needs of the applications. As blockchain and federated learning can be applied. The same goes for this research study on how 5G can offer such features to support blockchain in the proposed concept system. As the proposed concept system is for employees that apply flexible working arrangements, what 5G network can give to this proposed concept system?

Furthermore, the flexible working arrangement is basically an employee's work outside the organization. It requires the organization system to be decentralized (blockchain feature) as well can be accessed outside the organizations. According to Jain & Jain (2022), blockchain and 5G can increase the economic value of data sharing. This was due to blockchain features related to data transfer, sharing, and accessing data.

1.4. Aims of Study

In these current times, this study explores how organisations gauge employee performance when they have and planning on utilising Flexible Working Arrangements (FWA) – Work from Anywhere (WFA) and Flexible working hours (Flextime) and explores the potential for employing blockchain authentication technology for KPI systems in organisations with the help from 5G Network-Edge. Thus, developing the Blockchain KPI System can be a help in terms of understanding further on this research topic.

1.5. Research Objectives

RO 1 – To understand the organisation's readiness for implementing flexible working in the endemic phase/after Covid-19.
RO 2 – Examine the need to implement a Blockchain KPI System for flexible working during endemics.
RO 3 – To seek the support that can be gained from the Blockchain technology role to be used in the proposed concept KPI system.
RO 4 – Identity what are the relevant job scope that applicable for FWA during the endemic with the help of the proposed BC KPI System.
RO 5 – Identify if 5G can support the proposed concept system (Blockchain KPI System).
RO 6 – Examine flexible working arrangements that can affect employee performance.

1.6. Research Questions

RQ 1 – What is the current organisation's readiness for implementing flexible working in the endemic phase/after Covid-19?
RQ 2 – To what extent is there a need to implement a blockchain KPI system for flexible working during endemics?
RQ 3 – Does the role of BC help the proposed concept KPI system?
RQ 4 – What are the relevant job scopes that may apply for FWA during the endemic with the help of the proposed BC KPI System?
RQ 5 – Is 5G can support the proposed concept system (Blockchain KPI System)?
RQ 6 – How is employee performance affected by flexible working arrangements?

1.7. Significance of Study

Organisations in public and private sectors will profit from this study which includes HR officers and policymakers that may consider this as a strategic plan for future use. This research study will demonstrate in what way the proposed Blockchain of the KPI System may assist the organisation in monitoring the performance of its remote employees or flexible working arrangements (FWA) during the endemic.

1.8. Scope of Study

The Brunei-Muara district will be the sole subject of this study, and its scope will be limited to organisations in the public or private sectors that focus on the flexible working arrangements, work from anywhere and flextime.

1.9. Concrete Goals and Objectives

This research project aims to determine whether using information systems during endemics is relevant. The proposed KPI system ensures that workers work remotely or flexibly and complete their tasks according to their predetermined performance indicators as FWAs have been implemented.

Second, since they are accustomed to WFH during the lockdown, employees will find the system convenient if it is introduced in any organisation during this period and used for FWA.

1.10. Significance and Own Contributions

Today's information technology or information system trends include blockchain technology. Our research study concentrates primarily on how organisations use the suggested proposed Blockchain KPI System for FWA reasons during endemics, which may benefit workers who telecommute or have flexible schedules. Second, check to determine if the recommended system with FWA may help workers improve their output. This study helps determine whether adopting the suggested KPI system within an organisation for FWA during an endemic is relevant.

2. LITERATURE REVIEW

2.1. Introduction

The chapter will investigate the applicability of the research literature review's historical context - previous studies, including its results. Nonetheless, the research study focuses on the needs and relevancy of having organisation KPIs during post-Covid 19 or people might be called endemic. The use of traditional KPIs before Covid-19 struck the world. Due to technological evolvement, organisations might go for digitalisation. Invest in implementing systems that integrate the traditional KPI system with new technology. Hence, reviewing the past studies through journal articles has been conducted toward the KPI System. in addition, to understand the potential blockchain technology to be integrated with the KPI System to see the relevancy and compatibleness. Therefore, to better understand how the KPI system can be applied in an organisation or even connected with blockchain technology, it is crucial to identify the components in this chapter.

Because of the new nature of this research, it will be challenging to locate articles that are relevant to the research subjects. Use similar articles to overcome this challenge and become relevant to the research topic. As endemic Covid-19 has just come to light in the past months, there was difficulty in finding articles related to the use of FWAs in the endemic working environment.

Finding the relevant article for this topic was the first step in systematically evaluating the sparse literature on the subject, which was new and focused mostly on human resources and blockchain technology. The utilisation of related literature will support this research.

2.2. Review of Literature

2.2.1. Pandemic Covid-19 to Endemic Covid-19

A pneumonia outbreak of unknown cause was detected in Wuhan, Hubei Province, China, in December 2019. The new respiratory virus is known as acute respiratory syndrome (Sars syndrome) coronavirus two after genome analysis revealed it to be a novel coronavirus connected to SARS-CoV. (SARS-CoV-2). The World Health Organization declared a pandemic on March 12, 2020, due to the SARS-CoV-2 virus widespread distribution and the thousands of deaths brought on by Covid-19, a coronavirus disease. In terms of lost human lives, adverse economic effects, and rising poverty levels, this epidemic exacted a heavy price on the entire world (Ciotti, et al., 2020).

One of the effects of the pandemic is that a lockdown has been initiated, which can directly impact the perspectives of businesses, the economy, people, and others. A study conducted by Grimmer (2022) that focused on the scope of the Island State of Tasmania, in Australia, which narrowed to business owners of SMEs in retail and services during the first wave of Covid-19, found that; 1) despite nearly 80% of respondents saying they were confident in their company's survival going into 2021, over 65% of respondents reported a decline in sales throughout 2020, 2) even while businesses did not generally consider the level of environmental hostility as being particularly high, there was a significant correlation between perceptions of environmental hostility and judgments of organisational effectiveness and the degree of trust in business survival., 3) in Australia, the federal government's assistance and other incentive were regarded essential for business survival in 2020, with 75% of enterprises using the "JobKeeper" program; finally, 4) During the pandemic, businesses changed how they operated by introducing new goods and services, stepping up marketing efforts, shifting how they used technology, and emphasising "localness."

From business perspectives affected by Covid-19. When discussed internally in businesses, specifically among Human Resource practitioners, it has implications, challenges, opportunities, and direction for the organisation. Hamouche (2021) has conducted research focusing on the general literature review that broadens the management's scope of research by exploring the potential impact of Covid-19. The author has listed a few of the implications and challenges.

1. Working conditions – changes in working time, remuneration, physical condition, and mental demands. Due to the pandemic, most organisations have moved to FWA, which allowing workers to operate remotely. Not every organisation is suitable to implement work from home, such as manufacturing industries – which can lead to losing their jobs. Significant challenges have been identified.

a. Must have the necessary tools to perform remote working
b. Have effective communication for employees
c. Lack of interaction between employees

Hence, the suggested solution was to create virtual socialisation activities that can help employees keep communicating with their colleagues and, at some point, acquire tacit knowledge related to organisational development.

2. Staffing – due to Covid-19, organisations must reshape their dynamics, and different organisations have different repercussions. Downscaling, block recruitment and laying off employees were the challenges in staffing. From these issues, organisations have decided to hire flexible workers such as freelancers, gig economy or temporary workers.
3. Performance management – even when facing the Covid-19 crisis, employees were still required to perform. The main issues were the need to alter the performance management in the organisation, such as employee performance review and its incentives, in which some organisations unwillingly abandoned performance management. The only way to cope with this issue was by understanding the owner of the organisation and its respective managers.
4. Compensation management – financial incentives were the most crucial compensation during facing Covid-19. In addition, providing temporary paid sick leave and short- time compensation can help employees during their unhappy moments. The advantage of these kinds of benefits is to be implemented in industries that have not have these types of benefits.

From here, working flexibility provides employees with a platform to do their work, increasing productivity and performance. Ultimately, they are still entitled to compensation, such as bonuses.

Hence, the pandemic Covid-19 has currently transited to the endemic phase. According to Antia & Halloran (2021) the term "epidemic" might be used to contrast with the pathogen's ongoing viability.; often, at a lesser incidence, an endemic state implies to a pathogen's rapid spread within a community. In light of this, the virus may persist for a very long time at a low incidence than it did during the period of the epidemic if it does not go away. This can be called as endemic.

Figure 3. Influence of immunological effectiveness and infection prevalence on endemicity (Source: (Antia & Halloran, 2021))

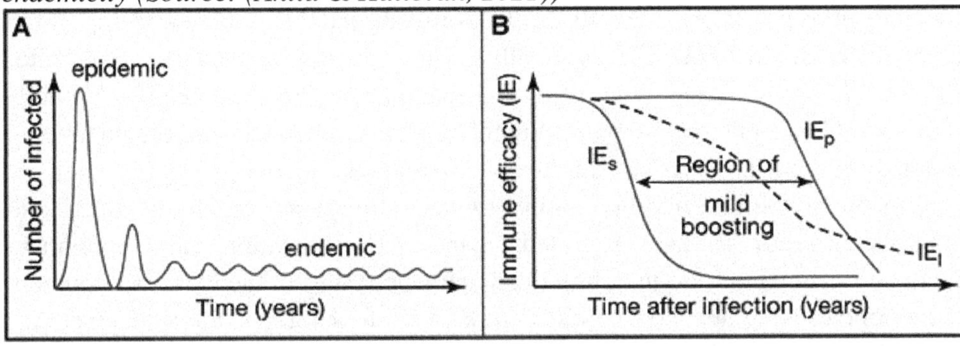

(A) The graph shows how the epidemic transforms into an endemic over time, excluding the intervention of the virus mutation from virus evolutions.

(B) Over time, it was anticipated that immunological effectiveness (IE) measurements would decline.

Covid-19 has impacted all levels and angles globally, nationally, or individually. Decision- makers were compelled to use and implement the spectrum of reactions as a continuing structure to manage the pandemic's unexpected character. Due to the transition from pandemic to endemic, the impacts were not excluded on society, technology, and higher learning institutions. The pandemic's effects on the world economy are due to production being locked down, closed borders, and the supply chain collapsing. When everyone is immune, the pandemic age will come to an end. Alternatively, the pandemic will continue and won't disappear as long as people resume their regular lives. Although the endemic phase is now being announced and living new norms, post-pandemic strategies must address both the pre- pandemic causes of this disparity and the "equality implications" of recovery and regeneration that begin with the vast financial disparities in the healthcare (Hadfield, 2022). Hence, it includes for HR to move forwards and be prepared based on experience from this Covid-19 with resilience strategies for the benefit of employees and organisations.

(Vyas, 2022) has conducted research on this "new normal" at work during post-Covid 19 which affects the work-life balance and labour markets. Vyas (2022) saw this Covid-19 as a catalyst for change – referring towards the future of working come into existence. Due to a pandemic crisis that acts as an emergency element, hence, emergency approach shall be in parallel. By changing certain policies to cope with the challenges that were brought about by this Covid-19. As one of the good things about Covid-19 is that it leads to accelerating digital transformation which this digitalization can be imperative for organizations that could be a solution for survivability. Digital transformation could help employees, especially non-manual workers. Vyas (2022) also argued that remote working would be popular during the endemic, especially for non-manual work but that is definitely not a solution for every type of job. As manual workers may need to continue their work. Consequently, the management of human resources and organizational sustainability may be at risk during the post-pandemic period.

Referring to the International Labour Organization report on Digitalization and Employment report in 2022, reported regarding Digitalization and Employment that the governments were handling the dynamic changes in the work environment where policies were needed to protect workers. Note that the skills levels that digital workers possessed are heterogeneous. Casual work and other non-traditional job arrangements are now prevalent. Since the COVID-19 epidemic, some people have adopted remote employment as the new norm, and digital entrepreneurship is now more important than ever for social and economic advancement. Additionally, e-formality is now a growing answer to the problems of fair labour and sustainable development. Inequalities between nations, industries, and employees are growing despite these efforts. In contrast, there were challenges in the context which includes employee relationships, employee skills and job quality. Hence, at the local, national, and international levels, efforts have been made by numerous stakeholders to promote just and equal work in the digital era. A few policies have been developed to ensure the quality of employment with regard to social security, workplace safety and health regulations, work hour restrictions, and access to data and privacy (Charles, Xia, & Coutts, 2022).

2.2.2. Flexible Working Arrangement (FWA)

Flexible Working Arrangements (FWAs) offer employees more control over their work hours, improving work-life balance and increasing organisational performance. The researchers have established two study subjects to examine the effects of FWAs on organizational performance as measured through both monetary and non-monetary indicators and while taking into account the employer versus the employee-driven perspective of FWA adoption. Their findings suggest that the employee-driven FWA policies produced better organisational performance. However, it was discovered that several employer-driven practices were strongly but unfavourably associated with organisational performance (Klindžić & Marić, 2019).

Flexible work arrangements include, but are not limited to, Weekend work, work shifts, overtime, annual hours employment, part-time work, job-sharing, flextime, seasonal employment, fixed-term contracts, work from home, telework, and compressed work weeks, all examples of flexible work arrangements and (Ray & Pana-Cryan,

2021) changing schedules. A business challenge is ensuring employees maintain a good work-life balance while delivering effective and efficient performance. Numerous businesses provide flexible work schedules to their workforce because of the benefits of flexibility for employers and employees. Significantly higher organisational and personnel performance is one of the most prevalent outcomes. It has been noted that the growth of digitisation in the working environment brought on by the existence of ICT, the global market, and trans-nationalisation takes resulted in significant alterations to the way people experience work, including the type of work done, the time spent on it, and the techniques employed to assess employees' performance within the company. Technological advancements have significantly influenced the emergence of 24-hour businesses and the ever-fuzzier lines separating work and play, making it easier to work remotely (Austin-Egole, et al., 2020).

Rahman, Kistyanto, & Surjanti (2020) conducted a study on preserving firm performance during the pandemic. This will give depth analysis to help create fitting work regulatory policies and encourage innovative work behaviour. This promotes research on how flexible work arrangements affect employee performance by looking into the innovative work practices of Indonesia's East Java region's banking industry employees. They discovered that creative work behaviour modulates the link between FWA and innovative work behaviour, which acts as a mediator between innovative work behaviour and employee performance. How flexible work arrangements are perceived by employees does not significantly affect their performance.

FWAs has significantly increased in implementation in organisation globally. FWA can allow flexibility privileges towards employees to perform their tasks, either flexible working hours or working from home as the standard practices nowadays (Weideman & Hofmeyr, 2021). The research study by Tasrin, Wahyuadianto, Pratiwi, & Masrully (2021) focuses on using FWA policies in the organisation based on different job characteristics – administration department, training department, competency department and research development. The researcher examined the Indonesian public sector's implementation of the FWAs policy using

case studies comprising qualitative and quasi-statistical data. The study concluded that each job's characteristics have a unique way of affecting the working style, employee performance, benefits and challenges of WFA. The job characteristics results as follows:

- Administration Department – Due to issues with accessibility to work-related objects, a lack of work autonomy, and a high reliance on office equipment, future FWA implementation should set up outside-the-office work-object accessibility for its employees, overcome the lack of work-related paraphernalia at home, design WFH-fit communication mechanisms because employees fancied direct communication, and pay particular attention to competency gaps among employees.

- Training Department – There are no issues with the work-object and work autonomy aspects due to the transition from traditional to online training and the support of knowledgeable employees accustomed to online and virtual platforms and applications for work. However, given its heavy reliance on office supplies, this department continues to have difficulties.
- Competency Assessment Department – It involves two groups of duties (WFO and WFH), calls for the suitable personnel, the proper assignment of duties, and positive workplace autonomy. It might therefore mix WFO and WFH. Additionally, as emloyees preferred using direct communication, employees preferred WFO.
- Research Department – This department could use full FWA because of the employees' high levels of workplace autonomy, better accessibility to work objects, proper work distribution, adequate individual competency, compatibility with virtual communication, sufficient work equipment, and sufficient self-management in the workplace.

The emergence of hybrid work was anticipated especially in entering the post-Covid-19 pandemic which makes this hybrid work part of the new normal. On contrary, there were a few important aspects that need to think of and considers adopting FWA in the organization which must be based on the types of work and job positions and at some point, the work did not require in-person involvement (Vyas, "New normal" at work in a post-COVID world: work– life balance and labor markets, 2022).

Henceforth, FWA policy implementation may differ at each business, industry, and organisation level. In addition, the proposed concept system of Blockchain KLPI system can

be integrated with the policies to identify whether the proposed concept system can be linked with FWA as a whole on how the system may help in improving employee performance through tracking features and which can provide convenience for employer's assurance that the employees working even through FWA.

2.2.3. Work from Anywhere (WFA)

Globalization and digital technology are progressing, and the workplace is changing in a variety of ways. Due to the advent of telecommuting, new work arrangements now allow employees to work from any location at any time such as from different office branches, hotels, or other places. Telecommuting is a different manner of working while travelling that is possible thanks to technology. Therefore, businesses need to seek out and comprehend the advantages of working remotely, and HR managers must consider including this in the human resources strategic plan (Narayanan, Menon, Plaisent, & Bernard, 2017).

Another term that can be used for people that work from anywhere especially now living in digital technology can be called "digital nomad". A research study has been conducted regarding the digital nomad lifestyle which refers to the capacity for people to conduct business through a laptop while travelling because they are not tied to an office. Based on the findings from interviewing thirty-eight people who applied digital nomads have profound that it touches rights, differences, leisure, employment, and surroundings. In contrast, it is clear from critical and empirical research that companies are enjoying a great degree of freedom as they are relieved of the obligation to provide full-time employment, benefits, office space, and paid vacation. As their insecure and competitive compensation is frequently falling and at the whim of an algorithm, employees are free to labour continuously (Thompson, 2019).

Employees may be able to work from anywhere or remotely through mediating of information, communication and technologies (ICT) – work from home was the most common way of WFA and/or anywhere else (multiple locations) including in café, libraries or in vehicles in one day. The findings show that working from home a full day can reduce travel time which increases the possibility of avoiding peak hour travel, eventually for work and non- work related. By working from different locations, employees can avoid travelling during peak hours which consumes their time (Stiles & Smart, 2021).

Working from anywhere or working remotely which does not require the employees to be in the office can be influenced by several drivers which include technology evolvement, and the Covid-19 lockdown which enhanced the use of working remotely. In the past, working remotely were for information-based work which now increase rapidly due to advances in videoconferencing, file sharing and cloud-based system. Looking back at previous research study, it indicates that working remotely may be challenging but with new findings, a call centre in China showed an increase in 13% of productivity for working remotely, while a study in the United Kingdom shows that only small changes in productivity happened by 40% and in United States of America studies – employers anticipated 5% increase in performance (Gifford, 2022). Thus, even the slightest increase in performance, proves that working from anywhere or remotely may help in the future with the innovative way of the working environment.

Having Covid-19 in this world and at a global scale people were entering the endemic phase, and remote working is seen to be an innovative way of working. Before Covid-19, technology was evolving which create a support platform for working remotely and during the Covid-19 lockdown, working remotely illustrates its feasibility for more job scope/positions to implement working remotely. Hence, there are in a need for HR officers and policymakers to investigate this as it provides implications towards the HR core. (Gifford, 2022).

2.2.3.1. Work from Home (WFH)

(OECD, 2020) stated that as the global still in a fight to cope with the health and economic crisis that was caused by Pandemic Covid-19, there was a need to come up with new and innovative ways for employees to keep on working especially when the government- imposed lockdown or partial lockdown. Advancing technology may indirectly help in provisioning this work from home or teleworking which gives employees the ability to work from home rather than in their traditional way of working – in the office (Abdullah, Rahmat, Zawawi, Khamsah, & Anuarsham, 2020). According to Abdullah et.al., (2020), their findings show that working from home leads to more advantages rather than disadvantages this shows that they came to the conclusion in employees prefer working from home because it brings convenience (the findings of the results shows the highest mean in the performance increase which is 4.03) – can increase working performance due to the existence of flexibility which employees able to work according to their pace and time and compare when working in the

office where time may be wasted because of break-time and communicate with colleagues. Hence, certain factors should be considered in adopting WFH such as in terms of communication, management side, working environment and technology involvement (Green, Tappin, & Bentley, 2020).

Research conducted by Galanti et al. (2021), Covid-19 has forced organisations to switch from the usual manner of working to working from home. Through analysing the cross- sectional study, researchers gathered data from an online questionnaire from 209 employees working from home during a pandemic to show that family-work conflict & social isolation among employees were negatively linked with WFH productivity and engagement, while strongly correlated with self-leadership. Family-work conflict and social isolation were negatively correlated with WFH stress, whereas autonomy and self-leadership had no effect. Hence, they have concluded that both personal and professional variables hinder and aid WFH during the Covid-19 pandemic.

Due to the pandemic, all industries were directly or indirectly affected by it. This includes the banking industry in the Republic of Indonesia, Jakarta. In a study conducted on businesses adjusting to the new normal era, factors affecting knowledge worker productivity while implementing new WFH practices become increasingly important. In addition, it examines the relationship between work-life balance (WLB) and job satisfaction and the direct effects of WFH on productivity in the Greater Jakarta area's banking sector. The researchers have found how WFH positively affects overall productivity, and that job satisfaction is a mediator factor between WFH and Productivity. However, results also indicated that WFH has a detrimental impact on WLB, defying the researchers' predictions (Prasetyaningtyas, Heryanto, Nurfauzi, & Tanjung, 2021).

For businesses that are in manufacturing sections, it's pretty difficult to impose WFH policies in their organisation. In a study conducted by Kitagawa et al. (2021) in Japan, the researchers tried to analyse productivity variations between people who work from home and those who don't, as well as potential causes of WFH-related productivity changes. Due to Covid-19, individuals' work has drastically changed due to the shift to telework (WFH). First, workers who worked from home saw productivity losses more than those who did not, according to research. Second, research analysis reveals that the main causes of productivity losses are subpar WFH installations and communication issues. Thirdly, researchers

discovered that employees who work from home have more significant mental health than those who cannot. Thus from here, it can be deduced that when WFH is initiated, it can help improve employees' WLB, which leads to better performance.

Another investigation into WFH during the pandemic from the viewpoint of the IT sector has also been done. The pandemic has caused harm to organisations, businesses, and employment in India, which compelled the organisation to alter its WFH rules to maintain business operations—especially in light of the lockdown that the governments imposed. Since the researcher gathered 526 IT industry specialists from throughout the world. The study indicated that two-thirds of IT workers reported higher productivity during WFH, including efficient use of commute time and raised expectations. Additionally, organisational elements, including autonomy, employee freedom, and a supportive atmosphere, contributed to weariness. (Patanjali & Bhatta, 2022).

There has been a study that was focusing working from home from the perspective of digital development services that develop software; the findings were monitoring work from home in 2020 with specific target companies that were in the USA, UK and Sweden which focuses on the productivity, job satisfaction, communication, efficiency, and flow of data efficiency. Šmite et. al., (2023) found that the engineers continue to self-reporting regarding productivity such as coding, and their work duties. Hence, based on the experienced that was gained from the work from home during COVID-19 has impacted the way of working as only 9% of engineers are willing to work in the office full time (Šmite, Moe, Klotins, & Gonzalez- Huerta, 2023).

Work-from-home policies do not exclude Malaysia and Indonesia. Focusing on employee performance and quality of life affected by Covid-19. WFH has its pros and cons for organisations and employees. Research conducted by Zainal Abiddin, Ibrahim, & Abdul Aziz (2022) found that the cons of implementing WFH were flexibility, retention, recruiting fresh talent, productivity, and motivation. On the other hand, the cons would be staff isolation, monitoring employees' performance, distraction, burnout, and mental health issues. Although the researcher has identified the pros and cons of WFH, WFH could increase the scope and impact of our work platform in light of all of the recent developments and technological improvements consistent with IR 4.0. Working from home has advantages for employees

everywhere, including (1) assistance needed, (2) staff training; (3) technological improvement and monitoring; (4) WFH guidelines; (5) direction-moving forward; and (6) gratitude.

Thus, more advantages can be gained from WFH during the Covid-19 crisis, this can say that there is a good indication that WFH may be able to work as well during the endemic as part of an innovative way of working (OECD, 2020). As most organisations have experienced in WFH, this shows an indicator that employees were likely to continue this WFH; but if not fully, at least there is some capacity provided – as WFH during Covid-19 sparks the innovation that developed organisations' capabilities enhancements. And implementing an information system can aid organisations in coping with the issues of WFH, especially in monitoring employee performance. To conclude, according to OECD (2020), the widespread of WFH can be seen as a permanent feature of working with better policies preparedness that can be based on the crisis times which also proves that WFH can provide more advantages and increase performances that can be used during not limit to pandemic only but in endemic and future times.

According to (Gifford, 2022), WFH may not be a feasible option for a number of employees as imposing WFH may require thinking due to only limited job positions and job scope that can apply WFH.

2.2.4. Flexible Working Hours (Flextime)

Flextime was defined by (Collins dictionary, n.d.) as a system that allows workers to begin or terminate their shifts whenever they like if they finish the entire amount of hours required. The importance of flexible work hours is growing in the workplace. As flexibility offers various benefits for employers and employees, lots of organisations offer flextime policies implemented in their organisations. Flexibility was integrated into the work to give employees the freedom to choose when, how much, and where to work because it benefits both employers and employees. The advantages of flexible working hours include recruiting and retaining employees and increased job satisfaction which can lead to higher work commitment. In opposition to that, when talking about flexible work schedules, trust will be an issue.

If managers cannot control their employees, flexible work schedules may lead to certain problems in the office (Shagvaliyeva & Yazdanifard, 2014).

Acknowledging the value of countering a balance between work and personal life motivates employees. Flextime employment arrangements have been identified as one of the central area's most popular strategies among Nairobi's commercial banks. The outcomes of this strategy regarding employee performance should be crucial in determining whether flextime contributes to these banks' more significant business goals. Given the strict requirements the banks in this locality have, this study aimed to determine the effects of flextime work arrangements on employee performance in commercial banks in Nairobi's central business district. Hence, it demonstrates that every employee regardless of their position, supports flextime and impacts employee performance (Mwebi & Kadaga, 2015).

Flexible work schedules have recently received attention from academics and practitioners alike to enhance organisational and employee performance. Numerous factors that are directly or indirectly related to the business' efficiency have been taken into consideration. Flexible work hours and flexibility impact organisational productivity, which has significant ramifications for all HR managers. It's crucial to remember that these decisions must be made strategically with the necessary support from resources and proper communication of those changes. Through work, the idea of High-Performance Systems (HPWS), which is central to improving performance in HRM, has some relevant connections with FWH. The flexibility that accommodates employees' choices and demands are inevitably more likely to aid firms and their employees in achieving performance-related goals (John, 2017).

Flexible working policies have become more prevalent due to the Covid-19 lockdown (Prager, Rhoads, & Martínez, 2022). Another study by Nerobkova et al. (2022) regards Flextime and full-time employees' welfare was compared before and after the Covid-19 outbreak in South Korea; this study – shows that offering full-time employees flexible hours may enhance their welfare. However, it's crucial to take the Covid-19 pandemic's potential effects on the workplace and staff well-being into account when deciding on working hours.

Covid-19 has had a significant effect on the worldwide labour market. It significantly explains the loss of norms in the workplace by changing the social structure of the workplace. Flextime includes changing and flexible working hours, job shifts, job sharing and compressed workweeks. Flextime policies, adopted by the majority of businesses during and after the coronavirus shutdown, will enable employees to maintain more effective work schedules than traditional hours. Flexible work schedules can be arranged by employees in coordination with

other departments. Therefore, having flextime can increase job productivity and efficiency which indirectly help to change organization cultures in the post-Covid-19. And in addition, this flexibility can help to adjust this so-called "red-tapism" that hinders the organization from performing in efficient and effective ways (Agba, Ocheni, & Agba, 2020).

Hence, it is an excellent step to consider implementing flextime, but the employee's welfare might be affected due to performance. Thus, the proposed concept system might help to encounter this gap in which the proposed concept system can track employee performance by considering employees' well-being.

2.2.5. Key Performance Indicators (KPIs)

Key performance indicators (KPIs) involve financial and non-financial systems of measurement that organisations measure and document their degree of achievement in achieving startegic goals that have already been established. Selecting the appropriate indicators for measuring is essential (Velimirović, Velimirović, & Stanković, 2011). In addition, research has been conducted by (Arso, Sfenrianto, & Wahyudi, 2018) regarding a change in traditional work to telework. It implies employing the balanced scorecard method, which involves financial views, customer views, organisation core process view, and learning and development view, to execute KPI measurement of its employees based on teleworking. The design concept made by KPI workers to allow telework at the company is based on the findings of this study. The results of the KPI employee test then revealed an increase in the employee KPI's average value of 0.295 points (9.47%) over the old KPI. As a result, it is advised that the organisation apply the employee KPI.

(Badawy, A.A. Abd El-Aziz, Idress, Hefny, & Hossam, 2016) Numerous academics have proposed various approaches for manually, semi-automatically, or automatically determining KPIs, which are employed in many disciplines. The study overviews multiple approaches for analysing and predicting essential performance measures (KPIs). In the business world, indicators and key performance indicators (KPIs) are mostly quantitative data that show the internal workings of an organisation. Four different categories of performance measurements exist:

1. Key result indicators (KRIs) show how you performed concerning a goal or crucial success component.
2. Result indicators (RIs): they provide feedback on your actions.
3. Performance indicators (PIs): These indicators provide instructions. KPIs provide instructions on how to improve performance significantly.

The Key Success Indicators (KSI), also known as Key Performance Indicators (KPIs), are financial and non-financial indicators that organisations use to show how successful organisations were in achieving long-term goals (Bala & Koxhaj, 2017). When the Prime Minister included KPIs in the ministers' cabinet as part of performance management in 2019, KPIs in Malaysia began to become popular. Since then, KPIs has also started to be used in the private sector. Employees who don't perform up to standard might be classified as having poor performance, leading to disciplinary actions and termination (Jamaluddin, Taher, & Yi, 2019). Due to challenges in measuring performance, including disruptions in performance-based pay brought on by Covid-19, many organisations are reducing or eliminating their usage of performance management. Performance management must be maintained and even strengthened during a crisis in order to convey a company's strategic direction, gather crucial business data, give individuals and workgroups constructive criticism, safeguard organisations from legal concerns, and retain top personnel. The Performance Promoter Score (PPS), a measure of performance, is introduced by the researcher as an addition to the well-known Net Promoter Score measurement from a marketing point of view. PPS is an idea that will be helpful even after the COVID-19 pandemic has ended. It is a realistic, relevant, convenient, and valuable performance indicator in times of crisis (Aguinis & Burgi-Tian, 2021). In addition, due to the evolution of the digital interconnected technology that can be utilized by employees that can be used especially working from home through a conceptual system that was Electronic Performance Monitoring (EPM); although sensing the negative effects as well. Based on the conceptual analysis and the findings that follow—which also take into account privacy, ethical, and cultural considerations; it discusses potential future study areas and the design implications for EPM systems (Kalischko & Riedl, 2021).

Employee performance is crucial for organizations. This includes during either pandemic or the endemic of Covid-19. Work practices in the "new normal" working environment have unique challenges towards certain organizations or the employees themselves. This includes some managers believing they are unable to supervise workers who are employed remotely,

lack of clarity on goals and output, monitoring employees if they are working at home, confidentiality issues, lack of digitalized paperwork and importantly in the performance perspective is that their will be a less engagement between employees which can lead to digital misunderstanding (Vyas, "New normal" at work in a post-COVID world: work–life balance and labor markets, 2022).

2.2.6. Information System

Developing a system requires depth understanding of what the Information System (IS) is all about and how to develop them. The understanding of the Information system is a critical aspect of this research study due to the development of a new set of systems which involves KPI systems for organisations and specific integration with Blockchain (BC) technology.

To develop an information system, it is required to have proper planning on how to develop it and decide what features to be includes. According to (Haramis, 1996), the initial stage of system development is called the System Requirements Definition (SRD). Nonetheless, it directly affects the other stages of the system development cycle, and the significance of this phase is apparent. The researcher discusses the SRD's purpose and goals, the tasks of analysing the current system and identifying the new requirements, and – most importantly – it suggests a process for performing the SRD that will result in an SRD report.

Before being developed, information systems must go through the Systems Development Life Cycle (SDLC) using the appropriate methodology. However, the project manager, systems analyst, system designer, and end users must collaborate closely for an information systems project to be thriving (Philip, Afolabi, Adeniran, Oluwatolani, & Ishaya, 2010). A design review's primary objective is to confirm that the stakeholders have a clear grasp of the design and can attest to the project team's comprehension of their needs and the project's direction. Because the phases of the Systems Development Life Cycle recur, improvements to the design can be made in the following cycle. The design phase should receive much attention because it is crucial to every project, regardless of approach. The five stages of the SDLC model—Analysis, Design, Implementation, Testing, and Evaluation—are defined in this fashion (Scroggins, 2014).

To further understand IS, a research study was conducted to examine the different views of defining IS. By analysing 34 literature reviews, (Boell & Cecez-Kecmanovic, 2015) concluded that there were four views of IS: technology, social, socio-technical, and process. A further definition can be found below:

1. Technology view – emphasise the value of IT in a business setting or the software used to process, store, and distribute data and information.
2. Social view – Emphasize the importance of IS's social component. Although they generally prioritise social aspects over technology, they nevertheless regularly recognise the significance of technology. The processes through which human actors produce, transmit, and assess information and give meaning to IS, as well as the social institutions and organisations that support and limit human agency, are consequently of the highest importance.
3. Socio-Technical view – Understand IS in terms of ongoing interactions between social and technical components. IS comprises technological and social elements and phenomena that develop because of their interaction.
4. Process view – The process view of IS emphasises the connection between IS and the specific information processing tasks they carry out and support. The

transformation of data into information or the dissemination and delivery of information are activities supported by IS. This relates IS to usage and action. Thus, it is common knowledge that Information System is associated with work-related tasks, supporting organisational goals, or problem-solving.

Employing the performance management method is a problem that organisations currently face. A management information system based on KPIs improves performance structure. Due to the utilisation of current information technology, it is vital to strengthen and expand mathematical security structures. As a result, efficiency will increase, and functionality will be more widely distributed. A significant calibration solution limitation must be adopted for the complexity of modern corporate management processes based on a limited amount of time, extensive financial analysis, and other data. It is concluded that with the creation of significant indicators of employee productivity and business performance, the automation challenge of industrial processes for firm performance management approach is described – a thorough description of the subsystems and comprehensive system performance management is based on the company's information structure. Many information technology organisations use the outcomes of the standard information system (AlRababah, AlShahrani, & Al-Kasasbeh, 2016).

Developing a new system is not easy; according to (Haramis, 1996), the system must be transparent and able to be presented to clients as part of the 16 steps of SRD procedures. Hence, once the system has been presented or perhaps having the prototypes is better for clients to test it, it can provide a better view through conducting User Acceptance Test (UAT). High-cost software project failures have primarily been linked to errors in the requirements specifications. Verifying requirements early in the development process, ideally before creating a functioning prototype, is very helpful in anticipating the workplace adoption of a new system based on user reviews of its specifications. Before users can provide assessments that correctly predict future user behaviour after workplace installation, they must have a direct, practical learning experience with at least a functional prototype of a new system. Therefore, it is important to gather input from end users based on their intended usage, perceived usefulness, and perceived ease of use. Therefore, conducting UAT at pre-prototype rather than post-prototype is advised (Davis & Venkatesh, 2004).

2.2.7. Blockchain (BC) Technology

Blockchain Technology (BC) simplifies asset tracking and transaction logging inside an organisation network using a decentralized, permanent database. An asset could be material or intangible. On a blockchain network, literally, everything of value may be recorded and transacted, lowering risk and increasing efficiency for all participants. (IBM, n.d.). Thanks to cryptography, blockchains offer distributed ledger management without the need for a central authority to enforce the. As a result, transaction histories and permanent records are created, which are exceedingly difficult to change or erase (Laurence, 2017). Although BC technology is frequently connected to the financial sector, it can also be used in other fields. Multiple advantages and features of BC technology include a tamper-resistant (Kombe, Ally, & Sam, 2018), increased functionality, ledger distributions, security, cost savings, and ease of supply chain management (Justinia, 2019).

Numerous sectors, including finance, healthcare, manufacturing, education, (Leible, Schlager, Schubotz, & Gipp, 2019), energy and economics (Alam, et al., 2021) implement blockchain applications to take advantage of the inimitable characteristics of technology provides organisation, credibility, and transparency. Application programming interfaces (APIs) are required for blockchain to connect off-chain (external) hardware and software to the

network, permitting data, communication, and exchange transmission across systems. For specialised uses, web services and other third-party applications will be able to interact with current blockchain processes and capabilities. Thus, the researchers have compiled the following list of pertinent attributes relevant to the open scientific use case after summarising the technology's properties: decentralisation, Cryptographic hashing, timestamping, immutability, consensus mechanism and access and governance system (Leible, Schlager, Schubotz, & Gipp, 2019).

Although blockchain technology is relatively new and can be seen as disruptive, there has been more exploitation of Blockchain Technology. In a study on employee performance with integration with Blockchain Technology towards a Smart City Governance by Sifah, et al., (2020), the researchers used Blockchain technology to develop an employee performance assessment system. The system has exploited the benefits of blockchain technology which involves decentralised systems, tamper-resistance, accountability, transparency, security, and reliability. The developed system applies a 3-chain model, which includes ID-Chain, Behaviour Chain and Credit Chain. Sifah et al. (2020) have used two specialised nodes – ID controller nodes and Evaluation Processing nodes which focus on creating and managing digital ID in the blockchain and storing digital formats of employees' assessment information, respectively. According to the findings, using Proof of Concept (PoC), the result shows that their system does a great job of precisely analysing people's performance and motivating them.

Understanding the different blockchain types is necessary in order to comprehend depth. The access, confidentiality, productivity, and adaptability that are demonstrated by various types of Blockchain technology may benefit enterprises, and these factors must be taken into account by organizations when developing this kind of organizational solutions (Monrat, Schele´n, & Andersson, 2020). According to

(Ostern, Holotiuk, & Moormann, 2022), there are three types of blockchain which are (1) Public blockchain which enables the reading of blockchain data by all nodes in a peer-to-peer network and the suggestion of new data entries, (2) Private blockchain which restricting nodes that have been configured by a central authority from reading blockchain data, sending and validating new data that has to be registered on the blockchain, and (3) Blockchain with permissions are better suitable for closed or mostly closed systems – this is because according to Monrat et.al., (2020) that it supports the claims of Blockchain technology features even better such as its ledger distributions, transacting anonymously which can be conducted by the parties that involve in the system

which can be verified automatically and stored data through cryptographic configuration without requiring a central authority.

There was a potential for 5G technologies that can be enabled by blockchain technology. This can be seen from a previous research study that was conducted by (Nguyen, Pathirana, Ding, & Seneviratne, 2020), the researchers explored and analyzed what blockchain technology can give its advantages towards 5G technologies that were based on the spectrum management, sharing of data, virtualization of network, privacy and security, etc. The blockchain may raise security and privacy issues, but the blockchain has a unique security feature which relates to cryptography. Hence, this could help 5G technologies to help secure the network as it distributed the trust models with a high access level especially when relates with convert such a system from centralized to decentralized. But in contrast, Nguyen et. al., (2020) have found that there were fundamental security weaknesses from the blockchain aspect if it involves 5G technologies. In addition, when it involves smart contracts where data leakage and system modifications can be altered as well. Although both blockchain and 5G technologies can help each other, according to Nguyen et. al., (2020) there are still flaws in both technology's integration.

Blockchain technology keeps advancing, and blockchain use in many sectors can be seen globally. It is required to stretch the understanding of blockchain technology integrated with human resources. Even though blockchain concepts may be seen as still in the developing phase or not all industries are able to utilise it yet, but there is a need for human resources officers or policymakers to take this as an opportunity that can provide efficient and effective ways to manage human resources. It is seen that technology does not novel towards human resources as there is lots of HR system out there but there is a need to utilise current technology to enable human resource leader to utilise them very well (Chillakuri & Attili, 2021). Adding more, Chillakuri, et.al., (2021) also found that the perspectives of performance management help in a way that can reduce manual work (documentation) and provide transparency – performance feedback, consultation, new performance approaches and others. Hence why, Chillakuri, et.al., (2021) stated that blockchain technology can help to manage performance which can reduce biases, validates stakeholders and perhaps have the ability to use 360-degree individual performance methods – individuals can view their real-time feedback and managers can control the access using role-based accessed.

The characteristics, roles, and advantages of Blockchain technology can be properly utilized for a better reason. A study on blockchain technology for preventing fraud through performance appraisal was conducted by Gerrardo et.al., (2022) by looking towards the job recruitment process on the applicant's documents or employee experience letters. Introducing the proposed system which can verify the applicant's documents using performance appraisal as 'proof of work' through blockchain technology can help to identify if there is any fraud as blockchain advantages create a system that is safe, tamper-proof, and real-time verifiable (Gerrardo, Harjoko, & Lo, 2022).

According to (Insider Intelligence, 2022), by 2024, the global blockchain market will be worth close to $17.9 billion, growing at a rate of 46.4% over the previous five years, on average. Thus, this can be seen as a breakthrough in utilising blockchain technology. The advantages of blockchain include preventing fraud instances, keeping records in – a distributed permanent directory, using blockchain technology for procurement, reducing expenses, requiring less time, and maintaining privacy (Javaid, Haleem, Singh, Khan, & Suman, 2021). Hence, the necessity for future research on this study, particularly in the human resource sector, is demonstrated by the researcher's publications, which show that the uses of blockchain technology have not yet been thoroughly investigated in the human resource field. This Blockchain is still relatively new and requires more exploration. This research study focuses on integrating blockchain technology with KPI systems, which raises concerns about security, dependability, interaction with KPI systems' current IT structures and intellectual property and addressing legal ambiguities (Ostern, Holotiuk, & Moormann, 2022).

Understanding the requirements of the KPIs system to monitor employees working during FWAs is vital because this research topic can be regarded as novel given the surge in the number of organisations implementing FWA, particularly during a pandemic and endemic situation. Additionally, this system will help businesses and employees because it will provide employers with productive workers, and employee performance, effectiveness, and efficiency might result in bonuses.

Based on past studies, there are still limited studies on FWA during the endemic using Blockchain technology as the integration module. Not much research has been conducted on FWA during the endemic. Furthermore, blockchain is still in development, and many industries try to explore how to utilise it (Chillakuri & Attili, 2021). Moreover, Tasrin, et.al., (2021) also mentioned that only certain jobs can use FWA. Henceforth, developing a system that tracks employees' performance while working from home can address the gaps that have been found. Tracking and storing data will be made possible via blockchain technology, which will be essential. Additionally, because the proposed concept system for KPI requires indicators to be implemented, we have chosen to leave it open and provide just broad suggestions for how the system might look and the kinds of KPI that the business might choose depending on the business nature and whether WFA, WFH or Flextime was implemented. This is because it's essential to recognise that every organisation operates according to a particular set of rules.

2.3. Underlying Theories

The research study is based on a blockchain-integrated employee performance management system. This integration creates the KPI system. As indicated, this suggested idea system aims to support companies and employees through this trying period as the Covid-19 pandemic sweeps the globe. Several theories will be used in this research topic which include (1) Self- determination theory, (2) Employee engagement theory, and (3) blockchain technology.

1) Self-Determination Theory

Self-determination theory involves motivation views and addresses the benefits of internal motivation and the disadvantages of external push. This implies that employees prefer to control their behaviour, and people would get unmotivated if anything made what did once enjoyable labour seem more like a chore than a freely chosen interest (Austin-Egole, et al., 2020).

2) Employee Engagement Theory

An important area of discussion in managerial theory and practice is employee engagement. However, there are still many differences in the concept, theory, influencing factors, and outcomes of employee engagement, and there is still no solid standard (Sun & Bunchapattanasakda, 2019). Employee engagement is a person's mental and emotional dedication to their job, teammates, and organisation (Quantum Workplace, n.d.). The impact of Covid-19 is still around. Work flexibility became a trend during Covid-19, and employee engagement was affected by it and indirectly affected employees' performances. Field

(Weideman & Hofmeyr, 2021) shows a positive relationship between FWAs and employee engagement. Hence, this can prove that employee engagement will significantly impact employee performance. But for now, what if the performance measurement tools use the proposed blockchain KPI system?

3) Blockchain Theory

Blockchain (BC) technologies exist from Bitcoin. Blockchain technology is heralded as the next big thing in business because it offers benefits, including data symmetry, responsibility for transactions, and data transparency. The main focus is how distributed networking and the functions of cryptography. On the Bitcoin network, every node holds a record of previously authorised transactions. Therefore, each machine independently verifies a new transaction uploaded in the network using information from its local database. The cryptographic hash of the entire chain is computed and published each time a new block is added. The blockchain system's (network's) data replication does not just include copying information from one machine to another. The network runs on a completely different system, ensuring that all devices eventually store the same data. The best feature of BC is that it is difficult to modify data in the blockchain, and if able, it can easily be detected due to previous data being stored in all blocks, and any changes in one block will not change for the whole block. The BC feature is the opposite of keeping data current database system (Cherukupally, 2021).

Blockchain technology can be exploited based on what the clients need. This research will focus on providing a platform for employees to still work even working remotely or with flexibility. Using BC characteristics can provide a better understanding of what the function is. Refer table below for further elaborations on the BC characteristics and its advantages.

Table 1. BC characteristics and advantages.

Blockchain Characteristics	Descriptions	Advantages
Open distributed ledgers	To avoid central authorities and making multiple ledgers (one ledgers available for all parties).	One truthful source.
Decentralised networks	The necessity for parties to be familiar with one another is avoided by not using massive central servers to manage and store data.	Transparency.
Less intermediaries	Avoiding third parties and facilitating execution at a low cost are made feasible by private and public keys (accessible to anybody who validates).	Cost limitation.
Real-time updates	In networks with multiple organizations, the ability to update all copies in real-time makes it useful.	Effective means of collaboration.
Transition validity	Any transaction will be recorded and kept by major nodes.	Traceability.

continued on following page

Table 1. Continued

Blockchain Characteristics	Descriptions	Advantages
Consensus validity	This consensus approach aids in preventing fraudulent behavior by having participants independently validate transactions.	Anti-fraud.
Immutability of data	Data integrity is improved via hash algorithms and cryptographic digital signatures, which also prevent block tampering.	Improved security.
Automation through Smart Contract	Configured settings that allow automatic executing of the operation with certain conditions are met.	Efficient.
Time-stamped and chronological blocks	Blocks in a blockchain are connected by time. They enable users to produce analytics using dynamic data.	Analytics support.

Source: Chillakuri and Attili (2021)

2.4. Gaps in the Literature Review

Many factors and concerns must be considered while attempting to understand the requirements and importance of building a KPI System in any firm while trying to implement the FWAs, particularly during this endemic Covid-19. Note that since the research topics are pretty new and the need for exploration of the issues, the literature review will show the possible link and connection between them. It is not easy to find literate reviews focusing on Blockchain KPI Systems. Some gaps were found after the previous study's analysis from the literature review. The gaps were as follows:

The first thing is about developing a Blockchain KPI system for an organisation. Of course, the need to understand the challenges of creating a new and integrating two elements into one system. Thus, the challenges are not limited to data, time, configuration and other features that determine what kind of KPI measurement tools shall be implemented in the proposed system.

Blockchain technology has become a trend, and organisation leaders are trying to learn and understand the potential benefits that it can provide. (Kombe, Ally, & Sam, 2018) mentioned that although blockchain technology has many potential applications, it is not yet apparent whether KPIs can be integrated with blockchain in the human resources sector. But looking back to, research conducted by Sifah et al., (2020) shows that blockchain can be used in many fields, especially when discussing smart cities or smart nations. For example, looking at the (MTIC, 2020) report on Digital Economy Masterplan 2025, where Brunei is focusing towards digitalisation, and one of its strategic thrusts was 'Industrial Digitalization', which focuses on Industrial Revolution 4.0 (IR4.0) technologies that can be developed and implemented in businesses and, supporting the strategic thrust number 2 of

'Government Digitaliztion'. From here, developing the proposed Blcockhain KPI system can help the government build smart nations. Assuming one firm started developing this and looking at its performance, this can be a step ahead for other organisations and government sectors to use it.

One way to close the gaps is to create a system that assesses how well FWA, WFA and Flextime workers perform. In all circumstances, blockchain technology will be crucial to data collection and archiving. Furthermore, the proposed system will be opted to leave it open because KPI requires indicators to be integrated into the proposed concept system, leaving just

general recommendations for how the system should appear and the kinds of KPI the business may choose. This is because it's crucial to recognise that each organisation's activities are different.

For developing the proposed concept system of Blockchain KPI system, through an understanding of information systems and blockchain technology, research on developing it was required. Thus, two options have been identified to develop the proposed concept system: coding development and an open-source website development platform such as WordPress.

Finally, survey questionnaires will be distributed to participants for completion to fill in the gaps. These will ask them about their thoughts, suggestions, and opinions regarding the proposed concept system and whether it can be implemented in an organisation for FWAs, especially in this endemics times.

2.5. Research Framework

Figure 4. Research Framework

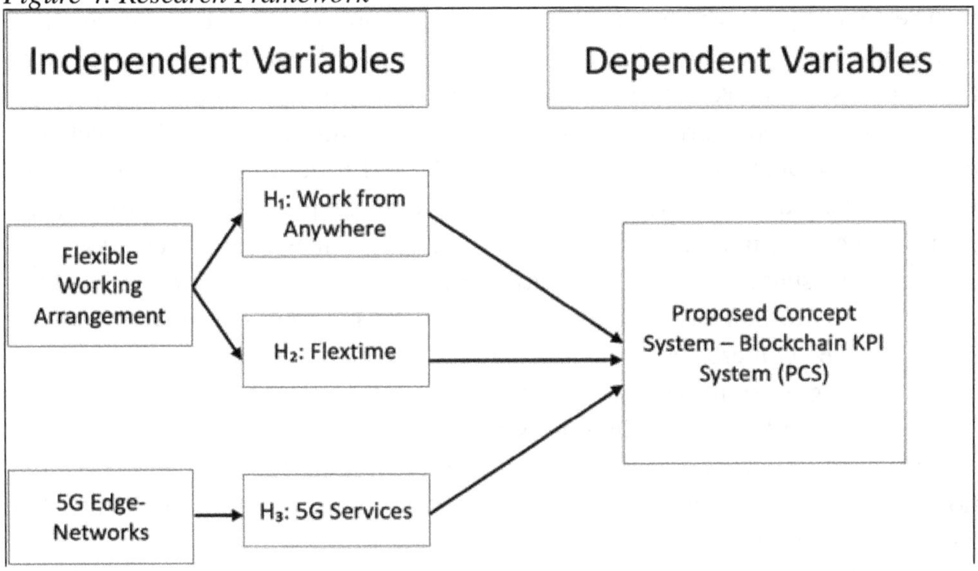

The Figure 4 above shows the research frameworks for this study. Work from Anywhere (WFA), Flextime (FLT) and 5G Services (5GS), because of the Covid-19 pandemic and current endemic phase, which has affected working practices, were independent factors in determining the scope of needs and the organisation's readiness for the proposed blockchain

KPI system's applicability. The blockchain KPI system that has been offered as a concept is one of the dependent variables that support the system that focuses on KPI when an endemic occurs.

2.6. Hypothesis Formulation

Based on the literature review above from past studies, no past studies mentioned the relationship between selected independent variables with the selected dependent variables; as this is a new research topic, it's pretty difficult to find past studies with the same concept and work of the area. This research topic can be considered new. Hence, this study aimed to identify the positive or negative correlation between the listed independent variables with the dependent variables – figure 3.

The independent variables are (1) Working from Anywhere, (2) Flexible Working Hours (Flextime), and (3) 5G Services (5GS). On the other hand, the dependent variable is the proposed concept system of the Blockchain KPI System.

H1: There is a significant relationship between Working from Anywhere with the proposed Blockchain KPI System

The first hypothesis, Work from Anywhere. Through the use of information, communication, and technology (ICT), employees are able to work remotely or from any location. Work from home was the most popular method of FWA, but it is also possible to work from numerous locations throughout the day, such as a café, a library, or a vehicle (Stiles & Smart, 2021). In addition, the ability to work from anywhere or remotely, which does not require people to be in the office, can be influenced by a number of factors, including the advancement of technology and the Covid-19 shutdown, which increased the usage of remote working. Working remotely used to be reserved for knowledge-based jobs, but because to improvements in video conferencing, file sharing, and cloud computing, this trend is now fast expanding (Gifford, 2022).

The use of WFH, especially during Covid-19, has become popular. As every country tried to move on to the endemic phase, working from home became optional. Still, some organisations are implementing WFH during post-Covid-19 or endemic. According to Chung

et al., (2020) mentioned that 86% of their respondents worked from home during the Covid-19 crisis and 43% of the respondents agreed that the respondents could focus on completing their work based on priorities.

Galanti et al., (2021) mentioned that WFH policies had been implemented, especially during Covid-19. Prasetyaningtyas et al., (2021) have indicated a correlation between WFH and employees' productivity. This shows that during Covid-19, the WFH policies have successfully been implemented. Thus, the gap that needs to be identified is how WFH correlate with employee performance during the endemic. Hence, Barbour, Menon, & Mannering (2021) stated that WFH would be utilised even post-Covid-19.

Employers and employees will benefit when the suggested concept system is implemented because it will make tracking employee performance easier. From there, the proposed concept system can be utilised to encourage employees to continue working and finish tasks within time.

H2: There is a significant relationship between Flexible work hours (Flextime) with the proposed Blockchain KPI System

Secondly, Flexible Working Hours (Flextime). This independent variable has been mentioned by Austin-Egole et al., (2020) as part of FWA policies that organisations can consider implementing in their organisations. All managers, and HR managers, in particular, must consider the impact of flexible work schedules and hours on the firm's effectiveness. As a result, there are some relevant connections between FWH and the notion of a High- Performance System (HPWS), which is crucial for improving performance in the HRM (John, 2017).

Every organisation is looking for ways to increase operational effectiveness. It is common knowledge that flexible organisational structures are among the most effective elements. The ability of the organisation to add or remove expensive and precious resources, such as recruiting employees for their skills and knowledge to perform precious work, is viewed as flexibility in this context. Hence, from the organisation's view, flextime can be seen as controlling employees' welfare and increasing their productivity or performance (Trigos & Doria, 2021).

Thus, when an organisation uses flextime as part of its HR policies, the proposed concept system may help track the employees' performance based on their productivity. Furthermore, timestamp features for check-in and check-out as part of the attendance in the employee performance review whether they could meet the daily working hours regardless of the provision of the flextime.

> H3: There is a significant relationship between 5G Communication Services with the proposed Blockchain KPI System.

5G communication services is an act of providing network services in the nations. The feature of 5G was providing a more speed internet connection which can be applied to devices that requires intense usage of internet connection. Securities are part of the 5G which can help enhance the integration of these technologies.

According to Nguyen et. al., (2020), 5G technologies and blockchain can support each other in terms of their security as 5G has its security while blockchain also has its security which is the cryptographic hash. But although it can support the integration between those two technologies, it has been observed that there were still flaws in the technology integration.

Blockchain technology is an innovative and advanced technology in this current era. Utilizing the edge networks of the 5G network can provide edge-to-edge protection of traffic networks which can be suited to any application due to its flexibility and ability to be fitted with the applications. Furthermore, there was one advantage that can be taken from 5G is integrating it with essential technologies such as blockchain and federated learning. This integration served the efficiency and security of any transaction that has been made. Thus, the blockchain transaction cannot be changed, this can benefit federated learning when it is across with 5G network (Rahmadika, Muhammad Firdaus, Jang, & Rhee, 2021).

Decentralization of blockchain can be viewed as the system can be accessed from anywhere without needing to be in the location to access the system. Thus, according to research by (Jain & Jain, 2022), blockchain and 5G can increase the economic value of data sharing. Its securities were a unique transformation technology which it served to validate the transaction, store information – distributed ledgers, and manage identities in a decentralised

manner. Blockchain provides strength for 5G which utilized the layer of security, integrity, and agreement mediation. This 5G can benefit the blockchain through involving node expansion, decentralisation and lowering block times, and IoT. As blockchain technology involves data transfer, sharing data and accessing data, the 5G can deliver more security.

Therefore, a 5G edge network can provide support for blockchain technologies from the perspective of securities. Although it supports blockchain technologies, there were still flaws or gaps that need to be confronted to ensure optimizing integration between these technologies.

2.7. Conclusion

This chapter uses information from previous studies to identify the research gaps and potential solutions to fill them. This chapter can also be utilised to pinpoint the research framework, which leads to the emergence of three hypotheses.

3. RESEARCH METHODOLOGY

3.1. Introduction

One of a study's most important elements is the research methodology. This will likely accomplish the study's objectives and might be extremely valuable in supplying answers to the research questions. The process of identifying, deciding on, processing, and evaluating data regarding a study topic is known as the research methodology.

3.2. Instrument Development

Identifying a comparable problem that only required research on a topic relevant to the study was challenging because it is quite a new topic. Determining the necessity for blockchain authentication of KPI performance towards FWAs during the endemic and its applicability required gathering primary data via surveys.

The primary method for data collection was through questionnaires. The questionnaires have their measurement. Specific measurement will be using Likert-Scale for each variable set of questions. And the last part of the questions will be about respondents' demographic information.

The first section of the questionnaires will be asked on Working from Anywhere (WFA) variables extracted from (Narayanamurthy & Tortorella, 2021), but not all the questions are relevant to this research study. This set of questions consists of six questions with a Cronbach Alpha of 0.805, answering them using a 5-point Likert-Scale (1 = Strongly Disagree and 5 = Strongly Agree). Next, for section two, for Flextime variables, the set of questions was extracted from (Mwebi & Kadaga, 2015), which consists of 9 questions which need to be answered using a 5-point Likert-Scale (1 = Strongly Disagree and 5 = Strongly Agree) where the Cronbach Alpha 0.805. For Section three, the questions will focus on employee performance, extracted from (Mwebi & Kadaga, 2015), consisting of nine questions where the Cronbach Alpha was 0.730 and expecting respondents to answer in 5-point Likert-Scale (1 = Strongly Disagree and 5 = Strongly Agree). In addition, this section will have a few questions regarding the type of KPI respondents currently uses. Section four will focus on the proposed concept system (BC KPI System), where the surveys will inquire about the proposed concept system, we are developing to collect feedback from respondents on what should be embraced

and what should not be implemented. The questions will be mapped out without extracting from previous studies, using a 5-point Likert-Scale as measurement and the need to conduct a Factor Analysis and Reliability test for this section. And for the last section will be asked about the demographics of respondents, which were extracted from (Narayanamurthy & Tortorella, 2021).

3.3. Data Collection

The process of acquiring information to learn more about the study subject is known as the data collection (Taherdoost, 2021). For collecting data needed for the study topic, it is required to identify the sampling population eligible to answer the questionnaires—using a non-random method to pick the sample, employing two significant conditions as our primary selection criteria. Respondents must first be employed in the public or private sectors. Second, employees must be aware of their annual performance targets to qualify for year-end bonuses. All responses should be assumed to be from a general officer, employer, or regular employee. It was anticipated that respondents in these roles would view their company more comprehensively and holistically, decreasing the possibility of having narrow perspectives of the current circumstance. There are several service organisations; therefore, ownership is neither restricted to the public nor the private sectors.

The questionnaires will be set up through Google Forms, which could help potential respondents easily answer for their convenience. The link to Google Forms will be distributed to potential responders through mass email, WhatsApp, Facebook and Instagram to reach more respondents randomly.

To support the findings for the research study other than questionnaires, another research method will be used: a data crawling method. Data crawling can be defined as the involvement of data mining that was sourced from different websites which is the approach to searching web links and attaining information from them (CE-GAL, n.d.). As the internet can be easily accessible and serve a variety of data and information – either its semi-organized or raw, the data can provide a wide range of information that can be collected and used, by all means using the data crawling method (Shamrat, Tasnim, Rahman, Nobel, & Hossain, 2020).

The procedures to conduct data crawling are as follows; extracting data from websites or social media such as Instagram, Reddit and LinkedIn reports and comments respectively. Once data extracted this data can be view in csv. format in which require to open in Excel for data cleaning. Once data cleaning has been conducted later on, Rapid Miner software will be used to analyze the collected data and seek to measure the accuracy of the respondent's perception on the readiness and willingness for FWA during endemic in general and try to find the related to Blockchain KPI system.

Figure 5. Data crawling process.

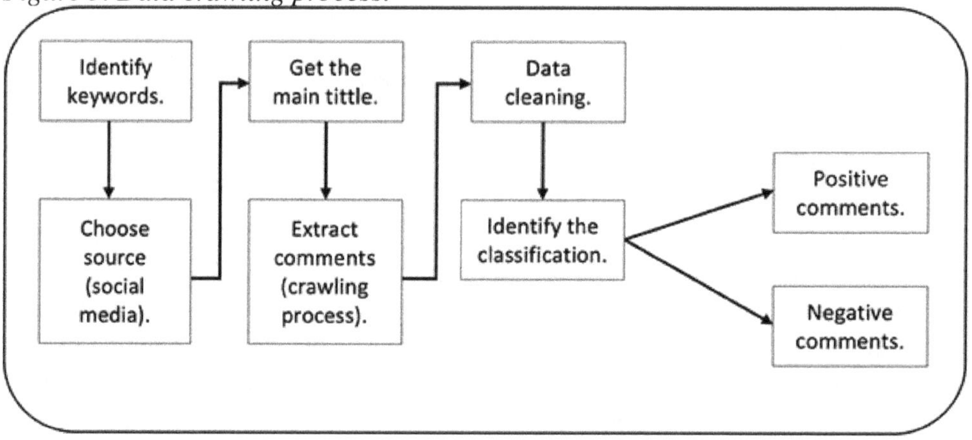

3.4. Measurement of Variables

As mentioned above, there were six sections to the questionnaire involved. Each set of questions will be explained the measurement of the variables, lists of questions and the reliability results (Cronbach's Alpha). There will be other question lists that need to be included and modified during the research study process.

There were items of questionnaires for independent variables and dependent variables. For all set of independent variables were reusing from other authors and extracted from several journal articles while for independent variables were original developed by this research author. On contrary, the dependent variables Proposed Concept System – Blockchain KPI System were not yet tested the Cronbach's Alpha analysis. Thus, the Cronbach's Alpha analysis result can be viewed in Chapter 5. The items of questionnaires can be view in Appendix 1. Thus, the heading of questions are as follows:

For dependent variables were developed by the research authors. There were 15 items that were listed.

For independent variables, the items of questionnaires for four independent variables were extracted from different author from different journal articles. The items of the questionnaires were as follows:

1. For Flexible Working Arrangement (FWA). The set items were extracted from Albion (2005). The questionnaires have eleven listed questions.
2. For Work from Anywhere (WFA). The set items were extracted from Narayanamurthy & Tortorella (2021). The questionnaires have six listed questions.
3. For Flextime (FLT). The set items were extracted from Mwebi & Kadaga (2015). The questionnaires have nine listed questions.
4. For Employee Performance (EMP). The set items were extracted from Mwebi & Kadaga (2015). The questionnaires have nine listed questions.
5. For 5G Communication Service (5GS). The questionnaires have fifteen listed questions.

For 5G questionnaires items which includes one independent variables (5G Communications Service – 5GS), 5G related awareness and 5G Information securities were extracted from several articles from Leu, Susanto, Chou, & Lin (2019), Leu, Tsai, Susanto, Gru, & You (2021), Yu, Susanto, Liu, Wu, & Leu (2022). Lu, Susanto, & Leu (2022), Jian, Chung, Susanto, & Leu (2022), & Hong, Susanto, & Leu (2022). While for demographic questionnaires items were extracted from Ray & Pana-Cryan (2021). More additional questions were developed to support the research study.

3.5. Statistical Method

The following statistical procedures are as follows:

1. Factor Analysis

Factor analysis (FA) allows to investigation of the fundamental dimensions that underpin the interactions between the many variables/items through the use of statistical techniques (Tavakol & Wetzel, 2020).

2. Reliability test or Cronbach Alpha Analysis

Cronbach's alpha measure's internal reliability, or how closely related a set of things are to one another. It serves as a measurement of scale dependability. Even if alpha has a "high" value, the metric might not be one-dimensional. Other analyses can be performed in order to show that the scale is unidimensional in addition to assessing its internal consistency (UCLA, n.d.).

3. Frequency Analysis

Frequency analysis is used to forecast the frequency of a variable phenomenon and assess how accurate the forecast was (Oosterbaan, 1994). Thus, the frequency of each variable in the sample or population, such as the split between men and women, is counted in frequency analysis. A branch of statistics called frequency analysis examines both the frequency and proportion of occurrences of events (Mishra, et al., 2019).

4. Normality Test

The normality test is an additional method for defining whether something is normal. To determine normalcy, apply the Shapiro-Wilk (S-W) or Kolmogorov-Smirnov (K-S) tests. This test can be given using the IBM SPSS software. To determine whether the scores are normally distributed, the null hypothesis compares the sample's scores to a group of scores that share the same standard deviation and mean (Ghasemi & Zahediasl, 2012).

5. Correlation Analysis

The correlation analysis describes the direction and the strength of the linear relationship between two variables. (Pallant, 2010).

3.6. Web-Based System Design (Blockchain KPI System)

This section will discuss the planning to design the web-based system design of the Blockchain KPI system. The proposed Blockchain KPI System can be viewed and edited by organisations, employers and employees using this proposed system.

The aim of designing and developing this proposed concept system is to preset and produce the prototype to illustrate how the proposed system will look and focus on the critical aspects of the blockchain KPI system, such as tracking features. The proposed system will be designed in the open-up platform as different organisations might use different KPI tools.

There was no prominent signal of KPI input for the designing process because the design was done purely for appearance purposes (interface). The qualities of blockchain technology will be incorporated into some of the features mentioned earlier and services. User profiles and timestamps were implemented using blockchain technology, creating a decentralised system. The blockchain technology plugin for WordPress can be used with the proposed idea system.

The software to develop the proposed design concept system will be XAMPP software as the web server. The database will use MySQL and WordPress as open-source website-building software for designing and installing relevant plugins.

3.7. Conclusion

The independent and dependent variables have been mentioned and explained regarding their measurement. The data collection will focus on random sampling but with the condition of working people focus on random sampling samples but with working people's needs. Thus, several statistical methods have been identified.

4. PROPOSED CONCEPT SYSTEM (BLOCKCHAIN KPI SYSTEM) DURING ENDEMIC

4.1. Introduction

This chapter will focus on explaining the proposed concept system where the system may be an aid for applying Flexible Working Arrangement (FWA) during the endemic phase. What it means here is that during the pandemic COVID-19, the practices of FWA were a trending practice in human resource policies. Thus, applying FWA during endemics or the new normal can be applied, but further research is required to enhance the loopholes. Hence, the proposed concept system was developed. The proposed concept system will carry the status of prototype only in which some functions were not working and the objective of having the proposed concept system was to showcase and help better understand the research topic.

4.2. Concept of Blockchain KPI System during Endemic

The blockchain KPI system after this will refer to as the 'Proposed Concept System' was focused on producing aid to support employees during the endemic. This proposed concept system focuses on tracking employees' work or tasks during FWA as the main of this research study. Forward, the proposed concept system will be based on general aspects as different organizations may use different modules in the KPI system, so, the proposed concept system will be developed as an open system in which organizations can use it using their respective modules.

The development of the proposed concept system will be using open-source website development software to design the system and install plugins for system modules through WordPress. Furthermore, XAMPP was used as a web server and Database Management System (DBMS) used MySQL for storing data.

The process to develop the proposed concept system was developed during research studies in the year 2022 and the proposed concept system was reused back to support this research studies which includes several processes includes design the system, testing and implementation.

4.3. Design of the Proposed Concept System

The design of this proposed concept system will include several functions and the screenshot of the design can be viewed in the Appendix Section. The design functions are as follows:

Table 2. Appendix showing design page functions.

Figure number	Design Page Function
14	Login Page for user
15	Dashboard Page
16	User Profile Page
17	Employee List Page

Below a several screenshots of the proposed concept design with its brief explanations, are as follows:

1. KPI Result Page

Figure 6. KPI Result Page

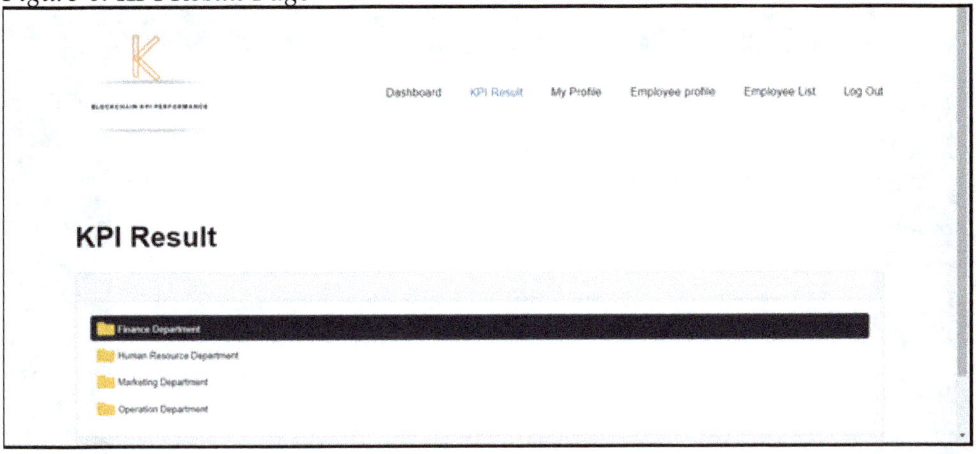

Figure 6 above illustrates the KPI Result page which can be clicked and accessed by clicking the KPI Result button from the header menu. The purpose of this web page existed, was to provide a document which can be downloaded by the users/ employees for their end-of- year KPI results based on perhaps the indicators that have been set especially for flexible working arrangements – work from anywhere and flextime. Once users click the download

button, the 'blockchain-hash' will be displayed before users can download the documents. Unfortunately, due to require to subscribed the plugin and it is require cost. Hence, due to that issue, the blockchain-has display will not be able to function.

2. Cryptographical Hash (Blockchain Features) Pop-Up

Figure 7. Cryptographical Hash (Blockchain Features) Pop-Up

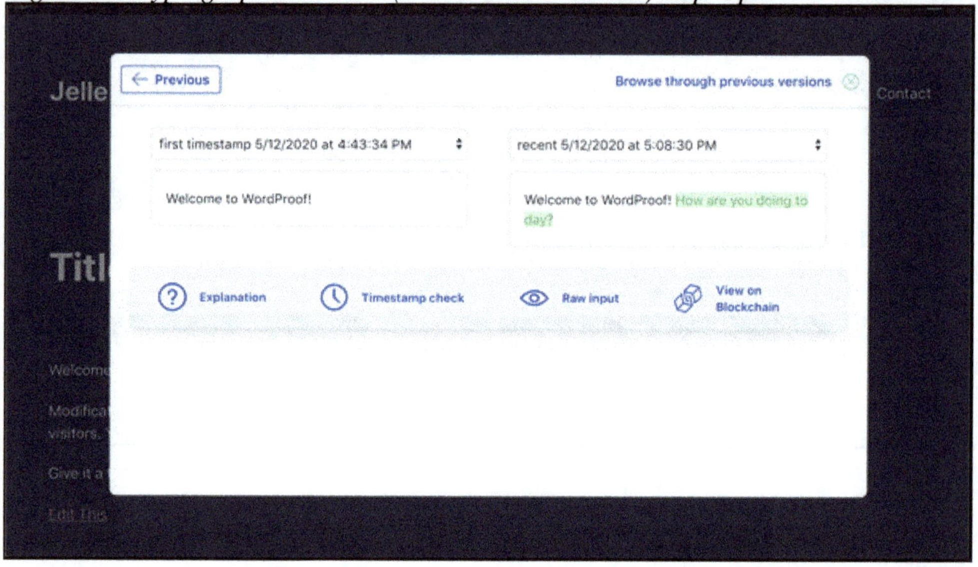

Figure 7 above, shows a pop-up display when users/employees try to download documents from the KPI Result webpage (Figure 6). Unfortunately, it require to subscribe the plugin and it is require cost. Hence, due to that issue, the blockchain-has display will not be able to function.

3. Timestamp Page

Figure 8. Timestamp Page

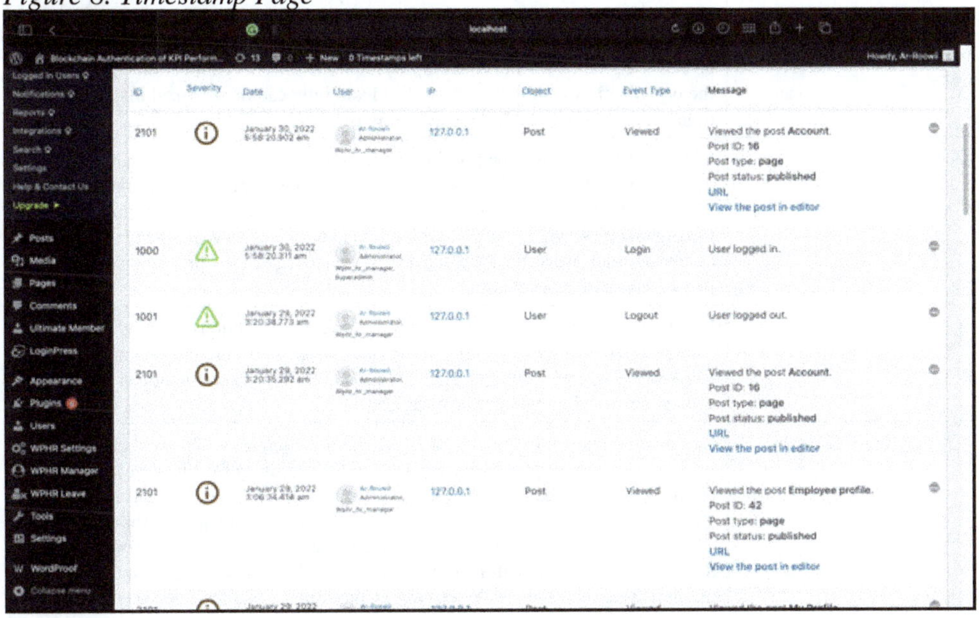

Figure 8 above shows the administrator dashboard which can be accessed by thc admins to view users/employee's login and log out time and what activities have been performed with its timestamp as well. By subscribing into this plugin monthly, it can provide organization a report that can be used to evaluate employees performance when in flexible working arrangements mode.

4.4. Blockchain Functions

The proposed concept system inclusive of Blockchain functions as part of the Blockchain KPI System. There are several functions of Blockchain and only a few of its functions were integrated into the proposed concept system.

Table 3. Blockchain functions explanations.

Blockchain Functions	Explanation
Decentralization	This function helps organizations especially employees where it can support the Flexible Working Arrangements. This can be supported for employees can have access to the proposed concept system from anywhere. The proposed can be accessed using Wi-Fi or an employee phone internet connection. As usually the organization system was centralised and only can be accessed inside the organization only (which not supporting the FWA).
Security	Unique credentials will be provided to the employees to log in and have access to the system when employees were working outside the organization. In addition, Blockchain technology provides more secure when interacting in the organization where once submitted it cannot be altered or amended by the owner or other users. Lastly, Blockchain technology offers private or semi-private types of blockchain.
Timestamp	Every time employees log in and logout system, transactions are made, and submission of files will be logged the timestamp. This is to ensure support the FWA working environments. Hence, human resource department can keep track if they are working outside the organization.
Cryptographical Hash	One of the important elements in Blockchain Technology. This will also be integrated in the proposed concept system for capturing the block or nodes of the transaction in the system. It also shows a verification of the transactions with details. Thus, any users want to amend or adding block after the transaction has been made by the owner of other users, the Hash feature will show the details and the details will be put publicly for other users to view. Note that publicly here means it can be viewed by other users that have access into the proposed concept system.

4.5. Blockchain KPI System Process Flow

Below the Figure 9 are the process flow from input to output based that shows what involves in every process.

Figure 9. Blockchain KPI System Process Flow.

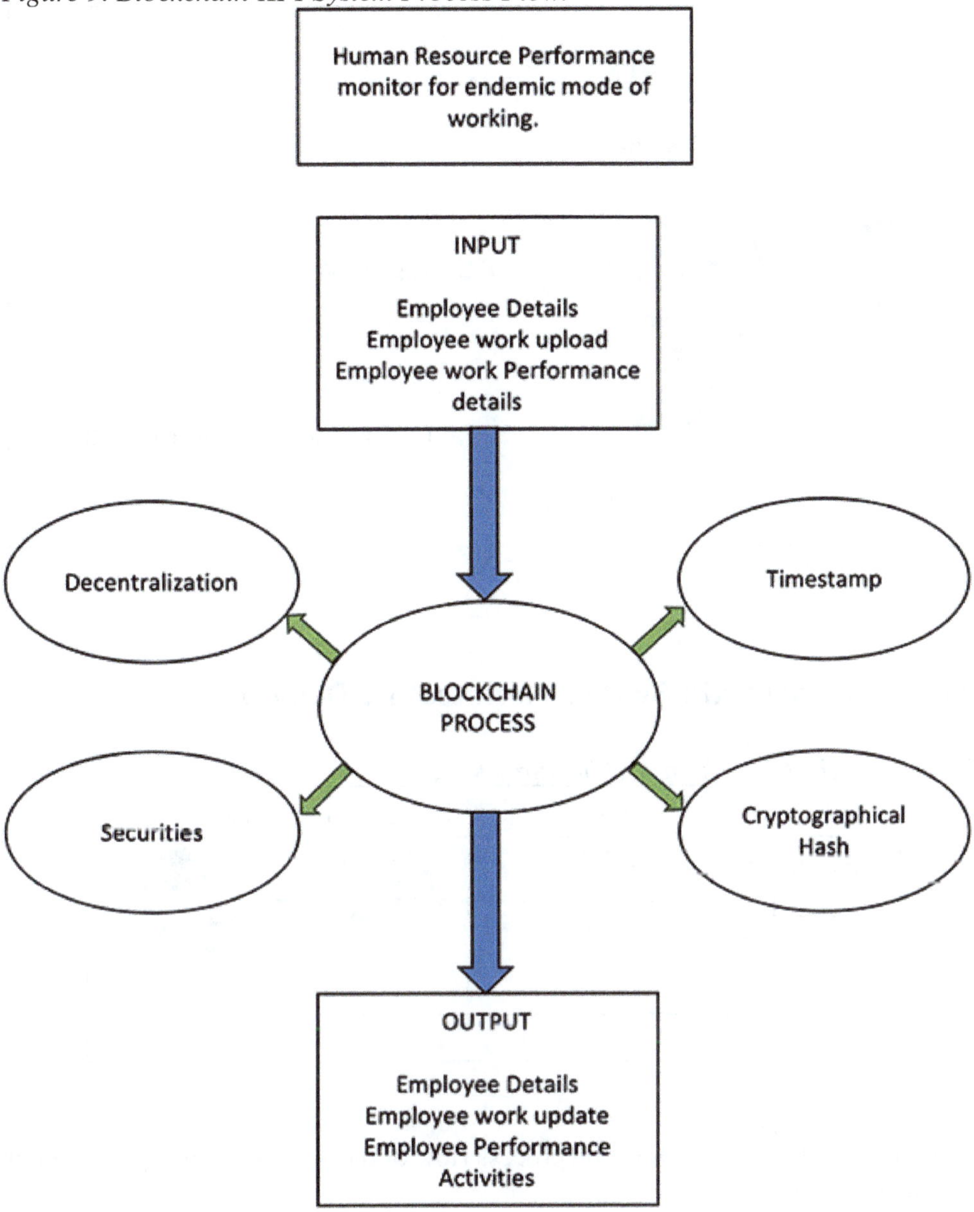

In addition, to get better understanding, there were several user's access parties' which includes Executive, Human Resource and Employees. Figure 10 shows the types of users and its annotations. Thus, the sigma of annotations of the system is:

Transaction Node (TN) = Σ x, y, z

Figure 10. User(s) Access annotations

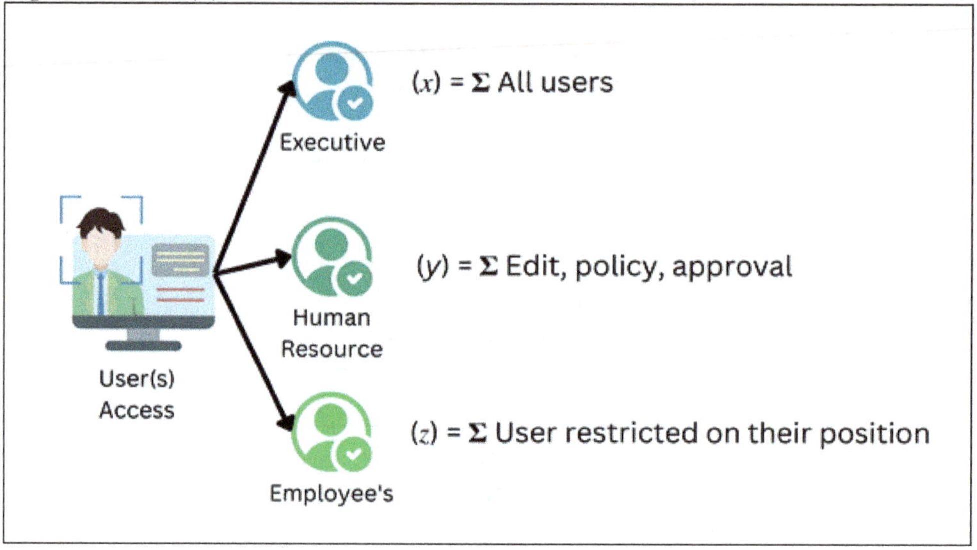

4.6. Blockchain KPI System Architecture Design

Figure 11. KPI Blockchain Architecture Design.

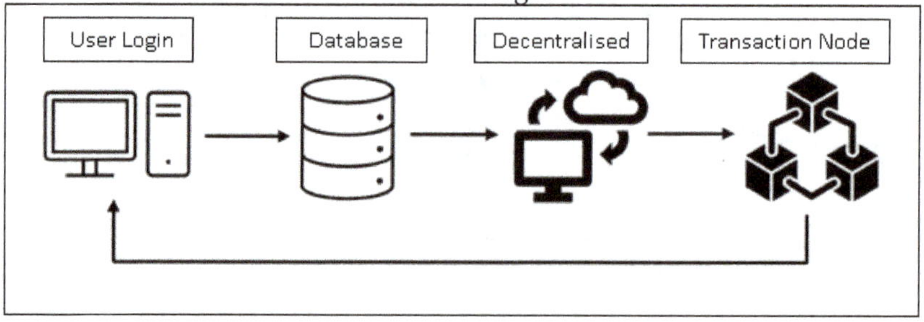

Figure 11 above shows how the process flow of the proposed concept system in architecture design point of view.

Technically, users' computers log in using their ID credentials to get access the server and led to the decentralized database. Once logged in, the user can get access to any files that have inside the system (depending on the restriction level). Thus, the blockchain technology will be captured once transactions have been made above the DBMS.

4.7. Conclusion

This chapter has explained in concept detail its figures process flow and system architecture design. Thus, it surely provides a better understanding of how the process of the proposed concept system works.

5. DATA ANALYSIS

5.1. Introduction

This chapter will discuss the findings and results from both primary and secondary research methodologies. The primary data collection method is using questionnaires. Hence, the results will be explained in detail further and the findings will be analysed using IBM SPSS Software.

Furthermore, the secondary data collection will be from data mining from social media. Hence, the results were based on the categorical aspect of whether assumptions from people are positive or negative towards Flexible Working Arrangements, Work from Anywhere, and Flextime. To analyse the data, RapidMiner software was used.

5.2. Data Management

Data collection was based on primary and secondary resources. As for primary data collection, the data were collected from questionnaires that were distributed to the working community as stated in the sampling requirement in Chapter 3. The data were collected from Google Forms and were able to extract into MS Excel. The duration of the opening for participants to answer the survey was two months. After such difficulties, only 50 participants participated in filling in the survey. Hence, it reached the minimum requirement for data analysis of 30 participants. The data cleaning process is also performed to ensure the quality of using the data to analyse and get quality results.

As for secondary resources, for literature review will be using published articles from any sources that can be accessed as long the journal article were related to the research study. For social media data mining, the chosen social media were Instagram, LinkedIn, and Reddit. The collected data were 1,024 comments. The base of social media will not be part of data filtering. Next, once comments from social media have been extracted, the data collected will be in the data cleaning process of removing unnecessary comments and identifying the category into positive and negative comments.

The data were only used in a collective manner and the data accessibility will be shared with only two people the author and the supervisor. The data will be stored in Google Drive.

5.3. Data Analysis

5.3.1. Cronbach Alpha Analysis

Due to several independent variables set of questionnaires were not known of its reliability, hence, reliability test or Cronbach Alpha test has been performed for the independent variables – 5G Services (5GS) and the dependent variables – proposed concept system (PCS) – Blockchain KPI System.

Table 4. Cronbach's Alpha Analysis.

Item set	Cronbach's Alpha	Cronbach's Alpha Based on standardized item	N of items
Independent Variables			
Work from Anywhere	.683	.696	5
Flextime	.752	.764	8
5G Services	.941	.945	23
Employee Performance**	.925	.929	8
Dependent Variables			
Proposed Concept System	.923	.935	15

**Not included for the hypothesis.

Table 4 shows the result of Cronbach's Alpha Analysis which shows that both variables were reliable. The indicator of reliability of the set of questionnaires must be more than 0.7. Thus, the reliability shows both variables having strong reliability.

5.3.2. Frequency Analysis

One of the descriptive statistical analyses is Frequency Analysis. Basically, it analyses the number of occurrences in that respondents have responded to the questionnaires. Thus, below are the Tables of frequency analysis:

Table 5. Demographic section.

Particular	Options	f	%	Options	f	%
Gender	Male	32	64%	Female	18	36%
Organization experience	< 5 years	27	54%	> 5 years	23	46%
Organization size	< 5,000 employees	45	90%	> 5,000 Employees	5	10%
Organization ownership	Public Sector	18	36%	Private Sector	32	64%
Org. degree of interaction	High	35	70%	Low	15	30%
Org. degree of labour	High	37	74%	Low	13	26%
Roles apply FWA	Yes	38	76%	No	12	24%
Want to implement FWA	Yes	46	92%	No	4	8%
During pandemic, entitle to	Yes	37	74%	No	13	26%
Endemic, apply FWA**	Yes	16	32.7%	No	33	67.3%
Agree FWA implemented	Yes	37	74%	No	13	26%

** Missing data by 1 respondent.

Table 5 shows the demographics of the participants that have participated in answering the survey questionnaires. A total of participants were 50 participants responded. The gender distribution, the highest was male with 32 participants (64%) and female were 23 participants (36%). The organization experience shows that most of the participants 54% (27 participants) were having less than 5 years working with the organization that 90% were having less than 5,000 employees. In terms of organization ownership, the highest were participants working in the private sector 32 out of 50 participants (64%) having much of a high degree of interactions and customization 60%, and the organization's degree of labour intensity was also high which contribute of 74% of 50 total of participants respectively.

From the perspective of Flexible Working Arrangement (FWA), participants' roles in the respective organization majority stated 'Yes', their role can be applied to the FWA mode of working with 38 participants (76%). Next, 92% of the participants stated 'Yes' that they wanted to implement FWA in their organization. During the pandemic COVID-19, the participants stated that they have entitled to apply for FWA 37 out of 50 participants (74%) while during the endemic, it reflects the opposite which only 16 out of 50 respondents (28.7%) can apply for FWA. But overall, from the participant's point of view, 37 respondents (94%) wanted to implement FWA during the endemic.

Table 6. Demographic (Job roles).

Job Roles	f	%
Officer	22	44%
Manager	4	8%
Supervisor	9	18%
Director	0	0%
Others	15	30%

Table 6 above shows the frequency of the participant's job roles in their organization. The highest of the respondents was Officer who contributes 22 participants (44%). The second highest was from the others category which accumulated different answers about participants' job roles which contributes to 15 participants (30%). The other job roles were clerk, support staff, admin, assistant manager, Marketing manager, Academic staff, Executive, i-Ready, operators and assistant. The third highest was the job role of supervisor which contributes 9 participants (18%), next was Manager which contribute to 4 respondents (8%). But the job role of the director was none that answer the questionnaires.

Table 7. Demographic (Organization sector).

Sector	f	%
Banking	11	22%
Oil and Gas	11	22%
Agriculture	0	0%
Transportation	1	2%
Others	27	64%

Table 7, from 50 of the total participants, 27 participants responded to Others (62.2%) as most of the sectors were not listed as part of the answer. Hence, the other sector was the Education sector, Finance sector, Government Sector, Medical sector, Estate sector, Retail sector, security and Fire Industry, and IT sector. The second highest was from the Banking sector and Oil and Gas sector of 11 respondents (22%) respectively, and lastly, only 1 respondent (2.7%) was from the Transportation sector.

Table 8. Work from Anywhere (WFA).

Code	Strongly disagree		Disagree		Neutral		Agree		Strongly agree	
	f	%	f	%	f	%	f	%	f	%
WFA1	2	4%	8	16%	**15**	**30%**	**15**	**30%**	10	20%
WFA2	1	2%	3	6%	14	28%	**19**	**38%**	13	26%
WFA3	0	0%	6	12%	**17**	**34%**	16	32%	11	22%
WFA4	0	0%	9	18%	10	20%	14	28%	**17**	**34%**
WFA5	6	12%	11	22%	**13**	**26%**	8	16%	12	24%

Table 8 above is referring to one of the independent variables. WFA4 shows the highest frequency answer of 'Strongly Agree' to the statement that was asked which contributes to 17 participants (34%). WFA1 shows the highest frequency for answering 'Neutral' and 'Agree' with 15 respondents (30%) both respectively. WFA2 show the highest frequency answer was for 'Agree' which reflects 38%. And the 'Neutral' answer for statements WFA3 and WFA 5 contributes 34% and 26% respectively.

Table 9. Flexible Working Hours (Flextime).

Code	Strongly disagree		Disagree		Neutral		Agree		Strongly agree	
	f	%	f	%	f	%	f	%	f	%
FLT1	9	18%	7	14%	**14**	**28%**	13	26%	7	14%
FLT2	4	8%	2	4%	**18**	**36%**	16	32%	10	20%
FLT3	1	2%	6	12%	18	36%	**20**	**40%**	5	10%
FLT4	1	2%	4	8%	**17**	**34%**	14	28%	14	28%
FLT5	1	2%	5	10%	16	32%	17	34%	11	22%
FLT6	3	6%	4	8%	**21**	**42%**	16	32%	6	12%
FLT7	10	20%	5	10%	**18**	**32%**	11	22%	8	16%
FLT8	2	4%	8	16%	**15**	**30%**	14	28%	11	22%

Table 9 above is the third independent variable. The highest frequency for FLT1, FLT2 FLT4, FLT6, FLT7, and FLT8 shows a 'Neutral' response while FLT3 the highest answer was 'Agree' to the statement asked with 40% and FLT5 also showed the highest answer was 'Agree' to the statement asked with 34% or 17 respondents.

Table 10. Employee Performance.

Code	Strongly disagree		Disagree		Neutral		Agree		Strongly agree	
	f	%	f	%	f	%	f	%	f	%
EMP1	2	4%	3	6%	**16**	**32%**	14	28%	15	30%
EMP2	2	4%	1	2%	15	30%	**23**	**46%**	9	18%
EMP3	1	2%	2	4%	12	24%	**27**	**54%**	8	16%
EMP4	2	4%	6	12%	12	24%	**19**	**38%**	11	22%
EMP5	1	2%	8	16%	13	26%	**19**	**38%**	9	18%
EMP6	2	4%	4	8%	16	32%	**20**	**40%**	8	16%
EMP7	1	2%	1	2%	18	36%	**21**	**42%**	9	18%
EMP8	1	2%	1	2%	10	20%	**26**	**52%**	12	24%

Table 10 shows the set of employees' performance questionnaires. For EMP1 the highest answer was 'Neutral' which reflects to 32%. While other than that just mentioned, the highest frequency answer was 'Agree'.

Table 11. Proposed concept system.

Code	Strongly disagree		Disagree		Neutral		Agree		Strongly agree	
	f	%	f	%	f	%	f	%	f	%
PCS1	0	0%	3	6%	7	14%	12	24%	**28**	**56%**
PCS2	3	6%	2	4%	8	16%	16	32%	**21**	**42%**
PCS3	1	2%	1	2%	12	24%	**18**	**36%**	**18**	**36%**
PCS4	8	16%	**14**	**28%**	12	24%	5	10%	11	22%
PCS5	4	8%	2	4%	**21**	**42%**	11	22%	12	24%
PCS6	2	4%	2	4%	**21**	**42%**	16	32%	9	18%
PCS7	2	4%	1	2%	**18**	**36%**	17	34%	12	24%
PCS8	2	4%	2	4%	13	26%	**21**	**42%**	12	24%
PCS9	0	0%	2	4%	20	40%	**21**	**42%**	7	14%
PCS10	0	0%	2	4%	**24**	**48%**	18	36%	6	12%
PCS11	0	0%	1	2%	**20**	**40%**	18	36%	11	22%
PCS12	0	0%	2	4%	**21**	**42%**	18	36%	9	18%
PCS13	0	0%	1	2%	**25**	**50%**	15	30%	9	18%
PCS14	0	0%	1	2%	**22**	**44%**	17	34%	10	20%
PCS15	0	0%	1	2%	**19**	**38%**	18	36%	12	24%

Table 11 above is the dependent variable for this research study. 9 statements that were asked (PCS5, PCS6, PCS7, PCS10, PCS11, PCS12, PCS13, PCS14 and PCS15) show the highest frequency answer was 'Neutral' towards the statement for the proposed concept system. while for PCS1 and PCS2 the highest frequency answer for both statements was 'Strongly Agree' which shows 54.1% and 40.5% respectively. And for the highest frequency of answers of 'Agree' were for statements PCS3, PCS8, and PCS9 with 36%, 42%, and 42% respectively.

Table 12. 5G Communication Service.

Code	Strongly disagree		Disagree		Neutral		Agree		Strongly agree	
	f	%	f	%	f	%	f	%	f	%
5GS1	3	6%	1	2%	9	18%	9	18%	**28**	**56%**
5GS2	2	4%	1	2%	10	20%	11	22%	**26**	**52%**
5GS3	2	4%	1	2%	7	14%	14	28%	**26**	**52%**
5GS4	2	4%	1	2%	8	16%	13	26%	**26**	**52%**
5GS5	5	10%	4	8%	**18**	**36%**	10	20%	13	26%
5GS6	4	8%	6	12%	**21**	**42%**	8	16%	11	22%
5GS7	1	2%	4	8%	**20**	**40%**	13	26%	12	24%
5GS8	2	4%	6	12%	13	26%	**18**	**36%**	11	22%
5GS9	1	2%	1	2%	10	20%	10	20%	**28**	**56%**
5GS10	1	2%	1	2%	8	16%	11	22%	**29**	**58%**
5GS11	1	2%	1	2%	6	12%	15	30%	**27**	**54%**
5GS12	1	2%	1	2%	9	18%	14	28%	**25**	**50%**
5GS13	1	2%	0	0%	6	12%	16	32%	**27**	**54%**
5GS14	1	2%	2	4%	12	24%	12	24%	**23**	**46%**
5GS15	1	2%	0	0%	13	26%	14	28%	**22**	**44%**
5GS16	2	4%	6	12%	**18**	**36%**	9	18%	15	30%
5GS17	3	6%	2	4%	10	20%	**18**	**36%**	17	34%
5GS18	2	4%	1	2%	15	30%	**18**	**36%**	14	28%
5GS19	2	4%	1	2%	9	18%	12	24%	**25**	**52%**
5GS20	2	4%	1	2%	8	16%	17	34%	**22**	**44%**
5GS21	2	4%	0	0%	10	20%	15	34%	**23**	**46%**
5GS22	1	2%	0	0%	12	24%	14	28%	**23**	**46%**
5GS23	2	4%	1	2%	10	20%	13	26%	**24**	**48%**

Table 12 above shows a set of questionnaires of 5G communication services. From the frequency analysis, the majority of participants responded to 'Strongly Agree' for all the statements that were asked except codes 5GS5, 5GS6, 5GS7, and 5GS16, in which the mentioned code was the highest answer was 'Neutral'. While for participants answering 'Agree' the majority came from codes 5GS8, 5GS17, and 5GS18.

Below starting from Table 13 to Table 24 will be a discussion on frequency analysis for Information Technology 5G-related awareness questions.

Table 13. Does the participant department/activity utilize the organization's information technology?

Particulars	f	%
Yes	43	86%
No	7	14%

Table 13 shows that 43 participants (86%) have utilized organization information technology while 7 participants (14%) have not utilized organization information technology.

Table 14. How often does the participant's department/activity utilize the information technology?

Particulars	f	%
Always	31	62%
Often	11	22%
Once in a while	8	16%
Never	0	0%

Table 14 shows that 31 participants (62%) have always utilized information technology while 11 participants (22%) utilized information technology often and 8 participants (16%) only utilized information technology once in a while.

Table 15. How often does the IT or any related people review the Management Information Technology?

Particulars	f	%
Often (Once every month)	31	62%
Daily	13	26%
Hourly	0	0%
Other	6	12%

Table 15 asked how often IT, or related parties review the Management Information Technology the highest number of participants responded 'Often (once every month)' which contributed to 31 participants (62%), and 13 participants (26%) respond to 'Daily'. On the other hand, 6 respondents (12%) responded 'Other' which reflects answers of 'only if needed', 'once every semester' and 'Not sure'.

Table 16. How long does the participants' organization been using the information technology? i.e. How long has this system been implemented?

Particulars	f	%
Less than 6 months	5	10%
6 months to 1 year	3	6%
1 – 2 years	5	10%
2 years and more	37	74%

Table 16 illustrates that the majority of the respondents have been using information technology '2 years and more' that is 37 participants (74%) while 5 participants (10%) has answer for each 'Less than 6 months', and '1 – 2 years' respectively. For '6 months to 1 year' was 3 participants (6%).

Table 17. Do participants have the right (authorization) to access the documents in the information technology?

Particulars	f	%
Yes	31	62%
No	19	38%

The Table 17 shows that in terms of rights of authroisation to access documents in information technology shows that 31 participants (62%) stated 'Yes' they have access while 19 participants (38%) stated 'No' they don't have authorization.

Table 18. Has the participants organization encountered any form of information security breaches? (Participants may choose more than one)

Particulars	f	%
System failure / data corruption	34	68%
Infection by viruses or malicious software	25	50%
Theft or fraud involving computers	10	20%
Attack by an authorised outsider / system hacked	20	40%
Misused of authorization access	19	38%

Table 18 shows what kind of information security breaches they have encountered. The highest answer was 'System failure/data corruption' which contributes to 34 responses (68%). The second highest was 'Infection by viruses or malicious software' with 25 responses (50%), next the third and fourth highest was 'Attack by an authorized outsider/system hacked' with 20 responses (40%) and 'Misused of authorization access' which respectively each contributing of 19 responds (38%). Finally, the least answer was 'Theft or fraud involving computers' where only 10 responds (20%).

Table 19. Does participant organization outsource to external providers for information security systems?

Particulars	f	%
Yes	38	76%
No	12	24%

Table 19 above shows that only 38 participation (76%) stated 'Yes' their organization has outsource their information security system, while 12 participations (24%) stated 'No'.

Table 20. What kind of information technology training does the participant's organization provide with?

Particulars	f	%
Information system basics	12	24%
Management and implementation training in information system	14	28%
Application information management / life cycle management	5	10%
Risk management and contingency planning	8	16%
None of the above	11	22%

Table 20 shows that the highest type of information technology training was the 'Management and implementation training in information system' that a response of 14 participants (28%) while 'none of the above' shows 11 respondents (22%). The next highest chosen answer was the training in 'Information system basics' which contributes to 12 respondents (24%), the fourth highest was the training in 'Risk management and contingency planning' from 8 respondents (16%) and the least answer was 'Application information management/life cycle management' with 5 respondents (10%).

Table 21. What is the standard procedure followed for the information security system in participants' respective organizations/departments? (Participants may choose more than one)

Particulars	f	%
Firewall	36	72%
Anti-virus	40	80%
Formal written information security policy documented	28	56%
Implemented AAA (Authentication, Authorization, Accounting) for all users	26	52%
Accounts and password individually	42	84%

Table 21 above shows the highest answer of the standard procedure of security system was 'Accounts and password individually' which shows 42 responses (84%). The second highest answer was using 'Anti-virus' have 40 responses (80%), and the third highest was 'Firewall' with 36 responses (72%). The fourth were formal written information security policy documented' have 28 responses (56%) and 'Implemented AAA (Authentication, Authorization, Accounting) have 26 responses (52%).

Table 22. What are the measures taken to mitigate information security system breaches?

Particulars	f	%
Restrict access to the internet at work	10	20%
Block access to inappropriate websites	26	52%
Block access to social networking sites	5	10%
Monitor websites / social through logs	9	18%

The table 22 shows the frequency of answering on method to mitigate information security breaches where the highest responds was 'Block access to inappropriate website' with 26 responds (52%), the second highest was 10 responds (20%) was

'Restrict access to the internet at work' while only 9 responds (18%) to 'Monitor websites / social through logs' and lastly with 5 responds (10%) to agree with 'Block access to social networking sites'.

Table 23. How do participants' organizations react to issues related to information security systems such as data breaches, information leakage and etc?

Particulars	f	%
Improvement on information security policies	26	52%
More investment on information security system	13	26%
Trainings on information system	11	22%

Table 23 shows the answer of how participant organization react to issues related to information security system which the highest answer was 'Improvement on information security policies' with 26 participation (52%), while the second highest method was 'More investment on information security system' that were agree by 13 respondents (26%) and the least answer was 'Training on information system' with only 11 participants (22%).

Table 24. What is the business process that is involved in using the information system? (Participants may choose more than one)

Particulars	f	%
Corporate website	35	70%
Corporate email	44	88%
Payment processing	34	68%
Payroll processing	37	74%
Sales and/or marketing	23	46%
Customer transaction processing	25	50%
Finance and accounting	30	60%
Office tools (e.g., Word processing)	35	70%
Data storage	37	74%

Table 24 above shows the business process in using an information system where the highest options were chosen was using 'Corporate email' having 44 responses (88%), while the second highest was 'Payroll processing' and 'Data storage' have the same response of 37 (74%), while 'Corporate website' and 'Office tool' having 35 responses (70%). Next, while options from 'Payment processing' has 34 responses (68%), for 'Finance and accounting' has 30 responses (60%). The second least frequent response was 'Customer transaction processing' having 25 responses (50%) and the lowest was 'Sales and/or marketing' contributing 23 responses (346%).

Below starting from Table 25 to Table 34 will be a discussion on frequency analysis for attitudes to 5G Information Security System questions.

Table 25. Does the participant organization assign Authentication IDs or access cards for employees to track from any unauthorized access?

Particulars	f	%
Yes	35	70%
No	15	30%

The table 25 shows that 35 participation (60%) stated 'Yes' they have been assigned to Authentication ID or access cards while 15 participants (30%) stated 'No'.

Table 26. If NO from Table n (above), how are unauthorized access detected?

Particulars	f	%
Role-based access into system	17	34%
Surveillance camera	9	18%
Biometrics	10	20%
Other	14	28%

Table 26 is the connection from Table n above, if the participant answers 'No', mostly they have detected unauthorized access with 'Role-based access into system' which contribute to 17 participants choosing this method (34%). For 'Biometrics' shows the responses of 10 participants (20%) while 'Surveillance camera' response of 9 participants (18%). As for 'Others' most of the answer was saying they have Authorization ID and half of them were unsure.

Table 27. Does the participant organization use any Remote Access network servers?

Particulars	f	%
Yes	41	82%
No	9	18%

Table 27 above shows that 41 participants (82%) stated 'Yes' they have use Remote Access Network while only 9 participants (18%) stated 'No'.

Table 28. What type of remote servers does the participant's organization implement?

Particulars	f	%
Virtual Private Network	20	40%
Dial-Up	1	2%
Wi-Fi	27	54%
Other	2	4%

Above Table 28 shows the responses on what kind of remote server participants used. The highest answer was 'Wi-Fi' with 27 responses (40%), and 30 respondents (40%) responds to 'Virtual Private Network' and 'Other' with the answer of special VPN and not applicable to their organization.

Table 29. Which global security standards does your organization adhere to?

Particulars	f	%
ISO	28	56%
COBIT	4	8%
Sarbones - Oxley	2	4%
Other	16	32%

Table 29 shows the highest answer for global security standards was 'ISO' with 28 respondents (56%), while 'Other' responds by 16 (32%) mentioning 13 participants stated unsure, 2 participants mentioned none, 1 participant mentioned no comments and 1 mentioned UKAS. While the least chosen was 'COBIT' with only 4 participants (8%).

Table 30. What database technologies does the participants' organization apply?

Particulars	f	%
Oracle	11	22%
PeopleSoft	6	12%
Microsoft SQL	19	38%
Other	14	28%

Table 30 above shows the highest answer for database technologies was 'Microsoft SQL' with 19 responses (38%), 'Oracle' responded by 11 participants (22%) and 6 participants (12%) chose 'Peoplesoft'. While 14 participants answered, 'Others' where 13 participants mentioned 'Unsure' and 1 participant mentioned 'Ding Talk'.

Table 31. Please state a brief reason for the choice(s) of database technology.

Particulars	f	%
User-friendly configuration and architecture	29	58%
Cost-savings	10	20%
Global recognition and awards	7	14%
Other	4	8%

Table 31 shows the highest reason for choosing database technology was 'User-friendly configuration and architecture' shows 29 participants (58%), while both options of 'cost savings' has 10 responses (20%) and 'Microsoft SQL' has 7 participants (18.9%). And the lease chosen options was 'Other' which reflect they do not know the reason.

Table 32. What are the kinds of security issues faced in recent years? (Participants may choose more than one)

Particulars	f	%
System failure or data corruption	34	68%
Infection by viruses and malicious software	25	50%
Theft or fraud of computers	10	20%
Theft or stolen information	12	24%
Attacks by an authorised outsider	26	52%
Others	5	10%

Table 32 above shows the frequency of answers on security issues in recent years. Where the highest type of security issue chosen was 'System failure and data corruption' with 34 responses (68%), while 'Attacks by an authorized outsider' was having 26 responses (52%), and the third highest was 'Infection by viruses and malicious software' having 25 responses (50%). Next 'Theft or stolen information' was responded to by 12 (24%). The 'Theft or fraud computers' was having 10 responses (20%), while 'Others' shows 5 responses (10%) which mentioned phishing emails and were not sure.

Table 33. What are the types of staff-related incidents that have occurred in recent years?

Particulars	f	%
Misuse of web access	14	28%
Misuse of email access	5	10%
Unauthorised access to system or data (e.g., using someone else's ID)	10	20%
Misuse of confidential information	7	14%
Loss or leakage of confidential information	11	22%
Others	3	6%

Table 33 above shows the frequency answer of staff-related incidents that showing the highest frequency was 'Misuse of web access' from 14 participants (28%), and the second highest frequency was 'Loss or leakage of confidential information system' with 11 participants (22%), third highest was 'Unauthorized access to system data' shows 10 participants responds (20%).

For 'Misused of confidential information' has 7 responses (14%), for 'Misuse of email access' shows 5 participants respond (10%) and the least frequency was 'Other' shows 3 responses (6%).

Table 34. How often do participants' organization update their anti-virus software?

Particulars	f	%
Once a year	18	36%
Once in six months	14	28%
Once a month	18	36%

Table 34 above shows the frequency of answers on the often participants' organization updates their anti-virus software. The highest was 'Once a year' and 'Once a month' with 18 participants (36%), and the least was 14 participants (28%) who chose 'Once in six months'.

5.3.3. Descriptive Analysis

Table 35. Descriptive Analysis results.

Particular	N	Min	Max	Mean	Std. Deviation	Skewness		Kurtosis	
PCS[1]	50	2.20	5.00	**3.7120**	.66373	.018	.337	-.219	.662
WFA[2]	50	2.00	5.00	**3.5720**	.73735	-.108	.337	-.338	.662
FLT[3]	50	1.50	4.50	**3.4050**	.67317	-.580	.337	.518	.662
EMP	50	1.00	5.00	**3.7025**	.77997	-.871	.337	1.941	.662
FGS	50	1.70	5.00	**4.0174**	.68627	-.982	.337	1.353	.662
Valid N (listwise)	50								

This descriptive statistics analysis focuses on finding participants' or respondents' answers from a cumulative point of view. The descriptive table above analysed five variables in which the first particular is the dependent variable, while the second, third, and fourth particulars were the independent variables for this research study. This descriptive analysis's average or mean scores were based on the 50 participants or respondents for the primary research methodology. Using IBM SPSS software to analyse the descriptive analysis. Detailed explanations of the mean for each variable are as follows:

i. The mean value for the dependent variable which refers to PCS[1] (Proposed Concept System – Blockchain KPI System) shows a value of 3.7120. It suggests that the majority of the respondent's responses in between Neutral to Agree towards the statements that were asked in the questionnaires. Hence, this shows that respondents or participants agreed with the statements of the questionnaire.
ii. The mean value for the independent variable which refers to WFA[2] (Work from Anywhere) shows a value of 3.5720. It suggests that the majority of the respondent's responses in between Neutral to Agree towards the statements that were asked in the questionnaires. Hence, this shows that respondents or participants agreed with the statements of the questionnaire.
iii. The mean value for the independent variable which refers to FLT[3] (Flextime) shows a value of 3.4050. It suggests that the majority of the respondent's responses in between Neutral to Agree towards the statements that were asked in the questionnaires. Hence,

this shows that respondents or participants agreed with the statements of the questionnaire.

iv. The mean value for this particular variable which refers to EMP[4] (Employee performance) shows a value of 3.7025. It suggests that the majority of the respondent's responses in between Neutral to Agree towards the statements that were asked in the questionnaires. Hence, this shows that respondents or participants agreed with the statements of the questionnaire.

v. The mean value for this particular variable which refers to FGS[5] (5G Services) shows a value of 4.0174. It suggests that the majority of the respondent's responses between Agree to Strongly Agree towards the statements that were asked in the questionnaires. Hence, this shows that respondents or participants agreed with the statements of the questionnaire.

5.3.4. Normality Test

Table 36. Normality Test for Independent Variables.

Particular	Kolmogorov-Smirnov[a]			Shapiro-Wilk		
	Statistics	dF	Sig	Statistics	dF	Sig
PCS[1]	.069	50	**.200***	.982	50	**.631**
WFA[2]	.099	50	**.200***	.976	50	**.403**
FLT[3]	.114	50	**.121**	.957	50	**.064**
5GS	.095	50	**.200***	.938	50	**.012**

*. This is a lower bound of the true significance.
a. Lilliefors Significance Correction

The above table (Table 36) shows the results of the normality test for both dependent and independent variables. Based on the significant value (Sig.) for the dependent variables of PCS[1], from Kolmogorov-Smirnov, the value is .200, while based on the Shapiro-Wilk the value is .631.

For independent variables of WFA[2], the Kolmogorov-Smirnov, the value is .200, while based on the Shapiro-Wilk the value is .403. Second independent variable of FLT[3], the Kolmogorov-Smirnov, the value is .121, while based on the Shapiro-Wilk the value is .064. And for 5GS[4], the Kolmogorov-Smirnov, the value is .200, while based on the Shapiro-Wilk the value is .012.

Thus, based on the normality test above, the results have shown that it is not normally distributed. This is because in order to have a normal distribution, the significant value should be less than 0.05. Although based on the results it's not normally distributed, according to (Ghasemi & Zahediasl, 2012), having enough sample or respondents from the primary questionnaires at least more than 30 to 50 respondents, the disruption of the normality should not be considered a major problem. In addition, Ghasemi & Zahediasi (2012) add that based on the Central Limit Theory, if the samples are more than 30 to 40 samples, it is considered a normal distribution.

5.3.5. Nonparametric Test

5.3.5.1. Based on Gender

Table 37. Nonparametric Test based on Gender.

	Test	Sig.	Decision
1. The distribution of WFA is the same across categories of gender.	Independent- Samples Mann-Whitney U Test	.345	Retain the null hypothesis.
2. The distribution of FLT is the same across categories of gender.	Independent- Samples Mann-Whitney U Test	.162	Retain the null hypothesis.
3. The distribution of 5GS is the same across categories of gender.	Independent- Samples Mann-Whitney U Test	.693	Retain the null hypothesis.

Looking at Table 37 above, the nonparametric test was tested towards the independent variables. Firstly, the distribution of Work from Anywhere (WFA) is the same category based on gender, the significant value is .345. Next, for the distribution of Flextime (FLT) in the same category based on gender, the significant value is .162. And finally, the distribution of 5G Services (5GS) is the same across categories based on gender, the significant value is .693. Thus, since the results have shown more than 0.05 for WFA, FLT, and 5GS; hence, the hypothesis is accepted.

5.3.5.2. Bases on Job Roles.

Table 38. Nonparametric Test based on Job Roles.

	Test	Sig.	Decision
1. The distribution of WFA is the same across categories of job roles.	Independent- Samples Mann-Whitney U Test	.537	Retain the null hypothesis.
2. The distribution of FLT is the same across categories of job roles.	Independent- Samples Mann-Whitney U Test	.893	Retain the null hypothesis.
3. The distribution of 5GS is the same across categories of job roles.	Independent- Samples Mann-Whitney U Test	.537	Retain the null hypothesis.

Table 38 above, the nonparametric test was tested towards the independent variables. Firstly, the distribution of Work from Anywhere (WFA) is the same category based on job roles, the significant value is .537. Next, for the distribution of Flextime (FLT) in the same category based on job roles, the significant value is .893. And finally, the distribution of 5G Services (5GS) is the same across categories based on job roles, the significant value is .537. Thus, since the results have shown more than 0.05 for WFA, FLT, and 5GS; hence, the hypothesis is accepted.

5.3.5.3. Based on Organization Experiences.

Table 39. Nonparametric Test based on Organization Experiences.

	Test	Sig.	Decision
1. The distribution of WFA is the same across categories of organization experiences.	Independent- Samples Mann-Whitney U Test	.891	Retain the null hypothesis.
2. The distribution of FLT is the same across categories of organization experiences.	Independent- Samples Mann-Whitney U Test	.777	Retain the null hypothesis.
3. The distribution of 5GS is the same across categories of organization experiences.	Independent- Samples Mann-Whitney U Test	.104	Retain the null hypothesis.

Table 39 above, the nonparametric test was tested towards the independent variables. Firstly, the distribution of Work from Anywhere (WFA) is the same category based on organization experiences, the significant value is .891. Next, for the distribution of Flextime (FLT) in the same category based on organization experiences, the significant value is .777. And finally, the distribution of 5G Services (5GS) is the same across categories based on organization experiences, the significant value is .104. Thus, since the results have shown more than 0.05 for WFA, FLT, and 5GS; hence, the hypothesis is accepted.

5.3.5.4. Based on Organization Size.

Table 40. Nonparametric Test based on Organization Size.

	Test	Sig.	Decision
1. The distribution of WFA is the same across categories of organization size.	Independent- Samples Mann- Whitney U Test	.376	Retain the null hypothesis.
2. The distribution of FLT is the same across categories of organization size.	Independent- Samples Mann- Whitney U Test	.683	Retain the null hypothesis.
3. The distribution of 5GS is the same across categories of organization size.	Independent- Samples Mann- Whitney U Test	.032	Retain the null hypothesis.

In Table 40 above, the nonparametric test was tested towards the independent variables. Firstly, the distribution of Work from Anywhere (WFA) is the same category based on organization size, the significant value is .376. Next, for the distribution of Flextime (FLT) in the same category based on organization size, the significant value is .683. And finally, the distribution of 5G Services (5GS) is the same across categories based on organization size, the significant value is .032. Thus, since the results have shown more than 0.05 for WFA and FLT hence, the hypothesis is accepted. For FLT, as the results show less than 0.05, hence, the hypothesis rejected.

5.3.5.5. Based on Working Sector.

Table 41. Nonparametric Test based on Working Sector.

	Test	Sig.	Decision
1. The distribution of WFA is the same across categories of the working sector.	Independent- Samples Mann- Whitney U Test	.964	Retain the null hypothesis.
2. The distribution of FLT is the same across categories of the working sector.	Independent- Samples Mann- Whitney U Test	.770	Retain the null hypothesis.
3. The distribution of 5GS is the same across categories of the working sector.	Independent- Samples Mann- Whitney U Test	.77	Retain the null hypothesis.

Table 41 above, the nonparametric test was tested towards the independent variables. Firstly, the distribution of Work from Anywhere (WFA) is the same category based on the working sector, the significant value is .864. Next, for the distribution of Flextime (FLT) in the same category based on the working sector, the significant value is .770. And finally, the distribution of 5G Services (5GS) is the same across categories based on the working sector, the significant value is .077. Thus, since the results have shown more than 0.05 for WFA, FLT and 5GS; hence, the hypothesis is accepted.

5.3.5.6. Based on Organization's degree of interaction and customization.

Table 42. Nonparametric Test based on organization's degree of interaction and customization.

	Test	Sig.	Decision
1. The distribution of WFA is the same across categories of the organization's degree of interaction and customization.	Independent- Samples Mann- Whitney U Test	.617	Retain the null hypothesis.
2. The distribution of FLT is the same across categories of the organization's degree of interaction and customization.	Independent- Samples Mann- Whitney U Test	.140	Retain the null hypothesis.
3. The distribution of 5GS is the same across categories of the organization's degree of interaction and customization.	Independent- Samples Mann- Whitney U Test	.059	Retain the null hypothesis.

Table 42 above, the nonparametric test was tested towards the independent variables. Firstly, the distribution of Work from Anywhere (WFA) is the same category based on the organization's degree of interaction and customization, the significant value is .617. Next, for the distribution of Flextime (FLT) in the same category based on the organization's degree of interaction and customization, the significant value is .140. And finally, the distribution of 5G Services (5GS) is the same across categories based on the organization's degree of interaction and customization, the significant value is .059. Thus, since the results have shown more than 0.05 for WFA, FLT and 5GS; hence, the hypothesis is accepted.

5.3.5.7. Based on the organization's degree of labour intensity.

Table 43. Nonparametric Test based on the organization's degree of labour intensity.

	Test	Sig.	Decision
1. The distribution of WFA is the same across categories of the organization's degree of labour intensity.	Independent- Samples Mann- Whitney U Test	.815	Retain the null hypothesis.
2. The distribution of FLT is the same across categories of the organization's degree of labour intensity.	Independent- Samples Mann- Whitney U Test	.78	Retain the null hypothesis.
3. The distribution of 5GS is the same across categories of the organization's degree of labour intensity.	Independent- Samples Mann- Whitney U Test	.426	Retain the null hypothesis.

Table 43 above, the nonparametric test was tested towards the independent variables. Firstly, the distribution of Work from Anywhere (WFA) is the same category based on the organization's degree of labour intensity, the significant value is .815. Next, for the distribution of Flextime (FLT) in the same category based on the organization's degree of labour intensity, the significant value is .078. And finally, the distribution of 5G Services (5GS) is the same across categories based on the organization's degree of labour intensity the significant value is .426. Thus, since the results have shown more than 0.05 for WFA, FLT and 5GS; hence, the hypothesis is accepted.

5.3.5.8. Based on FWA Application.

Table 44. Nonparametric Test based on FWA Application.

	Test	Sig.	Decision
1. The distribution of WFA is the same across categories of FWA Applications.	Independent- Samples Mann-Whitney U Test	.343	Retain the null hypothesis.
2. The distribution of FLT is the same across categories of FWA Applications.	Independent- Samples Mann-Whitney U Test	.393	Retain the null hypothesis.
3. The distribution of 5GS is the same across categories of FWA Applications.	Independent- Samples Mann-Whitney U Test	.641	Retain the null hypothesis.

Table 44 above, the nonparametric test was tested towards the independent variables. Firstly, the distribution of Work from Anywhere (WFA) is the same category based on FWA Applications, the significant value is .343. Next, for the distribution of Flextime (FLT) in the same category based on FWA Applications, the significant value is .393. And finally, the distribution of 5G Services (5GS) is the same across categories based on FWA Application's significant value is .641. Thus, since the results have shown more than 0.05 for WFA, FLT and 5GS; hence, the hypothesis is accepted.

5.3.5.9. Based on Job Roles for FWA Implementation.

Table 45. Nonparametric Test based on Job Roles for FWA Implementation.

	Test	Sig.	Decision
1. The distribution of WFA is the same across categories of Job Roles for FWA Implementation.	Independent- Samples Mann- Whitney U Test	.959	Retain the null hypothesis.
2. The distribution of FLT is the same across categories of Job Roles for FWA Implementation.	Independent- Samples Mann- Whitney U Test	.823	Retain the null hypothesis.
3. The distribution of 5GS is the same across categories of Job Roles for FWA Implementation.	Independent- Samples Mann- Whitney U Test	.097	Retain the null hypothesis.

Table 45 above, the nonparametric test was tested towards the independent variables. Firstly, the distribution of Work from Anywhere (WFA) is the same category based on Job Roles for FWA Implementation, the significant value is .959. Next, for the distribution of Flextime (FLT) in the same category based on Job Roles for FWA Implementation, the significant value is .823. And finally, the distribution of 5G Services (5GS) is the same across categories based on Job Roles for FWA Implementation significant value is .097. Thus, since the results have shown more than 0.05 for WFA, FLT and 5GS; hence, the hypothesis is accepted.

5.3.5.10. Based on the Pandemic FWA.

Table 46. Nonparametric Test based on FWA during the Pandemic.

	Test	Sig.	Decision
1. The distribution of WFA is the same across categories of FWA during the Pandemic.	Independent- Samples Mann- Whitney U Test	.004	Retain the null hypothesis.
2. The distribution of FLT is the same across categories of FWA during the Pandemic.	Independent- Samples Mann- Whitney U Test	.176	Retain the null hypothesis.
3. The distribution of 5GS is the same across categories of FWA during the Pandemic.	Independent- Samples Mann- Whitney U Test	.163	Retain the null hypothesis.

Table 46 above, the nonparametric test was tested towards the independent variables. Firstly, the distribution of Work from Anywhere (WFA) is the same category based on FWA during the pandemic for FWA Implementation, the significant value is .004. Next, for the distribution of Flextime (FLT) in the same category based on

FWA during the pandemic, the significant value is .176. And finally, the distribution of 5G Services (5GS) is the same across categories based on FWA during the pandemic significant value is .163. T Thus, since the results have shown more than 0.05 for FLT and 5GS; hence, the hypothesis is accepted. While for WFA, as it less than 0.05, the hypothesis is rejected.

5.3.5.11. Based on the Endemic FWA.

Table 47. Nonparametric Test based on FWA during the Endemic.

	Test	Sig.	Decision
1. The distribution of WFA is the same across categories of FWA during the Endemic.	Independent- Samples Mann- Whitney U Test	.822	Retain the null hypothesis.
2. The distribution of FLT is the same across categories of FWA during the Endemic.	Independent- Samples Mann- Whitney U Test	.290	Retain the null hypothesis.
3. The distribution of 5GS is the same across categories of FWA during the Endemic.	Independent- Samples Mann- Whitney U Test	.382	Retain the null hypothesis.

Table 47 above, the nonparametric test was tested towards the independent variables. Firstly, the distribution of Work from Anywhere (WFA) is the same category of FWA during the Endemic, the significant value is .822. Next, for the distribution of Flextime (FLT) in the same category of FWA during the Endemic, the significant value is .290. And finally, the distribution of 5G Services (5GS) is the same across categories of FWA during the Endemic the significant value is .382. Thus, since the results have shown more than 0.05 for WFA, FLT and 5GS; hence, the hypothesis is accepted.

5.3.5.12. Based on the Agree FWA implementation during the endemic.

Table 48. Nonparametric Test based on the Agree of FWA implementation during the endemic.

	Test	Sig.	Decision
1. The distribution of WFA is the same across categories of Agree FWA implementation during the endemic.	Independent- Samples Mann- Whitney U Test	.788	Retain the null hypothesis.
2. The distribution of FLT is the same across categories of Agree FWA implementation during the endemic.	Independent- Samples Mann- Whitney U Test	.533	Retain the null hypothesis.
3. The distribution of 5GS is the same across categories of Agree FWA implementation during the endemic.	Independent- Samples Mann- Whitney U Test	.671	Retain the null hypothesis.

Table 48 above, the nonparametric test was tested towards the independent variables. Firstly, the distribution of Work from Anywhere (WFA) is the same category across the Agree FWA implementation during the endemic, the significant value is .788. Next, for the distribution of Flextime (FLT) in the same category across the Agree FWA implementation during the endemic, the significant value is .533. And finally, the distribution of 5G Services (5GS) is the same category across the Agree FWA implementation during the endemic, the significant value is .671. Thus, since the results have shown more than 0.05 for FWA, WFA, and FLT; hence, the hypothesis is accepted.

5.3.6. Correlation Analysis.

This section focuses on analysing the dependent variable and independent variables correlation analysis relating to the Pearson Correlation. Theoretically, the correlation analysis, analyse or examines the independent variables to dependent variables – which refers to a one- to-one relationship. The correlation analysis will be using the average score of respondents or participants from questionnaires. Hence, the results and their interpretation are as follows:

Firstly, examining the correlation analysis of the dependent variables – The proposed Concept System (PCS) with the independent variables – Work from Anywhere (WFA).

Table 49. Correlation Analysis between PCS and WFA.

		Proposed Concept System (PCS) Dependent Variable	Work from Anywhere (WFA) Independent Variable
Proposed ConceptSystem (PCS) Dependent Variable	Pearson Correlation	1	**.287***
	Sig. (2-tailed)		.043
	N	50	50
Work from Anywhere (WFA) Independent Variable	Pearson Correlation	**.287***	1
	Sig. (2-tailed)	.043	
	N	50	50

*. Correlation is significant at the 0.05 level (2-tailed).

Based on Table 49 above, the Pearson Correlation coefficient value was .287 between the Proposed Concept System (PCS) and Working from Anywhere (WFA). The correlation value shows a low positive correlation or there was a positive relationship between the dependent variables (PCS) and the independent variable (WFA).

Secondly, examining the correlation analysis of the dependent variables – The proposed Concept System (PCS) with the independent variables – Flextime (FLT).

Table 50. Correlation Analysis between PCS and FLT.

		Proposed Concept System (PCS) Dependent Variable	Flextime (FLT) Independent Variable
Proposed Concept System (PCS) Dependent Variable	Pearson Correlation	1	**.175**
	Sig. (2-tailed)		.225
	N	50	50
Flextime(FLT) Independent Variable	Pearson Correlation	**.175**	1
	Sig. (2-tailed)	.225	
	N	50	50

Based on Table 50 above, the Pearson Correlation coefficient value was .175 between the Proposed Concept System (PCS) and Flextime (FLT). The correlation value shows a low positive correlation or there was a positive relationship between the dependent variables (PCS) and the independent variable (FLT).

Finally, examining the correlation analysis of the dependent variables – The proposed Concept System (PCS) with the independent variables – 5G Services.

Table 51. Correlation analysis between PCS and 5GS.

		Proposed Concept System (PCS) Dependent Variable	Flextime (FLT) Independent Variable
Proposed Concept System (PCS) Dependent Variable	Pearson Correlation	1	**.539****
	Sig. (2-tailed)		.000
	N	50	50
5G Services (5GS) Independent Variable	Pearson Correlation	**.539****	1
	Sig. (2-tailed)	.000	
	N	50	50

**. Correlation is significant at the 0.01 level (2-tailed).

Based on Table 51 above, the Pearson Correlation coefficient value was .539 between the Proposed Concept System (PCS) and 5G Services (5GS). The correlation value shows a low positive correlation or there was a positive relationship between the dependent variables (PCS) and the independent variable (5GS).

5.4. Data Analysis – Sentiment Analysis

The data sources came from different social media sources, including Instagram, Reddit, and LinkedIn. The method to find the related post will be based on finding the keywords 'Flexible Working Arrangement', 'Work from Anywhere', and 'Flextime' related to a flexible working arrangement. The scope of collecting the comments from social media will be general, focusing on understanding global comments regarding the mentioned search keywords.

The comments extracted were in total of more than 1,000 comments. After cleaning the data by removing bots' comments and unnecessary comments, the total comments were left with 1,024 comments that can be analysed. Hence, this sentiment analysis was conducted manually by categorizing the comments into the 'Positive', 'Negative', and 'Neutral' categories using MS Excel. Note that, the categorization comments were in terms of overall comments from the above keywords. Further description of those categories will be explained.

In addition, there will be several keywords that can act as an indicator to assign the comments into three categories.

Positive keywords: Yes, Agree, Save, Allow, Reduce, Increase and Less.
Negative keywords: No, Disagree, Expenses, Disallow, Increase, and More.
Neutral keywords: Depends, questions, and comparing.

Thus, the results and detailed explanation are as follows:

Table 52. Sentiment Analysis Results.

Category	Percentage (%)	Reviews
Positive	54.3%	Less commute. Save time. Reduce cost. Sustainability. Increase productivity. Increase efficiency. Family engagement increase. Time management. Rewards
Negative	22.3%	Management issues. Misunderstanding of the terms of FWA, WFA and Flexitime. More expenses. Not all jobs or sectors applied. Tax issues – internationalisation. Less interaction with co-workers. Mental health issues – anxiety, stress and becoming introverted. Social issues. Career progression.
Neutral	11.7%	Depends on the situation. Agree to disagree. Part-time working. Freelance works. Gig economy. Questioning situations
Not relevant	11.7%	Comments that are not related to FWA, WFA and Flexitime.

Table 52 above shows the results of sentiment analysis. From 1,023 comments, 54.3% show positive comments regarding the FWA, WFA, and Flextime. The factors that make social media users agree towards the FWA, WFA, and Flextime were one of them was less commuting. This is because in general, FWA provides advantages to employees to don't have to go to offices to do their jobs, hence, it provides convenience. Next, social media users mentioned saving time. They felt that they can save more time in the sense of not commuting to the office and doing at home. Hence, it also can reduce costs in terms of commuting (petrol). Hence, it can be led to a sustainability factor where it can reduce CO or Carbon Monoxide from car engines which can support the effort regarding the climate change issue. In addition, employees were doing their job from home or remotely, for them it increases their work productivity and increase work efficiency. While at it, employees were able to manage their time wisely by working and managing their families as well.

For the Negative category, the sentiment analysis results show a 22.3% reaction. Several key points were mentioned. Firstly, it leads to management issues. In general, the organization may be allowed employees to choose FWA but the working hour getting longer in addition, for the new hire, the organization mentioned mode of work was remote, but it only applies to several conditions. This could happen because the organization have a lack of knowledge on what is the actual meaning of FWA, WFA or Flextime. Not just that, not all types of jobs can apply for FWA, WFA or Flextime. On the other hand, from the perspective of employees, working from home, for example, they tend to spend more money to buy working equipment for working at home or working remotely. Furthermore, the negative aspects of this working remotely were mental health issues – anxiety, feeling disconnected or turning to an introverted personality. And the review aspects were for some of the employee's concerns were for their career progression. This could have happened because working not in the office could affect employees' performance hence, it leads to a lack of work supervision and lastly, it leads to disruption of employee career progression. Thus, this is the main factor that was found in what many people think about FWA, WFA or Flextime.

For the Neutral category, the sentiment analysis results show an 11.7% reaction to neutral. The reason users expressed their thought from a neutral perspective was that they agreed to disagree reaction in which they mentioned that it will depend on the situation such as types of jobs, organization policies and rules and regulations. Furthermore, social media users mentioned that perhaps freelance or gig economy workers were better suited to apply for FWA. And the statement of every question from social media comments was considered neutral because it does not reflect positive or negative reactions.

And finally, the Not Relevant category contributes to 11.7% which comments but does not directly point out the main keywords. Hence, these results were extracted after completing data cleaning by removing bots' comments and spam comments.

In conclusion for sentiment analysis, it shows there was significant positivity regarding the application and implementation of FWA, WFA or Flextime. It applies worldwide scope for this FWA. Although there were positives for the FWA aspects, thus, it does not exclude the negative aspects from people's opinions. For the neutral category, it seems that people's opinion of FWA was not well defined for them to get a better understanding, thus, they tend to show confusion on the application of the FWA in the organization. Finally, the worldwide perspective and opinions were showing a majority showing positive comments, hence, it shows that FWA can be applied in selected organizations.

5.5. Data Analysis – Additional Analysis

Further analysis for prediction based on the respondents from participants. One of the statements asked the participants if they agreed or not to implement FWA during the endemic. Based on frequency analysis in Table 10, the respondents show 74% agreed while 26% not agreed. Hence, prediction analysis was conducted to predict whether future do people agree to implement FWA during the endemic.

The process of this forecasting was using logistic regression. The reason for choosing logistic regression was to identify categorical variables of 'Yes' or 'No' towards the statement of whether participants/respondents agreed or not to implement FWA during endemic. The process of identifying the forecasting results includes:

1. Retrieved data – Using MS Excel primary data and imported in to RapidMiner software.
2. Discretize - This operator's primary function is bin generation. It thereby lowers the possible number of categories.
3. Replace missing value – The function of this operators was to replace any missing data in the datasets.
4. Set role – Making the target variables (Agreed or not to implement FWA during endemic) as the target forecasting.
5. Split data - this operator functions to split the data set into the trained data and test data with the ratio of 0.7:0.3.
6. Logistic regression – the decision of machine learning model.
7. Apply model – To get prediction based on the trained data from the learning algorithm.
8. Performance (Logistic Regression) – To provides evaluation based on performance criteria values.

Using RapidMiner analysis, performing logistic regression was the right method to perform prediction. Figure 12 shows the process flow.

Figure 12. Logistic Regression Process using RapidMiner.

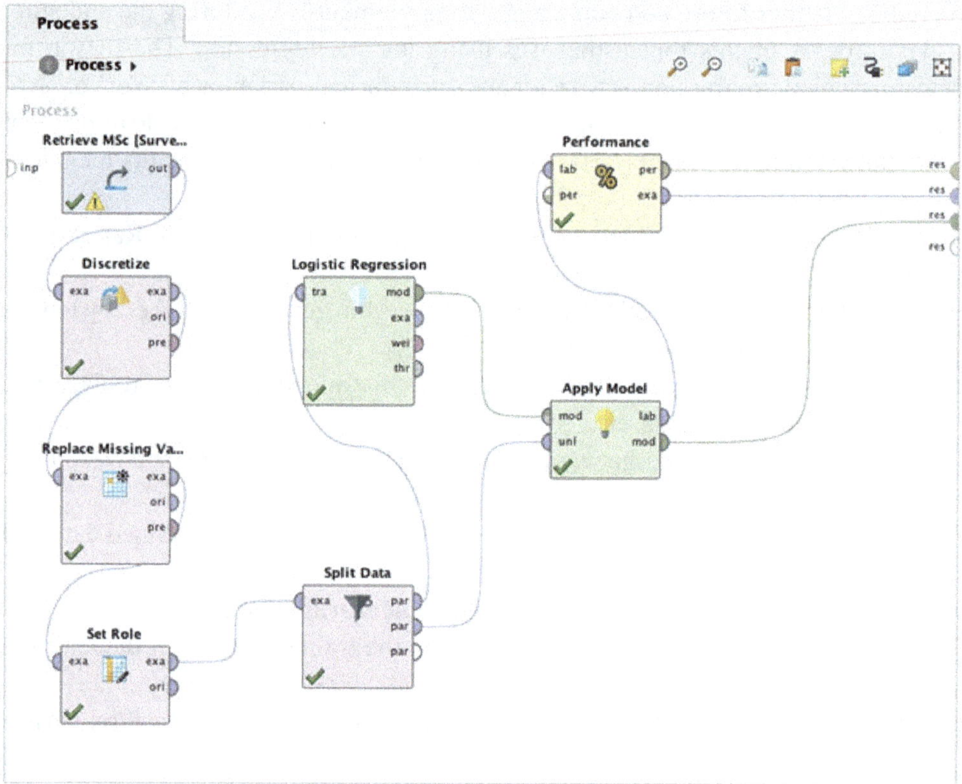

The results (Table 52) show a prediction of test data from 50 samples (17 samples), it shows positive results where 17 samples were predicted 'Agree' to the statements. Table 53 below shows the performance accuracy results. The results show an accuracy of 94.12%.

Hence, although the accuracy was quite high as to compare the ideal range of 75%- 85%, this accuracy still be valid because it's not overfitted.

Table 53. Logistic Regression Analysis Result (Accuracy).

	True Yes	True No	Class precision
Pred. Yes	16	1	.644
Pred. No	0	0	0.00%
Class recall	100.00%	49	

5.6. Hypothesis Statement

H_1: Work from Anywhere (WFA) has positive effects on Proposed Concept System (PCS – Blockchain KPI System).

- Based on analysing the correlation analysis (Table 49), for H_1, it shows a substantial positive effect relationship, thus, the hypothesis is accepted.

H_2: Flextime (FLT) has positive effects on Proposed Concept System (PCS – Blockchain KPI System).

- Based on analysing the correlation analysis (Table 50), for H_2, it shows a substantial positive effect relationship, thus, the hypothesis is accepted.

H_3: 5G Services has positive effects on Proposed Concept System (PCS – Blockchain KPI System).

- Based on analysing the correlation analysis (Table 51), for H_3, it shows a substantial positive effect relationship, thus, the hypothesis is accepted.

5.7. Conclusion

In this chapter, several analyses have been performed using several software as well. Using IBM SPSS software to analyse the primary data, using MS Excel to analyse the social media sentiment analysis, and finally, using RapidMiner software to perform prediction on the future agreement from respondents/participants regarding the implementation of flexible working arrangements in the organizations. Based on the analysis, it has been decided that H_1, H_2 and H_3 have shown a substantial positive relationship that was detected from Correlation Analysis. Thus, based on the results from this data analysis chapter, further discussion on the results will be portrayed in the next chapter, in addition to addressing the research questions, the limitations of this research study and as well future research needs.

6. DISCUSSION

6.1. Introduction

In this chapter, further discussion will be discussed that were based on the data analysis results from the previous chapter. The discussion will be focused on the research study of using Blockchain KPI System for Flexile Working Arrangements during the Endemic or post-Covid

19. This chapter will cover a brief and details discussion of the findings, its implications, and its limitation. In addition, future recommendations will also be portrayed in this chapter as well.

6.2. Summary of Findings

For this research study, four primary objectives were required to be met. Firstly, to understand the organization's/employees' readiness for implementing flexible working in the endemic phase. Secondly, to examine the need to implement a Blockchain KPI System (proposed concept system) for flexible working during the endemic. Thirdly, to seek the support that can be gained from the Blockchain technology role to be used in the proposed concept system and finally, to identify what are the relevant job scope applicable for FWA during the endemic with the help of the proposed BC KPI System. Thus, based on the mentioned primary objectives, several research questions were stated in Chapter 1 that needed to be answered to meet the research objectives. The research questions are as follows:

1. What is the current organization's/employees' readiness for implementing flexible working in the endemic phase/after COVID-19?
2. To what extent is there a need to implement a blockchain KPI system for flexible working during the endemic?
3. Does the role of Blockchain Technology help the proposed concept KPI System?
4. What are the relevant job scopes that may apply for FWA during the endemic with the help of the proposed Blockchain KPI System?
5. Is 5G can support the proposed concept system (Blockchain KPI System)?
6. How is employee performance affected by flexible working conditions?

To answer the research question, the use of results from the questionnaire finding and its data analysis from Chapter 5 will be used and the results summary is as follows.

6.3. Discussion of Findings

Research Question 1: What is the current organization's/employees' readiness for implementing flexible working in the endemic phase/after COVID-19?

COVID-19 has been an 'innovation' element for the working sector in the world. This is because it has changed the working dynamic environment. And the facts that due to back in the pandemic days, working from home has been practiced for two years. In Brunei Darussalam, the early endemic phase has been announced to end on 31st May 2022 and Brunei Darussalam entered the actual Endemic Phase on 1st June 2022. Meaning to say new normal will be started where everyone will get back to work normally and there will be a lack of work- from-home practice. In addition, with the recent announcement from World Health Organization (WHO) regarding COVID-19. On 5th May 2023, the Chief of WHO declared the end of

COVID-19 global health emergency. Hence, this showing that the world will enter new normal, and the working environment will also shift again; either applying the same concept of working during the pandemic or back to the office.

Organizations play an important role to take care of their employee's welfare. If the organization wanted to maintain a flexible working environment, organizations need a platform or a base to monitor employees whether they were working or not. Back in those pandemic days, the flexible working mode, the common type was working from home. During those times, everything was managed in 'emergency' response where the organization have to think about what to do to respond towards the change in the working environment. Most organization monitor their employees through the daily report and submitting tasks.

To answer research question 1, the first thing needs to understand the readiness was based on different perspectives sides; from the organization sides and employees' sides. From the organization's perspective, from empirical perspectives, during pandemic times, organizations may not have the option to ask their employees to work in the office as normal. But organizations have to abide by the policies that were put into implementation – due to the lockdown, organizations were advised to ask non-essential employees to work from home. This can be proven from Table 10 that during the pandemic employees were having flexible working arrangements with 74%. With lacking in terms of preparation which affects monitoring

employees working activities, would be considered a disadvantage for organizations. Organizations prefer their employees to work in the office where they can constantly monitor. In terms of answering the readiness, for the organization, the readiness, in general, was almost ready only with the condition of how to monitor employees. In addition, with the mindset of 'employees should work in the office' this could lead to resistance to change as well. furthermore, referring to Table 10, from data analysis, a statement during the endemic phase, shows only 32.7% were entitled to do flexible work during the endemic phase. This shows that the preferences from organizations were that they preferred to have employees work in the office.

To ensure the readiness for organizations to practice flexible working during the endemic, to provide an 'insurance' for the organization, what it means here was that organizations need something to ease their mind when allowing employees to work in flexible arrangements. That is why the proposed concept system (Blockchain KPI System) comes in. It helps organizations to monitor employees' work and at the same time, it has record transactions which cannot be modified or deleted. In which organization can be able to track employees working activities if in flexible working arrangements.

Blockchain technology can be integrated with a normal KPI system. Blockchain theory provides a better-decentralised system. Here it refers to employees can have access to their work outside the organization's premises. As of now, with Intranet, the system can only be accessed when employees were in the office connecting with the organization's Wi-Fi or connected to its intranet. This feature could help to increase the readiness level of the organization to implement a flexible working mode.

On the other hand, from employees' perspectives, the readiness to have flexible working arrangements was promising. Based on the statement of wanting to implement flexible working, 92% shows a positive sign that they wanted to implement it in their organization. In addition, with the support of agreeing the statement of implementing flexible working during the endemic shows 74% positive signs. The percentage itself indicates that employees were ready to have flexible working arrangements at a high level.

Furthermore, referring to sentiment analysis from Table 58, even social media shows a 54.3% positive on wanting flexible working arrangemenmt. Part of the reason was it less

commute which could save more time, at the same time reduce employees cost and most importantly it can increase employee's productivities and efficiency. Organizations wanted to see employees' performance, but flexible working also provides better job performance as well.

From a different angle, by using the proposed concept system (Blockchain KPI System) as the dependent variable, for Working from Anywhere (WFA) shows a positive relationship. The reason for this is that having the proposed concept system will definitely help the organisation to monitor and keep track of their employees. And employees were able to access and submit their work through the system as well. This same applies to Flextime (FLT) which has a positive relationship with the same reason as WFA. In addition, with the advanced network communication technologies, with the existence of 5G network, this 5G service can support the proposed concept system in terms of improving securities, efficiency, and accessible. Thus, from the results of the correlation, this can be considered as a recommendation for organizations to consider applying flexible working conditions.

In conclusion, organizations may be considered as ready to implement flexible working arrangements. The only challenge it faces was the platform to ensure its employees were working outside the office or at different times. The correlation results show that by having the proposed concept system support organizations to implement flexible working arrangements, the proposed concept system can be applied for Work from Anywhere types of flexible arrangements and Flextime as well. Employees were ready to change to flexible working arrangements starting from the organization to impose the changes. Finally, through predicting the future employee's preferences of working conditions, with the advanced rapid evolvement of technologies, flexible working arrangements show positive forecasting that employees preferred to work flexibly based on forecasting results from Table 59. Hence, it is suggested for organizations to consider and implement the changes.

Research Question 2: To what extent is there a need to implement a blockchain KPI System for flexible working conditions during the endemic?

Endemic phases have shifted back to normal from how people lived during the pandemic by disregarding the flexible work during the pandemic. During the pandemic times, there was a lot of research going on in all aspects of life which includes in human resource area as well. This is because in response to COVID-19 impacts towards the national and international levels affect people's lives and how people go to work.

According to Brunei Economic Outlook 2023 (Centre for Strategic and Policy Studies, 2023), having the high vaccination rates in Brunei Darussalam, has allowed people to transit into an endemic where Bruneian can get back to normal economic activities. Furthermore, even with the spread of the Omicron Variant, in terms of mobility restrictions were not stricken. This was due to almost 100% of Bruneians having at least two doses of COVID-19 vaccinations. In addition, the perspectives of the labour force in Brunei Darussalam show a declining rate of unemployment due to foreign workers deciding to go back to their country and when the post was vacant local people were hired. This shows a good improvement for Brunei Darussalam.

Blockchain technology elements may help the current organization's KPI system to be a better version. With its enhanced security, anti-fraudulent and its decentralization. This proposed concept system acted as a support system for the organization. From an empirical perspective, maybe organizations have more than one system for attendance, KPI monitoring and even work submission. So, by having this proposed concept system, it includes all of those modules. And the fact it offers better security.

The needs of blockchain KPI system can help the organization to monitor its employee when employees were working in flexible working conditions. Based on the data analysis, it shows 64% were working in the private sector. Having said that, in normal working conditions, an organization in the private sector also have their own KPI system that has been implemented. Moreover, the frequency analysis showed that 74% stated that their organization were having a high degree of labour intensity. What it means here is that the pacing of the work was quite high and it needs to be completed. For example, in the banking sector, employees need to handle clients' requests at a faster response because of to gain a competitive advantage. Thus, when employees were outside the premises, normally, they could not process the request unless they come to the office. On the other hand, the proposed concept system can be implemented for a trial period towards daily paid jobs for the public sector or the government.

In the employee performance that was based on flexible working condition point of view, it shows that employees were majority "Agree" in the statements that were asked in the questionnaires. It improved their attendance rate, productivity, creativity, teamwork, and ability to complete the task (refer to Table 16).

Furthermore, each organization have utilized an information system. it does not exclude the proposed concept system (Blockchain KPI System) which acts as an information system that can support the organization to improve its performance and efficiency. Table 19 shows that 86% were utilizing their organization's information system. Hence, in general, organizations actually can be considered as ready to improve their information system. This can be supported by the fact that no matter how often employees were using their organization's information system, from Table 20, it can be concluded that there were no employees were ever using the information system during working.

Moreover, based on the correlation analysis that was performed between FWA, WFA and FLT towards the proposed concept system shows an indication towards the needs of this proposed concept system when flexible working conditions were applied. Referring Table 55 to Table 57 shows that for Flexible Working Arrangements (FWA) with the proposed concept system, the results show a negative relationship with -.011. This indicates that the proposed concept system may not support the application of FWA. Hence, this cannot be finalized by stating that the Blockchain KPI System did not support the FWA because this was only based on the results that were generated statistically and the need to test the system to check the actual outcome. The second correlation between the Work from Anywhere (FWA) with the proposed concept system were showing a positive relationship, .287 was the result. This indicates that the proposed concept system can be applied in an organization as a support for employees that apply working from anywhere mode. And for the final correlation, between Flextime (FLT) with the proposed concept system, it also shows a positive correlation or positive relationship. Hence, it can be interpreted that the proposed concept system can be a support as well towards the organization that were applying for flextime working mode.

Research Question 3: Does the role of Blockchain Technology help the proposed concept KPI System?

An information system can be described as a platform that can collect data and information systems or/and can be accessed by several people for a particular purpose this information system has several features that can be applied that suit its purpose. Based on Table 19, shows that 86% use information systems. Hence, there's a belief that employees were well aware of what is information system does and what is the limit of information systems.

The proposed concept system (Blockchain KPI System) also can be considered an information system. But the proposed concept of the Blockchain KPI System has a distinctive difference from other information systems. The name of the proposed concept system itself shows the integration of the information system with Blockchain technology. Although this integration was hypothetically based, by understanding the role of blockchain technology, it can be combined or can be considered as an upgrade information system.

The role of blockchain includes decentralization, less involvement of third parties (securities issues), real-time updates, transaction validity, Cryptographical hash, smart contract, and recorded timestamp (time log).

The first role is decentralization. Based on a frequency analysis which can be referred to in Table 17 (Code: PCS9), it shows the highest response was 'Agree' with 42%. The result was based on a statement on blockchain role from the Flexible working condition point of view. Based on the results, it shows that participants/respondents agreed that flexible working mode can be done with having a decentralized system. The proposed concept system does not only focus on monitoring KPI, but it can be used for an organization's working system, hence, by having one system it can serve multiple functions. From an empirical view, an organization's information system can usually not be accessed from the outside of the organization. This is because the organization has its server and the organization's information system can only be accessed inside the organization through organization Wi-Fi access, Intranet or Internet cable connected to the organization server. This is the normal way of how information system work in the organization in which this is one of the major challenges for organizations to allow employees to work flexibly. How does this decentralisation help the proposed concept system? By changing the system from a centralized to a decentralised mode. When decentralization was initiated, employees that work flexibly can have access to the information system outside the organization.

The second role was less involved in third parties or enhancing security. Table 17 (Code: PCS10), shows 48% were 'Neutral', 36% were 'Agree' and 12% were 'Strongly Agree'. This shows that in the perspective of flexible working conditions, the participants/respondents were stating that Blockchain technology can enhance better security.

The common security problem for information systems was security breaches. Based on the research that was conducted, the highest types of system breaches were system failure or data corruption (68%). It's common to have system failure or system down or the data were corrupted. This is because the security in the system was not strong, and it can affect other functions as well. 50% were coming from viruses or malicious software. This always happens when employees received phishing emails and click the links. Once the links were clicked, viruses can be spread through employees' computers, and it is not possible if the virus can also spread the virus to the organization's information system. While 40% showed that the organization's information system was hacked, with 38% misused authorisation access and 20% were computers that involved theft and fraud.

Thus, for blockchain technology role, one of its best roles was its security. It is essential to understand the governance of blockchain technology. The governance involved public, permission or public types of blockchain. As the proposed concept system was only a prototype, hence, when the system was implemented, the system needed to be designed according to the organization's requirements whether the organization want to have open (public) or make it private or semi-private (permission) types of governance. Either way, having credentials issues with the related parties such as employees, can increase security. Furthermore, blockchain technologies were commonly used in the finance sector such as cryptocurrencies or Bitcoins. Hence, by that, security was enhanced using blockchain for organization information systems. Normally the standard procedure of security system was 84% based on individual accounts and passwords. Although the proposed concept system has the same features, the security will be more improved when the information system was integrated with blockchain technology.

The third blockchain role is real-time updates. What it means was that every transaction made in the system will show the updates in the system without delay. In Table 17 (Code: PCS11), 40% responded 'Neutral', 36% responded 'Agree' and 22% responded 'Strongly Agree'. This result of the analysis shows that participants/respondents were from Agree to Strongly Agree. It refers to that employees wanted to have real-time updates in order to get their work done.

The fourth and fifth roles were interconnected with each other which are transaction validity (Code: PCS12) and cryptographically hash (PCS13). Transaction validity is here referring to any transaction made it will validate first. Based on frequency analysis, it shows that participants/respondents were 42% 'Neutral', 36% 'Agree' and 18% 'Strongly Agree'. This indicates that for employees as long as their work was validated by the system employees were satisfied. For the Cryptographically hash role, based on frequency analysis it shows that 50% 'Neutral', 30% 'Agree' and 18% 'Strongly Agree'. This showcase that employees were also not really concerned about these functions but as long as their work was done it satisfies them. Furthermore, the function of cryptographical hash was to show that any transaction made by the 'node' was created and cannot be amended or modified. In addition, every transaction made everyone in the system able to access and view it.

The sixth role was the Smart contract. This smart contract role can be described in a simple description as a fixed configuration for the system. It does not need to request too much validation as the validation was configured at an early stage when developing the system. Based on the frequency analysis, it shows that 44% 'Neutral', 34% 'Agree' and 20% 'Strongly Agree' toward this blockchain role.

The last role was recorded timestamp. Based on the frequency analysis, it shows that participants/respondents were 38% 'Neutral', 36% 'Agree' and 24% 'Strongly Agree'. Hence, this shows that respondents acknowledge this role to be part of the proposed concept system. This is because, when implementing flexible working conditions, organizations need to know and calculate the time of entering the system and the time when they log out from the system. thus, this can be used as attendance as well and can be beneficial for organizations to monitor employees' KPIs as well.

In conclusion, based on the frequency itself alone, it indicates that participants/respondents were neutral to agree towards the implementation of the blockchain technology with the system as the roles themselves have good features that can help the proposed concept system to provide better support towards the organizations when employees were applying flexible working arrangements, work from anywhere and flextime.

Research Question 4: What are the relevant job scopes that may apply for FWA during the endemic with the help of the proposed Blockchain KPI System?

During the pandemic COVID-19, Brunei Darussalam also implemented a lockdown during both the first and second wave. Hence, the Brunei Darussalam government were encouraged to implement work from home for both the public and private sector.

Critical terms to understand when involving flexible working conditions, especially back then during the pandemic COVID-19 were the terms of essential and non-essential workers. Essential workers can be described as those workers that if they don't come to work it will affect the functions of the work society. For example, healthcare employees, delivery workers, government higher officers, constructors, and front liners for important economic sectors such as the banking sector. in contrast, non-essential workers can be described as those workers that can apply flexible working conditions because their jobs were not crucial which does not affect business operations, especially affecting health and safety elements. Examples of non-essential workers were administrators, manufacturers, retail clerks, or people that were working in the entertainment industry such as Cineplex, theme parks and others. Understanding this, portrayed that not all types of jobs or industries can apply flexible working conditions.

Understanding flexible working conditions, in simple terms, flexible work tells us that it can change working hours and working locations. And not all can apply these changes. Unless those who work in the gig economy such as freelance employees for an instant example.

Based on the data analysis that was performed, a statement was asked whether participants/respondents' job roles can be applied to the flexible working arrangement, 24% says 'No'. The major organisational sector that we are unable to apply for flexible working conditions were from Oil and Gas sector. This is understandable because the type of producing oil and gas sector manufactured was a continuous production type where the employees need to ensure the process of the manufacturing process was safe and completed. In addition, the perspectives of job roles include Officers, Supervisors, Assistants and Operators. From this, it shows that the oil and gas sector is one of the essential types of workers. Thus, in the oil and gas sector, not all employees under this sector can apply flexible working conditions. But from the empirical perspective, flextime was one of the perks given. For example, hypothetically, normal working hours were from 8 am to 5 pm. But if employees decided to enter the office at

9 am, then employees should finish at 6 pm. This was how the flextime was applied, as long as the hours of working per day were achieved, regardless of what time employees come to the office.

Another sector mentioned was the education sector. This is quite true because educators can be considered essential workers because they can affect the community as well. But the Pandemic COVID-19 shows that educators can educate their students online such as school system, and through third-party applications such as Zoom or MS Teams. This can be considered as work from anywhere (WFA).

Next, Security & Fire Industry as well as an essential sector. This type of job acts as a frontline for protecting and maintaining community security and stability. This kind of fieldwork will work flexibly as it requires standby.

On the other side, 76% of the participants/respondents were saying that their job roles were able to apply for flexible working conditions. Several types of job roles were mentioned. The majority of the answer was from the Banking sector. Several types of job positions such as managers, officers, supervisors, assistants and support staff. Moreover, the participants/respondents' answers also show the job roles as hoteliers, government employees, private hospitals, Insurance, construction workers, and transportation workers. As most of them come from stated job positions, logically, they were able to perform their work flexibly.

In conclusion, not all economic sectors can be applied for flexible working conditions. As the flexibility of working is still a subjective area of discussion and it was based on the types of jobs and the organization's working policies.

Research Question 5: Is 5G can support the proposed concept system (Blockchain KPI System)?

5G Network services were considered an innovation platform, allowing lots of technology to use the 5G services to perform the particular technologies to their potential level. Example of technology was IoT, AI and the Industrial Revolution 4.0 *IR 4.0).

Brunei Darussalam is also not excluded from having 5G Network implementation. In the current phase, the 5G Network services were in the trial phase where all telecommunication providers in Brunei have offered the people interested in trying out the 5G Network Services. The trial phase was started in mid-2022.

5G Network Services basically focuses on providing connection speed that can be utilized through cell services and Wi-Fi as well. Having a faster connection regardless of the mode, is definitely another reason why flexible working conditions may work if it is implemented. For instant example, to access the system, it provides faster login, quicker access to the tasks and quicker to submit the work to the system. Generally, from a business perspective, the business was competitive and by that means having implemented the system and with the help of 5G network services it shows how dynamic and competitive the organization were.

Based on the data analysis that was conducted, the descriptive analysis from Table 41, shows that the mean of FGS (5G Service) shows 4.0174 which indicates the participants/respondents agreed towards the 23 items that were asked.

5G Communication services were the next generation of communication services that support advanced technologies and future technologies. No matter what, 5G will still dominate the communication service in the next few years. 56% show that participants/respondents have the intention to use 5G network services once available. This can indicate that the people are ready and definitely working people automatically use 5G once it has been launched in the country. This should be the factor in measuring the readiness of the employees able to work flexibly.

As this proposed concept system requires to access the system either from a web service or perhaps in the future it can evolve into a mobile application, 5G communication service is a platform or the providers that allow access into the proposed concept system. The possibility of accessing service applications with the help of 5G network service shows 52% will want to access the service application. The reason for this perhaps it will help employees to be able to work more efficiently and productivity with the faster speed of the internet. Hence, 56% strongly agreed that with the help of this 5G network services, it can help employees to receive responses if any feedback was given from the employees. This will have happened with the help of blockchain technology through the KPI comments in the proposed concept system (Blockchain KPI System) to the employers for example and employers can provide their feedback in the system. The real-time update is part of blockchain technology and with the integration with 5G network service, it helps to get the real update once the transaction has been made without delay. This statement was strongly agreed by the respondent/participants where 58% said that using this 5G network service, it can make all business transaction process inputs swiftly. In addition, 54% strongly agreed that 5G network services allow employees to obtain information without delay. Through the proposed Blockchain KPI System, having faster internet speed, it can access the system in less than one second and retrieve all information based on the user access level without delay or lag due to the low speed of internet connectivity.

As the proposed concept system (Blockchain KPI system) were focused on providing ease for employers to track and monitor employees' work during flexible working condition regardless of whether it is a flexible working arrangement, work from anywhere or flextime, with the help from 5G network services, the system can be accessed from anywhere as long as the connectivity with the 5G network is connected, practically. The statement was supported by 46% of the participants/ respondents. Having said that, this can be a positive indicator that the 5G network can help employees to access the proposed concept system anywhere, although it's subjective to the area of the 5G network coverage. Furthermore, when the proposed concept system was implemented, and it can be accessed anywhere, it surely helps for the personal use of the employees and the business as well, which shows 52% strongly agreed with this statement. And 48% were ready to use the 5G network once it has been implemented.

The usage of the system can be supported by the 5G network. Thus, from an empirical perspective, organizations surely have their own information system as 86% of the employees have utilized their organization's information system. Thus, this high percentage shows that

employees are tech-savvy and able to use information systems. The proposed concept system can be considered a standard information system. Hence, this is nothing for the employees to learn and to cope with the system functions. 62%, of employees, have fully utilized their organization's information system and 74% of employees have experienced using their organization's information system for more than 2 years, hence, this can indicate that when the Blockchain KPI System is implemented, employees will positively utilise the system once they opted to change from the traditional way of working in the office to flexible working conditions.

In conclusion, the 5G communication services will undoubtedly help to run better the proposed concept system and support the initiatives of implementing flexible working arrangements. Moreover, the correlation analyses have shown that there was a positive relationship between the 5G communication services with the proposed concept system (Blockchain KPI System) by .532. In logical terms, technology can be integrated with another technology, hence, this factor may lead to providing the readiness of an organization to consider implementing flexible working conditions during the endemic.

Research Question 6: How is employee performance affected by flexible working conditions?

Employees are assets for any organization. This is because employees or people are the ones who run or operate the business, regardless of what type of business. Although speculation was roaming around with advanced technology of the Internet of Things (IoT), or Artificial Intelligence (AI) may change the workforce dynamic in the future. As for now, facing the phase after COVID-19 or the endemic phase. During back in pandemic time, especially during the lockdown, employees experienced work from home which can be categorized under flexible working conditions. Due to sudden work from home during the pandemic, the policies of working flexibly were not fully prepared in which there were still weaknesses in those policies, especially when monitoring employees' performance. This, with those experienced, can help to implement flexible working conditions during the endemic phase.

Employee performances were usually measured by Key Performance Indicators (KPIs). But different organizations may apply different KPIs. Thus, to understand better to measure the employee's performance for flexible working conditions during the endemic phase asked the participants/respondents for the primary research method – questionnaires. Several indicators have been asked from the perspective of flexible working conditions. Overall, the mean for employee performance was scored at 3.7025 which indicated towards Agree with all the indicators that were asked.

The first indicator relates to absenteeism. 32% of the participants/respondents mentioned 'Neutral'. This can be understandable, regardless of if it's a traditional way of working or flexible working, employee attendance is a relative subject which depends on the employee itself. From the organization side, basically to produce such policies or actions that could help to cope with high absenteeism in the organization. For flexible working conditions, with the help of the proposed Blockchain KPI System, will only provide a platform for employees to log in when they apply for flexible working. The proposed concept system will detect the log-in time and from there, the presents of employees will be counted. But with the help of organization policies, rules, and regulations, it could help to enhance better attendance and reduce absenteeism rate.

Another indicator was creativity. In the current way of quality working employees, creativity is one of the qualities that are required before hiring employees. 46% have shown 'Agree' that flexible working conditions can improve employees' creativity. When employees were applying flexible working, it can enhance work-life balance. When employees feel at ease, employees can enhance their creativity. For example, those whose jobs involve creativity quality, such as editor, photographer, or videographer. These kinds of jobs require lots of creativity, hence, that is why working according to the employee phase can improve creativity qualities. Furthermore, employee performance was based on the self-engagement theory in which self-instruction and discipline were part of the employees to perform their tasks. Logical sense, better performance, better acknowledgement and getting year-end bonuses.

Preparing the platform for employees to be able to perform work flexibly, perhaps can improve employees' commitment, which 54% shows agree towards the statement. The reason for this was the proposed concept system has a feature that can show the KPIs and results which can be viewed by other users too. Hence, from that point of view, employees tend to feel motivated to complete their work to get better performance results.

Teamwork is an essential quality that employees should possess. In a traditional working environment, employees can meet their colleagues to work together, discuss and come up with decisions for organisational purposes. Back during the pandemic COVID-19, it was rare to have better teamwork assessments due to social distancing and the need to be at home. But practising through virtual such as through video calls or virtual meetings can enhance little of teamwork. This can be done through sharing session, feedback, and suggestions, and perhaps playing games together to ensure teamwork or team chemistry are maintained. Hence 38% show a positive agreement that even flexible working conditions can also improve employees' teamwork.

The next indicator was workload. Without arguing, every job position has a different level of workload. It's a matter of individual disciplines managing their workload. Based on the sentiment analysis, from the positive feedback, by applying flexible working it can improve in managing the workload. This is because employees can assign task priorities which they can do according to their pace and as long as it is completed and on time. In addition, this can happen with the help of time management as well where they can manage their family matters from the start and can focus on work afterwards. According to the findings, 40% Agreed that

applying flexible working can improve managing workload. Furthermore, with the help of the proposed concept Blockchain KPI System, it provides an indicator of what to achieve and the work details which can be referred to as a guideline. In addition, it also can help to improve employees to attain set targets or to achieve the KPIs. By flexible working, employees can focus on priority first and the proposed concept system will mention the job tasks and what are the objectives. It was found that 42% Agree that flexible working can achieve the targets. For example, in project management, by working on the site compared to the office, employees get a better understanding of the issues and problems, which can be an advantage where the employees can settle it at that time. Thus, it can indicate that the project will run smoothly and efficiently. To support this claim, based on the findings indicate that 52% believe that flexible working can complete the tasks that have been scheduled.

In conclusion, flexible working arrangements can be applied as long as the organization know how to set the indicators to ensure the employees were working. With the support from the proposed concept system, it can help in monitoring and tracking employees' performance as well.

6.4. Findings Framework

Figure 9 below shows the framework based on the findings of this research study.

Figure 13. Findings Framework.

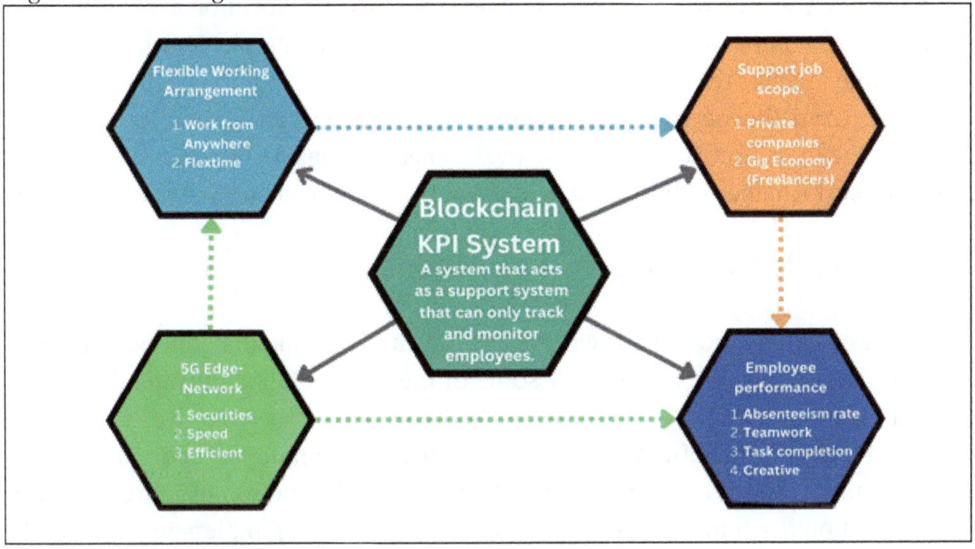

In overall, the proposed concept system (Blockchain KPI System) can support the flexible working arrangement as a whole due to it can monitor and track employee's performance if employees were applying flexible working arrangement wither work from anywhere or flextime. Moreover, the proposed concept system also can be applied by the private companies and gig economies business such as freelancers or a freelancer's start-up. Furthermore, the proposed concept system can use the employee performance indicators such as absents rate, teamwork, task completion and creativity as part of the KPI that can be implemented in the Blockchain KPI System. In addition, as people are moving towards better innovative technology advancement, the proposed concept system can utilize the existence of 5G network to ensure the system can be access at faster speed and without any delay if making any transactions.

From the perspective of 5G Edge-Network, it supports the FWA in the sense of providing a better connection speed and securities layer especially when it integrated with the Blockchain KPI System to easily accessed. Secondly, 5G Edge-Network can influence employee performance as well in terms of 5G network can provides efficient a platform for employees

working in flexible working arrangement which it influence the absenteeism rate, teamwork in collaborations work, task completion as part of employees primary KPI and creativity as well.

From the perspective of FWA, this can be applied by the private companies and as well as the gig economies work. In addition, freelancers' employees were able to enjoy the FWA work from anywhere such as from different location at project sites. As for private companies, maybe the best way is to apply flexible working – having the flextime to enter the office.

Lastly, from the perspective support the job scope can relates to employee performance indicator. Basically, here the connection was focus on identifying the employee performance indicator that need to be implement when FWA were initiated.

6.5. Implication of Study

In this research study, there will be several implications that can be extracted from this. It has positive benefits for some of the stakeholders, thus, the brief discussion follows.

The first that can benefit from this research study was employers or organizations. Basically, the proposed concept system (Blockchain KPI System) can help employees or organizations to monitor and track their employees during implementing flexible working policies which include Flexible Working Arrangements, Work from Anywhere or Flextime. How this can benefit organizations through blockchain technology – blockchain role as being stated in this chapter to answer research question 3 (RQ3). Organizations or employers will gain more benefits in terms of productivity and efficiency because when employees work in flexible working conditions, they can focus more to complete their tasks according to the pace as convenience were perks of flexible working conditions.

Secondly, positive implications towards employees. Employees were able to perform flexible working conditions by having the proposed concept system which provides and privileged to allow employees to work where they are comfortable as long their work can be completed. Not just focus on the perspective of doing the job, but it can provide employees with work-life balance as well. This can be proven from the sentiment analysis that was conducted, which shows that social media users were able to perform 'house duties' while they can complete the work from home, for instant example. Employees can save money because flexible working conditions can reduce the cost of commuting and time savings as well. For example, if employees were given flexible time, employees can be managed to settle their family matters first and can come to work with 100% focus. While for work from anywhere, employees can work while they are outstation for a short vacation to settle the important work. Moreover, for flexible working arrangements, perhaps the better example of that was Google. The employees can work anywhere in the building and not stick to their tables. They can work in the cafeteria, common room or anywhere inside the building. From the perspective of the proposed concept system, employees will feel secure with having the proposed concept system implemented. Because it can monitor their work and attendance, as these are both considered the critical or the primary way of measuring employees' KPI. When referring to KPI, relates to employees' annual performance and bonuses. Having the Blockchain KPI system implemented, can protect employees because the proof of working will be stored in the system. Furthermore,

decentralization of the proposed concept system allowed organizations to issue flexible working conditions and for employees to work flexibly.

Finally, positive implications towards economic standpoints. Understanding the work dynamic is crucial. At the current point, in the labour market, generation Z has started to penetrate. Understanding Generation Z is a crucial point because organizations need to understand the generation gaps as well. Most of Generation Z were tech-savvies and always try innovative things and challenged themselves. Through implementing flexible working conditions, generation Z can adapt quickly and perhaps increase the organization's productivity and efficiency which can lead to organization expansion and create more jobs towards local people. The unemployment rate can be less, and it helps the nation's economy to flourish. Moreover, the current working environment as well inclusive of gig economy types of work. For instant example type of gig economy job was freelance. Basically, freelancers can work anytime at any location prior to the employer's request. Moreover, by encouraging youth to open up a start-up business that can be done remotely, hende, hire employees that can work according to their paces and from any location as well.

On the negative side, the organization may need to test the proposed concept system to ensure its effectiveness. In addition, the resistance to change will be part of the negative implication which could lead to not having flexible working conditions to be implemented. Finally, not all jobs can apply flexible working conditions. This can impact the organization worse and perhaps could lead to protests because of unfairness. Especially having essential and non-essential workers in the same organization who can and cannot be entitled to flexible working conditions, including flexible working arrangements, working from any location or even flextime.

6.6. Limitations

Several limitations were encountered during performing this research study. Firstly, it's quite difficult to find journal articles that are related to the research topics. Especially, that are directed relations in between flexible working arrangements, work from anywhere and flextime to the proposed concept system – Blockchain KPI System. Secondly, to get a minimum of 100 participants to participate in the research survey. Due to the target scope being the working population, it is quite hard for the potential participants to answer the survey because of their working situations. Furthermore, time constraints to conduct the research were quite limited. The proposed concept system was designed and developed during the undergraduate period and reused for this research study. Due to a lack of time and skills, the proposed concept system will be the same.

6.7. Future Research Suggestions

The working environment may change in the future. Traditional ways of working will be started to shift into something else like flexible working conditions. This was proven during the Pandemic COVID-19 when everything changed so fast and the traditional way of doing things also disappear slowly. Moreover, KPIs may be changed into a different way of measuring employee performance. These changes can be supported by the evolution of technologies. Blockchain technology may be new at this period, but new technology discoveries may be forecast in the next few years. For example, the evolution of quantum technology. Furthermore, generation Z will take over the working environment. Thus, future research suggestions can focus on finding the type of jobs and sectors that can implement flexible working conditions. With advanced technology, it will help to monitor employees' KPIs when flexible working conditions are implemented. Finally, does Generation Z want to have flexible working conditions while monitored by the KPI system? Anything that makes an organization adapt to a certain period of time in the future, requires research as early as possible to ensure organization readiness towards the impacts of future dynamic changes towards the organization as a whole. The current opportunities that can be grasp is for a start-up that have business remotely which can hire employees and work from any location, this can be a good movement for coping with unemployment rate and to ensure that new generation will not depends on government.

6.8. Conclusion

The conclusion in this chapter, all the research questions were managed to be answered. As for research question one, the readiness was there and only required the steps from the organization to improve their working policies and implement flexible working conditions. For research question two, the extent of the need to implement a blockchain KPI system can be considered as a support system that help the organization to monitor and track employees working performance when flexible working conditions were applied. The third research question shows that all blockchain technology roles that were integrated into the proposed concept system were considered to help the system without any major disagreement towards the proposed concept system as a whole. Fourth research question shows that not all job types or every organization sector can apply for flexible working conditions. But it shows a high percentage that most of it can apply for flexible working conditions. The fifth research question focus on the 5G Network Edge. Without doubts, the 5G communication services will help to run better the proposed concept system and support the initiatives of implementing flexible working arrangements. Finally, the sixth research questions, flexible working arrangements can be applied as long as the organization know how to set the indicators to ensure the employees were working.

Based on the discussion, the implication of this research study has been explained in the perspectives of positive and negative points of view that affect organizations, employees, and the economy. With that, future research suggestions have been stated in this chapter.

7. CONCLUSION

The whole world has entered a new normal condition where the Pandemic COVID-19 has been passed to new chapters of all people, which is called as Endemic phase. During the pandemic COVID-19, flexible working arrangements were utilized in order to cater for the country's lockdown, especially working from home. As work from home was initiated, some people may be comfortable with it, and some are not. Based on those statements, the primary objective of this research study was to embrace KPI performance using blockchain technology for flexible working arrangements during the endemic, especially in Brunei Darussalam.

The dependent variables which were the proposed concept system (Blockchain KPI System) have been tested with three independent variables that were related to flexible working conditions. The Pearson correlation shows a positive relationship between the proposed concept system with work from anywhere, flextime and 5G Services with the proposed concept system has a good positive relationship. With the support from the primary questionnaires, it shows that respondents were 'Neutral' to 'Agree' towards the proposed concept system. Hence, it can be said that the proposed concept system was accepted by the participants/respondents.

To conclude, the needs to implement flexible working arrangements were still a subjective matter where it requires the organization's capacities to implement it. Hence, the proposed concept system will only act as a support system to monitor and track employees working performance if flexible working arrangements were applied. Furthermore, through the entering endemic phase, it slowly shifts back to the normal way of working, but the organization should learn what happens during the pandemic period as a preparation for future challenges.

APPENDIX

Items of Questionnaires

Flexibility in work arrangements is the first independent variable. The items are as follows, and it is measured in accordance with measurements made by Albion (2005):

Table 54. FWA independent variables lists of questions.

Code	Items
FWA1 (R)	I cannot afford the loss of pay associated with the most flexible work options. (R)
FWA2 (R)	Flexible work options do not suit me because they tend to make me feel disconnected from the workplace. (R)
FWA3 (R)	Working shorter hours would negatively impact my career progress within the organisations. (R)
FWA4	Working more flexible hours is essential for me in order to attend to family responsibilities.
FWA5	Flexible working arrangements are essential for me in order to participate in family and social events.
FWA6	Flexible working arrangements enable me to focus more on the job when I am at the workplace
FWA7 (R)	People at my workplace react negatively to people using flexible working arrangements. (R)
FWA8 (R)	People using flexible working arrangements usually have less commitment to their work roles. (R)
FWA9 (R)	People using flexible working arrangements often miss important work events or communications, such as staff meetings, training sessions, important notices, etc. (R)
FWA10	I would not be able to do paid work at all if I could not use flexible work arrangements.

Work from Anywhere is the second independent variable. The items are as follows, and it is measured in accordance with measurements made by (Narayanamurthy & Tortorella, 2021):

Table 55. WFA independent variables lists of questions.

Code	Items
WFA1	I have more frequently used websites to communicate with my suppliers, customers and/or team members.
WFA2	My work environment is neat and organized.
WFA3	My work environment allows presents the necessary infrastructure to support activities.
WFA4	My work environment allows me to properly concentrate and focus on my daily duties.
WFA5	My work environment allows me to have a flexible routine (i.e., flexible hours).

Flexible working hours or Flextime is the third independent variable. The items are as follows, and it is measured in accordance with measurements made by (Mwebi & Kadaga, 2015):

Table 56. Flextime independent variables lists of questions.

Code	Items
FLT1	Jobs allows to change working hours
FLT2	Flextime has off duty
FLT3	Flextime coordinated and supervised
FLT4	Flextime allows early work completion
FLT5	Flextime reduced settlings-in time wastage
FLT6	Flextime allows covering colleagues
FLT7	Flextime allows late sign-ins
FLT8	Flextime improves duty attendance

For section four, on employee performance, the items are as follows, and it is measured in accordance with measurements made by (Mwebi & Kadaga, 2015):

Table 57. Employee performance lists of questions.

Code	Items
EMP1	Employee abseentism reduced.
EMP2	Employee improved creativity.
EMP3	Employee work commitment enhanced.
EMP4	Employee improved teamwork.
EMP5	Employee improved customer service level.
EMP6	Employee improved workload management.
EMP7	Employee able to attain set targets.
EMP8	Employee able to complete schedule tasks.

The proposed concept system – Blockchain KPI system is the dependent variable. The items are as follows, and it is measured in accordance with measurements towards employee performance and employees' blockchain knowledge. In addition, few questions were coming from the author. Thus, this set of questions needs to be conducted a factor analysis and Cronbach Alpha analysis for reliability.

Table 58. Proposed Concept System dependent variables lists of questions.

Code	Items
PCS1	I am aware that I need to achieve my target to get entitled to year-end bonuses.
PCS2	I do have a KPI system implemented in my organization.
PCS3	I am aware that having a KPI system can help me track my yearly bonuses.
PCS4	I do know what Blockchain Technology is.
PCS5	I see the releveance to implement the proposed concept system in my organization.
PCS6	I see the relevance to implement the proposed concept system in my organization during this endemic period.
PCS7	I see the relevance to implement the proposed concept system in my organization even in more Covid-19.
PCS8	I agree that the proposed concept system should be implemented in my organizations.
PCS9	I agree that BC roles (decentralized system) can help in supporting the proposed concept KPI System.
PCS10	I agree that BC roles (less involvement of third parties) can help in supporting the proposed concept KPI System.
PCS11	I agree that BC roles (real-time updates) can help in supporting in the proposed concept KPI System.
PCS12	I agree that BC roles (transaction validity) can help in supporting in the proposed concept KPI System.

continued on following page

Table 58. Continued

Code	Items
PCS13	I agree that BC roles (cryptographical hash – immutability of data) can help in supporting in the proposed concept KPI System.
PCS14	I agree that BC roles (smart contract) can help in supporting in the proposed concept KPI System.
PCS15	I agree that BC roles (recorded the time-stamped) can help in supporting in the proposed concept KPI System

Next section will be asking on participant perception towards 5G communication services.

Table 59. 5G Communication Services lists of questions.

Code	Items
5GS1	If the 5G services available, I have the intention to use it.
5GS2	I intend to use 5G for my daily use in the future.
5GS3	I will use 5G in the future to access services and applications.
5GS4	I expect my use of 5G to continue in the future.
5GS5	In general, it will be risky to give confidential information using 5G network.
5GS6	5G will allow unauthorized third-party access to my mobile phone.
5GS7	There will be too much uncertainty associated with giving information using 5G network.
5GS8	I am concerned that 5G will raise some general privacy issues.
5GS9	In using 5G, it will provide fast response to my feedback.
5GS10	In using 5G, it will process my input swiftly.
5GS111	5G communication service will allow me to obtain information without being delayed.
5GS12	With 5G communication services, I will always keep up with the world.
5GS13	5G communication services will allow me to access information at the best moment for me.
5GS14	5G communication services will be practical because I can use them without difficulty wherever I am.
5GS15	Using 5G communication services will help me to reach my target information regardless of where it comes from.
5GS16	People who influence my behaviour will think that I should use 5G communication services.
5GS17	People who are important to me will support me to use 5G communication services.
5GS18	People whose views I respect support the use of 5G communication services.
5GS19	Using 5G communication services is a good idea for my personal use / study / work / businesses.
5GS20	The idea of adopting 5G communication services is appealing to me.

continued on following page

Table 59. Continued

Code	Items
5GS21	I would feel positive towards adopting 5G communication services.
5GS22	Working with/using 5G communication services will be fun/interesting.
5GS23	I look forward to those aspect of my life that require me to make full use 5G communication services.

The next section will be asking about information technology 5G related awareness.

Table 60.

List of questions	Remarks
Does your department/activity utilize the organization information technology?	Yes or No.
How often does your department/activity utilize the information technology?	Always, often, once in a while or never.
How often does the IT or any related people review the Management's information technology?	Often (once every month), daily, hourly or others.
How long have your organization been using the information technology? i.e. How long have this system been implemented?	Less than 6 months, 6 months to 1 year, 1- 2 years or 2 years and more.
Do you have the right (authorization) access the documents in the information technology?	Yes or No.
Has your organization encountered any form of information security breaches? (You may choose more than one).	System failure/data corruption, Infection by viruses or malicious software, Theft or fraud involving computers, Attack by an authorized outsider/ system hacked or Misused of authorization access.
Does your organization outsource to external providers for information security system?	Yes or No.
What kind of information technology training does your organization provide you with?	Information system basics, Management and implementation training in information system, Application information management / life cycle management, Risk management, and contingency planning or none of the above.
What is the standard procedure followed for information security system in your respective organization/ department? (You may choose more than once).	Firewall, Anti-virus, formal written information security policy documented, Implement AAA (Authentication, Authorization, Accounting) for all users, or Accounts and password individually.
What are the measures taken to mitigate information security system breach?	Restrict access to the internet at work, Block access to inappropriate websites, Block access to social networking sites or Monitor websites / socials through logs.

continued on following page

Table 60. Continued

List of questions	Remarks
How does your organization react to issues related to information security system such as security breach, information leakage and etc?	Improvement on information security policies, More investment on information security system or Training on information security system.
What are the business processes that are involved by using the information system? (You may choose more than one).	Corporate website, Corporate email, Payment processing, Payroll processing, Sales and/or marketing, Customer transaction processing, Finance and accounting, Office tools (e.g. Word processing) or Data storage.

The next section will be asking about participant attitudes towards 5G information security systems.

Table 61.

List of questions	Remarks
Does your company assign Authentication ID or access card for employees to track from any unauthorized access?	Yes or No.
If No, how are unauthorized access are detected?	Role-based access into systems, Surveillance camera, Biometrics or Others with specify.
Does your company use any Remote Access Network servers?	Yes or No.
What type of remote servers does your organization implement?	Virtual Private Network (VPN), Dial-Up, Wi-Fi, or Other with specify.
Which global security standards does your organization adhere to?	ISO, COBIT, Sarbones – Oxley or Other with specify.
What database technologies does your company apply?	Oracle, PeopleSoft, Microsoft SQL, or Other with specify.
Please state brief reason for choices(s) of database technology:	User-friendly configuration and architecture, Cost-saving, Global recognition and awards or Others with specify.
What are the kinds of security issues faced in recent years? (Please tick wherever appropriate, you can tick more than once).	System failure or data corruption, Infection by viruses and malicious software, Theft or fraud of computers, Theft or stolen information, Attacks by an unauthorized outsider or Others with specify
What are the types of staff-related incidents that have occurred in recent years?	Misuse of web access, Misuse of email access, Unauthorized access to systems or data (e.g., using someone else's ID), Misuse of confidential information, loss or leakage of confidential information or Other with specify
How often does your organization update its anti-virus software?	Once a year, Once in six months or Once a month

For the final section, on demographics, the items are as follows, and it is measured in accordance with measurements made by (Ray & Pana-Cryan, 2021):

Table 62.

List of questions	Remarks			
Genders	Male or Female			
Respondents' roles	Supervisor, Director	Coordinator,	Manager	or
Organization Experience	<5 years or >5 years			
Organization size	<5,000 employees or >5,000 employees			
Orgniaztions ownership	Public or Private			
Organizations sector	Open questions or possible limited list of few sectors			
Organization degree of interaction and customization	Low or high			
Orgnization degree of labour intensity	Low or high			
Organization type	Transnational or national			

Adding more questionnaires for the demographics section that was orchestrated by the author:

Table 63.

List of questions	Remarks
Are your roles can apply to FWA?	Yes or No.
IF answer above no, provide reason why.	Open-ended answer.
Do you want to have FWA implemented?	Yes or No.
During pandemic time, do you entitle to FWA?	Yes or No.
Do you agree that FWA should be implemented during endemic?	Yes or No.

To further investigation, subjective questionnaires will be asked and the list is below:

List of Questions

What are the respondent's suggestions towards the proposed concept KPI System? Any suggestions.

Figure 14. Login Page for the user

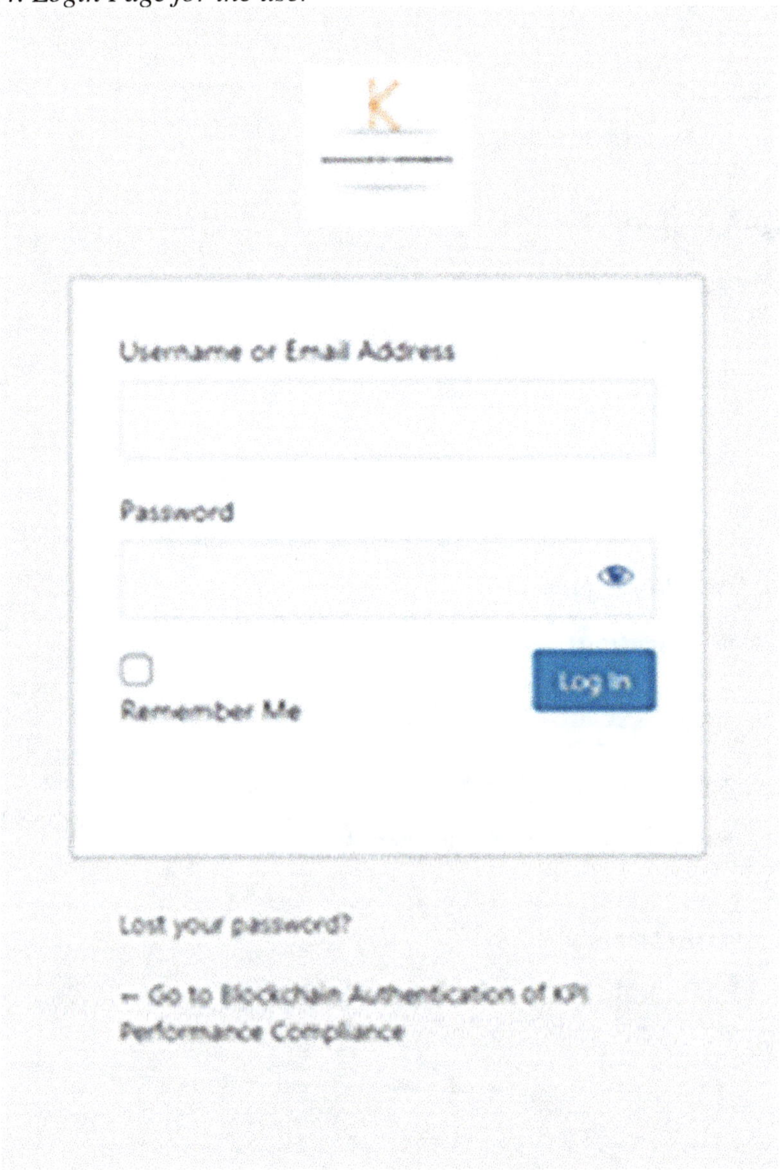

Figure 15. Dashboard Page

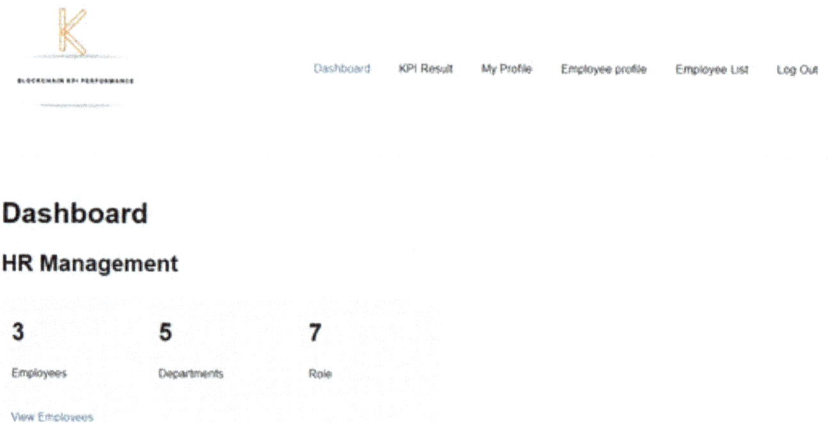

Figure 16. User Profile Page

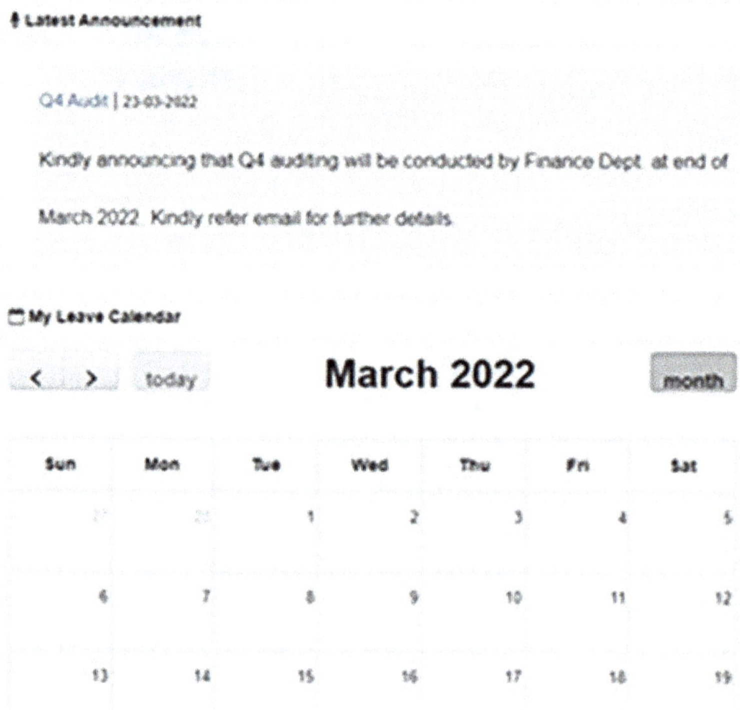

Figure 17. Employee List Page

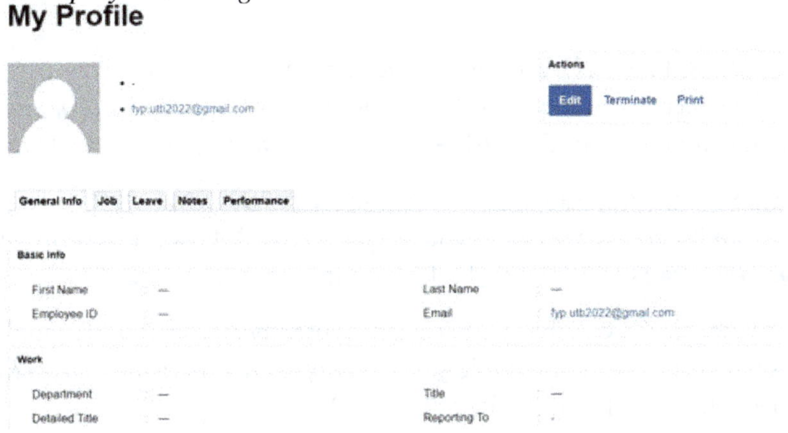

REFERENCES

Abdullah, N., Rahmat, N., Zawawi, F., Khamsah, M., & Anuarsham, A. (2020). Coping with post covid-19: can work from home be a new norm? *European Journal of Social Sciences Studies, 5*(6), 61-81. DOI: 10.46827/ejsss.v5i6.933

Aczel, B., Kovacs, M., Lippe, T., & Szaszi, B. (2021, March 25). Researchers working from home: Benefits and challenges. (T. U. Johnson Chun-Sing Cheung, Ed.) *Plos One, 16*(3), 1-13. DOI: 10.1371/journal.pone.0249127

Agba, A., Ocheni, S., & Agba, M. S. (2020, September). COVID-19 and the World of Work Dynamics: A Critical Review. *Journal of Educational and Social Research, 10*(5), 119-130. DOI: 10.36941/jesr-2020-0093

Aguinis, H., & Burgi-Tian, J. (2021). Measuring performance during crises and beyond: The Performance Promoter Score. *Business Horizons, 64*(1), 149–160. DOI: 10.1016/j.bushor.2020.09.001

Alam, S., Shuaib, M., Khan, W. Z., Garg, S., Kaddoum, G., Hossain, M., & Zikria, Y. B. (2021). Blockchain-based Initiatives: Current state and challenges. *Computer Networks, 198*, 1–20. DOI: 10.1016/j.comnet.2021.108395

Albion, M. (2005). A Measure of Attitudes Towards Flexible Work Options. *Australian Journal of Management, 29*(2), 275–294. DOI: 10.1177/031289620402900207

AlRababah, A., AlShahrani, A., & Al-Kasasbeh, B. (2016). Efficiency Model of Information Systems as an Implementation of Key Performance Indicators. *International Journal of Computer Science and Network Security, 16*(12), 139-143. Retrieved from https://www.researchgate.net/publication/316689258_Efficiency_Model_of_Information_Systems_as_an_Implementation_of_Key_Performance_Indicators

Antia, R., & Halloran, M. (2021). Transition to endemicity: Understanding COVID-19. *A Cell Press Journal, 54*(10), 2172-2176. DOI: 10.1016/j.immuni.2021.09.019

Arso, S. S., Sfenrianto, S., & Wahyudi, M. (2018). Employee Performance Measurement in Teleworking Using Balanced Scorecard. *International Journal of Electrical and Computer Engineering, 8*(6), 5178–5184. DOI: 10.11591/ijece.v8i6.pp5178-5184

Asih, L., Purba, H., & Sitorus, T. (2020). Key Performance Indicators: A Systematic Literature Review. *Journal of Strategy and Performance Management, 8*(4), 142–155. https://www.researchgate.net/publication/344493860_KEY_PERFORMANCE_INDICATORS_A_SYSTEMATIC_LITERATURE_REVIEW

Austin-Egole, Ifeyinwa, S., Iheriohanma, E.B.J, Chinedu, & Nwokorie. (2020). Flexible Working Arrangments and Organizational Performance: An Overview. *IOSR Journal Of Humanities And Social Science (IOSR-JHSS), 25*, 50-59. DOI:DOI: 10.9790/0837- 2505065059

Badawy, M., Abd El-Aziz, A. A., Idress, A., Hefny, H., & Hossam, S. (2016). A survey on exploring key performance indicators. *Future Computing and Informatics Journal, 1*(1-2), 47–52. DOI: 10.1016/j.fcij.2016.04.001

Bala, A., & Koxhaj, P. (2017). Key Performance Indicators (KPIs) in the Change Management of Public Administration. *European Scientific Journal, 13*(4), 278–283. DOI: 10.19044/esj.2017.v13n4p278

Barbour, N., Menon, N., & Mannering, F. (2021). A statistical assessment of work-from-home participation during different stages of the COVID-19 pandemic. *Transportation Research Interdisciplinary Perspectives, 11*, 1–9. DOI: 10.1016/j.trip.2021.100441

Bhatti, M., Awan, H., & Razaq, Z. (2014). 11). The key performance indicators (KPIs) and their impact on overall organizational performance. *Quality & Quantity*, •••, 48. DOI:10.1007/s11135-013-9945-y

Bienstock, J., LaPerla, J., & Seaman, C. (2020). The Flexible Work Arrangements in a Post Covid-19 Universe. *Review of Business Research, 20*(2), 41–52. Advance online publication. DOI: 10.18374/RBR-20-2.4

Boell, S., & Cecez-Kecmanovic, D. (2015). What is an Information System? *48th Hawaii International Conference on System Sciences*, (pp. 4959-4968). DOI: 10.1109/HICSS.2015.587

Borneo Bulletin. (2022, May 24). *Early Endemic Phase ends May 31*. Retrieved December 26, 2022 from Borneo Bulletin: https://borneobulletin.com.bn/early-endemic-phase-ends- may-31/

BruCERT. (2021). *BruCERT Survey on Studying/Working From Home 2021*. From https://csb.gov.bn/sites/default/files/pdf/2021_WFH_Survey_Report.pdf

Casino, F., Dasaklis, T., & Patsakis, C. (2019). A systematic literature review of blockchain- based applications: Current status, classification and open issues. *Telematics and Informatics, 36*, 55–81. DOI: 10.1016/j.tele.2018.11.006

Castrillon, C. (2022, March 23). *Why Flexible Work Boosts Employee Productivity*. Retrieved October 31, 2022 from Forbes: https://www.forbes.com/sites/carolinecastrillon/2022/03/23/why-flexible-work- boosts-employee-productivity/?sh=585736f06e4b

CB INSIGHTS. (2022, March 9). *2370 Banking is only the beginning: 65 big industries blockchain could transform*. Retrieved December 1, 2022 from CB INSIGHTS: https://www.cbinsights.com/research/industries-disrupted-blockchain/

CEGAL. (n.d.). *Data Crawling*. Retrieved January 6, 2023 from CEGAL: https://www.cegal.com/en/dictionary/datacrawling

Centre for Strategic and Policy Studies. (2023). *Brunei Economic Outlook 2023*. Centre for Strategic and Policy Studies.

Charles, L., Xia, S., & Coutts, A. (2022). *Digitalization and Employment*. International Labour Orgniazation. Retrieved from: https://www.ilo.org/wcmsp5/groups/public/--- ed_emp/documents/publication/wcms_854353.pdf

Chen, H. (2020). *Using Blockchain for improving communication efficiency and cooperation: the case of port logistics*. Degree of Master Thesis, Faculty of Computing, Blekinge Institute of Technology, 371 79 Karlskrona, Sweden. Retrieved from https://www.diva- portal.org/smash/get/diva2:1412835/FULLTEXT02

Cherukupally, S. (2021). Chapter 3 Blockchain technology: Theory and practice. (Arni S.R, Srinivasa Rao, & C.R. Rao, Eds.) *Handbook of Statistics, 44*, 75-103. https://doi.org/DOI: 10.1016/bs.host.2020.10.001

Chillakuri, B., & Attili, V. (2021). Role of blockchain in HR's response to new-normal. *The International Journal of Organizational Analysis*, •••, 1–21. DOI: 10.1108/IJOA-08-2020-2363

Chung, H., Seo, H., Forbes, S., & Birkett, H. (2020). *Working from home during the covid-19 lockdown: Changing preferences and the future of work*. Retrieved from https://kar.kent.ac.uk/83896/

Ciotti, M., Ciccozzi, M., Terrinoni, A., Jiang, W.-C., Wang, C.-B., & Bernardini, S. (2020). The COVID-19 pandemic. *Critical Reviews in Clinical Laboratory Sciences*, *57*(6), 365–388. DOI: 10.1080/10408363.2020.1783198

Collins dictionary. (n.d.). *Definition of 'flextime'*. Retrieved October 14, 2022 from Collins dictionary: https://www.collinsdictionary.com/dictionary/english/flextime

Cranfield University, School of Management. (2008). *Flexible Working adn Performance*. Retrieved from https://www.workingfamilies.org.uk/wp- content/uploads/2014/09/Flexible-Working-Performance-2008.pdf

Davidescu, A. A., Apostu, S.-A., Paul, A., & Casuneanu, I. (2020). Work Flexibility, Job Satisfaction, and Job Performance among Romanian Employees— Implications for Sustainable Human Resource Management. *Sustainability (Basel), 12*(15), 1–53. DOI: 10.3390/su12156086

Davis, F., & Venkatesh, V. (2004, February). Toward Preprototype User Acceptance Testing of New Information Systems: Implications for Software Project Management. *IEEE Transactions on Engineering Management, 51*(1), 31–46. DOI: 10.1109/TEM.2003.822468

De, R., Pandey, N., & Pal, A. (2020, June 9). Impact of digital surge during Covid-19 pandemic: A viewpoint on research T and practice. *International Journal of Information Management, 1-5*, 102171. Advance online publication. DOI: 10.1016/j.ijinfomgt.2020.102171

Eliaçık, E. (2022, May 17). *What is the role of blockchain in the world today?* Retrieved December 17, 2022 from DATACONOMY: https://dataconomy.com/2022/05/blockchain-use-cases-2022/

Faisal, F. (2021, October 26). *Framework to shift from pandemic to endemic state.* Retrieved December 21, 2022 from Borneo Bulletin: https://borneobulletin.com.bn/framework- to-shift-from-pandemic-to-endemic-state/

Gad, A., Mosa, D., Abualigah, L., & Abohany, A. (2022). Emerging Trends in Blockchain Technology and Applications: A Review and Outlook. *Journal of King Saud University. Computer and Information Sciences, 34*(9), 6719–6742. DOI: 10.1016/j.jksuci.2022.03.007

Galanti, T., Guidetti, G., Mazzei, E., Zappala', S., & Toscano, F. (2021). Work From Home During the COVID-19 Outbreak: The Impact on Employees' Remote Work Productivity, Engagement, and Stress. *Journal of Occupational and Environmental Medicine, 63*(7), e426–e432. DOI: 10.1097/JOM.0000000000002236

Gerrardo, B. A., Harjoko, A., & Lo, N.-W. (2022, April). On the Design of a Blockchain-based Fraud-prevention Performance Appraisal System. *Indonesian Journal of Computing and Cybernetics Systems, 16*(2), 137–148. DOI: 10.22146/ijccs.67669

Ghasemi, A., & Zahediasl, S. (2012). Normality Tests for Statistical Analysis: A Guide for Non-Statisticians. *International Journal of Endocrinology and Metabolism, 10*(2), 486–489. DOI: 10.5812/ijem.3505

Gifford, J. (2022). Remote working: Unprecedented increase and a developing research agenda. *Human Resource Development International*, *25*(2), 105–113. DOI: 10.1080/13678868.2022.2049108

Gilbert, N. (2022, November 5). *51 Critical Blockchain Statistics: 2022 Data Analysis & Market Share*. Retrieved December 1, 2022 from Finances Online: Reviews for Busisness: https://financesonline.com/blockchain-statistics/

Green, N., Tappin, D., & Bentley, T. (2020). Working from home before, during and after the Covid-19 pandemic: Implications for workers and organisations. *New Zealand Journal of Employment Relations*, *45*(2), 5–16. DOI: 10.24135/nzjer.v45i2.19

Grimmer, L. (2022). Lessons from the COVID19 pandemic: The case of retail and consumer service firms. *Journal of Retailing and Consumer Services*, *68*, 1–11. DOI: 10.1016/j.jretconser.2022.103012

Hadfield, A. (2022). From pandemic to endemic? Learning lessons from global contagion. *Journal of Chinese Economic and Business Studies*, *20*(3), 225–233. DOI: 10.1080/14765284.2021.2024486

Hamouche, S. (2021). Human resource management and the COVID-19 crisis: Implications, challenges, opportunities, and the future organizational directions. *Journal of Management & Organization*, •••, 1–16. DOI: 10.1017/jmo.2021.15

Han, S. (2021, August 10). *COVID-19: Gov't issues guidelines on working from home*. Retrieved December 21, 2022 from The Scoop: https://thescoop.co/2021/08/10/covid- 19-govt-issues-guidelines-on-working-from-home/

Han, S. (2021, October 21). *COVID-19: Brunei unveils lockdown exit plan*. Retrieved December 26, 2022 from The Scoop: https://thescoop.co/2021/10/26/covid-19-brunei- unveils-lockdown-exit-plan/

Haramis, G. E. (1996). Information systems requirements definition: rules and guidelines. *IFAC Proceedings, 29*(2), 113-118. DOI: 10.1016/S1474-6670(17)43787-6

Hart, M. (2019, July 26). *What Does WFH Mean? A Quick Guide*. Retrieved September 9, 2022 from Owl Labs: https://resources.owllabs.com/blog/wfh-meaning

Hasan, F. F. (2018). A Review Study of Information Systems. *International Journal of Computer Applications*, *179*(8), 15–19. DOI: 10.5120/ijca2018916307

Hayat, M. (2021, January 07). *Most Read of 2020: Brunei Darussalam: An Unexpected COVID-19 Success Story*. Retrieved December 21, 2022 from Australian Outlook: https://www.internationalaffairs.org.au/australianoutlook/brunei-darussalam-an - unexpected-covid-19-success-story/

Hong, Z.-Q., Susanto, H., & Leu, Z.-Q. (2022). A Q-Learning Based Downlink Scheduling Algorithm for Multiple Traffics in 5G NR Systems. *In Innovative Mobile and Internet Services in Ubiquitous Computing: Proceedings of the 15th International Conference on Innovative Mobile and Internet Services in Ubiquitous Computing (IMIS-2021)* (pp. 393-402). Springer International Publishing. https://doi.org/DOI: 10.1007/978-3-030-79728-7_39

IBM. (n.d.). *What is blockchain technology?* Retrieved October 11, 2022 from IBM: https://www.ibm.com/topics/what-is-blockchain

Insider Intelligence. (2022, April 15). *The growing list of applications and use cases of blockchain technology in business and life Share on social.* Retrieved October 14, 2022 from Insider Intelligence: https://www.insiderintelligence.com/insights/blockchain-technology-applications-use- cases/

Jain, G., & Jain, A. (2022). Blockchain for 5G-enabled networks in healthcare service based on several aspects. *Blockchain Applications for Healthcare Informatics*, 471-493. DOI: 10.1016/B978-0-323-90615-9.00018-9

Jamaluddin, S. Z., Taher, M., & Yi, N. S. (2019). Key performance indicators and employment contracts in Malaysia: a legal analysis. *IIUM Law Journal, 27*(2), 549-569. https://doi.org/10.31436/iiumlj.v27i2.430

Javaid, M., Haleem, A., Singh, R. P., Khan, S., & Suman, R. (2021). Blockchain technology applications for Industry 4.0: A literature-based review. *Blockchain: Research and Application, 2*(4), 1–11. DOI: 10.1016/j.bcra.2021.100027

Jian, Y. C., Chung, M. S., Susanto, H., & Leu, F. Y. (2022, June). 5G Base Station Scheduling. In Innovative Mobile and Internet Services in Ubiquitous Computing: Proceedings of the 16th International Conference on Innovative Mobile and Internet Services in Ubiquitous Computing (IMIS-2022) (pp. 315-324). Cham: Springer International Publishing.

John, W. (2017). Flexible Working Hours and Organizational Productivity: Exploring the Potential Linkage. *AIMA Journal of Management & Research, 11*(4), 1-7. Retrieved from https://apps.aima.in/ejournal_new/articlesPDF/waseem-john.pdf

Johnson, R., & Gueutal, H. (2011). *Transforming HR Through Technology - SHRM.* Retrieved December 2, 2022 from SHRM: https://www.shrm.org/hr-today/trends -and- forecasting/special-reports-and-expert-views/documents/hr-technology.pdf

Justinia, T. (2019). Blockchain Technologies: Opportunities for Solving Real-World Problems in Healthcare and Biomedical Sciences. *Acta Informatica Medica, 27*(4), 284–291. DOI: 10.5455/aim.2019.27.284-291

Kalischko, T., & Riedl, R. (2021). Electronic Performance Monitoring in the Digital Workplace: Conceptualization, Review of Effects and Moderators, and Future Research Opportunities. *Frontiers in Psychology, 12*, 633031. Advance online publication. DOI: 10.3389/fpsyg.2021.633031

Kitagawa, R., Kuroda, S., Okudaira, H., & Owan, H. (2021). Working from home and productivity under the COVID-19 pandemic: Using survey data of four manufacturing firms. *PLoS ONE, 16*(12), 1-24. https://doi.org/. pone.0261761DOI: 10.1371/journal

Klindžić, M., & Marić, M. (2019). Flexible Work Arrangements and Organizational Performance – The Difference between Employee and Employer-Driven Practices. *Društvena istraživanja, 28*(1), 89-108. https://doi.org/DOI: 10.5559/di.28.1.05

Kombe, C., Ally, M., & Sam, A. (2018). A review on healthcare information systems and consensus protocols in blockchain technology. *International Journal of Advanced Technology and Engineering Exploration, 5*(49), 473–483. DOI: 10.19101/IJATEE.2018.547023

Laurence, T. (2017). *Blockchain For Dummies*. John Wiley & Sons, Inc.

Leible, S., Schlager, S., Schubotz, M., & Gipp, B. (2019). A Review on Blockchain Technology and Blockchain Projects Fostering Open Science. *Front. Blockchain, 2*(16), 1–28. DOI: 10.3389/fbloc.2019.00016

Leu, F.-Y., Susanto, H., Chou, P.-H., & Lin, J.-W. (2019). Migration of Edge Computing Services in 5G Networks–Firewall as a Service Example. *In Advances on Broadband and Wireless Computing, Communication and Applications: Proceedings of the 13th International Conference on Broadband and Wireless Computing, Communication and Applications (BWCCA-2018)* (pp. 578-585). Springer International Publishing. https://doi.org/DOI: 10.1007/978-3-030-02613-4_52

Leu, F.-Y., Tsai, K.-L., Susanto, H., Gu, C.-Y., & You, I. (2021). A fault tolerant mechanism for UE authentication in 5G networks. *Mobile Networks and Applications, 26*(4), 1650–1667. DOI: 10.1007/s11036-019-01502-5

Lu, Y.-S., Susanto, H., & Leu, F.-Y. (2022). Asymmetric Cryptography Among Different 5G Core Networks. *In Innovative Mobile and Internet Services in Ubiquitous Computing: Proceedings of the 16th International Conference on Innovative Mobile and Internet Services in Ubiquitous Computing (IMIS-2022)* (pp. 325-333). Springer International Publishing. https://doi.org/DOI: 10.1007/978-3-031-08819-3_34

Lund, S., Madgavkar, A., Manyika, J., & Smit, S. (2020, November 23). *What's next for remote work: An analysis of 2,000 tasks, 800 jobs, and nine countries.* Retrieved January 3, 2023 from McKinsey Global Institute: https://www.mckinsey .com/featured- insights/future-of-work/whats-next-for-remote-work-an-analysis-of-2000-tasks-800- jobs-and-nine-countries

Ministry of Health. Brunei Darussalam. (2020). *Detection of the first case of covid-19 infection in Brunei Darussalam.* Press Release, Bandar Seri Begawan.

Mishra, P., Pandey, C., Singh, U., Gupta, A., Sahu, C., & Keshri, A. (2019). Descriptive Statistics and Normality Tests for Statistical Data. *Annals of Cardiac Anaesthesia*, *22*(1), 67–72. DOI: 10.4103/aca.ACA_157_18

Monrat, A. A., Schele´n, O., & Andersson, K. (2020). Performance Evaluation of Permissioned Blockchain Platforms. *2020 IEEE Asia-Pacific Conference on Computer Science and Data Engineering (CSDE)* (pp. 1-8). Gold Coast, Australia: IEEE. DOI: DOI: 10.1109/CSDE50874.2020.9411380

MTIC. (2020). *Digital Economy Masterplan 2025.* Retrieved October 16, 2022 from Digital Economy Council: https://www.mtic.gov.bn/DE2025/documents/Digital%20 Economy%20Masterplan%2 02025.pdf

Mwebi, M. B., & Kadaga, M. N. (2015). Effects of Flextime Work Arrangement on Employee Performance in Nairobi CBD Commercial Banks. *International Journal of Novel Research in Marketing Management and Economics*, *2*(3), 111–121. https://www.noveltyjournals.com/upload/paper/Effects%20of%20Flextime%20 Work- 423.pdf

Narayanamurthy, G., & Tortorella, G. (2021). Impact of COVID-19 outbreak on employee performance – Moderating role of industry 4.0 base technologies. *International Journal of Production Economics*, *234*, 1–10. DOI: 10.1016/j.ijpe.2021.108075

Narayanan, L., Menon, S., Plaisent, M., & Bernard, P. (2017). Telecommuting: The Work Anywhere, Anyplace, Anytime Organization in the 21st Century. *Journal of Marketing Management*, *8*(2), 47–54. https://gsmi-ijgb.com/wp- content/uploads/ JMM-V8-N2-P04-Lakshmi-Narayanan-Telecommuting.pdf

Nerobkova, N., Park, Y. S., Park, E.-C., & Jang, S.-Y. (2022, July 11). The Association between Working Hours Flexibility and Well-Being Prior to and during COVID-19 in South Korea. *International Journal of Environmental Research and Public Health*, *19*(14), 1–11. DOI: 10.3390/ijerph19148438

Nguyen, D., Pathirana, P., Ding, M., & Seneviratne, A. (2020). Blockchain for 5G and beyond networks: A state of the art survey. *Journal of Network and Computer Applications*, *166*, 1–38. DOI: 10.1016/j.jnca.2020.102693

OECD. (2020, September 20). *Productivity gains from teleworking in the post COVID-19 era: How can public policies make it happen?* Retrieved October 31, 2022 from OECD Policy Responses to Coronavirus (COVID-19): https://www .oecd.org/coronavirus/policy-responses/productivity-gains-from- teleworking-in-the-post-covid-19-era-a5d52e99/

Oosterbaan, R. (1994). Frequency and regression analysis. In *Drainage Principles and Applications* (3rd revised Edition ed., pp. 175-223).

Ostern, N. K., Holotiuk, F., & Moormann, J. (2022). Organizations' approaches to blockchain: A critical realist perspective. *Information & Management*, *59*(7), 1–14. DOI: 10.1016/j.im.2021.103552

Pallant, J. (2010). *SPSS survival manual: a step by step guide to data analysis using SPSS* (7th Edition ed.). Routledge.

Patanjali, S., & Bhatta, N. (2022). Work from Home During the Pandemic: The Impact of Organizational Factors on the Productivity of Employees in the IT Industry. *Vision*, •••, 1-13. https://doi.org/10.1177/09722629221074137

Philip, A., Afolabi, B., Adeniran, O., Oluwatolani, O., & Ishaya, G. (2010). Towards an Efficient Information Systems Development Process and Management: A Review of Challenges and Proposed Strategies. *Journal of Software Engineering and Applications*, *3*(10), 983–989. DOI: 10.4236/jsea.2010.310115

Prager, F., Rhoads, M., & Martínez, J. (2022). The COVID-19 economic shutdown and the future of flexible workplace practices in the South Bay region of Los Angeles County. *Transport Policy*, *125*, 241–255. DOI: 10.1016/j.tranpol.2022.06.004

Prasetyaningtyas, S. W., Heryanto, C., Nurfauzi, N. F., & Tanjung, S. B. (2021). The effect of work from home on employee productivity in banking industry. *Journal of Applied Management (JAM)*, *19*(3), 507-521. http://dx.doi.org/10.21776/ub.jam .2021.019.03.05

Prime Minister Office. Brunei Darussalam. (2021, October 26). *National Covid-19 Recovery Plan.* Retrieved Decemebr 21, 2022 from Prime Minister Office, Brunei Darussalam: https://www.pmo.gov.bn/SiteCollectionDocuments/covid19/National -COVID-19- Recovery-Framework.pdf

Quantum Workplace. (n.d.). *What is Employee Engagement? What, Why, and How to Improve It.* Retrieved October 16, 2022 from Quantum Workplace: https://www.quantumworkplace.com/future-of-work/what-is-employee-engagement-definition

Rahmadika, S., Firdaus, M., Jang, S., & Rhee, K.-H. (2021). Blockchain-Enabled 5G Edge Networks and Beyond: An Intelligent Cross-Silo Federated Learning Approach. *Security and Communication Networks, 2021*, 1–14. DOI: 10.1155/2021/5550153

Rahman, M., Kistyanto, A., & Surjanti, J. (2020). Flexible Work Arrangements in Covid-19 Pandemic Era, Influence Employee Peformance: The Mediating Role of Innovative Work Behaviour. *International Journal of Management Innovation & Entrepreneurial Research*, *6*(2), 10–22. DOI: 10.18510/ijmier.2020.622

Ray, T., & Pana-Cryan, R. (2021, March). Work Flexibility and Work-Related Well-Being. *International Journal of Environmental Research and Public Health, 18*(6), 1–17. DOI: 10.3390/ijerph18063254

Scroggins, R. (2014). SDLC and Development Methodologies. *Global Journal of Computer Science and Technology: C Software & Data Engineering, 14*(7). Retrieved from https://computerresearch.org/index.php/computer/article/view/148

Shagvaliyeva, S., & Yazdanifard, R. (2014). Impact of Flexible Working Hours on Work-Life Balance. *American Journal of Industrial and Business Management*, *4*(1), 20–23. DOI: 10.4236/ajibm.2014.41004

Shamrat, F., Tasnim, Z., Rahman, A., Nobel, N. I., & Hossain, S. A. (2020, January). An effective implementation of web crawling technology to retrieve data from the world wide web (WWW). *International Journal of Scientific & Technology*, *9*(1), 1252–1256. http://www.ijstr.org/final-print/jan2020/An-Effective-Implementation-Of-Web-Crawling-Technology-To-Retrieve-Data-From-The-World-Wide-Web-www.pdf

Sifah, E. B., Xia, H., Cobblah, C. N., Xia, Q., Gao, J., & Du, X. (2020). BEMPAS: A Decentralized Employee Performance Assessment System Based on Blockchain for Smart City Governance. *IEEE Access, 8*, 99528-99539. doi: 10.1109/ACCESS.2020.2997650

Singh, E., & Bakshi, E. (2018). Human Resource Management System(HRMS)- The Effects and Organizational Performance. *International Journal of Advance Research in Science and Engineering*, *7*(3), 137–145. http://www.ijarse.com/images/fullpdf/1521196206_Vedant634ijarse.pdf

Šmite, D., Moe, N. B., Klotins, E., & Gonzalez-Huerta, J. (2023). From forced Working-From-Home to voluntary working-from-anywhere: Two revolutions in telework. *Journal of Systems and Software*, *195*, 1–10. DOI: 10.1016/j.jss.2022.111509

Stiles, J., & Smart, M. (2021). Working at home and elsewhere: Daily work location, telework, and travel among United States knowledge workers. *Transportation*, *48*(5), 2461–2491. DOI: 10.1007/s11116-020-10136-6

Sun, L., & Bunchapattanasakda, C. (2019). Employee Engagement: A Literature Review. *International Journal of Human Resource Studies*, *9*(1), 63–80. DOI: 10.5296/ijhrs.v9i1.14167

Taherdoost, H. (2021). Data Collection Methods and Tools for Research; A Step-by-Step Guide to Choose Data Collection Technique for Academic and Business Research Projects. *International Journal of Academic Research in Management*, *10*(1), 10–38. https://www.researchgate.net/publication/359596426_Data_Collection_Methods_and_Tools_for_Research_A_Step-by-Step_Guide_to_Choose_Data_Collection_Technique_for_Academic_and_Business_Research_Projects

Tasrin, K., Wahyuadianto, A., Pratiwi, & Masrully. (2021). Evaluation Study of the Implementation of Flexible Working Arrangement in Public Sector Organization during Covid-19 Pandemic. *BISNIS & BIROKRASI: Jurnal Ilmu Administrasi dan Organisasi, 28*(3), 143-157. DOI: 10.20476/jbb.v28i3.1274

Tavakol, M., & Wetzel, A. (2020). Factor Analysis: A means for theory and instrument development in support of construct validity. *International Journal of Medical Education*, *11*, 245–247. DOI: 10.5116/ijme.5f96.0f4a

Thompson, B. Y. (2019). The Digital Nomad Lifestyle: (Remote) Work/Leisure Balance, Privilege, and Constructed Community. *International Journal of the Sociology of Leisure*, *2*(1-2), 27–42. DOI: 10.1007/s41978-018-00030-y

Timely. (2018, April 18). *KPIs for measuring employee performance*. Retrieved November 1, 2022 from Timely blog: https://timelyapp.com/blog/kpis-for-measuring-employee-performance

Trigos, F., & Doria, M. (2021, June 22). *The Benefits of Flexible Work in the Post-Covid-19 Era: The Transdisciplinary Flextime Hiring Method (TFHM) considers both employee and company needs*. Retrieved November 5, 2022 from Egade Ideas - Thought Leadership in Action: https://egade.tec.mx/en/egade-ideas/research/benefits-flexible- work-post-covid-19-era

UCLA. (n.d.). *What does Cronbach's alpha mean? | SPSS FAQ*. Retrieved October 26, 2022 from UCLA Advanced Research Computing Statistical Methods and Data Analytics: https://stats.oarc.ucla.edu/spss/faq/what-does-cronbachs-alpha-mean/

Velimirović, D., Velimirović, M., & Stanković, R. (2011, March). Role and importance of key performance indicators measurement. *Serbian Journal of Management, 6*, 63-72. DOI:10.5937/sjm1101063V

Vyas, L. (2022). "New normal" at work in a post-COVID world: Work–life balance and labor markets. *Policy and Society*, *41*(1), 155–167. DOI: 10.1093/polsoc/puab011

Vyas, L., & Butakhieo, N. (2021, December 23). The impact of working from home during COVID-19 on work and life domains: An exploratory study on Hong Kong. *Policy Design and Practice*, *4*(1), 59–76. DOI: 10.1080/25741292.2020.1863560

Wang, T., Li, N., & Li, H. (2021). Design and development of human resource management computer system for enterprise employees. *PLoS One*, *16*(12), 1–21. DOI: 10.1371/journal.pone.0261594

Weideman, M., & Hofmeyr, K. (2021). Corrigendum: The influence of flexible work arrangements on employee engagement: An exploratory study. *SA Journal of Human Resource Management*, *19*(0), 1–18. DOI: 10.4102/sajhrm.v19i0.1522

WHO. (2020, March 13). Clinical management of severe acute respiratory infection (SARI) when COVID-19 disease is suspected. 2.

Wishart, J. (2022, August 25). *Why are KPIs Important? The Importance of KPIs*. Retrieved November 1, 2022 from Rhythm Systems: https://www.rhythmsystems.com/blog/5-reasons-why-you-need-kpis-infographic

Wong, A. (2021, August 10). *Brunei tightens control measures amid new surge of COVID-19 cases*. Retrieved December 21, 2022 from Biz Brunei: https://www.bizbrunei.com/2021/08/brunei-tightens-control-measures-amid-new- surge-of-covid-19-cases/

World Health Organization. (2022). Strategic *Preparedness, Readiness and Response Plan to End the Global Covid-19 EMeergency in 2022*. Geneva: World Health Organization. Retrieved from https://www.who.int/publications/i/item/WHO-WHE-SPP-2022.1

Wu, Y.-C., Chen, C.-S., & Chan, Y.-J. (2020, March). The outbreak of COVID-19: An overview. *Journal of the Chinese Medical Association*, *83*(3), 217–220. DOI: 10.1097/JCMA.0000000000000270

Xiao, Y., Becerik-Gerber, B., Lucas, G., & Roll, S. (2021, March). Impacts of Working From Home During COVID-19 Pandemic on Physical and Mental Well-Being of Office Workstation Users. *Journal of Occupational and Environmental Medicine, 63*(3), 181–190. DOI: 10.1097/JOM.0000000000002097

Yu, P.-H., Susanto, H., Liu, L.-X., Wu, S.-J., & Leu, F.-Y. (2022). The Implementation of Dynamical Shortest Path and Resource Management for Network Slicing in 5G Networks. *In Advances on Broad-Band Wireless Computing, Communication and Applications: Proceedings of the 16th International Conference on Broad-Band Wireless Computing, Communication and Applications (BWCCA-2021)* (pp. 206-215). Springer International Publishing.

Zainal Abiddin, N., Ibrahim, I., & Abdul Aziz, S. A. (2022). A Literature Review of Work From Home Phenomenon During COVID-19 Toward Employees' Performance and Quality of Life in Malaysia and Indonesia. *Frontiers in Psychology, 13*, 1–8. DOI: 10.3389/fpsyg.2022.819860

Chapter 8
Autonomous Systems in Agriculture: An Innovation-Based Framework

Ananya Pandey
https://orcid.org/0000-0002-2419-6314
Christ University, Bangalore, India

ABSTRACT

The emergence of autonomous systems in agriculture signifies a transformative change in global food production, propelled by developments in artificial intelligence, robotics, and data analytics. This chapter suggests a thorough innovation framework that brings together technological, organizational, institutional, economic, social, and environmental aspects to steer the sustainable development and implementation of autonomous agricultural technologies. The chapter examines essential facilitators and obstacles to innovation, such as infrastructure deficiencies, digital literacy, and regulatory challenges, by analyzing historical trends, case studies, and policy landscapes. It stresses ethical and inclusive innovation to guarantee the involvement of smallholders and ecological resilience. This framework acts as a strategic resource for researchers, practitioners, and policymakers who seek to connect digital transformation in agriculture with sustainability objectives, especially those outlined by the UN Sustainable Development Goals (SDGs).

INTRODUCTION

A profound transformation is taking place in the agriculture sector, fueled by the integration of digital technologies and autonomous systems that hold the promise of revolutionizing traditional farming practices. With increasing worries about

DOI: 10.4018/979-8-3373-8607-2.ch008

food security, climate change, labor shortages, and environmental degradation, the advent of autonomous systems—such as AI-driven tractors, drone-assisted crop monitoring, robotic harvesters, and autonomous irrigation networks—has generated considerable worldwide interest (Liakos et al., 2018; Wolfert et al., 2017). The goal of these innovations is to boost productivity, accuracy, and sustainability in agriculture, allowing farmers to manage resources more effectively and lessen their environmental impact. . The emergence of what is frequently referred to as "Agriculture 4.0" marks a new paradigm in which cyber-physical systems and machine intelligence merge with conventional farming practices, resulting in data-driven, adaptive, and autonomous agricultural systems (Klerkx et al., 2019). This technological shift is not just incremental; it has the potential to be transformative by reducing reliance on manual labor, optimizing input usage, and facilitating real-time decision-making. National and international initiatives, including the United Nations' Sustainable Development Goals (SDGs), particularly SDG 2 (Zero Hunger) and SDG 12 (Responsible Consumption and Production) (United Nations, 2015), further accelerate the global momentum toward sustainable and intelligent farming by promoting digital innovation in food systems.

Nevertheless, there are numerous ongoing and complex challenges that hinder the acceptance and successful use of autonomous systems in farming. A major problem is found in the disjointed innovation environment, where advances in technology frequently surpass farmers'—particularly smallholders'—capabilities to embrace and adjust to these modifications (Zhang et al., 2021). Although high-income countries with advanced infrastructure and supportive policies have started to implement autonomous systems at scale, many regions, especially in the Global South, face challenges due to inadequate digital infrastructure, limited access to capital, and a lack of digital literacy (Rose et al., 2021). Moreover, incorporating autonomous technologies into current agricultural practices brings up issues related to interoperability, cybersecurity, ethical dilemmas regarding data ownership and privacy, and the possibility of job displacement for rural workers. It is increasingly acknowledged that just having advanced technologies available does not ensure their successful implementation or social acceptance. In this context, innovation is not solely technical; it is profoundly rooted in social, institutional, and environmental contexts (Schut et al., 2016). The absence of a comprehensive innovation framework that considers the interconnected dimensions—technological, organizational, institutional, economic, social, and environmental—has resulted in misalignments between the supply of innovation (from developers and policy actors) and its demand (from users and beneficiaries), resulting in less-than-ideal outcomes and resistance to change.

This chapter aims to propose a comprehensive innovation framework specifically designed for autonomous systems in agriculture, considering these challenges and opportunities. The framework seeks to connect technological progress with systemic adoption by placing autonomous agricultural innovations in a wider socio-technical context. It aims to express the main elements, facilitators, and obstacles of innovation at various levels, providing a multidimensional perspective for evaluating and directing the advancement, dissemination, and management of autonomous systems in agriculture. This chapter examines the technological architecture of autonomy as well as the institutional ecosystems, governance mechanisms, and socio-environmental implications that influence their deployment. This chapter enhances the understanding of how innovation in autonomous farming can be leveraged for an equitable, sustainable, and efficient transformation of agriculture by integrating theoretical perspectives from innovation systems theory, digital agriculture literature, and sustainability science. The scope includes an analytical review of current technological trends, empirical case studies from both developed and developing countries, and a critical examination of policy and regulatory landscapes that influence innovation trajectories. This chapter aims to make the scholars, practitioners, and policymakers aware about the strategic pathways and governance tools needed to foster an inclusive and resilient adoption of autonomous systems in agriculture.

CONCEPTUAL FRAMEWORK

In agriculture, autonomous systems embody a revolutionary change in food cultivation, management, and distribution, propelled by technological convergence and systemic innovation. According to Bechar & Vigneault (2017), these systems are characterized as self-operating technological solutions that carry out agricultural tasks—like seeding, weeding, irrigation, harvesting, and monitoring—without the need for constant human involvement. Instead, they rely on a combination of sensor data, AI, machine learning (ML), and mechanical automation. Autonomous agricultural systems can be classified into four main categories: ground-based robotics (such as autonomous tractors, weeders, and harvesters), aerial platforms (including drones and unmanned aerial vehicles for crop monitoring), smart irrigation and fertilization systems (which automate water and nutrient delivery based on sensor data), and decision-support systems (like AI-driven platforms for predicting crop yield and diagnosing diseases) (Zhang et al., 2022). These systems function within a dynamic ecosystem of enabling technologies that underpin their functionality and adaptability. These enabling technologies are fundamentally powered by Artificial Intelligence (AI), which enables autonomous systems to replicate cognitive functions like learning and problem-solving through methods such as pattern recognition, predictive analytics, and optimization algorithms. In the field of precision agriculture, AI plays an especially crucial role, as real-time decision-making enhances efficiency and resource use (Kamilaris & Prenafeta-Boldú, 2018). Machine Learning (ML), a branch of AI, is closely linked to AI. It enables systems to enhance their performance over time by learning from extensive and varied agricultural datasets, such as weather patterns, crop health images, and soil moisture levels. The Internet of Things (IoT) enhances these systems by linking field devices—like moisture sensors, pH meters, and weather stations—to cloud platforms, facilitating smooth data transfer and automation (Wolfert et al., 2017).

Robotics is vital for carrying out agricultural tasks that require great precision and consistency and are labor-intensive, which decreases the need for human workers and boosts productivity (Liakos et al., 2018). Drones, also known as Unmanned Aerial Vehicles (UAVs), play a crucial role in aerial surveillance, mapping, and crop scouting, especially on large-scale farms where conventional monitoring methods are impractical. At the same time, Global Positioning Systems (GPS) and Geographic Information Systems (GIS) enable geo-referenced analysis of agricultural activities and spatial variability, aiding in site-specific interventions and providing sub-meter tracking of autonomous machines. Finally, Edge computing is becoming a crucial technology by handling data locally on the farm instead of depending solely on cloud computing. This reduces latency and allows for real-time responses in essential decision-making processes (Sarangi et al., 2023). In order to comprehend the direction of these technological advancements, it is crucial to situate them within the context of innovation theory, especially regarding agri-tech. The approach to agricultural innovation has transitioned from linear adoption models to intricate co-evolution systems that encompass various stakeholders, feedback loops, and contextual variables. Joseph Schumpeter's early theories of creative destruction and technological innovation have evolved into contemporary models like the National Innovation System (NIS) and the Triple Helix model, which highlight the interactive roles of academia, industry, and government in nurturing innovation ecosystems (Etzkowitz & Leydesdorff, 2000). Innovation in agriculture goes beyond just introducing new technology; it requires a systemic transformation that encompasses practices, institutions, and socio-cultural norms. This wider perspective is in accordance with the theory of agricultural innovation systems (AIS), which emphasizes the networks of organizations, individuals, and institutions that foster innovation through knowledge co-production, experimentation, and mutual learning (Klerkx et al., 2019).

The idea of socio-technical systems is closely connected to this systemic perspective, taking into account the social and technological aspects of innovation. According to the socio-technical perspective, technology adoption in agriculture is influenced by a combination of factors beyond just technical performance, including institutional arrangements, regulatory environments, market dynamics, user behavior, and cultural values (Geels, 2004). Such socio-technical configurations embed autonomous agricultural systems, where complex interactions among farmers, policymakers, researchers, agri-tech companies, and civil society negotiate innovation pathways. As an illustration, the implementation of self-driving tractors is affected by elements like the dimensions of the farm, availability of digital resources, proficiency of farmers, and permission from regulators. This exemplifies that something being technologically feasible does not guarantee its broad uptake. This underscores the necessity for systemic innovation, which entails reconfiguring entire systems—such as production, distribution, and governance structures—through coordinated technological, institutional, and behavioral changes (Smith & Stirling, 2010). In the context of the climate crisis, systemic innovation takes on particular importance for agriculture, which must boost productivity while lowering its environmental impact and enhancing resilience to climate change. If integrated into inclusive and sustainable innovation frameworks, autonomous systems can potentially make a substantial contribution to such a transformation.

EVOLUTION OF AUTONOMOUS SYSTEM IN AGRICULTURE

One of the most important changes in human history is the transition from agriculture based on intensive labor to highly advanced, technology-driven systems. Historically, the first significant wave of innovation was mechanization, which began in the 19th century with the introduction of steam-powered tractors and later machines using internal combustion engines. According to Pingali (2007), these advancements transformed productivity and diminished the need for human labor. This transition was further expedited by the Green Revolution of the mid-20th century, which amalgamated chemical inputs with mechanical innovations like combine harvesters, resulting in considerable yield increases (Evenson & Gollin, 2003). Nonetheless, mechanization by itself could not meet the increasing demands for sustainability, resource efficiency, and labor shortages. This gap led to the rise of precision agriculture in the late 20th century. Precision agriculture brought about a paradigm shift by utilizing GPS technologies, remote sensing, and data analytics to tailor inputs such as water, fertilizers, and pesticides to site-specific conditions (Gebbers & Adamchuk, 2010). Precision agriculture improved efficiency and minimized waste by customizing farming practices to fit micro-environments. Despite this, the decision-making and operations during this phase were still largely dependent on human involvement, making it more of a semi-automated approach than a genuinely autonomous system. The sector began its transition from automation to autonomy only in the 2010s, with the integration of AI, machine learning, and robotics.

In agriculture, the shift from automation to autonomy is characterized by machines acquiring the capacity to sense, make decisions, and take actions independently of human supervision. AI algorithms that analyze data from sensors, drones, and satellite imagery enable this transformation by making real-time decisions regarding planting, irrigation, harvesting, and pest control (Shamshiri et al., 2018). New technologies such as autonomous tractors, robotic weeders, and drone-based crop monitors not only carry out tasks but also learn and adapt to changing field conditions (Roldán et al., 2018). Traditional automation systems operate based on pre-set instructions, whereas autonomous systems integrate feedback loops and predictive analytics to enhance their performance over time. This transformation is especially beneficial for tackling issues like workforce shortages, fluctuations in climate, and the necessity of sustainable intensification. On a global scale, this technological transformation has progressed along uneven paths, influenced by key trends and milestones that have shaped adoption in different regions. In the US, initial leadership in precision agriculture established a foundation for swift innovation in autonomous systems. In 2017, John Deere acquired Blue River Technology, marking a significant milestone by incorporating computer vision and machine learning into large-scale agricultural equipment (John Deere, 2017). In the U.S., particularly in California, autonomous tractors and robotic harvesters have been deployed for specialty crops like strawberries and lettuce (Pedersen et al., 2020). Japan's government is actively backing robotic farming innovations due to the limitations imposed by an aging rural population and scarce arable land. Firms such as Kubota and Yanmar have created self-operating rice planters and harvesters, with the aid of regulatory sandboxes that permit real-world trials (Nanseki et al., 2018). At the same time, due to its emphasis on advanced horticulture, the Netherlands has emerged as a worldwide frontrunner in autonomous greenhouse systems. Research institutions and startups in the Netherlands have led the way in developing AI-controlled climate systems, robotic pollinators, and automated vertical farms, resulting in a transformation of agricultural productivity per square meter (Berkhout et al., 2020).

Australia is another leading country in this area, particularly in broadacre and remote farming. The continent's extensive land area and limited labor supply have made the use of autonomous machinery a necessity rather than an option. The development of swarm robotics by the Australian Centre for Field Robotics has facilitated the coordination of planting and weeding tasks across extensive farmlands using multiple small robots (Underwood et al., 2017). In Western Australia, the Australian grains industry has adopted driverless tractors and drone surveillance, thanks to connectivity infrastructure that enables real-time data exchange.

The emergence of autonomous agriculture is underscored by these worldwide advances, which emphasize the necessity of converging several technological fields—robotics, data science, mechatronics, and connectivity infrastructure. They also show how the speed and course of innovation are affected by regional needs, resource limitations, and institutional backing. Despite the considerable progress made by high-income countries, a digital divide persists that restricts access to these technologies in developing regions. Nonetheless, new developments in affordable sensor systems and open-source platforms are starting to make access more democratic, possibly paving the way for a more inclusive evolution in the coming decades.

Even with these progressions, the path to completely autonomous farming is still in motion. Challenges that persist include those pertaining to system interoperability, data ownership, cybersecurity, and legal liability (Bronson & Knezevic, 2016). Furthermore, the socio-economic impact—especially on smallholders and rural workers—requires thorough examination to prevent worsening inequality. Up to this point, however, evolution has highlighted a clear path: moving from the replacement of mechanized labor to the development of intelligent, self-regulating agricultural ecosystems that offer the potential to improve productivity, sustainability, and resilience in response to global food security challenges.

COMPONENTS OF INNOVATIVE FRAMEWORK

The innovation framework for autonomous systems in agriculture can be viewed as a multidimensional construct that includes technological, organizational, institutional, economic, social, and environmental layers. Every layer plays a role in the overall functionality, sustainability, and scalability of autonomous agricultural innovations. These layers interact with one another in a dynamic manner, affecting how technology is integrated into farming practices and its resulting effects.

Technological Layer

Autonomy in agriculture is based at the technological layer on a collection of interconnected tools such as sensors, platforms, and machine learning models. Advanced sensors—like LiDAR, multispectral cameras, and environmental probes—gather real-time information on soil moisture, nutrient levels, crop health, and weather patterns. This data is essential for decision-making (Liakos et al., 2018). Integrated platforms that facilitate real-time observation and automated response mechanisms process these data streams, thereby aiding precision farming. To optimize planting schedules, pest control, irrigation, and harvesting, models of machine learning (ML) and artificial intelligence (AI) analyze these enormous datasets. It is essential for enhancing productivity and minimizing input use (Kamilaris & Prenafeta-Boldú, 2018) to have AI-driven decision-making capabilities that enable predictive analytics and adaptive responses. A significant challenge and opportunity for innovation lies in ensuring these technologies can work together within agricultural ecosystems—where cloud computing, edge devices, and robotics must come together.

Organizational Layer

The organizational layer encompasses the structural and operational arrangements that allow farmers and agribusinesses to manage and integrate autonomous systems. This layer is primarily focused on digital farm management systems (FMS), which serve as platforms for data aggregation from multiple sources and offer dashboards for decision-making, inventory tracking, and compliance monitoring (Zhang et al., 2020). These FMS platforms frequently integrate IoT capabilities, AI analytics, and cloud services, serving as the digital foundation for smart agriculture. Moreover, digital ecosystems that promote collaboration among farmers, agri-tech companies, researchers, and policymakers have proven vital for speeding up the spread of innovation. The transition to collaborative, networked organizational models that facilitate scalable and user-centered autonomous solutions is exemplified by open innovation platforms, agricultural innovation hubs, and data-sharing consortia. Nonetheless, the integration may be impeded by organizational inertia, restricted digital capacity, and an absence of change management strategies in contexts of smallholder and traditional farming.

Institutional Layer

The institutional layer encompasses the formal and informal rules, norms, and governance mechanisms that influence innovation processes. Regulatory frameworks for autonomous agricultural systems must tackle various issues, such as liability in the event of machine failure, standards for machine-to-machine communication, and safety protocols for human-robot interaction (Lowenberg-DeBoer et al., 2020). IP (intellectual property) rights are crucial, especially for safeguarding proprietary algorithms, data-driven innovations, and robotic designs. Simultaneously, excessively restrictive IP regimes can hinder open-source collaboration and small-scale innovation.To ensure compatibility, reliability, and cross-border regulatory alignment, it is essential to adhere to international standards developed by organizations such as ISO and the Food and Agriculture Organization (FAO). In addition, data governance frameworks—encompassing data ownership, privacy, and security—need to adapt to the unique characteristics of agricultural data, which is frequently co-produced by farmers, machines, and third-party platforms (Bronson, 2019).

Economic Layer

Regarding the economic layer, the innovation framework takes into account the financial viability, cost-effectiveness, and market readiness of autonomous systems. Small and medium-scale farmers are often deterred from adopting robotic harvesters, autonomous tractors, and AI platforms due to their high upfront capital costs (van der Burg et al., 2021). Moreover, the creation of insurance products, subsidy schemes, and venture capital interest in agri-tech startups affects the speed and magnitude of innovation. Market readiness assessments are instrumental in evaluating the demand-side receptivity and adequacy of distribution infrastructure, ensuring that innovations are not only technically sound but also economically sustainable and accessible.

Social Layer

The social layer encompasses human factors like skills development, social acceptance, and considerations of equity. Autonomous systems necessitate a workforce proficient in digital and technical skills—spanning machine operation, software analytics, and remote sensing interpretation (Eastwood et al., 2019). To equip farmers and rural youth for the digital transformation, educational institutions, extension services, and vocational training programs need to adjust their curricula.It is also essential to achieve social acceptance; doubts about data misuse, job displacement, and excessive reliance on technology can lead to resistance in farming communities. Furthermore, the rural-urban digital divide—evident in differences in broadband access, technological literacy, and institutional backing—intensifies inequalities in the adoption of innovation. It is crucial for socially inclusive innovation that autonomous technologies cater to a variety of user groups, such as smallholders, women, and indigenous communities (Carolan, 2020).

Environmental Layer

Lastly, the environmental layer incorporates issues of sustainability and ecological effects. Autonomous systems can contribute to sustainability by increasing input efficiency, lowering carbon emissions, and maintaining soil health. As an example, autonomous sprayers that utilize computer vision can apply herbicides with precision, leading to a significant decrease in both chemical usage and runoff (Shamshiri et al., 2018). Robotic weeders and seeders can reduce soil disturbance and promote regenerative farming practices. It is essential to incorporate sustainability metrics—including energy consumption, greenhouse gas (GHG) emissions, water usage, and biodiversity impact—into the design and assessment of autonomous systems. Eco-design and adherence to sustainability standards such as ISO 14001 can be informed by lifecycle assessments and environmental audits. Moreover, agroecosystems impacted by extreme weather events, resource scarcity, and soil degradation can enhance their resilience through the use of adaptive technologies that respond to climate variability.

BARRIERS AND LIMITATIONS TO INNOVATION IN AGRICULTURE

Various factors that can either facilitate or hinder the process play a role in determining the innovation trajectory, scalability, and long-term sustainability of autonomous systems in agriculture. This is true for their adoption as well. A key factor is the targeted funding of research and development (R&D), which drives technological advances in machine learning, computer vision, and robotics designed for agricultural activities like seeding, weeding, harvesting, and soil monitoring. Experimentation with autonomous tractors, drone surveillance systems, and robotic harvesters has been catalyzed by government-sponsored programs, academic-industry partnerships, and private sector innovation hubs (Zhang et al., 2020). As an example, companies such as John Deere and AGCO have made substantial investments in research and development to create smart machinery that incorporates sensors and can operate with little human involvement.. Open data ecosystems also play a crucial role in complementing R&D by providing agronomic, meteorological, and geospatial datasets that enable the development and implementation of autonomous technologies. Open data frameworks boost predictive analytics and real-time decision-making by facilitating data-sharing among stakeholders like farmers, tech developers, and policy agencies (Bronson & Knezevic, 2016). In this context, programs such as the Global Open Data for Agriculture and Nutrition (GODAN) serve as examples of how transparency and interoperability can drive digital transformation in agriculture. In addition, policy incentives such as subsidies for adopting technology, tax breaks for R&D investments, and grants for smart farming act as strong motivators for farmers and agricultural businesses to investigate autonomous solutions. Financial risk linked to the initial deployment of nascent technologies can be mitigated through national and regional policy tools, which can also lend these technologies institutional legitimacy.

Although these facilitators exist, various obstacles impede the broad adoption and fair distribution of autonomous farming systems. Interoperability issues remain a core challenge, particularly when equipment from different manufacturers or data from diverse platforms cannot communicate smoothly. Due to the absence of standardized data formats, limitations imposed by proprietary software, and the use of non-uniform communication protocols, technological silos are created that reduce efficiency and scalability (Eastwood et al., 2019). As an example, a robotic weeder created by one manufacturer might not align with the drone surveillance system of another, thereby diminishing the systemic coherence required for autonomous farming ecosystems. Interoperability is closely tied to the challenge of insufficient infrastructure, especially in rural and developing areas where digital connectivity is limited. Infrastructural deficiencies like unreliable power supplies, limited broadband penetration, and lack of edge computing facilities compromise the internet connectivity, GPS accuracy, and cloud computing capabilities that autonomous systems depend on (Rose et al., 2021). This digital gap continues regional inequalities and poses a risk of confining the advantages of autonomous innovation to regions that are already technologically advanced. Digital literacy represents another significant barrier, impacting farmers' and agricultural workers' ability to engage with, troubleshoot, or make modifications to autonomous technologies. Even when infrastructure and tools are available, insufficient training, technical assistance, and user-friendly interfaces can result in these systems being unused or underused (Balafoutis et al., 2017). Digital literacy includes not just technical expertise but also comprehension of data privacy implications, algorithmic decision-making, and maintenance routines—all crucial for responsible and sustainable use.

Besides technological and operational aspects, the implementation of autonomous agricultural systems must address risk and uncertainty management. Autonomous systems, unlike conventional machinery, utilize artificial intelligence to make context-sensitive decisions. This can lead to unpredictable behavior in novel or extreme conditions, such as unpredictable weather, unfamiliar terrain, or unanticipated crop variants. System malfunctions, cyber-physical attacks, or faulty algorithmic inputs can also pose risks, resulting in yield losses or safety hazards (Rotz et al., 2019). Uncertain ROI, extended payback periods, and unclear regulatory compliance deepen the reluctance of both farmers and investors. In order to reduce these risks, innovation frameworks should include solid testing environments, fail-safe protocols, and adaptive regulatory sandboxes that allow for iterative learning and safe experimentation (Pivoto et al., 2019). Insurance models customized for agri-tech risks, along with digital risk evaluation tools, can significantly contribute to establishing resilience and trust in autonomous systems.

Finally, ethical considerations and legal liability must be addressed in any thorough assessment of innovation in autonomous agriculture. A significant ethical dilemma concerns data ownership: who possesses the data produced by autonomous machines, and what are the methods of its storage, access, and monetization? Farmers frequently voice worries about the imbalance of power between themselves and major agri-tech companies that gather and sell farm-level data without clear consent processes (Wiseman et al., 2019). To safeguard farmers' rights, legal structures must guarantee data sovereignty, informed consent, and benefit-sharing. Furthermore, in the case of a malfunctioning machine or crop destruction, it is unclear who should be held responsible—does liability fall on the producer of the machine, the developer of the software, the operator of the farm, or the provider of the data? The lack of clear legal precedents or standardized liability frameworks raises the perceived risk associated with autonomous systems (Marinoudi et al., 2019).

POLICY, GOVERNANCE AND STANDARDS

As autonomous systems become more integrated into agriculture, there is a need for a strong and adaptable policy framework that can steer innovation and reduce associated risks. Globally, existing policy mechanisms have been characterized by fragmentation and reactivity, frequently trailing behind technological advancements. For example, although the United States Department of Agriculture (USDA) and the European Union's Common Agricultural Policy (CAP) have included structures to support digital innovation, these frameworks seldom tackle the specificities and intricacies of autonomous technologies, such as machine-to-machine communication, edge-based decision-making, and AI-driven crop optimization (Eastwood et al., 2019). National standards and regulatory agencies frequently concentrate on general agricultural mechanization, resulting in considerable governance gaps concerning machine autonomy levels, accountability for decision-making errors, and system interoperability. This has led to an uneven uptake of autonomous systems, which is often obstructed by doubts about regulations and a failure to conform to global best practices.

The necessity for international collaboration and the alignment of standards is paramount. The absence of harmonized protocols for autonomous systems across different jurisdictions results in inefficiencies, data silos, and duplicated compliance efforts, as agricultural supply chains become increasingly global. While there have been multilateral initiatives led by organizations like the Food and Agriculture Organization (FAO) and the International Organization for Standardization (ISO) to establish frameworks, their widespread adoption has been sluggish. ISO 18497, which focuses on safety protocols for highly automated agricultural machinery, serves as a foundation; however, its voluntary nature and limited national enforcement have reduced its effectiveness (FAO, 2021). To ensure cross-border functionality and interoperability, there is a distinct necessity for globally coordinated protocols that include technical, legal, and ethical standards. It is important that these standards take into account the contextual differences in infrastructure, data governance, and user capabilities between high-income and low-income agricultural economies (Rotz et al., 2019).

Models for governance regarding data ownership, cybersecurity, and AI regulation in autonomous agriculture are still lacking development. Current frameworks often lack clarity on who owns the data collected by autonomous systems — whether it is the farmer, the equipment manufacturer, or the platform provider. This uncertainty deters data sharing and erodes trust, particularly among smallholder farmers (Bronson, 2019). Moreover, as autonomous systems depend on real-time data exchange to a great extent, they are especially susceptible to cybersecurity threats. A breach can lead to data theft as well as physical harm via system manipulation, including the sabotage of irrigation or pest control functions. While existing cybersecurity policies like the EU's Cybersecurity Act and the U.S. National Institute of Standards and Technology (NIST) guidelines offer general protections, they do not include specific provisions for the agricultural sector (Wolfert et al., 2017). At the same time, regulation of AI-based decision-making in farming equipment is still at an early stage. In agricultural contexts, particularly in low-data regions where AI models may not perform well, there is minimal examination of algorithmic transparency, fairness, or bias.

Evidence-based policymaking is crucial for tackling these challenges. Regulations should be based on empirical research and stakeholder consultation, with a focus on inclusivity, equity, and sustainability, according to policymakers. It is necessary for policies to create incentives for open data ecosystems, foster public-private partnerships, and aid in the development of farmers' digital literacy skills. Regulatory sandboxes can be especially useful for enabling real-world experimentation under supervision, which promotes iterative learning and policy refinement (OECD, 2021). Additionally, it is essential for coherent governance that agricultural departments, technology ministries, and data protection authorities coordinate across sectors. Ultimately, the policy landscape needs to shift from reactive regulation to proactive governance, guided by foresight tools, scenario planning, and continuous evaluation for the ethical and effective use of autonomous systems in agriculture.

INNOVATION TRAJECTORIES AND FUTURE DIRECTIONS

The convergence of cutting-edge technologies is shaping the future of autonomous systems in agriculture, promising to transform farming practices into hyper-efficient, sustainable, and intelligent operations. Swarm robotics and synthetic biology are two of the horizon technologies with the most promise. Swarm robotics draws inspiration from the collective behavior observed in nature (e.g., bees or ants) and entails the use of fleets of small, inexpensive autonomous robots that can work together to perform tasks like planting, weeding, and harvesting (Dorigo et al., 2020). These systems provide scalability and resilience, especially in decentralized farming models and across variable terrains. Meanwhile, synthetic biology converges with automation through the engineering of crops and microbes to improve nitrogen fixation, pest resistance, and resource efficiency. This reduces reliance on chemical inputs and facilitates real-time bio-sensing for autonomous decision-making (Cameron et al., 2014). By merging these biological innovations with robotic and AI systems, the functional capabilities of autonomous agriculture could be significantly enhanced.

Alongside these developments in biology and robotics, the importance of digital twins, blockchain, and cloud-edge computing synergies is growing significantly.

Digital twins—virtual representations of physical systems in real time—facilitate dynamic monitoring and predictive analysis for crop growth, soil health, and machinery performance. These systems, when integrated with cloud-edge architectures, can facilitate low-latency, high-accuracy decision-making across extensive agricultural environments, particularly in situations of limited connectivity (Fuller et al., 2020). Blockchain strengthens data integrity, traceability, and trust throughout the agri-supply chain, guaranteeing that transactions, sources of inputs, and sustainability metrics can be verified (Tripoli & Schmidhuber, 2018). The combination of these technologies results in a strong digital infrastructure that provides autonomous systems with transparency, scalability, and security. With the advancement of innovation, it becomes crucial to create inclusive routes that correspond with wider sustainability objectives. Inclusive innovation involves the co-design and deployment of technologies that are accessible to smallholder farmers, Indigenous communities, and underrepresented stakeholders in both developed and developing areas. This method encompasses capacity building, participatory governance, open-source platforms, and gender-responsive design (FAO, 2022). In addition, aligning with sustainability necessitates that self-sufficient farming systems mitigate their environmental impact—by means of precision application of inputs, minimizing tillage, and promoting biodiversity—while also fostering food security and socio-economic equity. To prevent worsening digital divides or ecological degradation, an integrated sustainability framework needs to be incorporated into innovation trajectories.

As we look ahead to 2030 and beyond, multiple scenarios arise that showcase the varied futures of autonomous agriculture. In a hopeful "techno-green" vision, autonomous systems are seamlessly incorporated into regenerative agriculture practices, leading to high yields, low emissions, and improved ecosystem services. In a contrasting "dual-speed" scenario, industrialized nations experience rapid adoption, while smallholders in the Global South encounter marginalization because of infrastructure and policy deficiencies. A more dystopian "platform consolidation" scenario forewarns of digital monopolies taking over the agri-food system, where autonomy and sovereignty are compromised by data asymmetries and algorithmic biases (Rotz et al., 2019). To navigate these potential futures, we need anticipatory governance, ethical foresight, and participatory innovation policies that emphasize resilience, justice, and planetary health. Ultimately, the development of autonomous agricultural systems will rely not only on technological advances but also on the governance, adoption, and integration of innovation within wider socio-ecological systems. Over the next ten years, we will have an unparalleled chance to establish ethical, sustainable, and inclusive principles as fundamental to agricultural automation. It is essential for policymakers, technologists, and farmers to work together to guarantee that the autonomy we create for machines does not undermine the agency of those who provide sustenance for the planet.

CONCLUSION AND RECOMMENDATIONS

Incorporating autonomous systems into agricultural practices signifies a crucial change in food production, management, and distribution. This chapter has explored the development of these technologies, ranging from early automation to intelligent and adaptive systems driven by artificial intelligence (AI), machine learning (ML), and the Internet of Things (IoT). This study's critical finding is that although autonomous technologies could transform agriculture for the better by improving productivity, resource efficiency, and environmental sustainability, their uptake is inconsistent and complicated by a variety of challenges. These encompass technical constraints, infrastructural shortcomings, regulatory uncertainties, data privacy issues, and socio-economic disparities, especially in the contexts of smallholder and resource-constrained farming. This chapter has put forward a holistic innovation framework to tackle these complexities, comprising six interrelated layers: technological, organizational, institutional, economic, social, and environmental. This framework highlights the necessity of systems thinking when it comes to the design, implementation, and governance of autonomous agricultural systems.

The suggested innovation framework acts as both a diagnostic and prescriptive tool. The technological layer fundamentally deals with the incorporation of AI-driven machinery, drone systems, sensor networks, and edge-cloud computing to facilitate real-time decision-making. The focus of the organizational layer is on restructuring farm management systems and digital ecosystems to facilitate automation. The institutional layer emphasizes the necessity of strong regulatory frameworks, data governance standards, and protections for intellectual property that can adapt to fast-paced technological change (Rotz et al., 2019). Investment models, return-on-innovation metrics, and inclusive financing pathways are considered in the economic layer to guarantee wide-ranging access to these systems. Digital literacy, labor transitions, and capacity-building are emphasized in the social layer, particularly for marginalized communities. Lastly, the environmental layer incorporates sustainability metrics like carbon footprint reduction, soil health monitoring, and water-use optimization to guarantee that innovation is in line with Sustainable Development Goals (SDGs), especially SDG 2 (Zero Hunger) and SDG 12 (Responsible Consumption and Production) (FAO, 2022).

This framework has ramifications for academic research, practical application, and public policy. The framework provides researchers with a multidisciplinary schema to investigate technological innovation as part of a dynamic agri-food system shaped by institutional norms and ecological constraints, rather than in isolation. It promotes future research that takes transdisciplinary approaches to innovation, integrating perspectives from engineering, law, sociology, and environmental science. The framework can assist technology developers, agritech startups, and farming cooperatives in creating user-centric solutions that are scalable and adaptable to various geographical contexts. Practitioners can improve the effectiveness and acceptability of autonomous systems by incorporating the framework into participatory co-design processes (Rose et al., 2021). Meanwhile, there are calls for policymakers to promote conducive environments by means of intelligent subsidies, investments in digital infrastructure, the establishment of ethical AI standards, and international collaboration aimed at aligning cross-border regulations. It is crucial to align policies in this way in order to reduce differences in access and ensure that the advantages of automation do not worsen existing inequalities in rural areas. Ultimately, the sustainable and fair adoption of autonomous systems in agriculture depends not just on advanced technology, but also on fostering an inclusive innovation ecosystem. It is essential to make deliberate efforts to democratize access to technology, uphold data justice, and collaboratively create value in various agricultural contexts. Rather than seeing autonomous systems simply as tools for enhancing productivity, we should recognize them as facilitators of regenerative, resilient, and equitable food systems. Realizing this vision will necessitate a fundamental change in approach—one that reconciles digital innovation with socio-environmental responsibility and prioritizes the perspectives of farmers, particularly smallholders, in the process of technological change. Thus, the innovation framework put forth in this document serves not only as a roadmap for the future of autonomous agriculture but also as a call to action for systemic change.

REFERENCES

Balafoutis, A., Beck, B., Fountas, S., Vangeyte, J., Van Der Wal, T., Soto, I., & Gemtos, T. A. (2017). Precision agriculture technologies positively contribute to GHG emissions mitigation, farm productivity and economics. *Sustainability (Basel), 9*(8), 1339. DOI: 10.3390/su9081339

Bechar, A., & Vigneault, C. (2017). Agricultural robots for field operations: Current status and future trends. *Biosystems Engineering, 149*, 94–111. DOI: 10.1016/j.biosystemseng.2016.06.014

Berkhout, P., van Galen, M., & van Tongeren, F. (2020). *The Future of Food: Smart Farming and Sustainable Agriculture*. Wageningen Economic Research.

Bronson, K. (2019). Looking through a responsible innovation lens at uneven engagements with digital farming. *NJAS Wageningen Journal of Life Sciences, 90-91*(1), 100294. DOI: 10.1016/j.njas.2019.03.001

Bronson, K., & Knezevic, I. (2016). Big Data in food and agriculture. *Big Data & Society, 3*(1), 1–5. DOI: 10.1177/2053951716648174

Cameron, D. E., Bashor, C. J., & Collins, J. J. (2014). A brief history of synthetic biology. *Nature Reviews. Microbiology, 12*(5), 381–390. DOI: 10.1038/nrmicro3239 PMID: 24686414

Carolan, M. (2020). Automated agrifood futures: Robotics, labor and the distributive politics of digital agriculture. *The Journal of Peasant Studies, 47*(1), 184–207. DOI: 10.1080/03066150.2019.1584189

Dorigo, M., Birattari, M., & Brambilla, M. (2020). Swarm robotics. *Scholarpedia Journal, 9*(1), 1463. DOI: 10.4249/scholarpedia.1463 PMID: 33298518

Eastwood, C., Klerkx, L., Ayre, M., & Dela Rue, B. (2019). Managing socio-ethical challenges in the development of smart farming: From a fragmented to a comprehensive approach for responsible innovation. *Journal of Agricultural & Environmental Ethics, 32*(5), 741–768. DOI: 10.1007/s10806-017-9704-5

Etzkowitz, H., & Leydesdorff, L. (2000). The dynamics of innovation: From National Systems and "Mode 2" to a Triple Helix of university–industry–government relations. *Research Policy, 29*(2), 109–123. DOI: 10.1016/S0048-7333(99)00055-4

Evenson, R. E., & Gollin, D. (2003). Assessing the impact of the Green Revolution, 1960 to 2000. *Science, 300*(5620), 758–762. DOI: 10.1126/science.1078710 PMID: 12730592

FAO. (2021). *The digitalization of the agriculture sector: A global overview*. Food and Agriculture Organization of the United Nations.

FAO. (2022). *Digital agriculture: Technology, innovation and inclusive development*. Food and Agriculture Organization of the United Nations.

Fuller, A., Fan, Z., Day, C., & Barlow, C. (2020). Digital twin: Enabling technologies, challenges and open research. *IEEE Access : Practical Innovations, Open Solutions*, *8*, 108952–108971. DOI: 10.1109/ACCESS.2020.2998358

Gebbers, R., & Adamchuk, V. I. (2010). Precision agriculture and food security. *Science*, *327*(5967), 828–831. DOI: 10.1126/science.1183899 PMID: 20150492

Geels, F. W. (2004). From sectoral systems of innovation to socio-technical systems: Insights about dynamics and change from sociology and institutional theory. *Research Policy*, *33*(6–7), 897–920. DOI: 10.1016/j.respol.2004.01.015

John Deere. (2017). *John Deere acquires Blue River Technology*. https://www.deere.com/en/our-company/news-and-announcements/news-releases/2017/corporate/john-deere-acquires-blue-river-technology/

Kamilaris, A., & Prenafeta-Boldú, F. X. (2018). Deep learning in agriculture: A survey. *Computers and Electronics in Agriculture*, *147*, 70–90. DOI: 10.1016/j.compag.2018.02.016

Klerkx, L., Jakku, E., & Labarthe, P. (2019). A review of social science on digital agriculture, smart farming and agriculture 4.0: New contributions and a future research agenda. *NJAS Wageningen Journal of Life Sciences*, *90-91*(1), 100315. DOI: 10.1016/j.njas.2019.100315

Liakos, K. G., Busato, P., Moshou, D., Pearson, S., & Bochtis, D. (2018). Machine learning in agriculture: A review. *Sensors (Basel)*, *18*(8), 2674. DOI: 10.3390/s18082674 PMID: 30110960

Lowenberg-DeBoer, J., Huang, I., Grigoriadis, V., & Blackmore, S. (2020). Economics of robot use in arable farming: Lessons from the first twenty years. *Precision Agriculture*, *21*(6), 1249–1272. DOI: 10.1007/s11119-019-09667-5

Marinoudi, V., Sørensen, C. G., Pearson, S., & Bochtis, D. (2019). Robotics and labour in agriculture: A context consideration. *Biosystems Engineering*, *184*, 111–121. DOI: 10.1016/j.biosystemseng.2019.06.013

Nanseki, T., Shiratsuchi, H., & Mizoguchi, T. (2018). Smart agriculture in Japan. *IFAC-PapersOnLine*, *51*(17), 6–11. DOI: 10.1016/j.ifacol.2018.08.002

OECD. (2021). *Regulatory sandboxes and innovation in agriculture*. Organisation for Economic Co-operation and Development.

Pedersen, S. M., Fountas, S., Have, H., & Blackmore, S. (2020). Agricultural robots—System analysis and economic feasibility. *Precision Agriculture*, *21*, 1473–1491. DOI: 10.1007/s11119-020-09736-0

Pingali, P. (2007). Agricultural mechanization: Adoption patterns and economic impact. *Handbook of Agricultural Economics*, 3, 2779–2805. https://doi.org/DOI: 10.1016/S1574-0072(06)03054-2

Pivoto, D., Waquil, P. D., Talamini, E., Finocchio, C. P. S., Dalla Corte, V. F., & de Vargas Mores, G. (2019). Scientific development of smart farming technologies and their application in Brazil. *Information Processing in Agriculture*, *6*(1), 15–34. DOI: 10.1016/j.inpa.2018.08.002

Roldán, J. J., Peña-Tapia, E., de León, J., & García-Aunon, P. (2018). Autonomous robotics in precision agriculture: A review. *Robotics (Basel, Switzerland)*, *7*(4), 48. DOI: 10.3390/robotics7040048

Rose, D. C., Wheeler, R., Winter, M., Lobley, M., & Chivers, C. A. (2021). Farming and agri-tech: Developing a responsible innovation agenda for smart agriculture. *Frontiers in Sustainable Food Systems*, *5*, 671276. DOI: 10.3389/fsufs.2021.671276

Rotz, S., Gravely, E., Mosby, I., Duncan, E., Finnis, E., Horgan, M., LeBlanc, J., Martin, R., Neufeld, H. T., Nixon, A., Pant, L., Shalla, V., & Fraser, E. D. G. (2019). Automated pastures and the digital divide: How agricultural technologies are shaping labour and rural communities. *Journal of Rural Studies*, *68*, 112 122. DOI: 10.1016/j.jrurstud.2019.01.023

Sarangi, S., Chatterjee, A., & Balasubramanian, V. (2023). Edge computing for smart agriculture: Architecture, applications, and challenges. *Computers and Electronics in Agriculture*, *209*, 107880. DOI: 10.1016/j.compag.2023.107880

Schut, M., Klerkx, L., Sartas, M., Lamers, D., Mc Campbell, M., Ogbonna, I., Kaushik, P., Atta-Krah, K., & Leeuwis, C. (2016). Innovation platforms: Experiences with their institutional embedding in agricultural research for development. *Experimental Agriculture*, *52*(4), 537–561. DOI: 10.1017/S001447971500023X

Shamshiri, R. R., Kalantari, F., & Ting, K. C.. (2018). Advances in greenhouse automation and controlled environment agriculture: A transition to plant factories and urban agriculture. *International Journal of Agricultural and Biological Engineering*, *11*(1), 1–22. DOI: 10.25165/j.ijabe.20181101.3210

Smith, A., & Stirling, A. (2010). The politics of social-ecological resilience and sustainable socio-technical transitions. *Ecology and Society, 15*(1), 11. DOI: 10.5751/ES-03218-150111

Tripoli, M., & Schmidhuber, J. (2018). *Emerging opportunities for the application of blockchain in the agri-food industry.* FAO and ITC.

Underwood, J., Wendel, A., McCool, C., & Walsh, D. (2017). The future of autonomous farming. *IEEE Potentials, 36*(6), 19–24. DOI: 10.1109/MPOT.2017.2704158

United Nations. (2015). *Transforming our world: The 2030 Agenda for Sustainable Development.* https://sdgs.un.org/2030agenda

van der Burg, S., Bogaardt, M. J., & Wolfert, S. (2021). Ethics of smart farming: Current questions and directions for responsible innovation towards the future. *NJAS Wageningen Journal of Life Sciences, 90-91*, 100289. DOI: 10.1016/j.njas.2019.100289

Wiseman, L., Sanderson, J., Zhang, A., & Jakku, E. (2019). Farmers and their data: An examination of farmers' reluctance to share their data through the lens of the laws impacting smart farming. *NJAS Wageningen Journal of Life Sciences, 90-91*(1), 100301. DOI: 10.1016/j.njas.2019.04.007

Wolfert, S., Ge, L., Verdouw, C., & Bogaardt, M.-J. (2017). Big Data in Smart Farming – A review. *Agricultural Systems, 153*, 69–80. DOI: 10.1016/j.agsy.2017.01.023

Zhang, Q., Reid, J. F., & Noguchi, N. (2020). *Agricultural automation: Fundamentals and practices.* CRC Press.

Zhang, Y., Geng, L., Tang, Y., & Zhao, Y. (2022). Development of autonomous agricultural machinery and intelligent equipment: A review. *Computers and Electronics in Agriculture, 199*, 107128. DOI: 10.1016/j.compag.2022.107128

Zhang, Y., Wang, H., Wang, J., & Cao, Z. (2020). Smart agriculture based on cloud computing and IOT. *Journal of Sensors, 2020*, 1–10. DOI: 10.1155/2020/2970143

Zhang, Y., Xie, H., Liu, T., & Chen, D. (2021). A review of digital agricultural technologies and their applications. *Intelligent Agriculture, 1*(1), 18–25. DOI: 10.1016/j.inag.2021.08.002

KEY TERMS AND DEFINITIONS

Agricultural Robotics: Robots designed specifically for agricultural applications, including autonomous tractors, harvesters, drones, and weeding machines, which enhance productivity and reduce labor dependency.

Autonomous Agricultural Systems: Integrated technological solutions that operate independently or with minimal human intervention to perform farming tasks such as planting, irrigation, harvesting, and monitoring crop health using robotics, AI, and sensors.

Digital Twin in Agriculture: A virtual replica of a farm or agricultural process that simulates real-world conditions using real-time data, allowing farmers to optimize operations and predict outcomes through modeling and analysis.

Machine Learning in Agriculture: The application of algorithms and statistical models to analyze agricultural data for tasks such as crop yield prediction, pest detection, and soil quality assessment, enabling smarter decision-making.

Precision Agriculture: A farming management concept that utilizes data-driven technologies (e.g., GPS, IoT sensors, drones) to optimize field-level management regarding crop farming, improving efficiency and reducing waste.

Sustainability in Agriculture: Practices aimed at maintaining productivity while minimizing environmental impact, conserving resources, and supporting long-term farm viability.

Chapter 9
Navigating Organizational Culture Shifts in the Modern Business Landscape

Sakshi Mann
https://orcid.org/0009-0002-8238-5268
Indira Institute of Management, India

ABSTRACT

Organizational culture is a key driver of business success, but it needs to adapt to keep up with the pace of technological advancement, changing workforce demographics, and market pressures. This chapter examines key cultural change drivers such as digitalization, AI, hybrid work arrangements, and diversity and inclusion. It covers underlying theories such as Schein's Model and Hofstede's Cultural Dimensions, as well as practical case studies of successful and unsuccessful cultural transformation. Employee engagement, change management practices, and leadership role are quoted as essential to lasting change. The chapter ends by highlighting the importance of cultural agility and ethical leadership in successfully adapting to the future of work.

1. INTRODUCTION

Organizational culture is the cornerstone of any company, influencing its values, behaviours, and long-term success. As companies compete in an era of accelerated change, cultural adaptability has emerged as a prime driver of long-term sustainability. Dated, rigid corporate cultures that thrived in the past during stable environments are now under intense pressure to transform due to technological change, globalization,

DOI: 10.4018/979-8-3373-8607-2.ch009

changes in the composition of the workforce, and changing employee expectations. Organizations that fail to recognize and react to these cultural shifts will become obsolete, disengage employees, and strategic misalignment.

This chapter addresses organizational culture change dynamics, their causes, successful change strategies, leadership and employee commitment. This chapter, grounded in real-life examples and theoretical models, is a full business guide to cultural change management in today's competitive business world.

1.1 Organizational Culture Understanding

Organizational culture is the set of shared values, norms, and beliefs that influence the manner in which employees communicate and make decisions. Organizational culture is the cornerstone of an organization's identity and affects a significant number of business activities, such as leadership, employee behaviour, decision-making, and customer relationships.

1.1.1 Organizational Culture Definition and Characteristics

Organizational culture can be thought of as a collection of values, assumptions, and beliefs which guide the way individuals behave within an organization. Organizational culture has been conceptualized as "the way things are done around here." Organizational culture is determined by several important determinants:

- **Core Values:** The organizational beliefs that dictate decision-making and behaviour.
- **Patterns and Expectations:** The unwritten guidelines that decide what is proper conduct and relations.
- **Leadership Influence**: Leadership power to set standards of culture and lead by example.
- **Work Environment:** The physical and psychological determinants that affect the way employees undertake their work.
- **Communication Patterns:** How information flows around in the organization, impacting transparency and collaboration.

1.1.2 Why Organizational Culture Is Important

A robust organizational culture gives employees a sense of belonging and purpose, resulting in increased engagement, productivity, and innovation. Well-cultured organizations tend to outperform others in terms of finances, customer satisfaction, and employee retention. A toxic or misaligned culture, on the other hand, results in high turnover, resistance to change, and ethics problems.

1.2 The Requirement for Cultural Flexibility

In today's fast-paced business era, organizations can't remain static. Cultural agility is a call for companies to stay effective, competitive, and viable in the face of shocks from the external environment.

1.2.1 The Impact of Digital Transformation

With the emergence of digital technologies, AI, and automation, the workplaces are being transformed at their very foundation. The traditional top-down models are being replaced by responsive, technology-driven models that need a culture of continuous learning, collaboration, and innovation. Without integrating digital transformation into the organizational culture, any organization becomes inefficient and outdated.

For example, Google and Amazon have developed data-driven decision-making, experimentation, and agility cultures. On the other hand, companies that are resistant to embracing technology are besieged by inefficiencies and stagnation.

1.2.2 Employee Demographics and Evolving Employee Expectations

Today's workforce is more diverse than ever with various generations introducing different values and expectations. Their workers, from Millennials and Gen Z generations, value mission-oriented work, flexibility, and diversity, making traditional management and corporate pyramid structures difficult.

Organizations have to transform their cultures to address these shifting expectations by creating:

- **Work-Life Integration:** Providing telework options, flexible work hours, and mental health support.
- **Diversity, Equity, and Inclusion (DEI):** Creating inclusive environments in which diverse employees are respected and empowered.
- **Collaborative Decision-Making:** Involving employees to provide suggestions and contribute to developing company policies.

Such organizations as Netflix and Microsoft have managed to transform their culture in order to recruit and retain young professionals by focusing on openness, employee autonomy, and ongoing feedback processes.

1.3 Critical Drivers of Changes in Organizational Culture

Cultural shifts are not in a vacuum; they are initiated by internal and external factors that compel businesses to re-examine their core values and business models.

1.3.1 Exogenous Drivers of Cultural Change

Several macro-environmental factors contribute to cultural shifts, including:

- **Technological Disruption**: With increasing reliance on automation, big data, and AI, cultural transformation towards innovation and digital literacy is required.
- **Globalization:** As businesses expand to transnational markets, they must make their cultures adaptable to manage diverse cultural perspectives and business attitudes.
- **Economic and Market Pressures:** Unforeseen shifts in consumer trends, competition, and financial markets require cultural adaptability to remain competitive.
- **Social and Political Movements:** Social justice movements and corporate social responsibility initiatives have compelled organizations to reframe their ethical responsibilities and values.

1.3.2 Cultural Change Drivers Internal

Organizations are further affected by developments internally and become culturally changed by:

- **Leadership Transitions:** New directions, priorities, and cultural expectations accompany new leadership.
- **Mergers and Acquisitions:** Integrating different organizational cultures is challenging and requires a strategic realignment.
- **Employee Engagement and Feedback:** Strong employee voice has the potential to bring about cultural change by identifying areas of change and instilling change.

For instance, when Satya Nadella took over as the CEO of Microsoft, he guided the company through a cultural shift from a competitive, hard-nosed culture to one cantered on collaboration, empathy, and innovation. As a result of that, Microsoft became a global technology leader once again.

1.4 Addressing Cultural Shift Challenges

Even though cultural change is required, organizations usually have great trouble changing.

1.4.1 Resistance to Change

Managers and staff accustomed to traditional ways can oppose cultural change because they are hesitant, insecure about their employment, or doubt new approaches. This can be overcome by good communication, change management, and involving employees in decision-making.

1.4.2 New Values That Are In-Line with Business Objectives

An effective cultural transformation has to be directed toward an organization's general vision and goals. When the cultural transformation is interfering with business priorities, it brings about confusion and lack of interest among employees. Leaders should make sure that the cultural evolution is driving long-term business goals.

1.4.3 Consistency in Global Operations

Multinational firms struggle to achieve a uniform culture geographically. Local traditions and laws might necessitate an asymmetric implementation approach on the basis of maintaining central organizational values.

1.5 Structure of the Chapter

This chapter will examine the different facets of organizational culture changes in more detail. The following sections will discuss:

- **Theoretical Models of Cultural Change** – Discussion of typical theories of how and why change happens in organizations.
- **Tactics for Effective Cultural Transformation** – Reviewing change management procedures, leadership, and best practices for cultural change management.

- **Cultural Transformation Case Studies** – Studying real case studies of companies which have implemented or failed to implement cultural transformation.
- **Implications for Leadership and Business** Strategy – Describing the broader implications of cultural transformation on organizational performance and long-term growth.

By the end of this chapter, readers will have a full understanding of how to identify, practice, and sustain cultural changes in contemporary business environments.

2. UNDERSTANDING ORGANIZATIONAL CULTURE

Organizational culture is a multifaceted and complex concept that plays a significant role in the internal dynamics and external relations of an organization. Organizational culture comprises common norms, values, and beliefs that determine the practices and behaviour of an organization. Organizational culture requires a deep understanding by leaders and stakeholders who wish to establish an enabling environment for the achievement of strategic objectives.

2.1 Description and Organisational Culture Constituents

Organizational culture is the collective mind programming that distinguishes members of a particular organization from members of another organization. It is a system of shared values, assumptions, and beliefs that shape the manner in which people behave in organizations. The shared values influence the people in the organization greatly and shape the manner in which they dress, the manner in which they behave, and the manner in which they perform their work.

These are the fundamental components of organizational culture:

- **Artefacts:** They are the visible and tangible features of an organization, including dress code, office design, rituals, and ceremonies. Artefacts are the outward manifestations of culture and are normally easy to see but difficult to interpret correctly.
- **Espoused Values:** These are the stated values and norms which an organization would like to embrace. These may be found in mission statements, corporate philosophies, and official statements. There can typically be a gap between espoused values and enactment within the firm.
- **Underlying Basic Assumptions:** These are the deeply rooted, taken-for-granted habits that are usually unconscious but constitute the substance of

culture. They are the assumptions employees have about their job and the company that shape behaviour without needing explanation.

2.2 Organizational Culture Theories and Frameworks

Several theories and frameworks have been developed to study and understand organizational culture. These models provide an insight into how culture is developed, maintained, and can be altered.

2.2.1 Edgar Schein's Organizational Culture Model

Edgar Schein, a renowned organizational psychologist, suggested a model explaining three levels of organizational culture (Schein, 1983). The model provides a structured approach to understanding how culture influences organizational behaviour, knowledge sharing, and decision-making. The study suggests that organizational culture is a driving force that influences knowledge management practices and human capital development, as it provides a setting that is favourable to innovation and competitive advantage (Perez & de Pablos, 2003).

1. **Artefacts and Behaviours**: This is the level that includes all the physical objects of an organization that you can touch, hear, and see. It includes the physical setting, language, technology, products, and tangible rituals. While artefacts are observable, they are hard to understand unless you look below the surface levels of culture. Organizations whose artefacts are aligned with their strategic objectives can enhance knowledge-sharing processes, enabling continuous learning culture.
2. **Espoused Values:** These are the officially proclaimed values and norms that an organization asserts to follow. They are a model of behaviour and a guide to making decisions for employees. But there may be discrepancies between what is asserted and what exactly is practiced. Perez & de Pablos (2003) believe that a well-articulated culture that includes knowledge management tools can bridge this gap, so that espoused values are translated into concrete behaviours that render an organization competitive.
3. **Basic Underlying Assumptions**: At the most basic level, these are the unconscious, assumed values and beliefs that actually drive organizational behaviour. These are embedded deeply and typically difficult to modify. Studies conclude that companies with advanced, knowledge-based cultures can leverage these assumptions in the creation of innovation, flexibility, and sustainable competitive advantage (Perez & de Pablos, 2003).

Schein's model highlights the point that in order to comprehend an organization's culture as a whole, one has to go beyond visible artefacts as well as espoused values in order to find the underlying assumptions that actually shape behaviour. Furthermore, the intersection of knowledge management and cultural models can greatly improve organizational competitiveness by making sure that intellectual capital is maximized.

2.2.2 Hofstede's Cultural Dimensions Theory

Geert Hofstede's Cultural Dimensions Theory is a theory applied to describe differences in culture between countries and how these affect organizational behaviour. Through an IBM employee survey of over 50 countries, Hofstede discovered six dimensions of national culture (Hofstede, 2011):

1. **Power Distance Index (PDI):** This dimension measures to what extent less powerful members of an organization embrace and expect the power to be unevenly distributed. High PDI cultures are okay with hierarchical systems without questioning much, while low PDI cultures subscribe to equality and participative decision-making.
2. **Individualism vs. Collectivism (IDV)**: This dimension measures the degree to which societies are organized for individuals and groups. Individualist cultures focus on personal success and individual rights, whereas collectivist cultures focus on group harmony and collective good.
3. **Masculinity vs. Femininity (MAS):** This dimension deals with the difference between emotional roles of the sexes. Masculine cultures focus on competitiveness, assertiveness, and material success, while feminine cultures focus on relationships, quality of life, and care for the weak.
4. **Uncertainty Avoidance Index (UAI):** It is the degree to which the members of a culture are threatened by unknown or uncertain situations. A high UAI culture has a rigorous code of conduct and is less tolerant of deviant behaviours or attitudes, whereas a low UAI culture is more relaxed and tolerant of change.
5. **Long-Term vs. Short-Term Orientation (LTO):** LTO refers to the time orientation of society. Long-term societies are concerned with future rewards, perseverance, and saving, while short-term societies are concerned with traditions, the current social order, and respecting social obligations.
6. **Indulgence vs. Restraint (IVR):** This dimension reflects the degree to which societal norms provide citizens with liberty in the satisfaction of their human needs. Indulgent societies allow relatively unrestricted satisfaction of basic human needs related to enjoying life and having fun, and restrained societies restrict satisfaction of needs and direct it through stringent social norms.

Hofstede's model is credited with describing how cultural differences can affect organizational practices, communication, and management styles across different countries.

2.2.3 Teal Organizations (Frederic Laloux)

Frederic Laloux employed the term "Teal Organizations" in his book "Reinventing Organizations," referring to a new model of organizational development. According to Laloux, organizations have evolved through various stages, and each stage is identified by a different colour:

- **Red Organizations:** These are defined by authoritarian leadership and survival orientation.
- **Amber Organizations:** Marked by formal roles and hierarchical structures, emphasizing stability and control.
- **Orange Organizations:** Driven by competition, innovation, and the necessity to deliver results.

2.2.4 Ambidextrous Organizations (Tushman & O'Reilly)

Ambidextrous organizations, a theory advanced by Michael Tushman and Charles O'Reilly, are companies capable of contemporaneously pursuing incremental (evolutionary) and discontinuous (revolutionary) innovations. This dual capability enables companies to take advantage of existing competence and explore new channels and, therefore, sustain long-term performance and responsiveness in turbulent markets. The key characteristics of ambidextrous organizations are:

- **Structural Differentiation:** Ambidextrous companies typically have separate units or teams for exploratory and exploitative activities. Exploratory units are loose-structured experiment- and innovation-focused, while exploitative units are improvement-of-existing-process- and efficiency-focused with more structured systems.
- **Senior Leadership Integration:** Even with structural segregation, one senior leadership team facilitates coordination of exploratory and exploitative activities. Leaders ensure balancing of resource allocation, setting consistent strategies, and fostering a culture that supports innovation and operational excellence.
- **Cultural Ambidexterity:** Shared organizational culture that is aligned and adaptable is important. Such a culture helps employees embrace change and

innovation while remaining committed to the organisation's core values and operational goals.

2.3 How Culture Affects Organizational Strategy and Performance

Organizational culture is a driver of performance and a strategic enabler. A strong, responsive culture can power higher employee engagement, higher productivity, and higher alignment with organizational goals. A misaligned or toxic culture, by contrast, can lead to low morale, high turnover, and strategic failure.

Main ways in which culture affects performance and strategy are:

- **Decision-Making:** Culture will determine whether decision-making is centralized or decentralized, affecting responsiveness and agility.
- **Innovation:** Those societies that have a culture of risk-taking and learning from mistakes will be more innovative.
- **Communication:** Open cultures facilitate open communication, which reduces misunderstandings and fosters cooperation.
- **Employee Conduct**: Employee conduct is influenced by shared norms and values, affecting customer service, quality, and performance.

Knowledge of organizational culture and deliberate design by leadership is significant

3. KEY DRIVERS OF ORGANIZATIONAL CULTURE CHANGES

Organisational culture keeps evolving continuously as a result of various internal and external influences. In the era of technology, organisations are undergoing unprecedented changes that influence how employees engage, contribute, and work towards organisational goals. Several drivers influence such cultural transformations, including technological innovation, employee demographics and aspirations, socio-political and economic forces, and competitive forces. All the drivers exert significant influences on the contemporary workplace.

3.1 Technological Developments

Technology has transformed organizational culture, reshaping the way work is executed, managed, and measured. The convergence of artificial intelligence (AI), automation, and digitalization, as well as the proliferation of remote and hybrid work styles, has reshaped work environments at the very core.

3.1.1 Artificial Intelligence, Automation, and Digital Transformation

The rapid emergence of AI and automation has revolutionized conventional work processes, and it has created a paradigm shift in organizational culture. AI-based decision-making, predictive analytics, and machine learning solutions have mechanized processes, minimizing human intervention in routine tasks. Organizations that use AI have redesigned their workplaces and are focusing more on data-driven insights, cross-functional collaboration, and continuous learning.

Furthermore, digital transformation initiatives have accelerated the adoption of cloud computing, big data, and enterprise resource planning (ERP) systems that have enhanced organizational productivity and work convenience (Westerman et al., 2019). The organizations that do not change themselves to keep up with these changes will end up being outdated because digital disruption keeps on redefining companies.

3.1.2 Remote Work and Hybrid Work Models

The COVID-19 pandemic leapfrogged the adoption of remote and hybrid work models, propelling the traditional way of thinking about work culture. Businesses have moved towards flexible work patterns, necessitating a digital-first culture, improved cyber security practices, and efficient virtual collaboration tools.

Remote work has redefined employee commitment and organizational communication, promoting greater use of virtual meetings, asynchronous work, and computerized project management software (Gajendran & Harrison, 2007). Hybrid work arrangements have also prompted organizations to redesign the workplace, adopt flexible work policies, and focus on employee health. Organizations that adapt successfully to these will develop a more flexible and inclusive work environment.

3.2 Workforce Demographics and Expectations

Workforce demographics and employee aspirations are changing organizational culture in today's time. Millennials and Gen Z employees have been brought up with different perspectives on work-life balance, meaningful work, and workplace belongingness. Organizations are also placing greater emphasis on diversity, equity, and inclusion (DEI) initiatives to develop a diverse and innovative workforce.

3.2.1 Millennial and Gen Z Workforce Values

Millennials and Gen Z employees prioritize meaningful work, career development, and work-life integration over traditional hierarchical structures (Meister & Willyerd, 2010). They expect open leadership, team-oriented work environments, and continuous learning opportunities. Unlike previous generations, these employees embrace flat organizational structures, open communication, and flexible work arrangements.

Firms that align their corporate values with these workforce expectations are able to foster employee retention, engagement, and productivity. This shift to meaningful work also signifies the significance of corporate social responsibility (CSR) and ethical business practices.

3.2.2 Diversity, Equity, and Inclusion (DEI) Factors

The demand for inclusive and diverse workspaces has grown, influencing organizational cultural norms and policies. Diverse teams have been said to enhance performance, make better decisions, and create innovation (Hunt et al., 2018). Organizations now emphasize DEI initiatives through targeted recruitment practices, inclusive leadership, and unconscious bias training.

Efforts of equity and inclusion extend beyond demographic diversity to embrace neurodiversity, accessibility, and psychological safety (Edmondson, 2018). Organizations that embed DEI principles in organizational culture will be able to recruit better talent and attain a sustainable competitive edge in the marketplace.

3.3 Socio-Political and Economic Factors

Global socio-political and economic pressures influence corporate culture through the influence of business strategy, regulatory environments, and ethics. Companies have to be responsive and resilient in the face of globalization, changing markets, and changing regulatory requirements.

3.3.1 Market Dynamics and Globalization

Globalization has unified economies and provided cross-cultural cooperation and expanded marketplace opportunities. Since organizations are operating in various regions, they must establish inclusive and adaptable workplace cultures that can incorporate various cultural worldview perspectives.

Furthermore, economic shifts, including inflation pressure and supply chain interruption, require companies to create flexible work arrangements and strategic talent. Companies that possess cultural adaptability and innovation built into their organizational structure are best positioned to address marketplace uncertainty.

3.3.2 Regulatory and Ethical Requirements for Change

Regulators and governments continue to have strict compliance rules, which affect organizational policy and company governance. Ethical issues such as environmental, social, and governance (ESG) policies are increasingly becoming mainstream corporate strategy. Organizations need to be transparent, accountable, and sustainable in order to support changing regulatory aspirations.

In addition, ethical issues regarding data privacy, AI bias, and algorithmic decision-making have led organizations to embrace robust ethical frameworks for technology adoption. Strong ethical grounding generates trust among stakeholders, customers, and employees.

3.4 Competitive Pressures and Market Forces

Competitive market forces compel organizations to constantly shift their culture in order to remain up to date. Customer-centric strategies, and the necessity for innovation and responsiveness, compel organizations to prioritize flexibility and strategic change.

3.4.1 Customer-Focused Strategies

Organizations are finding customer experience a strategic competitive advantage. Customer-focused cultures believe in personalized interactions, data-driven and responsive service models and individualized interactions (Lemon & Verhoef, 2016). Amazon and Tesla are some of the companies that have shifted market expectations by being constantly innovative and customer-focused.

Employees are delivering fantastic customer experiences, and that requires a culture of responsibility, empowerment, and collaboration. Companies that make customer obsession a part of their institutional DNA are likely to thrive in the long term.

3.4.2 Need for Innovation and Flexibility

Innovation is a pillar of modern organizational culture. Organizations need to develop a culture of experimentation, risk-taking, and continuous learning to stay ahead of the curve. Agile methods, design thinking, and cross-functional collaboration are now the determinants of organizational success.

During a time of increased technological revolution, the enterprises that cultivate innovation and entrepreneurship will keep growing. Organizational heads must cultivate an environment that sustains innovation, resilience, and transformational leadership.

4. STRATEGIES FOR CULTURAL TRANSFORMATION

Organizational culture is dynamic and, in the long term, will have to adapt to external business environments, employees' expectations, and technological change. Changing culture, however, requires strategic planning, effective change management, and leadership. Some of the major strategies for cultural change that have been discussed in this section include acknowledging the requirement for change, applying existing models of change management, balancing innovation and tradition, overcoming resistance to change, and encouraging open communication.

4.1 Establishing the Need for Change

Before cultural change, organizations must see the necessity for change. There are a number of signs of the necessity for cultural transformation, including low employee engagement, low innovation, high turnover, customer dissatisfaction, or strategic goal misalignment (Imperatori, 2017). Cultural audits, employee opinion surveys, and benchmarking against industry standards can be employed to determine areas of necessity for transformation.

Leaders must be aware whether the dominant culture will facilitate organizational flexibility, competitive success, and sustainability. Cultural transformation will fail if there is no clear understanding of the cultural landscape. Aligning business goals with cultural transformation ensures relevance and support from stakeholders (Kotter, 2012).

4.2 Change Management Models

To be able to effectively transform culture, organizations can apply well-proven change management models. Two of the most celebrated models are Kotter's 8-Step Change Model and Lewin's Change Management Model.

4.2.1 Kotter's 8-Step Change Model

John Kotter (2012) also developed an eight-step process of effective change leadership. This model provides a step-by-step approach to cultural change:

1. **Instil a sense of** urgency – Leaders must convey the imperative for cultural change by illustrating the risks of complacency.
2. **Establish a guiding coalition** – An influential group of stakeholders must drive change initiatives.
3. **Create a vision and strategy** – Having the desired cultural shift in place aligns efforts.
4. **Communicate the change vision –** Repeated messaging reinforces the significance of cultural evolution.
5. **Mobilize employees for widespread action** – Giving resources and eliminating obstacles facilitates participation.
6. **Generate short-term wins** – Short-term success builds momentum and generates commitment.
7. **Consolidate gains and introduce further change** – Maintaining progress avoids a return to previous cultural practices.
8. **Ground new strategies in the culture** – Placing change in policies, behaviour, and leadership practices guarantees sustainability.

Kotter's model works for significant long-term culture changes that need systematic execution and continuous leadership support.

4.2.2 Lewin's Change Management Model

Kurt Lewin (1947) outlined a three-stage model of change management:

1. **Unfreeze** – Organizations must disrupt existing cultural norms, making employees aware of the need for transformation.
2. **Change** – New values, attitudes, and behaviour must be brought in and instilled through modelling, communication, and training by the leadership.
3. **Refreeze** – After cultural change has been implemented, it needs to be embedded in policies, performance management, and reward systems.

Lewin's model is best suited for organizations that must transition from deeply entrenched traditional cultures to more adaptive, dynamic cultures.

4.3 Balancing Tradition with Innovation

Cultural transformation is not a matter of abandoning all the traditional values but of reconciling tradition and innovation. Cultures that are historically rooted must find core values that remain relevant and embrace new practices for enhancing flexibility (Schein, 2010).

A strategic response includes:

- **Identifying non-negotiable cultural elements** – Retaining core principles that define the organization's identity.
- **Incremental innovation introduction** – Introducing incremental innovations that are aligned with traditional values to minimize disruption.
- **Enable intergenerational collaboration** – Merge the experience of older workers and bring in new ideas from younger generations.

Firms such as IBM and Microsoft have survived through cultural change by upholding central ethical values while encouraging digital innovation (Gates, 2021).

4.4 Overcoming Resistance to Change

Resistance to cultural change will be the greatest challenge organizations will encounter. Employees will likely fear the unknown, be suspicious of management motives, or be resistant to shifting expectations (Oreg et al., 2011). Organizations can employ the following to overcome resistance:

- **Engage employees early** – Employee involvement in the change process makes them feel more like owners.
- **Transparency in addressing problems** – Clear articulation of why change is needed eliminates ambiguity.
- **Provide training and support** – Equipping employees with new skills diminishes fear and builds confidence in change management.
- **Reward adaptation** – Rewarding adaptation incentivizes learning about new cultural behaviours.

Netflix and Google organizational case studies highlight that it leads to smoother transitions by developing a culture of psychological safety and flexibility (Edmondson, 2018).

4.5 Communication and Transparency in Cultural Transitions

Effective communication is needed for successful cultural transformation. Trust, reducing uncertainty, and inducing wholehearted commitment result from openness (Clampitt et al., 2000). Organizations have to:

- **Utilize multiple communication channels** – The use of town halls, internal publications, and websites offers widespread dissemination.
- **Foster two-way communication** – Feedback loops allow the employees to voice their opinions and participate in the change process.
- **Storytelling practice** – Telling stories of success and client testimonials evoke the spirit of cultural change.

Leaders who communicate honestly and frequently create a culture of openness and engagement, driving effective change initiatives.

5. LEADERSHIP'S ROLE IN CULTURAL CHANGE

Leadership is responsible for developing, maintaining, and changing organizational culture. Leaders themselves determine the tone of values, behaviours, and norms within an organization, and accordingly, the employees' interaction and alignment with the company's purpose are determined. Cultural transformation is most effective when leaders lead the transformation visibly, model the desired behaviour, and establish a climate for innovation and ethical decision-making. This section discusses the most important leadership styles that facilitate cultural transformation, the leaders as culture champions, leadership-led transformation case studies, and the role of ethical leadership in cultural transformations.

5.1 Transformational and Transactional Leadership

Two most prevalent leadership styles lead to cultural change: transformational and transactional leadership.

5.1.1 Transformational Leadership

Transformational leaders motivate and empower employees to embrace change, generating innovation and lasting cultural change (Bass, 1990). Transformational leaders have four traits:

- **Idealized Influence:** Portraying themselves as models and establishing high standards of ethics and performance.
- **Inspirational Motivation:** Creating an inspiring vision for the future.
- **Intellectually Stimulating:** Encouraging innovative thinking and problem-solving.
- **Individualized Consideration:** Fostering employees' career growth and well-being.

Companies like Microsoft under Satya Nadella are the best examples of transformational leadership. Nadella changed the culture of Microsoft from a fixed one to a growth mind-set, promoting collaboration, learning, and customer-centric innovation (Ibarra et al., 2018). He promoted empathy, learning, and flexibility, demonstrating that transformational leadership is about continuous self-development and emotional intelligence.

5.1.2 Transactional Leadership

Transactional leaders are interested in creating order, efficiency, and performance through formal reward and punishment (Burns, 1978). Transactional leadership is effective in stable organizations but may not be the optimal means to shift culture. Transactional leadership involves:

- **Contingent Rewards:** Offering rewards for achieving set goals.
- **Active Management by Exception:** Deviation correction and performance monitoring.
- **Passive Management by Exception**: Correcting issues only when necessary (Avolio & Bass, 2004).

While stability is facilitated by transactional leadership, transformational leadership is most appropriate to spearhead cultural change. However, some form of both, merging the strengths of both methods, may be optimal, depending on the organization.

5.2 Leaders as Culture Champions

For cultural change to be effective, leaders must be champions, encouraging and affirming new cultural norms. Among the most critical tactics for leaders to drive cultural change are:

- **Developing and Enfranchising a Defining Vision**: Leaders must define why there is a call for culture change and how it sustains organizational success (Kotter, 2012).
- **Leading by Example:** Leaders will be more likely to adopt new cultural norms if they lead by example (Schein, 2010).
- **Empowering Employees:** Encouraging participation and ownership leads to commitment to cultural transformation (Yukl, 2013).
- **Creating a Feedback Culture:** Feedback loops and open communication ensure flexibility and alignment (Edmondson, 2018).

Leaders must also realize cultural change is a process that does not happen overnight. They must be patient and persistent and employ good communications and tie incentives to new cultural expectations.

5.3 Leadership-Driven Cultural Transformation Case Studies

5.3.1 Satya Nadella at Microsoft

When Satya Nadella became the CEO of Microsoft in 2014, he knew that the company had to go through a cultural transformation. Microsoft had developed a competitive in-house culture that discouraged collaboration and innovation. Nadella adopted the growth mind-set, focusing on learning, collaboration, and customer-led innovation (Ibarra et al., 2018). By changing the leadership practices and infusing these values in performance management and development programs, Microsoft was made agile and innovative. His leadership style focused on continuous learning, inclusion, and customer-first thinking, proving that cultural transformation is as much a product of strategic vision as it is of emotional intelligence.

5.3.2 Transformation of IBM under Lou Gerstner

In the early 1990s, IBM was financially struggling due to its culture of resistance to change and top-down structure. IBM's CEO in 1993, Lou Gerstner, led the culture transformation by shifting IBM's focus from hardware to services and customer orientation (Gerstner, 2002). Gerstner encouraged cross-functional working, implemented performance-based reward schemes, and reshaped leadership expectations for IBM, ultimately reversing the company's competitive performance. His leadership stressed the significance of convergence of culture, strategy, and business operations.

5.3.3 Netflix's Cultural Evolution

Netflix, under Reed Hastings, developed a distinctive culture of freedom and accountability with focus on high performance and outcomes (McCord, 2018). Hastings created radical transparency, ongoing feedback, and results culture, which helped Netflix stay nimble in the rapidly evolving entertainment business. Netflix's success is an example of how leadership is able to induce cultural transformation in perpetuating ongoing innovation and leadership in the marketplace.

5.4 The Importance of Ethical Leadership in Culture Transitions

Ethical leadership is required for cultural change so that change is paired with integrity, justice, and corporate accountability (Brown & Treviño, 2006). Ethical leaders:

- **Establish Trust:** Honesty and transparency build the employees' trust in the change process (Mayer et al., 1995).
- **Promote Inclusion:** Balanced policies and DEI initiatives create cultural transformation (Klein, 2020).
- **Encourage Accountability**: Ethical leadership supports adherence to organizational values and social norms (Treviño et al., 2000).
- **Lead Sustainable Change:** Ethical leaders value long-term cultural well-being more than fleeting success (Ciulla, 2014).

Ethics-based leaders build an organizational culture of integrity, inclusiveness, and long-term sustainability. Ethical leadership not only results in employee engagement but also in corporate reputation and stakeholder trust.

In addition, ethical leadership is critical in addressing resistance to cultural change. Employees can resist change because they are uncertain or in doubt about leadership intentions. Ethical leaders solve these issues by making transparent decisions, practicing open communication, and treating all employees equally.

6. EMPLOYEE ENGAGEMENT AND CULTURAL CHANGES

Organizational culture also plays the role of influencing employee motivation, engagement, and productivity. When employees undergo changes in norms, communication, expectations, and leadership at the workplace through cultural change, smooth transition is ensured through intentional strategies with high levels of engagement, less resistance, and alignment of employees with new organizational values. The following is a description of the effect of cultural change on employees, how positive engagement can be achieved, HR's role in enabling cultural change, and resistance measurement and management.

6.1 Effect on Employees of Cultural Change

Cultural change can profoundly alter the work life, beliefs, and employee behaviour. Some employees view change as an opportunity for growth while others resist or fear change. Some of the key effects cultural changes have on employees are:

- **Emotional Reactions**: Workers can have feelings of enthusiasm and motivation but also of concern and frustration. Change can dismantle routine and blur job security, expectations, and relationships. Emotions should be managed by employers through open communications, counseling, and stress-reduction programs.
- **Workplace Dynamics Changes**: Cultural changes typically lead to changes in communication, teamwork, and leadership interactions. Employees might need to adapt to new leadership styles, reporting lines, or habits of teamwork. Properly managed, these changes can increase teamwork and innovation but, if poorly managed, can lead to disengagement and confusion.
- **Increased or Decreased Engagement**: Cultural change is managed, and its impact on engagement is determined. The employees who are involved in the process and are aware of the reason for the change will be likely to stay engaged (Edmondson, 2019). The employees who are not involved or heard will disengage. Organizations must engage employees actively through communication, participative decision-making, and feedback mechanisms to sustain engagement.
- **Career Development Opportunities:** Cultural change is often followed by new learning opportunities, career development programs, and role enlargements (Yukl, 2013). Workers who see personal benefit in the change will be more likely to accept it. Career mapping, mentoring, and leadership development can help employees map their career development with the new cultural direction.

Understanding these effects makes it possible for organizations to pre-empt staff anxiety and design interventions that enhance engagement during cultural transitions.

6.2 Strategies for Promoting Healthy Engagement

In order to make cultural changes result in positive results, organizations need to have strategic programs that effectively engage employees. The most important strategies are:

6.2.1. Clear Communication

Open and honest communication is required to build employee trust and minimize resistance. Leaders should:

- Explain the reason behind the cultural shift and how it aids organizational goals (Kotter, 2012).
- Provide regular updates through town hall meetings, newsletters, and social media.
- Foster two-way communication in which employees can offer feedback, share concerns, and pose questions.
- Utilize stories and anecdotes to make the cultural transition concrete and meaningful.

6.2.2 Involvement and participation of employees

Employees will be more likely to accept cultural change when they are engaged in the process of building it. Companies can:

- Create cross-functional teams to collect employee input and co-create cultural initiatives.
- Enable staff members to act as change ambassadors to drive new cultural norms.
- Involve workers in pilot projects or feedback sessions before mass roll-out of reforms (Edmondson, 2018).
- Organize workshops and brainstorming sessions to collectively create workplace culture and policies that suit the new culture.

6.2.3 Leadership Support and Role Modelling

Leaders should model the values and behaviours desired in the culture. These are:

- Commitment to change by action being in line with organizational values.

- Identification and recognition of employees who adopt and sustain the cultural change.
- Offering counselling and guidance to employees with difficulty adjusting to new norms.
- Leaders being encouraged to have coaching conversations with employees to deal with issues and promote a commitment to the cultural change.

6.2.4 Training and Development

Organizations need to invest in learning programs that allow workers to acquire the skills they need to thrive in the new culture. They are:

- Organizing workshops on resilience, emotional intelligence, and flexibility.
- Providing training in emerging technology, procedures, and leadership requirements.
- Ensuring ongoing education via e-learning platforms and continuing professional development initiatives (Yukl, 2013).
- Creating experiential learning exercises such as role-playing and case study discussions to strengthen values.

6.2.5 Incentives and Appreciation

Rewarding and acknowledging employees for embracing cultural change encourages good behaviour. Best practice is:

- Developing reward systems that acknowledge employees' efforts in cultural change.
- Connecting performance rewards with cultural congruence.
- Providing career development opportunities to employees who demonstrate leadership in cultural change initiatives (McCord, 2018).
- Creating a peer reward system in which employees reward people who actively demonstrate the new culture.

6.3 HR's Role in Facilitating Cultural Change

HR is at the forefront of sustaining and propelling cultural transformation. These are:

6.3.1 Harmonization of HR Policy with New Cultural Values

HR must revamp procedures and policies to fit the new organizational culture. This means revamping performance management systems, hiring standards, and work policies. HR policy consistency and cultural expectations enhance credibility for the change initiative.

6.3.2 Enabling Change Management Initiatives

HR must spearhead cultural change programs by:

- Change readiness surveys to determine potential issues.
- Modifying formal change management models, i.e., Kotter's 8-Step Model or Lewin's Change Model.
- Providing long-term employee support and development throughout the change (Kotter, 2012).
- Designing the workshop and experience-based learning sessions to enable the employees to learn and accept the new norms.

6.3.3 Encouraging Employee Well-being

Cultural change is stressful; HR must address the welfare of employees through:

- Promoting work-life balance by flexible working.
- Offering mental health services and counselling.
- Creating a psychologically safe environment in which the employees feel appreciated and listened to (Edmondson, 2018).
- Organizing team-building activities and wellness programs to enhance relationships and emotional resilience.

6.3.4 Establishing a Feedback Culture

HR should establish mechanisms for continuous feedback, including:

- Employee focus groups and surveys to assess the extent of engagement.
- Offering anonymous means of providing feedback to highlight shortcomings and areas needing improvement.
- Ongoing review and refinement of cultural programs through employee feedback (McCord, 2018).

- Conducting open forums in which employees discuss problems and offer solutions together.

6.4 Measurement and Management of Resistance

6.4.1 Identifying Resistance Early

Organizations need to track the most important indicators of resistance, including:

- Increased turnover or absenteeism.
- Lower productivity and engagement ratings.
- Negative worker comments and resistance to becoming involved with change efforts (Kotter, 2012).
- Monitoring daily conversations and social activities to identify underlying problems.

6.4.2 Handling Employee Grievances

To counteract resistance, organizations need to:

- One-on-one talks to learn specific concerns.
- Provide promises of career development opportunities and job security.
- Provide individualized assistance for employees having challenges with adaptation.
- Leverage mentoring and coaching programs to help employees overcome cultural change phobias.

7. CASE STUDIES: SUCCESSES AND FAILURES IN CULTURAL TRANSFORMATION

Organizational culture is a key determinant of a company's long-term success or failure. Culture dictates how employees interact with one another, how decisions are made, and how companies react to change. Companies with a robust, adaptive culture thrive, while those that neglect cultural misalignment reap catastrophic results. Examples from the real world illuminate how cultural transformation can be a strategic asset or liability. Two success stories—Netflix's constant reinvention and Microsoft's turnaround under Satya Nadella—and two cautionary tales—Boeing's struggle with safety and accountability and Wells Fargo's struggle to regain trust after scandal—are covered in this section.

7.1 Success Stories

A well-defined and dynamic organizational culture can be the key to sustaining a competitive edge. The following two companies demonstrate how cultural transformation has led to business success and long-term growth.

7.1.1 Netflix: Continuous Innovation and Flexibility

Netflix's evolution from a DVD rental company to a streaming giant is a testament to the power of cultural responsiveness. Founded in 1997, Netflix initially disrupted the home entertainment industry with its DVD-by-mail business. The largest cultural shift for the company, however, took place in the early 2000s when it recognized the future of the industry through digital streaming and moved to an online subscription model in 2007 (McCord, 2018). This shift enabled Netflix to surpass its competitors like Blockbuster, which could not foresee the future of the industry.

One of the most defining aspects of Netflix's culture is its risk-taking and innovative culture. Netflix fosters a work culture in which experimentation is fostered and failure is embraced as a chance to learn (Keating, 2012). This has led to trailblazing initiatives such as AI-based content recommendation and the release of original content, beginning with House of Cards in 2013.

The "Netflix Culture Deck," which is an expression of company values, instills values in people like independence and accountability, excellence, and honesty. People enjoy a good degree of liberty but are totally answerable for what they do. Unlike typical hierarchical firms, Netflix is relatively flexible and geared toward making instant decisions and staying agile (Hastings & Meyer, 2020). Flexibility, on its part, has provided Netflix with room to adapt effectively to industry fluctuations and consumer trends.

In the time of the COVID-19 pandemic, Netflix's robust culture of flexibility was once again evident. With lockdowns happening all around the world, causing demand for home entertainment to surge, the company promptly moved its content pipeline and production schedules to provide uninterrupted service. The flexibility, complemented by a culture of innovation and responsiveness, has enabled Netflix to continue in its market position as a leading streaming company.

7.1.2 Microsoft: Satya Nadella's Cultural Transformation

Satya Nadella's Microsoft makeover ranks as one of the greatest business culture overhauls of all time. Before Nadella became CEO in 2014, Microsoft was regarded as stuck in a rigid and intensely competitive in-house culture that suppressed collaboration and innovation. Under Steve Ballmer, the firm had been focused on

Windows and Office software but was lagging behind competitors in cloud computing and mobile technology.

Nadella ushered in a change of culture by embracing a "growth mindset," a term coined by psychologist Carol Dweck. This led employees to accept learning, try new things, and view failure as a part of the process of innovation. By eliminating the dominant "know-it-all" culture and adopting a "learn-it-all" culture, Microsoft saw an explosion of innovation and teamwork.

One of Nadella's greatest culture changes was breaking down silos from within. Before he came on board as CEO, Microsoft departments operated in silos, resulting in inefficiency and wasted potential. He encouraged cross-functional collaboration, which opened the door to successful projects such as Microsoft Teams, expansion of the Azure cloud platform, and strategic acquisitions such as LinkedIn and GitHub.

The second major shift was Microsoft's commitment to diversity and inclusion. Nadella emphasized empathy as a leadership principle and fostered an environment where inclusive perspectives are valued. Microsoft had initiatives for fostering greater inclusion of underrepresented groups and inclusive corporate culture. This resulted in enhanced employee satisfaction and engagement that drove Microsoft to business success financially (Fenwick, Kaal, & Vermeulen, 2019).

From a commercial point of view, the cultural transformation reaped great rewards. Microsoft's market capitalization hit over $1 trillion in 2019, and the company emerged as a runaway success in cloud computing, artificial intelligence, and enterprise solutions. This achievement highlights the role of cultural transformation in business growth and sustainability.

7.2 Failures and Challenges

While a few organizations are successful due to cultural transformation, others fail due to misplaced priorities, ethical collapses, or inaction. The following two case studies illustrate the consequences of mismanagement of culture.

7.2.1 Boeing: Safety and Accountability Challenges

Boeing's recent history is a cautionary tale of how a toxic culture can lead to spectacular failures. The aerospace giant experienced disastrous reputational and financial losses following the Lion Air Flight 610 and Ethiopian Airlines Flight 302 crashes, both of which involved the 737 MAX. The two plane crashes killed 346 individuals and led to global condemnation of Boeing's safety culture.

Investigations showed that the corporate culture of Boeing had turned towards shareholder value and cost-cutting as opposed to engineering excellence. Boeing's rushed development of the Manoeuvring Characteristics Augmentation System

(MCAS) and failure to address safety concerns have been proven. Internal reports suggested that the employees knew the risks but were under pressure to keep up with production schedules (Herkert, Borenstein, & Miller, 2020).

These issues were compounded by another crisis for Boeing in January 2024 when an Alaska Airlines Boeing 737 MAX experienced uncontrolled decompression while in flight because of a fuselage panel that was not properly secured. This, combined with ongoing quality control issues, eroded confidence in Boeing's management and regulatory oversight.

Legislative confrontations also intensify. In March 2025, a federal judge permitted shareholders to bring a class-action suit, alleging Boeing's deceptive statements artificially elevated stock prices at the expense of safety. These challenges underscore the risks of a culture that places profits ahead of moral accountability and safety.

7.2.2 Wells Fargo: Restoring Trust after the Scandal

Wells Fargo’s fraudulent accounts scandal is another example of how a toxic culture can lead to organizational downfall. The scandal, which erupted in 2016, revealed that employees had opened millions of unauthorized accounts to meet aggressive sales targets. This breach of trust resulted in substantial fines, regulatory penalties, and reputational damage.

The reason for this crisis was a culture of high-pressure selling in which unethical behavior was rewarded. Employees were set impossible performance targets, and failure to meet these targets led to dismissal. Pressure created a culture in which fraud had become widespread and ultimately eroded the trust of the customers.

In response, Wells Fargo abolished sales quotas and reformed leadership. But trust has proved difficult to regain. The bank continues to struggle with regulatory oversight and continued reputational damage. Even with cultural reform, Wells Fargo is a textbook case of the depth to which entrenched cultural deficiencies can leave a lasting impact.

7.3 Conclusion

These case studies also recognize the profound impact of organizational culture on success or failure. Netflix and Microsoft show how expansion and long-term viability can be achieved through fostering a culture of innovation, learning, and moral leadership. Boeing and Wells Fargo show how culture mismanagement, particularly when ethics and safety are breached, can lead to calamitous financial and reputational setbacks. Organizations should reconcile their values with their strategic goals to be able to forge a culture that guarantees trust, accountability, and long-term prosperity.

8. MEASURING THE IMPACT OF CULTURAL CHANGES

Cultural transformation is a complex, ongoing process, and measurement is key to long-term success. Cultural transformation adopting organizations must be able to determine if their effort results in meaningful improvement in employee engagement, business operations performance, and enterprise-wide business performance. For that purpose, they must have a systematic process based on qualitative and quantitative measures.

Cultural changes impact the majority of aspects of an organization, from leadership performance to employee morale, customer satisfaction, and financial performance. Measurement strategies need to be implemented to prevent distraction of organizations from transformational initiatives and strategic agendas. The most critical measures utilized in measuring cultural changes are elaborated below, such as Key Performance Indicators (KPIs) of cultural change, employee satisfaction and engagement measures, organizational performance measures, and systems of continuous feedback.

8.1 Cultural Change Key Performance Indicators (KPIs)

Key Performance Indicators (KPIs) are quantifiable indicators to gauge the success of cultural transformation programs. Unlike financial KPIs, cultural KPIs are more interested in the employees' behaviour, leaders' performance, and alignment of company values and working practices.

8.1.1 Defining Effective Cultural KPIs

Good cultural KPIs ought to:

- **Organizational values aligned:** The measures must be aligned with the mission and long-term goals of the company.
- **Measurable and trackable:** Organizations should establish baseline measurements and assess progress periodically.
- **Actionable:** The findings derived should inform decision-making and policy reform.

8.1.2 Cultural Transformation KPIs in Widespread Use

Several KPIs help assess the success of cultural shifts, including:

1. **Employee Turnover Rate:** Decrease in voluntary turnover indicates that employees are more dedicated and in sync with the company culture.
2. **Employee Net Promoter Score (eNPS)**: It calculates the likelihood of employees referring the company to work for them.
3. **Leadership Effectiveness Scores:** Employees' perceptions of leadership can inform if management succeeds in embodying and promoting cultural values.
4. **Diversity and Inclusion Metrics:** Diversity of the workforce, pay equity, and inclusion survey data measurements help measure cultural progress.
5. **Ethical Compliance Indicators**: Companies with strong ethical cultures will have fewer compliance breakdowns and whistle blower concerns.

An equally balanced set of cultural KPIs gives businesses a clear picture of whether their transformation activities result in positive results.

8.2 Employee Satisfaction and Engagement Measures

Employee engagement is a key measure of an organization's cultural health. Engaged employees are more productive, creative, and dedicated to the success of the company. Measuring the level of engagement gives insight into whether cultural efforts are resonating with employees.

8.2.1 Employee Engagement Surveys

Organizations typically administer employee engagement surveys to measure employee attitudes. These surveys generally record:

- **Job satisfaction**: Are the workers satisfied with their job?
- **Organizational commitment:** Will the employees remain with the company in the long term?
- **Leadership trust:** Is the leadership and vision of the organization trusted by employees?
- **Work-life balance:** Are staff members burning out because of cultural misalignment?

Data from surveys assists business organizations in determining areas of concern and initiating change for enhancing the company culture.

8.2.2 Pulse Surveys and Real-Time Feedback

While yearly engagement surveys give a general snapshot, pulse surveys give immediate feedback on employee morale. These brief, regular surveys measure immediate responses to culture programs. They enable organizations to make quick changes in line with changing employee needs.

8.2.3 Exit Interviews and Stay Interviews

- Exit interviews offer useful feedback regarding why employees are leaving, which assists organizations in determining cultural vulnerabilities.
- Stay interviews truly quantify why individuals want to remain and what motivates satisfaction in the culture.

By integrating results from pulse surveys, engagement surveys, and interviews, organizations can make evidence-based changes to cultural transformation initiatives.

8.3 Organizational Performance Indicators

Along with employee engagement, cultural transformation ought to be manifest in measurable improvements in business performance. Cultural transformation ought to raise levels of innovation, productivity, and customer satisfaction while lowering workplace conflict and inefficiency.

8.3.1 Indicators of Productivity and Innovation

Organizations should assess how cultural change impacts productivity and innovation by tracking:

- **Levels of employee productivity:** Are employees more productive and cooperative?
- **Measures of innovation**: Did novel product ideas, process innovation, or patents presented increase?
- **Cross-functional collaboration:** Are different departments working together better?

For example, Satya Nadella's cultural shift at Microsoft focused on innovation and collaboration, leading to successful innovation in the form of Microsoft Teams and Azure.

8.3.2 Customer Satisfaction and Brand Reputation

A positive corporate culture will probably lead to better customer experiences. Firms need to track:

- **Customer Net Promoter Score (NPS):** Are customers enjoying better service and interaction?
- **Reputation surveys of brands:** Are employees and customers positively discussing the firm?
- **Customer retention rates:** Are cultural changes building customer loyalty?

For instance, companies like Zappos and Southwest Airlines have created sturdy cultures that directly influence customer service interactions (Hsieh, 2010).

8.3.3 Financial Performance Indicators

While profitability is not the sole objective of cultural transformation, good cultures tend to produce better financial performance. Organizations must keep an eye on:

- Revenue growth
- Market share growth
- Stock price performance

For example, the cultural emphasis at Netflix on innovation and flexibility has driven consistent financial advancement, with impressive annual revenue growth (Hastings & Meyer, 2020).

8.4 Continuous Culture Audits and Feedback

Cultural change is not a static affair—it needs ongoing monitoring, adjustment, and reinforcement. Ongoing feedback loops and periodic culture audits keep organizations aligned with their desired cultural outcomes.

8.4.1 Culture Audits

A culture audit is a scientific analysis that determines if the cultural values of an organization are compatible with its functions. These audits may include:

- Focus groups and employee interviews
- HR policy and practice analysis

- Leadership decision making and behaviours check

Culture audits allow companies to determine what is said and what is done and to act accordingly.

8.4.2 360-Degree Leadership Feedback

A 360-degree feedback process evaluates leaders according to peer, subordinate, and supervisor feedback. Feedback is utilized to determine whether leadership behaviour is supportive of desired cultural change.

For example, Google uses 360-degree feedback to enable its culture of ongoing learning and psychological safety (Edmondson, 2018).

8.4.3 AI and People Analytics to Measure Culture

AI-based people analytics are utilized by leading companies to track cultural trends. AI technology scans the tone of employees in emails, surveys, and collaboration tools to provide instant feedback on cultural shifts (Davenport & Harris, 2007).

For example, companies like IBM and Microsoft use AI-driven analytics to understand how culture influences employee performance and employee retention.

8.5 Conclusion

It is essential to measure the impact of cultural changes to ensure organizational growth and responsiveness. Organizations need to use a mix of KPIs, employee engagement data, performance metrics, and continuous feedback mechanisms to gauge the success of cultural change programs. Netflix, Microsoft, and Google are examples of how strategic cultural alignment is the recipe for long-term success, while Boeing and Wells Fargo failures are examples of the dangers of cultural measurement neglect.

With the development of sound measurement systems, organizations can be confident that cultural change leads to more committed employees, increased productivity, improved customer relationships, and overall business resilience in a dynamic corporate landscape.

9. BUSINESS IMPLICATIONS AND FUTURE TRENDS

Organizational culture is a dynamic process that is shaped by technological change, changes in the demographics of the workforce, and economic change globally. The digital age, characterized by artificial intelligence (AI), automation, and virtual work, has brought new challenges and opportunities for modelling workplace culture. As the organizations experience this change, they must make sure that cultural transformations are aligned with strategic objectives while maintaining employee engagement and inclusion. This section discusses the evolution of organizational culture, the role of AI and automation, and long-term sustainability of cultural change.

9.1 The Digital Age and the Future of Organizational Culture

The growing application of technology in business processes has had a profound impact on organizational culture. Workplace conventions are changing, and businesses are forced to reconsider how they promote collaboration, engagement, and innovation.

1. The Rise of Remote and Hybrid Work

The COVID-19 pandemic accelerated the transition to remote and hybrid work models, which have now become the norm for many organizations. According to a McKinsey report (2022), 90% of businesses worldwide have embraced some form of remote work, necessitating a shift in organizational culture to support virtual collaboration. However, maintaining a cohesive and engaged workforce in remote settings requires deliberate efforts:

- **Virtual Team-Building and Engagement:** Companies must establish positive connections among staff through regular virtual check-ins, virtual team-building, and online collaboration tools (Sull, Sull, & Zweig, 2022).
- **Outcome-Based Performance Measurement:** The old productivity measures in terms of office presence are being shifted to performance-based measures. Workers are now measured by what they produce and deliver, not by how many hours they put in.
- **Cultural Challenges of Remote Work:** While it is advantageous, remote work can lead to reduced social interaction, increased isolation, and communication breakdown. Organisations must tackle these problems in advance by developing a psychological safety and trust culture (Bloom, Liang, Roberts, & Ying, 2015).

2. Digital Fluency and Staff Mobility

In the age of digitalization, companies need to make the workforce digitally literate and able to learn new technology. According to the World Economic Forum

(2023), more than 50% of all employees will need to be reskilled by 2030 as a result of the speed of technological change. Companies can be ready for this change by:

- Cultivating a growth mind-set, whereby employees embrace lifelong learning and adaptability (Dweck, 2006).
- In investing in continuous learning initiatives, such as micro learning modules and AI-based customized learning platforms (Brynjolfsson & McAfee, 2014).
- Fostering a knowledge-sharing culture where workers can learn from and teach each other (Edmondson, 2018).

3. Diversity, Equity, and Inclusion (DEI) in a Digital Workplace

The age of digitalization has connected workplaces more internationally, and thus, inclusivity is the call of the hour. Organizations focusing on DEI programs are rewarded with higher innovation and employee engagement (Canals & Heukamp, 2019) AI-based solutions are assisting organizations in creating an inclusive environment by:

- Reducing hiring bias through AI-powered recruitment software that analyses job applications objectively.
- Expanding work accessibility for individuals with disabilities through voice-controlled technology and accessible AI tools.
- Adopting diverse workplaces through data analytics to measure diversity metrics and employee attitudes.

9.2 AI and Automation and Their Role in Influencing Workplace Culture

Artificial intelligence and automation are transforming workplace culture at its foundation by influencing decision-making, the employee experience, and organizational values. With these technologies making work more productive, businesses must balance people with automation.

1. AI-Based Decision Making

AI-based analytics are being used more and more in all HR operations such as talent sourcing, performance, and employee engagement measurement. AI assists organizations to:

- Track employee attitudes through real-time feedback systems that track morale and workplace engagement (Davenport & Harris, 2007).
- Improve decision-making by predicting employee turnover trends and providing personalized career development recommendations.
- Determine skill gaps in the workforce and recommend focused training programs.

But AI decision-making also has ethical obligations. Companies need to make sure that AI tools are transparent, non-discriminatory, and used responsibly so that discriminatory practices can be prevented.

2. Enhancing Employee Experience with AI

Artificial intelligence-based virtual assistants, chatbots, and HR automation software are improving the employee experience by offering real-time support. Some of these are:

- HelloID AI-powered HR chatbots that guide employees through leave, benefits, and career questions.
- Artificial Intelligence-powered training platforms to tailor training programs according to workers' performance levels and learning processes.
- Employee sentiment analysis software that measures employee feedback and flags areas that need managerial action.

3. Balancing Automation with People-Centric Leadership

As AI enhances efficiency, over-automation can make workplace interaction more personalized. Managers need to ensure that technology supports, rather than substitutes for, human connections within the workplace. A few of the most important strategies include:

- Encouraging open communication and enabling human interaction despite automated work processes.
- Making sure AI is utilized responsibly by engaging employees in the dialogue regarding AI use in decision-making.
- Sustaining human involvement in such areas as performance appraisals and conflict resolution.

9.3 Long-term sustainability of cultural change

Cultural transformation must be lasting if organizations are to maintain a competitive edge. Successful organizations that institutionalize cultural transformation are rewarded with extended endurance and flexibility.

1. Leadership Commitment to Cultural Evolution

Long-term cultural change needs leadership engagement at every level. Leaders need to:

- Demonstrate wanted behaviors and embody cultural values (Kotter, 2012).
- Regularly reinforce cultural values through stories, reward systems, and truthful communication (Edmondson, 2018).
- Realignment according to employee input to keep cultural changes up-to-date.

2. Imbedding Culture in Organizational DNA

In order to sustain cultural change, businesses must embed cultural values into policies, training initiatives, and reward systems. Successful cultural assimilation is seen in the following:

- Netflix culture of innovation, where accountability and transparency are valued (Hastings & Meyer, 2020).
- Google's culture of learning, built around ongoing improvement and psychological safety (Edmondson, 2018).
- Zappos customer dedication culture, enabling individuals to put customer satisfaction first (Hsieh, 2010).

3. Future Workplaces: Resilience and Adaptability

The future of work is uncertain, with economic and technological shocks reconfiguring business environments. Organisations must develop resilience by:

- Facilitating business strategy and labour flexibility.
- Investing in mental well-being and mental health programs to assist employees in transition.
- Becoming a culture of experimentation, where staff are not afraid to try out things without fearing mistakes (Dweck, 2006).

The future organizational culture will be influenced by digital transformation, AI adoption, and sustainable leadership. As automation and remote work persist, workplaces will keep changing, and companies must make ethical AI adoption, employee engagement, and inclusive leadership a priority. By embedding cultural values in long-term strategies, organizations can build lasting resilience and flexibility in a more dynamic business world.

10. CONCLUSION

Organizational culture is one of the cornerstones of business success, dictating everything from productivity and employee motivation to planning and overall corporate performance. As the business environment has become more complex and uncertain, an ability to adjust cultural paradigms to changing realities has become a predictor of long-term survival. Throughout the chapter, the complexity of organizational culture, cultural drivers for change, models of transformation, leadership's role in the transformation, employee involvement, and cultural transformation initiative measurement have been addressed.

The modern business world is shaped by increasing technological change, shifting workforce demographics, increasing globalization, and shifting regulatory and ethical standards. The intersection of artificial intelligence, automation, and digitalization has reshaped workplace design, with remote and hybrid work arrangements on the rise. At the same time, new generations of employees, such as Millennials and Gen Z, bring new values and expectations, necessitating workplaces that are inclusive, diverse, flexible, and purposeful. These, and external socio-political and economic drivers, necessitate an active response to cultural evolution and not reactive adaptation.

Effective cultural change management entails a strategic and systematic process. Change management theories like Kotter's 8-Step Change Model and Lewin's Change Management Model present guidelines for successful transition. Nevertheless, cultural change is not so much about new policies or new practices—about sustained and long-term commitment on the part of leaders and workers. Leaders themselves need to become cultural champions who live the values that they desire to instil in their respective organizations. Leadership is the take-home message that the case studies in this chapter emphasize, particularly in cultural reinvention, with the Microsoft under Satya Nadella case exhibiting how an empathetic, growth-oriented leadership strategy can change a whole organization. On the contrary, failures like Boeing's issues with culture reflect the dangers of putting short-term profits ahead of ethical accountability and employee welfare.

Employee engagement is the second most critical driver of culture change. Employees are the most critical drivers of culture, and their buy-in is needed for lasting change. Organizations need to facilitate open communication, offer upskilling and development opportunities, and spaces where employees are listened to and valued. Resistance to change is a natural human inclination, but by employing open communication, participative decision-making, and ongoing support, organizations are able to reduce resistance and develop a flexible workforce.

The success of cultural changes also needs to be measured. The organizations need to set crisp Key Performance Indicators (KPIs), conduct employee satisfaction surveys, monitor engagement levels, and audit their culture regularly to ensure that it is aligned to strategic objectives. Cultural change is a continuous improvement process, and to drive and shape desired values and behaviours, continuous feedback loops need to be incorporated.

Organizational culture in the next few years will be shaped by ongoing technology innovation, growing emphasis on sustainability and social responsibility, and shifting workforce expectations. Organizations that become culturally agile—blending innovation and heritage, digital transformation and human leadership, and form and flexibility—will be better positioned to navigate waves of future disruption and stay competitive.

In brief, organizational culture and work nature will continue to change, and flexibility will become a business skill. Leaders and HR professionals need to make cultural alignment to business strategy their top priority so that their organizations are resilient, innovative, and inclusive. The companies that succeed in creating a dynamic, values-based culture will not only survive the new business climate but thrive in the midst of change.

REFERENCES

Avolio, B. J., & Bass, B. M. (2004). *MLQ: Multifactor leadership questionnaire*. Mind Garden.

Bass, B. M. (1990). From transactional to transformational leadership: Learning to share the vision. *Organizational Dynamics, 18*(3), 19–31. DOI: 10.1016/0090-2616(90)90061-S

Bloom, N., Liang, J., Roberts, J., & Ying, Z. J. (2015). Does working from home work? Evidence from a Chinese experiment. *The Quarterly Journal of Economics, 130*(1), 165–218. DOI: 10.1093/qje/qju032

Brown, M. E., & Treviño, L. K. (2006). Ethical leadership: A review and future directions. *The Leadership Quarterly, 17*(6), 595–616. DOI: 10.1016/j.leaqua.2006.10.004

. Brynjolfsson, E., & McAfee, A. (2014). The second machine age: Work, progress, and prosperity in a time of brilliant technologies. WW Norton & company.

Burns, J. M. (1978). *Leadership*. Harper & Row.

Canals, J., & Heukamp, F. (Eds.). (2019). *The future of management in an AI world: redefining purpose and strategy in the fourth industrial revolution*. Springer Nature.

Clampitt, P. G., DeKoch, R. J., & Cashman, T. (2000). A strategy for communicating about uncertainty. *The Academy of Management Perspectives, 14*(4), 41–57. DOI: 10.5465/ame.2000.3979815

Davenport, T. H., & Harris, J. G. (2007). Competing on analytics: The new science of Winning. Harvard business review press. *Language, 15*(217), 24.

Dweck, C. S. (2006). *Mindset: The new psychology of success*. Random house.

Edmondson, A. C. (2018). *The fearless organization: Creating psychological safety in the workplace for learning, innovation, and growth*. John Wiley & Sons.

Fenwick, M., Kaal, W. A., & Vermeulen, E. P. (2019). The" Unmediated" and" Tech-Driven" Corporate Governance of Today's Winning Companies. *NYUJL & Bus., 16*, 75.

Gajendran, R. S., & Harrison, D. A. (2007). The good, the bad, and the unknown about telecommuting: Meta-analysis of psychological mediators and individual consequences. *The Journal of Applied Psychology, 92*(6), 1524–1541. DOI: 10.1037/0021-9010.92.6.1524 PMID: 18020794

Gates, B. (2021). *How to avoid a climate disaster: the solutions we have and the breakthroughs we need.* Vintage.

Gerstner, L. V. (2002). *Who says elephants can't dance? Inside IBM's historic turnaround.* HarperCollins Publishers.

Hastings, R., & Meyer, E. (2020). *No rules rules: Netflix and the culture of reinvention.* Random house.

Hofstede, G. (2011). Dimensionalizing cultures: The Hofstede model in context. *Online Readings in Psychology and Culture, 2*(1), 8. DOI: 10.9707/2307-0919.1014

Hsieh, T. (2010). *Delivering happiness: A path to profits, passion, and purpose.* Grand Central Publishing.

. Hunt, V., Prince, S., Dixon-Fyle, S., & Yee, L. (2018). Delivering through diversity.

Ibarra, H., Rattan, A., & Johnston, A. (2018). *Satya Nadella at Microsoft: Instilling a growth mindset.* London Business School.

Imperatori, B. (2017). *Engagement and disengagement at work: Drivers and organizational practices to sustain employee passion and performance.* Springer. DOI: 10.1007/978-3-319-51886-2

Keating, G. (2012). *Netflixed: The epic battle for America's eyeballs.* Penguin.

Klein, M. (2020). Leadership characteristics in the era of digital transformation. *Business & Management Studies: An International Journal, 8*(1), 883–902. DOI: 10.15295/bmij.v8i1.1441

. Kotter, J. P. (2012). Leading change. Harvard business press.

Lemon, K. N., & Verhoef, P. C. (2016). Understanding customer experience throughout the customer journey. *Journal of Marketing, 80*(6), 69–96. DOI: 10.1509/jm.15.0420

Mayer, R. C., Davis, J. H., & Schoorman, F. D. (1995). An integrative model of organizational trust. *Academy of Management Review, 20*(3), 709–734. DOI: 10.2307/258792

McCord, P. (2018). *Powerful: Building a culture of freedom and responsibility.* Tom Rath.

Meister, J. C., & Willyerd, K. (2010). *The 2020 workplace: How innovative companies attract, develop, and keep tomorrow's employees today.* Harper Collins.

Oreg, S., Vakola, M., & Armenakis, A. (2011). Change recipients' reactions to organizational change: A 60-year review of quantitative studies. *The Journal of Applied Behavioral Science*, *47*(4), 461–524. DOI: 10.1177/0021886310396550

Perez, J. R., & de Pablos, P. O. (2003). Knowledge management and organizational competitiveness: A framework for human capital analysis. *Journal of Knowledge Management*, *7*(3), 82–91. DOI: 10.1108/13673270310485640

. Schein, E. H. (1983). Organizational culture: A dynamic model.

Schein, E. H. (2010). *Organizational culture and leadership* (Vol. 2). John Wiley & Sons.

Sull, D., Sull, C., & Zweig, B. (2022). Toxic culture is driving the great resignation. *MIT Sloan Management Review*.

Treviño, L. K., Hartman, L. P., & Brown, M. (2000). Moral person and moral manager: How executives develop a reputation for ethical leadership. *California Management Review*, *42*(4), 128–142. DOI: 10.2307/41166057

Westerman, G., Soule, D. L., & Eswaran, A. (2019). Building digital-ready culture in traditional organizations. *MIT Sloan Management Review*, *60*(4).

Yukl, G. (2013). *Leadership in organizations* (8th ed.). Pearson.

Compilation of References

Abdelgafar, B. (2018). *Public policy: Beyond traditional jurisprudence: A Maqasid approach*. International Institute of Islamic Thought. DOI: 10.2307/j.ctvkc6778

Abdul-Khalil, S., Abdul-Rahman, S., Mutalib, S., Kamarudin, S. I., & Kamaruddin, S. S. (2023). A review on object detection forautonomous mobile robot. *IAES International Journal of Artificial Intelligence, 12*(3), 1033–1043. DOI: 10.11591/ijai.v12.i3.pp1033-1043

Abdullah, N., Rahmat, N., Zawawi, F., Khamsah, M., & Anuarsham, A. (2020). Coping with post covid-19: can work from home be a new norm? *European Journal of Social Sciences Studies, 5*(6), 61-81. DOI: 10.46827/ejsss.v5i6.933

Abraham, S. (2023). *The future of fashion is here: Integration of AI in marketing practices of leading fashion retail businesses*. In Toronto Metropolitan University.

Aczel, B., Kovacs, M., Lippe, T., & Szaszi, B. (2021, March 25). Researchers working from home: Benefits and challenges. (T. U. Johnson Chun-Sing Cheung, Ed.) *Plos One, 16*(3), 1-13. DOI: 10.1371/journal.pone.0249127

AG. A. G., Su, H. K., & Kuo, W. K. (2023, June). Unleashing Potential of Employees through Artificial Intelligence. In *2023 IEEE 5th Eurasia Conference on Biomedical Engineering, Healthcare and Sustainability (ECBIOS)* (pp. 204-206). IEEE.

Agba, A., Ocheni, S., & Agba, M. S. (2020, September). COVID-19 and the World of Work Dynamics: A Critical Review. *Journal of Educational and Social Research, 10*(5), 119-130. DOI: 10.36941/jesr-2020-0093

Agnihotri, A., Pavitra, K. H., Balusamy, B., Maurya, A., & Bibhakar, P. (2023). Artificial intelligence shaping talent intelligence and talent acquisition for smart employee management. EAI Endorsed Trans. Internet Things, 10.

Aguinis, H., & Burgi-Tian, J. (2021). Measuring performance during crises and beyond: The Performance Promoter Score. *Business Horizons*, *64*(1), 149–160. DOI: 10.1016/j.bushor.2020.09.001

Ahdadou, M., Aajly, A., & Tahrouch, M. (2024). Enhancing corporate governance through AI: A systematic literature review. *Technology Analysis and Strategic Management*, ●●●, 1–14.

Alam, S., Shuaib, M., Khan, W. Z., Garg, S., Kaddoum, G., Hossain, M., & Zikria, Y. B. (2021). Blockchain-based Initiatives: Current state and challenges. *Computer Networks*, *198*, 1–20. DOI: 10.1016/j.comnet.2021.108395

Al-Ansi, A., Al-Ansi, A. M., Muthanna, A., & Koucheryavy, A. (2024). Blockchain technology integration in service migration to 6Gcommunication networks: A comprehensive review. *Indonesian Journal of Electrical Engineering and Computer Science*, *34*(3), 1654–1664. DOI: 10.11591/ijeecs.v34.i3.pp1654-1664

Albion, M. (2005). A Measure of Attitudes Towards Flexible Work Options. *Australian Journal of Management*, *29*(2), 275–294. DOI: 10.1177/031289620402900207

Ali, S., Kumar, V., & Breazeal, C. (2023). AI Audit: A card game to reflect on everyday AI systems. *Proceedings of the AAAI Conference on Artificial Intelligence*, *37*(13), 15981–15989. DOI: 10.1609/aaai.v37i13.26897

Al-kfairy, M., Shuhaiber, A., Al-khatib, A. W., Alrabaee, S., & Khaddaj, S. (2024). Understanding Trust Drivers of S-commerce. *Heliyon*, *10*(1), e23332. DOI: 10.1016/j.heliyon.2023.e23332 PMID: 38163094

AlRababah, A., AlShahrani, A., & Al-Kasasbeh, B. (2016). Efficiency Model of Information Systems as an Implementation of Key Performance Indicators. *International Journal of Computer Science and Network Security, 16*(12), 139-143. Retrieved from https://www.researchgate.net/publication/316689258_Efficiency_Model_of_Information_Systems_as_an_Implementation_of_Key_Performance_Indicators

Al-Raeei, M. (2025). The smart future for sustainable development: Artificial intelligence solutions for sustainable urbanization. *Sustainable Development (Bradford)*, *33*(1), 508–517. DOI: 10.1002/sd.3131

Angwin, J., Larson, J., Mattu, S., & Kirchner, L. (2016). Machine bias: There's software used across the country to predict future criminals. And it's biased against Blacks. *ProPublica*. https://www.propublica.org/article/machine-bias-risk-assessments-in-criminal-sentencing

Anjorin, K. F., Raji, M. A., Olodo, H. B., & Oyeyemi, O. P. (2024). Harnessing artificial intelligence to develop strategic marketing goals. Int. j. *Manag. Entrep. Res*, *6*(5), 1625–1650.

Antia, R., & Halloran, M. (2021). Transition to endemicity: Understanding COVID-19. *A Cell Press Journal, 54*(10), 2172-2176. DOI: 10.1016/j.immuni.2021.09.019

Appannan, J. S., Mohd Said, R., Ong, T. S., & Senik, R. (2023). Promoting sustainable development through strategies, environmental management accounting and environmental performance. *Business Strategy and the Environment*, *32*(4), 1914–1930. DOI: 10.1002/bse.3227

Arso, S. S., Sfenrianto, S., & Wahyudi, M. (2018). Employee Performance Measurement in Teleworking Using Balanced Scorecard. *International Journal of Electrical and Computer Engineering*, *8*(6), 5178–5184. DOI: 10.11591/ijece.v8i6.pp5178-5184

Asefa, K., Kant, D. S., & Debela, K. L. (2023, November). Effect of Transformational Leadership on Organizational Performance: The Mediating Role of Employee Commitment and Expert Systems (AI) Inclusion in Ethiopia. In *2023 International Conference on Communication, Security and Artificial Intelligence (ICCSAI)* (pp. 305–310). IEEE. DOI: 10.1109/ICCSAI59793.2023.10421269

Asih, L., Purba, H., & Sitorus, T. (2020). Key Performance Indicators: A Systematic Literature Review. *Journal of Strategy and Performance Management*, *8*(4), 142–155. https://www.researchgate.net/publication/344493860_KEY_PERFORMANCE_INDICATORS_A_SYSTEMATIC_LITERATURE_REVIEW

Attar, R. W., Almusharraf, A., Alfawaz, A., & Hajli, N. (2022). New Trends in E-Commerce Research: Linking Social Commerce and Sharing Commerce: A Systematic Literature Review. *Sustainability (Basel)*, *14*(23), 16024. DOI: 10.3390/su142316024

Auda, J. (2008). *Maqasid al-Shariah as philosophy of Islamic law: A systems approach*. International Institute of Islamic Thought. DOI: 10.2307/j.ctvkc67tg

Auda, J. (2008). *Maqasid al-Shariah: A beginner's guide*. International Institute of Islamic Thought. DOI: 10.2307/j.ctvkc67c6

Austin-Egole, Ifeyinwa, S., Iheriohanma, E.B.J, Chinedu, & Nwokorie. (2020). Flexible Working Arrangments and Organizational Performance: An Overview. *IOSR Journal Of Humanities And Social Science (IOSR-JHSS)*, *25*, 50-59. DOI:DOI: 10.9790/0837- 2505065059

Avolio, B. J., & Bass, B. M. (2004). *MLQ: Multifactor leadership questionnaire*. Mind Garden.

Baabdullah, A. M. (2024). Generative conversational AI agent for managerial practices: The role of IQ dimensions, novelty seeking and ethical concerns. *Technological Forecasting and Social Change*, *198*, 122951. DOI: 10.1016/j.techfore.2023.122951

Babor, T., Caulkins, J., Edwards, G., Fischer, B., Foxcroft, D., Humphreys, K., & Strang, J. (2018). *Drug policy and the public good* (2nd ed.). Oxford University Press. DOI: 10.1093/oso/9780198818014.001.0001

Badawy, M., Abd El-Aziz, A. A., Idress, A., Hefny, H., & Hossam, S. (2016). A survey on exploring key performance indicators. *Future Computing and Informatics Journal*, *1*(1-2), 47–52. DOI: 10.1016/j.fcij.2016.04.001

Bala, A., & Koxhaj, P. (2017). Key Performance Indicators (KPIs) in the Change Management of Public Administration. *European Scientific Journal*, *13*(4), 278–283. DOI: 10.19044/esj.2017.v13n4p278

Balafoutis, A., Beck, B., Fountas, S., Vangeyte, J., Van Der Wal, T., Soto, I., & Gemtos, T. A. (2017). Precision agriculture technologies positively contribute to GHG emissions mitigation, farm productivity and economics. *Sustainability (Basel)*, *9*(8), 1339. DOI: 10.3390/su9081339

Balasubramaniam, N., Kauppinen, M., & Kujala Sari and Hiekkanen, K. (2020). Ethical guidelines for solving ethical issues and developing AI systems. In Product-Focused Software Process Improvement (pp. 331–346). Springer International Publishing.

Bankins, S., Ocampo, A. C., Marrone, M., Restubog, S. L. D., & Woo, S. E. (2024). A multilevel review of artificial intelligence in organizations: Implications for organizational behavior research and practice. *Journal of Organizational Behavior*, *45*(2), 159–182. DOI: 10.1002/job.2735

Barbour, N., Menon, N., & Mannering, F. (2021). A statistical assessment of work-from-home participation during different stages of the COVID-19 pandemic. *Transportation Research Interdisciplinary Perspectives*, *11*, 1–9. DOI: 10.1016/j.trip.2021.100441

Bass, B. M. (1990). From transactional to transformational leadership: Learning to share the vision. *Organizational Dynamics*, *18*(3), 19–31. DOI: 10.1016/0090-2616(90)90061-S

Baumgartner, R. J., & Ebner, D. (2010). Corporate sustainability strategies: Sustainability profiles and maturity levels. *Sustainable Development (Bradford)*, *18*(2), 76–89. DOI: 10.1002/sd.447

Bechar, A., & Vigneault, C. (2017). Agricultural robots for field operations: Current status and future trends. *Biosystems Engineering*, *149*, 94–111. DOI: 10.1016/j.biosystemseng.2016.06.014

Behare, N., Lakhani, D. Y., Vasmatkar, A., Waghulkar, S., Sayankar, V. N., Naik, A., . . . Behare, S. N. (2025). AI-Powered Personalization: Revolutionizing Mobile Commerce for Enhanced Customer Experiences. In *Leveraging AI for Effective Digital Relationship Marketing* (pp. 163-198). IGI Global. DOI: 10.4018/979-8-3693-5340-0.ch006

Berkhout, P., van Galen, M., & van Tongeren, F. (2020). *The Future of Food: Smart Farming and Sustainable Agriculture*. Wageningen Economic Research.

Bewley-Taylor, D., & Jelsma, M. (2016). Regime change: Re-visiting the 1961 Single Convention on Narcotic Drugs. *The International Journal on Drug Policy*, *23*(1), 72–81. DOI: 10.1016/j.drugpo.2011.08.003

Bhalerao, K., Kumar, A., Kumar, A., & Pujari, P. (2022). A study of barriers and benefits of artificial intelligence adoption in small and medium enterprise. *Academy of Marketing Studies Journal*, *26*(1), 1–6.

Bhatt, P. (2022). AI adoption in the hiring process – important criteria and extent of AI adoption. Foresight, ahead-of-print(ahead-of-print).

Bhatti, M., Awan, H., & Razaq, Z. (2014). 11). The key performance indicators (KPIs) and their impact on overall organizational performance. *Quality & Quantity*, •••, 48. DOI:10.1007/s11135-013-9945-y

Bhuiyan, M. S. (2024). The role of AI-enhanced personalization in customer experiences. *Journal of Computer Science and Technology Studies*, *6*(1), 162–169. DOI: 10.32996/jcsts.2024.6.1.17

Bienstock, J., LaPerla, J., & Seaman, C. (2020). The Flexible Work Arrangements in a Post Covid-19 Universe. *Review of Business Research*, *20*(2), 41–52. Advance online publication. DOI: 10.18374/RBR-20-2.4

Bin Rashid, A., & Kausik, M. A. K. (2024, December). AI revolutionizing industries worldwide: A comprehensive overview of its diverseapplications. *Hybrid Advances*, *7*, 100277. DOI: 10.1016/j.hybadv.2024.100277

Bisnis, K. U. M. K. M. (2025). *Survei Ungkap 97% UMKM di Indonesia Rasakan Manfaat AI untuk Bisnis*. 2025. Retrieved July from https://bisniskumkm.com/survei-ungkap-97-umkm-di-indonesia-rasakan-manfaat-ai-untuk-bisnis

Bloom, N., Liang, J., Roberts, J., & Ying, Z. J. (2015). Does working from home work? Evidence from a Chinese experiment. *The Quarterly Journal of Economics, 130*(1), 165–218. DOI: 10.1093/qje/qju032

Boell, S., & Cecez-Kecmanovic, D. (2015). What is an Information System? *48th Hawaii International Conference on System Sciences*, (pp. 4959-4968). DOI: 10.1109/HICSS.2015.587

Boesl, D. B., & Liepert, B. (2016, October). 4 Robotic Revolutions-Proposing a holistic phase model describing future disruptions in the evolution of robotics and automation and the rise of a new Generation 'R'of Robotic Natives. In *2016 IEEE/RSJ International Conference on Intelligent Robots and Systems (IROS)* (pp. 1262-1267). IEEE. DOI: 10.1109/IROS.2016.7759209

Boettke, P., Coyne, C., & Hall, A. (2013). Keep Off the Grass: The Economics of Prohibition and U.S. Drug Policy. *Oregon Law Review, 91*(4), 1075–1077.

Bolukbasi, T., Chang, K.-W., Zou, J., Saligrama, V., & Kalai, A. (2016). Man is to computer programmer as woman is to homemaker? Debiasing word embeddings. *Advances in Neural Information Processing Systems, 29*, 4349–4357.

Borneo Bulletin. (2022, May 24). *Early Endemic Phase ends May 31*. Retrieved December 26, 2022 from Borneo Bulletin: https://borneobulletin.com.bn/early-endemic-phase-ends- may-31/

Breidbach, C. F., & Maglio, P. (2020). Accountable algorithms? The ethical implications of data-driven business models. *Journal of Service Management, 31*(2), 163–185. DOI: 10.1108/JOSM-03-2019-0073

Brock, J. K.-U., & von Wangenheim, F. (2019). Demystifying AI: What digital transformation leaders can teach you about realistic artificial intelligence. *California Management Review, 61*(4), 110–134. DOI: 10.1177/1536504219865226

Bronson, K. (2019). Looking through a responsible innovation lens at uneven engagements with digital farming. *NJAS Wageningen Journal of Life Sciences, 90-91*(1), 100294. DOI: 10.1016/j.njas.2019.03.001

Bronson, K., & Knezevic, I. (2016). Big Data in food and agriculture. *Big Data & Society, 3*(1), 1–5. DOI: 10.1177/2053951716648174

Brown, M. E., & Treviño, L. K. (2006). Ethical leadership: A review and future directions. *The Leadership Quarterly, 17*(6), 595–616. DOI: 10.1016/j.leaqua.2006.10.004

BruCERT. (2021). *BruCERT Survey on Studying/Working From Home 2021*. From https://csb.gov.bn/sites/default/files/pdf/2021_WFH_Survey_Report.pdf

Brunnbauer, M. (2023). How top-down AI introduction leads to incremental business improvement. *Proceedings of the Annual Hawaii International Conference on System Sciences*. DOI: 10.24251/HICSS.2023.745

Burns, J. M. (1978). *Leadership*. Harper & Row.

Buttow, C. V. (2025). Data-Driven Policy Making and Its Impacts on Regulation: A Study of the OECD Vision in the Light of Data Critical Studies. *European Journal of Risk Regulation, 16*(1), 114–132. DOI: 10.1017/err.2024.73

Caiza, G., Sanguña, V., Tusa, N., Masaquiza, V., Ortiz, A., & Garcia, M. V. (2024). Navigating governmental choices: A comprehensive review of artificial Intelligence's impact on decision-making. *Informatics (MDPI), 11*(3), 64. DOI: 10.3390/informatics11030064

Cameron, D. E., Bashor, C. J., & Collins, J. J. (2014). A brief history of synthetic biology. *Nature Reviews. Microbiology, 12*(5), 381–390. DOI: 10.1038/nrmicro3239 PMID: 24686414

Canals, J., & Heukamp, F. (Eds.). (2019). *The future of management in an AI world: redefining purpose and strategy in the fourth industrial revolution*. Springer Nature.

Carolan, M. (2020). Automated agrifood futures: Robotics, labor and the distributive politics of digital agriculture. *The Journal of Peasant Studies, 47*(1), 184–207. DOI: 10.1080/03066150.2019.1584189

Cascella, M., Guerra, C., De Feo, R., Cerrone, V., & Farah, S. (2024). Cross-sectional study on medical attitude towards artificial intelligence use in fibromyalgia: Insights from the annual thinking lab on fibromyalgia syndrome (ATLAS 2024). *Translational Medicine @ UniSa, 26*(2), 153–163. DOI: 10.37825/2239-9747.1066

Casino, F., Dasaklis, T., & Patsakis, C. (2019). A systematic literature review of blockchain- based applications: Current status, classification and open issues. *Telematics and Informatics, 36*, 55–81. DOI: 10.1016/j.tele.2018.11.006

Castrillon, C. (2022, March 23). *Why Flexible Work Boosts Employee Productivity*. Retrieved October 31, 2022 from Forbes: https://www.forbes.com/sites/carolinecastrillon/2022/03/23/why-flexible-work- boosts-employee-productivity/?sh=585736f06e4b

Cath, C. (2018). Governing artificial intelligence: Ethical, legal and technical opportunities and challenges. *Philosophical Transactions. Series A, Mathematical, Physical, and Engineering Sciences, 376*(2133), 20180080. DOI: 10.1098/rsta.2018.0080

CB INSIGHTS. (2022, March 9). *2370 Banking is only the beginning: 65 big industries blockchain could transform*. Retrieved December 1, 2022 from CB INSIGHTS: https://www.cbinsights.com/research/industries-disrupted-blockchain/

CEGAL. (n.d.). *Data Crawling*. Retrieved January 6, 2023 from CEGAL: https://www.cegal.com/en/dictionary/datacrawling

Centre for Strategic and Policy Studies. (2023). *Brunei Economic Outlook 2023*. Centre for Strategic and Policy Studies.

Chaibi, A., & Zaiem, I. (2022). Doctor resistance of artificial intelligence in healthcare. *International Journal of Healthcare Information Systems and Informatics*, *17*(1), 1–13. DOI: 10.4018/IJHISI.315618

Chapra, M. U. (2019). *The future of economics: An Islamic perspective* (New ed.). The Islamic Foundation.

Charaan, R. D., Mallad, A., Maram, B., Mamodiya, U., & Nidhya, M. S. (2025). 3D Modelling and Printing in Smart Transportation System. In *Driving Green Transportation System Through Artificial Intelligence and Automation: Approaches, Technologies and Applications* (pp. 411–422). Springer Nature Switzerland. DOI: 10.1007/978-3-031-72617-0_22

Charles, L., Xia, S., & Coutts, A. (2022). *Digitalization and Employment*. International Labour Orgniazation. Retrieved from: https://www.ilo.org/wcmsp5/groups/public/--- ed_emp/documents/publication/wcms_854353.pdf

Chen, H. (2020). *Using Blockchain for improving communication efficiency and cooperation: the case of port logistics*. Degree of Master Thesis, Faculty of Computing, Blekinge Institute of Technology, 371 79 Karlskrona, Sweden. Retrieved from https://www.diva- portal.org/smash/get/diva2:1412835/FULLTEXT02

Chen, Y., & Biswas, M. I. (2021). Turning crisis into opportunities: How a firm can enrich its business operations using artificial intelligence and big data during COVID-19. *Sustainability (Basel)*, *13*(22), 12656. DOI: 10.3390/su132212656

Chen, Y.-C., Ahn, M. J., & Wang, Y.-F. (2023). Artificial intelligence and public values: Value impacts and governance in the public sector. *Sustainability (Basel)*, *15*(6), 4796. DOI: 10.3390/su15064796

Cheong, B. C. (2024). Transparency and accountability in AI systems: Safeguarding wellbeing in the age of algorithmic decision-making. *Frontiers in Human Dynamics*, *6*, 1421273. DOI: 10.3389/fhumd.2024.1421273

Cherukupally, S. (2021). Chapter 3 Blockchain technology: Theory and practice. (Arni S.R, Srinivasa Rao, & C.R. Rao, Eds.) *Handbook of Statistics, 44*, 75-103. https://doi.org/DOI: 10.1016/bs.host.2020.10.001

Chillakuri, B., & Attili, V. (2021). Role of blockchain in HR's response to new-normal. *The International Journal of Organizational Analysis*, •••, 1–21. DOI: 10.1108/IJOA-08-2020-2363

Chung, H., Seo, H., Forbes, S., & Birkett, H. (2020). *Working from home during the covid-19 lockdown: Changing preferences and the future of work.* Retrieved from https://kar.kent.ac.uk/83896/

Chy, M. K. H., & Buadi, O. N. (2024). Role of machine learning in policy making and evaluation. *International Journal of Innovative Science and Research Technology (IJISRT), 0 [].*DOI: 10.38124/ijisrt/IJISRT24OCT687

Ciotti, M., Ciccozzi, M., Terrinoni, A., Jiang, W.-C., Wang, C.-B., & Bernardini, S. (2020). The COVID-19 pandemic. *Critical Reviews in Clinical Laboratory Sciences, 57*(6), 365–388. DOI: 10.1080/10408363.2020.1783198

Clampitt, P. G., DeKoch, R. J., & Cashman, T. (2000). A strategy for communicating about uncertainty. *The Academy of Management Perspectives, 14*(4), 41–57. DOI: 10.5465/ame.2000.3979815

Collins dictionary. (n.d.). *Definition of 'flextime'.* Retrieved October 14, 2022 from Collins dictionary: https://www.collinsdictionary.com/dictionary/english/flextime

Cranfield University, School of Management. (2008). *Flexible Working adn Performance.* Retrieved from https://www.workingfamilies.org.uk/wp- content/ uploads/2014/09/Flexible-Working-Performance-2008.pdf

Csete, J., Kamarulzaman, A., Kazatchkine, M., Altice, F., Balicki, M., Buxton, J., & Wolfe, D. (2016). Public health and international drug policy. *Lancet, 387*(10026), 1427–1480. DOI: 10.1016/S0140-6736(16)00619-X

Davenport, T. H., & Harris, J. G. (2007). Competing on analytics: The new science of Winning. Harvard business review press. *Language, 15*(217), 24.

Davidescu, A. A., Apostu, S.-A., Paul, A., & Casuneanu, I. (2020). Work Flexibility, Job Satisfaction, and Job Performance among Romanian Employees— Implications for Sustainable Human Resource Management. *Sustainability (Basel), 12*(15), 1–53. DOI: 10.3390/su12156086

Davis, F., & Venkatesh, V. (2004, February). Toward Preprototype User Acceptance Testing of New Information Systems: Implications for Software Project Management. *IEEE Transactions on Engineering Management, 51*(1), 31–46. DOI: 10.1109/TEM.2003.822468

De, R., Pandey, N., & Pal, A. (2020, June 9). Impact of digital surge during Covid-19 pandemic: A viewpoint on research T and practice. *International Journal of Information Management, 1-5*, 102171. Advance online publication. DOI: 10.1016/j.ijinfomgt.2020.102171

Deshmukh, P., & Tare, H. (2024). Green marketing and corporate social responsibility: A review of business practices. *Multidisciplinary Reviews, 7*(3), 2024059–2024059. DOI: 10.31893/multirev.2024059

Di Stefano, A. G., Ruta, M., & Masera, G. (2023). Advanced digital tools for data-informed and performance-driven design: A review of building energy consumption forecasting models based on machine learning. *Applied Sciences (Basel, Switzerland), 13*(24), 12981. DOI: 10.3390/app132412981

Di Vaio, A., Palladino, R., Hassan, R., & Escobar, O. (2020). Artificial intelligence and business models in thesustainable development goals perspective: A systematic literature review. *Journal of Business Research, 121*, 283–314. DOI: 10.1016/j.jbusres.2020.08.019

Dignum, V., Baldoni, M., Baroglio, C., Caon, M., Chatila, R., Dennis, L., Génova, G., Haim, G., Kließ, M. S., Lopez-Sanchez, M., Micalizio, R., Pavón, J., Slavkovik, M., Smakman, M., van Steenbergen, M., Tedeschi, S., van der Toree, L., Villata, S., & de Wildt, T. (2018, December). Ethics by design. Proceedings of the 2018 AAAI/ACM Conference on AI, Ethics, and Society. DOI: 10.1145/3278721.3278745

Domisch, S., Kakouei, K., Martínez-López, J., Bagstad, K. J., Magrach, A., Balbi, S., Villa, F., Funk, A., Hein, T., Borg-wardt, F., Hermoso, V., Jähnig, S. C., & Langhans, S. D. (2019). Social equity shapes zone-selection: Balancing aquatic biodiversity conservation and ecosystem services delivery in the transboundary DanubeRiver Basin. *The Science of the Total Environment, 656*, 797–807. DOI: 10.1016/j.scitotenv.2018.11.348

Dorigo, M., Birattari, M., & Brambilla, M. (2020). Swarm robotics. *Scholarpedia Journal, 9*(1), 1463. DOI: 10.4249/scholarpedia.1463 PMID: 33298518

Dressel, J., & Farid, H. (2018). The accuracy, fairness, and limits of predicting recidivism. *Science Advances, 4*(1), eaao5580. Advance online publication. DOI: 10.1126/sciadv.aao5580

Dutta, D., Mishra, S. K., & Tyagi, D. (2023). Augmented employee voice and employee engagement using artificial intelligence-enabled chatbots: A field study. *International Journal of Human Resource Management, 34*(12), 2451–2480. DOI: 10.1080/09585192.2022.2085525

Dweck, C. S. (2006). *Mindset: The new psychology of success*. Random house.

Dwivedi, Y. K., Hughes, L., Ismagilova, E., Aarts, G., Coombs, C., Crick, T., Duan, Y., Dwivedi, R., Edwards, J., Eirug, A., Galanos, V., Ilavarasan, P. V., Janssen, M., Jones, P., Kar, A. K., Kizgin, H., Kronemann, B., Lal, B., Lucini, B., & Williams, M. D. (2021). Artificial Intelligence (AI): Multidisciplinary perspectives on emerging challenges, opportunities, and agenda for research, practice and policy. *International Journal of Information Management, 57*, 101994. DOI: 10.1016/j.ijinfomgt.2019.08.002

Dyllick, T., & Hockerts, K. (2002). Beyond the business case for corporate sustainability. *Business Strategy and the Environment, 11*(2), 130–141. DOI: 10.1002/bse.323

Eastwood, N., Fox, E., & Rosmarin, A. (2016). *A quiet revolution: Drug decriminalisation across the globe.* Release. https://www.release.org.uk/publications/quiet-revolution-drug-decriminalisation-across-globe

Eastwood, C., Klerkx, L., Ayre, M., & Dela Rue, B. (2019). Managing socio-ethical challenges in the development of smart farming: From a fragmented to a comprehensive approach for responsible innovation. *Journal of Agricultural & Environmental Ethics, 32*(5), 741–768. DOI: 10.1007/s10806-017-9704-5

Ebrahimi, P., Khajeheian, D., & Fekete-Farkas, M. (2021). A SEM-NCA Approach towards Social Networks Marketing: Evaluating Consumers' Sustainable Purchase Behavior with the Moderating Role of Eco-Friendly Attitude. *International Journal of Environmental Research and Public Health, 18*(24), 13276. DOI: 10.3390/ijerph182413276 PMID: 34948884

Edilia, S., & Larasati, N. D. (2023). Innovative approaches in business development strategies through artificial intelligence technology. *Itsdi, 5*(1), 84–90. DOI: 10.34306/itsdi.v5i1.612

Edmondson, A. C. (2018). *The fearless organization: Creating psychological safety in the workplace for learning, innovation, and growth.* John Wiley & Sons.

Eklof, J., Snis, U., Hamelryck, T., Grima, A., & Ronning, O. (2024). AI Implementation and Capability Development in Manufacturing: An Action Research Case.

El Hammoumi, A., Seghyar, N., El Hammoumi, A. M., & El Ouali, A. (2024, December). The Impact of Artificial Intelligence on Employee Adaptability to Remote Work. In *2024 3rd International Conference on Embedded Systems and Artificial Intelligence (ESAI)* (pp. 1-5). IEEE. DOI: 10.1109/ESAI62891.2024.10913897

Eliaçık, E. (2022, May 17). *What is the role of blockchain in the world today?* Retrieved December 17, 2022 from DATACONOMY: https://dataconomy.com/2022/05/blockchain-use-cases-2022/

Elmahjub, E. (2023). Artificial Intelligence (AI) in Islamic Ethics: Towards pluralist ethical benchmarking for AI. *Philosophy & Technology*, *36*(4), 1–24. DOI: 10.1007/s13347-023-00668-x

Elsyra, N. (2023). The role of artificial intelligence in government services: a systematic literature review. *Open access indonesia journal of social sciences, 6*(3), 998-1003.

Essays, A. A. (2022, July 29). A problem statement of Robotics Technologies Information Technology Essay. UK Essay.

Etzkowitz, H., & Leydesdorff, L. (2000). The dynamics of innovation: From National Systems and "Mode 2" to a Triple Helix of university–industry–government relations. *Research Policy*, *29*(2), 109–123. DOI: 10.1016/S0048-7333(99)00055-4

Evenson, R. E., & Gollin, D. (2003). Assessing the impact of the Green Revolution, 1960 to 2000. *Science*, *300*(5620), 758–762. DOI: 10.1126/science.1078710 PMID: 12730592

Faisal, F. (2021, October 26). *Framework to shift from pandemic to endemic state.* Retrieved December 21, 2022 from Borneo Bulletin: https://borneobulletin.com.bn/framework- to-shift-from-pandemic-to-endemic-state/

FAO. (2021). *The digitalization of the agriculture sector: A global overview*. Food and Agriculture Organization of the United Nations.

FAO. (2022). *Digital agriculture: Technology, innovation and inclusive development*. Food and Agriculture Organization of the United Nations.

Farayola, O. A., Abdul, A. A., Irabor, B. O., & Okeleke, E. C. (2023). Innovative Business Models driven by Ai technologies: A review. Comput. Sci. IT Res. j., 4(2), 85–110.

Fenwick, M., Kaal, W. A., & Vermeulen, E. P. (2019). The" Unmediated" and" Tech-Driven" Corporate Governance of Today's Winning Companies. *NYUJL & Bus.*, *16*, 75.

Fuller, A., Fan, Z., Day, C., & Barlow, C. (2020). Digital twin: Enabling technologies, challenges and open research. *IEEE Access : Practical Innovations, Open Solutions*, *8*, 108952–108971. DOI: 10.1109/ACCESS.2020.2998358

Gad, A., Mosa, D., Abualigah, L., & Abohany, A. (2022). Emerging Trends in Blockchain Technology and Applications: A Review and Outlook. *Journal of King Saud University. Computer and Information Sciences*, *34*(9), 6719–6742. DOI: 10.1016/j.jksuci.2022.03.007

Gafni, R., Aviv, I., Kantsepolsky, B., Sherman, S., Rika, H., Itzkovich, Y., & Barger, A. (2024). Objectivity by design: The impact of AI-driven approach on employees' soft skills evaluation. *Information and Software Technology*, *170*, 107430. DOI: 10.1016/j.infsof.2024.107430

Gajendran, R. S., & Harrison, D. A. (2007). The good, the bad, and the unknown about telecommuting: Meta-analysis of psychological mediators and individual consequences. *The Journal of Applied Psychology*, *92*(6), 1524–1541. DOI: 10.1037/0021-9010.92.6.1524 PMID: 18020794

Galanti, T., Guidetti, G., Mazzei, E., Zappala', S., & Toscano, F. (2021). Work From Home During the COVID-19 Outbreak: The Impact on Employees' Remote Work Productivity, Engagement, and Stress. *Journal of Occupational and Environmental Medicine*, *63*(7), e426–e432. DOI: 10.1097/JOM.0000000000002236

Garbuio, M., & Lin, N. (2019). Artificial intelligence as a growth engine for health care startups: Emerging business models. *California Management Review*, *61*(2), 59–83. DOI: 10.1177/0008125618811931

Gates, B. (2021). *How to avoid a climate disaster: the solutions we have and the breakthroughs we need*. Vintage.

Gazi, M. A. I., Rahman, M. K. H., Masud, A. A., Amin, M. B., Chaity, N. S., Senathirajah, A. R. B. S., & Abdullah, M. (2024). AI capability and sustainable performance: Unveiling the mediating effects of organizational creativity and green innovation with knowledge sharing culture as a moderator. *Sustainability (Basel)*, *16*(17), 7466. DOI: 10.3390/su16177466

Gebbers, R., & Adamchuk, V. I. (2010). Precision agriculture and food security. *Science*, *327*(5967), 828–831. DOI: 10.1126/science.1183899 PMID: 20150492

Geels, F. W. (2004). From sectoral systems of innovation to socio-technical systems: Insights about dynamics and change from sociology and institutional theory. *Research Policy*, *33*(6–7), 897–920. DOI: 10.1016/j.respol.2004.01.015

Geissbauer, R., Schrauf, S., Berttram, P., & Cheraghi, F. (2017). Digital Factories 2020: Shaping the future of manufacturing. *URL: https://www.*

Gerrardo, B. A., Harjoko, A., & Lo, N.-W. (2022, April). On the Design of a Blockchain-based Fraud-prevention Performance Appraisal System. *Indonesian Journal of Computing and Cybernetics Systems*, *16*(2), 137–148. DOI: 10.22146/ijccs.67669

Gerstner, L. V. (2002). *Who says elephants can't dance? Inside IBM's historic turnaround*. HarperCollins Publishers.

Ghani, E. K., Ariffin, N., & Sukmadilaga, C. (2022). Factors influencing artificial intelligence adoption in publicly listed manufacturing companies: A technology, organisation, and environment approach. International Journal of Applied Economics. *Finance And*, *14*(2), 108–117.

Ghasemi, A., & Zahediasl, S. (2012). Normality Tests for Statistical Analysis: A Guide for Non-Statisticians. *International Journal of Endocrinology and Metabolism*, *10*(2), 486–489. DOI: 10.5812/ijem.3505

Gifford, J. (2022). Remote working: Unprecedented increase and a developing research agenda. *Human Resource Development International*, *25*(2), 105–113. DOI: 10.1080/13678868.2022.2049108

Gilbert, N. (2022, November 5). *51 Critical Blockchain Statistics: 2022 Data Analysis & Market Share*. Retrieved December 1, 2022 from Finances Online: Reviews for Busisness: https://financesonline.com/blockchain-statistics/

Giri, C., Jain, S., Zeng, X., & Bruniaux, P. (2019). A detailed review of artificial intelligence applied in the fashion and apparel industry. *IEEE Access : Practical Innovations, Open Solutions*, *7*, 95376–95396. DOI: 10.1109/ACCESS.2019.2928979

Global Commission on Drug Policy. (2021). *Time to end prohibition. Geneva: Global Commission on Drug Policy*. https://www.globalcommissionondrugs.org/reports/time-to-end-prohibition

Gomes, P., Verçosa, L., Melo, F., Silva, V., Filho, C. B., & Bezerra, B. (2022). Artificial intelligence-based methods for business processes: A systematic literature review. *Applied Sciences (Basel, Switzerland)*, *12*(5), 2314. DOI: 10.3390/app12052314

Greene, D., Hoffmann, A. L., & Stark, L. (2019). Better, nicer, clearer, fairer: A critical assessment of the movement for ethical artificial intelligence and machine learning. *Proceedings of the 52nd Hawaii International Conference on System Sciences*. DOI: 10.24251/HICSS.2019.258

Green, N., Tappin, D., & Bentley, T. (2020). Working from home before, during and after the Covid-19 pandemic: Implications for workers and organisations. *New Zealand Journal of Employment Relations*, *45*(2), 5–16. DOI: 10.24135/nzjer.v45i2.19

Griffin, L. (2024). The power of social content: Transforming digital commerce. *Journal of Digital & Social Media Marketing*, *12*(2), 129–140. DOI: 10.69554/LSZN9443

Grimmer, L. (2022). Lessons from the COVID19 pandemic: The case of retail and consumer service firms. *Journal of Retailing and Consumer Services*, *68*, 1–11. DOI: 10.1016/j.jretconser.2022.103012

Gudigantala, N., Madhavaram, S., & Bicen, P. (2023). An AI decision-making framework for business value maximization. *AI Magazine*, *44*(1), 67–84. DOI: 10.1002/aaai.12076

Gupta, S., Langhans, S. D., Domisch, S., Fuso-Nerini, F., Felländer, A., Battaglini, M., Tegmark, M., & Vinuesa, R. (2021). *Assessing whether artificial intelligence is an enabler or an inhibitor of sustainability at indicator level*. Transp Eng. DOI: 10.1016/j.treng.2021.100064

Hadfield, A. (2022). From pandemic to endemic? Learning lessons from global contagion. *Journal of Chinese Economic and Business Studies*, *20*(3), 225–233. DOI: 10.1080/14765284.2021.2024486

Haefner, N., Wincent, J., Parida, V., & Gassmann, O. (2021). Artificial intelligence and innovation management:A review, framework. *Technological Forecasting and Social Change*, *162*, 120392. DOI: 10.1016/j.techfore.2020.120392

Haftor, D. M., Costa Climent, R., & Lundström, J. E. (2021). How machine learning activates data network effects in business models: Theory advancement through an industrial case of promoting ecological sustain-ability. *Journal of Business Research*, *131*, 196–205. DOI: 10.1016/j.jbusres.2021.04.015

Haidegger, T., Mai, V., Mörch, C. M., Boesl, D. O., Jacobs, A., Khamis, A., & Vanderborght, B. (2023). Robotics: Enabler and inhibitor of the sustainable development goals. *Sustainable Production and Consumption*, *43*, 422–434. DOI: 10.1016/j.spc.2023.11.011

Hamouche, S. (2021). Human resource management and the COVID-19 crisis: Implications, challenges, opportunities, and the future organizational directions. *Journal of Management & Organization*, •••, 1–16. DOI: 10.1017/jmo.2021.15

Han, S. (2021, August 10). *COVID-19: Gov't issues guidelines on working from home*. Retrieved December 21, 2022 from The Scoop: https://thescoop.co/2021/08/10/covid- 19-govt-issues-guidelines-on-working-from-home/

Han, S. (2021, October 21). *COVID-19: Brunei unveils lockdown exit plan*. Retrieved December 26, 2022 from The Scoop: https://thescoop.co/2021/10/26/covid-19-brunei- unveils-lockdown-exit-plan/

Haramis, G. E. (1996). Information systems requirements definition: rules and guidelines. *IFAC Proceedings, 29*(2), 113-118. DOI: 10.1016/S1474-6670(17)43787-6

Harm Reduction International. (2023). *The global state of harm reduction 2023*. Harm Reduction International.

Hart, M. (2019, July 26). *What Does WFH Mean? A Quick Guide*. Retrieved September 9, 2022 from Owl Labs: https://resources.owllabs.com/blog/wfh-meaning

Hasan, F. F. (2018). A Review Study of Information Systems. *International Journal of Computer Applications*, *179*(8), 15–19. DOI: 10.5120/ijca2018916307

Hastings, R., & Meyer, E. (2020). *No rules rules: Netflix and the culture of reinvention*. Random house.

Hayat, M. (2021, January 07). *Most Read of 2020: Brunei Darussalam: An Unexpected COVID-19 Success Story*. Retrieved December 21, 2022 from Australian Outlook: https://www.internationalaffairs.org.au/australianoutlook/brunei-darussalam-an - unexpected-covid-19-success-story/

Hofstede, G. (2011). Dimensionalizing cultures: The Hofstede model in context. *Online Readings in Psychology and Culture*, *2*(1), 8. DOI: 10.9707/2307-0919.1014

Hong, Z.-Q., Susanto, H., & Leu, Z.-Q. (2022). A Q-Learning Based Downlink Scheduling Algorithm for Multiple Traffics in 5G NR Systems. *In Innovative Mobile and Internet Services in Ubiquitous Computing: Proceedings of the 15th International Conference on Innovative Mobile and Internet Services in Ubiquitous Computing (IMIS-2021)* (pp. 393-402). Springer International Publishing. https://doi.org/DOI: 10.1007/978-3-030-79728-7_39

Hsieh, T. (2010). *Delivering happiness: A path to profits, passion, and purpose*. Grand Central Publishing.

Huang, Z., Lim, H. Y.-F., Ow, J. T., Sun, S. H.-L., & Chow, A. (2024). Doctors' perception on the ethical use of AI-enabled clinical decision support systems for antibiotic prescribing recommendations in Singapore. *Frontiers in Public Health*, *12*, 1420032. DOI: 10.3389/fpubh.2024.1420032

Ibarra, H., Rattan, A., & Johnston, A. (2018). *Satya Nadella at Microsoft: Instilling a growth mindset*. London Business School.

IBM. (n.d.). *What is blockchain technology?* Retrieved October 11, 2022 from IBM: https://www.ibm.com/topics/what-is-blockchain

Ikpe, E. O. (2024). Adoption and implementation of artificial intelligence in small businesses in selected developing countries. *Journal of Health, Applied Sciences & Management, 8*(1), 26–34-26–34. DOI: 10.4314/johasam.v8i1.3

Imperatori, B. (2017). *Engagement and disengagement at work: Drivers and organizational practices to sustain employee passion and performance*. Springer. DOI: 10.1007/978-3-319-51886-2

Insider Intelligence. (2022, April 15). *The growing list of applications and use cases of blockchain technology in business and life Share on social*. Retrieved October 14, 2022 from Insider Intelligence: https://www.insiderintelligence.com/insights/blockchain-technology-applications-use- cases/

Islamic World Educational, Scientific and Cultural Organization. (2024). *Riyadh charter on ethics of artificial intelligence*. ICESCO.

Iyelolu, T. V., Agu, E. E., Idemudia, C., & Ijomah, T. I. (2024). Driving SME innovation with AI solutions: overcoming adoption barriers and future growth opportunities. *International Journal of Science Technology Research Archive, 7*(1), 036-054. DOI: 10.53771/ijstra.2024.7.1.0055

Jagatheesaperumal, S. K., Rahouti, M., Ahmad, K., Al-Fuqaha, A., & Guizani, M. (2021). The duo of artificial intelligence and big data for industry 4.0: Applications, techniques, challenges, and future research directions. *IEEE Internet of Things Journal, 9*(15), 12861–12885. DOI: 10.1109/JIOT.2021.3139827

Jain, G., & Jain, A. (2022). Blockchain for 5G-enabled networks in healthcare service based on several aspects. *Blockchain Applications for Healthcare Informatics*, 471-493. DOI: 10.1016/B978-0-323-90615-9.00018-9

Jamaluddin, S. Z., Taher, M., & Yi, N. S. (2019). Key performance indicators and employment contracts in Malaysia: a legal analysis. *IIUM Law Journal, 27*(2), 549-569. https://doi.org/10.31436/iiumlj.v27i2.430

Javaid, M., Haleem, A., Singh, R. P., Khan, S., & Suman, R. (2021). Blockchain technology applications for Industry 4.0: A literature-based review. *Blockchain: Research and Application, 2*(4), 1–11. DOI: 10.1016/j.bcra.2021.100027

Jayakumar, M., Jenefa, L., Badrinarayanan, M. K., Sarah, K. S., Kumar, A., & Kumar, R. M. (2024, December). Exploring Organizational Adoption of Innovative Technologies in Consumer Online Purchase. In *2024 International Conference on Emerging Research in Computational Science (ICERCS)* (pp. 1-6). IEEE. DOI: 10.1109/ICERCS63125.2024.10895563

Jayakumar, M., Jenefa, L., Mishra, N., Kumar, A., & Sumitha, S. (2024, December). Artificial Intelligence In Digital Marketing Platform: Impact In Consumer Buying Behaviour. In *2024 International Conference on Emerging Research in Computational Science (ICERCS)* (pp. 1-6). IEEE.

Jayakumar, M., Kumar, A., Ganesh, K. S., & Jenefa, L. (2024, December). Impact of AI for Online Shopping through Enhancing Personalised Recommendations. In *2024 International Conference on Emerging Research in Computational Science (ICERCS)* (pp. 1-6). IEEE. DOI: 10.1109/ICERCS63125.2024.10894946

Jenefa, L., & Jayakumar, M. (2025). Digital Transformation Challenges: Adaptation to AI Technologies in Service Marketing. In *Strategic Workforce Reskilling in Service Marketing* (pp. 111-132). IGI Global Scientific Publishing.

Jenefa, L., Jayakumar, M., Catherine, S., Kumar, S. A., Tripathi, R., & Jeevitha, M. The Application of Artificial Intelligence and Robotics in Healthcare Services. In *Revolutionizing Healthcare Services* (pp. 27–45). CRC Press. DOI: 10.1201/9781003531272-3

Jenefa, L., Kanchana, K., Jayakumar, M., & Kumar, A. (2024, December). The Impact of Artificial Intelligence for Developing Supply Chain Collaboration Performance: An Empirical Investigation. In *2024 International Conference on Emerging Research in Computational Science (ICERCS)* (pp. 1-4). IEEE. DOI: 10.1109/ICERCS63125.2024.10894938

Jenefa, L., Kumar, A., Yiong, B. L. C., Jayakumar, M., & Sakthivel, M. (2024, November). The Implementation of Artificial Intelligence Tools In Retail Sector Among Consumers-A New Evolution Traditional to Morden. In *2024 International Conference on Electronic Systems and Intelligent Computing (ICESIC)* (pp. 220-223). IEEE. DOI: 10.1109/ICESIC61777.2024.10846326

Jian, Y. C., Chung, M. S., Susanto, H., & Leu, F. Y. (2022, June). 5G Base Station Scheduling. In Innovative Mobile and Internet Services in Ubiquitous Computing: Proceedings of the 16th International Conference on Innovative Mobile and Internet Services in Ubiquitous Computing (IMIS-2022) (pp. 315-324). Cham: Springer International Publishing.

Jobin, A., Ienca, M., & Vayena, E. (2019). The global landscape of AI ethics guidelines. *Nature Machine Intelligence*, *1*(9), 389–399. DOI: 10.1038/s42256-019-0088-2

John Deere. (2017). *John Deere acquires Blue River Technology*. https://www.deere.com/en/our-company/news-and-announcements/news-releases/2017/corporate/john-deere-acquires-blue-river-technology/

John, W. (2017). Flexible Working Hours and Organizational Productivity: Exploring the Potential Linkage. *AIMA Journal of Management & Research, 11*(4), 1-7. Retrieved from https://apps.aima.in/ejournal_new/articlesPDF/waseem-john.pdf

John, M. M., Olsson, H. H., & Bosch, J. (2023). Towards an AI-driven business development framework: A multi-case study. *Journal of Software (Malden, MA)*, *35*(6), e2432. DOI: 10.1002/smr.2432

Johnson, R., & Gueutal, H. (2011). *Transforming HR Through Technology - SHRM*. Retrieved December 2, 2022 from SHRM: https://www.shrm.org/hr-today/trends-and- forecasting/special-reports-and-expert-views/documents/hr-technology.pdf

Josimovski, S., Ivanovska, L. P., & Dodevski, D. (2023). Understanding the consumer dynamics of AI in north Macedonian E-business. *Econ. Cult.*, *20*(2), 64–75. DOI: 10.2478/jec-2023-0016

Justinia, T. (2019). Blockchain Technologies: Opportunities for Solving Real-World Problems in Healthcare and Biomedical Sciences. *Acta Informatica Medica*, *27*(4), 284–291. DOI: 10.5455/aim.2019.27.284-291

Kalischko, T., & Riedl, R. (2021). Electronic Performance Monitoring in the Digital Workplace: Conceptualization, Review of Effects and Moderators, and Future Research Opportunities. *Frontiers in Psychology*, *12*, 633031. Advance online publication. DOI: 10.3389/fpsyg.2021.633031

Kamali, M. H. (2009). *Shari'ah law: An introduction*. Oneworld Publications.

Kamilaris, A., & Prenafeta-Boldú, F. X. (2018). Deep learning in agriculture: A survey. *Computers and Electronics in Agriculture*, *147*, 70–90. DOI: 10.1016/j.compag.2018.02.016

Karunakaran, S., Hemasundari, M., Suguna, R., & Thandauthapani, A. (2024). Integrating AI and ML for dynamic pricing strategies: Innovations in marketing analytics and revenue management. *2024 International Conference on Power, Energy, Control and Transmission Systems (ICPECTS)*, Chennai, India. DOI: 10.1109/ICPECTS62210.2024.10780375

Kassa, B. Y., & Worku, E. K. (2025). The impact of artificial intelligence on organizational performance: The mediating role of employee productivity. *Journal of Open Innovation*, *11*(1), 100474. DOI: 10.1016/j.joitmc.2025.100474

Keating, G. (2012). *Netflixed: The epic battle for America's eyeballs*. Penguin.

Kedi, W. E., Ejimuda, C., Idemudia, C., & Ijomah, T. I. (2024a). AI Chatbot integration in SME marketing platforms: Improving customer interaction and service efficiency. *International Journal of Management & Entrepreneurship Research*, *6*(7), 2332–2341. DOI: 10.51594/ijmer.v6i7.1327

Kedi, W. E., Ejimuda, C., Idemudia, C., & Ijomah, T. I. (2024b). Machine learning software for optimizing SME social media marketing campaigns. *Computer Science & IT Research Journal*, *5*(7), 1634–1647. DOI: 10.51594/csitrj.v5i7.1349

Khamis, A., Meng, J., Wang, J., Azar, A. T., Prestes, E., Takács, Á., & Haidegger, T. (2021). Robotics and intelligent systems against a pandemic. *Acta Polytechnica Hungarica*, *18*(5), 13–35. DOI: 10.12700/APH.18.5.2021.5.3

Khan, M. A. (2024). Understanding the Impact of Artificial Intelligence (AI) on Traditional Businesses in Indonesia. *Journal of Management Studies Development*, *3*(02), 146–158. DOI: 10.56741/jmsd.v3i02.584

Kinder, T., Stenvall, J., Koskimies, E., Webb, H., & Janenova, S. (2023). Local public services and the ethical deployment of artificial intelligence. *Government Information Quarterly*, *40*(4), 101865. DOI: 10.1016/j.giq.2023.101865

Kitagawa, R., Kuroda, S., Okudaira, H., & Owan, H. (2021). Working from home and productivity under the COVID-19 pandemic: Using survey data of four manufacturing firms. *PLoS ONE, 16*(12), 1-24. https://doi.org/. pone.0261761DOI: 10.1371/journal

Kleinberg, J., Lakkaraju, H., Leskovec, J., Ludwig, J., & Mullainathan, S. (2018). Human decisions and machine predictions. *The Quarterly Journal of Economics*, *133*(1), 237–293. DOI: 10.1093/qje/qjx032

Klein, M. (2020). Leadership characteristics in the era of digital transformation. *Business & Management Studies: An International Journal*, *8*(1), 883–902. DOI: 10.15295/bmij.v8i1.1441

Klerkx, L., Jakku, E., & Labarthe, P. (2019). A review of social science on digital agriculture, smart farming and agriculture 4.0: New contributions and a future research agenda. *NJAS Wageningen Journal of Life Sciences*, *90-91*(1), 100315. DOI: 10.1016/j.njas.2019.100315

Klindžić, M., & Marić, M. (2019). Flexible Work Arrangements and Organizational Performance – The Difference between Employee and Employer-Driven Practices. *Društvena istraživanja, 28*(1), 89-108. https://doi.org/DOI: 10.5559/di.28.1.05

Kombe, C., Ally, M., & Sam, A. (2018). A review on healthcare information systems and consensus protocols in blockchain technology. *International Journal of Advanced Technology and Engineering Exploration, 5*(49), 473–483. DOI: 10.19101/IJATEE.2018.547023

Kong, H., Yin, Z., Baruch, Y., & Yuan, Y. (2023). The impact of trust in AI on career sustainability: The role of employee–AI collaboration and protean career orientation. *Journal of Vocational Behavior, 146*, 103928. DOI: 10.1016/j.jvb.2023.103928

Koren, I., Jarke, M., Michael, J., Heithoff, M., Tacke Genannt Unterberg, L., Stachon, M., & van der Aalst, W. M. (2024, May). Navigating the Data Model Divide in Smart Manufacturing: An Empirical Investigation for Enhanced AI Integration. In *International Conference on Business Process Modeling, Development and Support* (pp. 275-290). Cham: Springer Nature Switzerland. DOI: 10.1007/978-3-031-61007-3_21

Kragic, D., Gustafson, J., Karaoguz, H., Jensfelt, P., & Krug, R. (1970, January 1). Interactive, collaborative robots: Challenges and opportunities. *IJCAI (United States).*

Kramer, M. A., Leavens, A., & Scarlat, A. (2024). Harnessing AI for efficient analysis of complex policy documents: a case study of Executive Order 14110. *arXiv preprint arXiv:2406.06657.*

Krishnan, L. R. K. (2022). Impact of Using AI in Manufacturing Industries. *Journal of the International Academy for Case Studies, 28.*

Kurrahman, T., Ming, T. F., K., L. M., Kanchana, S., & and Tseng, M.-L. (2025). Generative AI capabilities for green supply chain management improvement: extended dynamic capabilities view. *International Journal of Logistics Research and Applications*, 1-28. DOI: 10.1080/13675567.2025.2479006

Kushwah, U. (2024). The role of artificial intelligence in personalizing consumer experiences: A study on predictive analytics in the e-commerce sector. *Vidhyayana - An International Multidisciplinary Peer-Reviewed E-Journal, 10*(1), 298-320. https://j.vidhyayanaejournal.org/index.php/journal/article/view/1961

Lainjo, B. (2024). The role of artificial intelligence in achieving the United Nations sustainable development goals. *Journal of Sustainable Development, 17*(5), 1–30. DOI: 10.5539/jsd.v17n5p30

Laurence, T. (2017). *Blockchain For Dummies*. John Wiley & Sons, Inc.

Lee, J., Suh, T., Roy, D., & Baucus, M. (2019). Emerging technology and business model innovation: The case of artificial intelligence. *Journal of Open Innovation*, *5*(3), 44. DOI: 10.3390/joitmc5030044

Leible, S., Schlager, S., Schubotz, M., & Gipp, B. (2019). A Review on Blockchain Technology and Blockchain Projects Fostering Open Science. *Front. Blockchain*, *2*(16), 1–28. DOI: 10.3389/fbloc.2019.00016

Lemon, K. N., & Verhoef, P. C. (2016). Understanding customer experience throughout the customer journey. *Journal of Marketing*, *80*(6), 69–96. DOI: 10.1509/jm.15.0420

Leong, L.-Y., Hew, T. S., Ooi, K.-B., Hajli, N., & Tan, G. W.-H. (2024). Revisiting the social commerce paradigm: The social commerce (SC) framework and a research agenda. *Internet Research*, *34*(4), 1346–1393. DOI: 10.1108/INTR-08-2022-0657

Leu, F.-Y., Susanto, H., Chou, P.-H., & Lin, J.-W. (2019). Migration of Edge Computing Services in 5G Networks–Firewall as a Service Example. *In Advances on Broadband and Wireless Computing, Communication and Applications: Proceedings of the 13th International Conference on Broadband and Wireless Computing, Communication and Applications (BWCCA-2018)* (pp. 578-585). Springer International Publishing. https://doi.org/DOI: 10.1007/978-3-030-02613-4_52

Leu, F.-Y., Tsai, K.-L., Susanto, H., Gu, C.-Y., & You, I. (2021). A fault tolerant mechanism for UE authentication in 5G networks. *Mobile Networks and Applications*, *26*(4), 1650–1667. DOI: 10.1007/s11036-019-01502-5

Levy, K., Chasalow, K. E., & Riley, S. (2021). Algorithms and decision-making in the public sector. *Annual Review of Law and Social Science*, *17*(1), 309–334. DOI: 10.1146/annurev-lawsocsci-041221-023808

Liakos, K. G., Busato, P., Moshou, D., Pearson, S., & Bochtis, D. (2018). Machine learning in agriculture: A review. *Sensors (Basel)*, *18*(8), 2674. DOI: 10.3390/s18082674 PMID: 30110960

Liang, X., Rasheed, U., Cai, J., Wibranek, B., & Awolusi, I. (2024). Impacts of collaborative robots on construction work performance and worker perception: Experimental analysis of human–robot collaborative wood assembly. *Journal of Construction Engineering and Management*, *150*(8), 04024087. DOI: 10.1061/JCEMD4.COENG-14390

Liao, S.-H., Widowati, R., & Hsieh, Y.-C. (2021). Investigating online social media users' behaviors for social commerce recommendations. *Technology in Society*, *66*, 101655. DOI: 10.1016/j.techsoc.2021.101655

Lloyd, K. (2018). Bias amplification in artificial intelligence systems. *arXiv preprint arXiv:1809.07842*.

Loi, M., & Spielkamp, M. (2021). Towards accountability in the use of artificial intelligence for public administrations. Proceedings of the 2021 AAAI/ACM Conference on AI, Ethics, and Society DOI: 10.1145/3461702.3462631

Lowenberg-DeBoer, J., Huang, I., Grigoriadis, V., & Blackmore, S. (2020). Economics of robot use in arable farming: Lessons from the first twenty years. *Precision Agriculture*, *21*(6), 1249–1272. DOI: 10.1007/s11119-019-09667-5

Lund, S., Madgavkar, A., Manyika, J., & Smit, S. (2020, November 23). *What's next for remote work: An analysis of 2,000 tasks, 800 jobs, and nine countries*. Retrieved January 3, 2023 from McKinsey Global Institute: https://www.mckinsey.com/featured- insights/future-of-work/whats-next-for-remote-work-an-analysis-of-2000-tasks-800- jobs-and-nine-countries

Lu, Y.-S., Susanto, H., & Leu, F.-Y. (2022). Asymmetric Cryptography Among Different 5G Core Networks. *In Innovative Mobile and Internet Services in Ubiquitous Computing: Proceedings of the 16th International Conference on Innovative Mobile and Internet Services in Ubiquitous Computing (IMIS-2022)* (pp. 325-333). Springer International Publishing. https://doi.org/DOI: 10.1007/978-3-031-08819-3_34

Machado, H., Silva, S., & Neiva, L. (2025). Publics' views on ethical challenges of artificial intelligence: A scoping review. *AI and Ethics*, *5*(1), 139–167. DOI: 10.1007/s43681-023-00387-1

Magableh, I. K., Mahrouq, M. H., Ta'Amnha, M. A., & Riyadh, H. A. (2024). The Role of Marketing Artificial Intelligence in Enhancing Sustainable Financial Performance of Medium-Sized Enterprises Through Customer Engagement and Data-Driven Decision-Making. *Sustainability (Basel)*, *16*(24), 11279. DOI: 10.3390/su162411279

Malik, A. (2024). A study on the relationship of artificial intelligence applications in HR processes for assessing employee engagement, performance, and job security. *International Review of Management and Marketing*, *14*(5), 216–221. DOI: 10.32479/irmm.16838

Malik, A., Budhwar, P., & Kazmi, B. A. (2023). Artificial intelligence (AI)-assisted HRM: Towards an extended strategic framework. *Human Resource Management Review*, *33*(1), 100940. DOI: 10.1016/j.hrmr.2022.100940

Marichamy, D., Sankar, M., Sivaprakash, P., Chithambaramani, R., Charaan, R. D., & Ithayan, J. V. (2024, August). Machine Learning Based Abnormal Human Behaviour Detection. In *2024 Second International Conference on Intelligent Cyber Physical Systems and Internet of Things (ICoICI)* (pp. 1155-1159). IEEE. DOI: 10.1109/ICoICI62503.2024.10696376

Marinoudi, V., Sørensen, C. G., Pearson, S., & Bochtis, D. (2019). Robotics and labour in agriculture: A context consideration. *Biosystems Engineering*, *184*, 111–121. DOI: 10.1016/j.biosystemseng.2019.06.013

Masih, N., Sriratanaviriyakul, N., El-Den, J., & Azam, S. (2018, June). The role of knowledge sharing on employees' innovation initiatives. In *Proceedings of the 8th International Workshop on Computer Science and Engineering*, Bangkok, Thailand (pp. 28–30). DOI: 10.2139/ssrn.3212950

Mayer, R. C., Davis, J. H., & Schoorman, F. D. (1995). An integrative model of organizational trust. *Academy of Management Review*, *20*(3), 709–734. DOI: 10.2307/258792

McCord, P. (2018). *Powerful: Building a culture of freedom and responsibility*. Tom Rath.

Meister, J. C., & Willyerd, K. (2010). *The 2020 workplace: How innovative companies attract, develop, and keep tomorrow's employees today*. Harper Collins.

Michael, O. (2025). Maximising the Potentials of Small and Medium Scale Business Enterprises in Developing Nations Through the Use of Artificial Intelligence: AI Adoption by SMEs in the Developing Nations. In *The Future of Small Business in Industry 5.0* (pp. 215-246). IGI Global Scientific Publishing. DOI: 10.4018/979-8-3693-7362-0.ch009

Mikhaylov, S. J., Esteve, M., & Campion, A. (2018). Artificial intelligence for the public sector: Opportunities and challenges of cross-sector collaboration. *Philosophical Transactions. Series A, Mathematical, Physical, and Engineering Sciences*, *376*(2128), 20170357. DOI: 10.1098/rsta.2017.0357 PMID: 30082303

Ministry of Health. Brunei Darussalam. (2020). *Detection of the first case of covid-19 infection in Brunei Darussalam*. Press Release, Bandar Seri Begawan.

Mishra, P., Pandey, C., Singh, U., Gupta, A., Sahu, C., & Keshri, A. (2019). Descriptive Statistics and Normality Tests for Statistical Data. *Annals of Cardiac Anaesthesia*, *22*(1), 67–72. DOI: 10.4103/aca.ACA_157_18

Misra, S. K., Das, S., Gupta, S., & Sharma, S. K. (2020). Public policy and regulatory challenges of artificial intelligence (AI). *International Working Conference on Transfer and Diffusion of IT* DOI: 10.1007/978-3-030-64849-7_10

Monrat, A. A., Schele´n, O., & Andersson, K. (2020). Performance Evaluation of Permissioned Blockchain Platforms. *2020 IEEE Asia-Pacific Conference on Computer Science and Data Engineering (CSDE)* (pp. 1-8). Gold Coast, Australia: IEEE. DOI: DOI: 10.1109/CSDE50874.2020.9411380

MTIC. (2020). *Digital Economy Masterplan 2025.* Retrieved October 16, 2022 from Digital Economy Council: https://www.mtic.gov.bn/DE2025/documents/Digital%20 Economy%20Masterplan%2 02025.pdf

Mubdir, G. A., Hashim, S., Ayob, A. H., & Rosli, N. (2025). Exploring Customer Engagement in Social Commerce: A Literature Review of Frameworks, Pathways, and Emerging Trends. *Engineering, Technology &. Applied Scientific Research, 15*(2), 20601–20608. DOI: 10.48084/etasr.9452

Mwebi, M. B., & Kadaga, M. N. (2015). Effects of Flextime Work Arrangement on Employee Performance in Nairobi CBD Commercial Banks. *International Journal of Novel Research in Marketing Management and Economics*, *2*(3), 111–121. https://www.noveltyjournals.com/upload/paper/Effects%20of%20Flextime%20 Work- 423.pdf

Nanseki, T., Shiratsuchi, H., & Mizoguchi, T. (2018). Smart agriculture in Japan. *IFAC-PapersOnLine*, *51*(17), 6–11. DOI: 10.1016/j.ifacol.2018.08.002

Narayanamurthy, G., & Tortorella, G. (2021). Impact of COVID-19 outbreak on employee performance – Moderating role of industry 4.0 base technologies. *International Journal of Production Economics*, *234*, 1–10. DOI: 10.1016/j.ijpe.2021.108075

Narayanan, L., Menon, S., Plaisent, M., & Bernard, P. (2017). Telecommuting: The Work Anywhere, Anyplace, Anytime Organization in the 21st Century. *Journal of Marketing Management*, *8*(2), 47–54. https://gsmi-ijgb.com/wp- content/uploads/ JMM-V8-N2-P04-Lakshmi-Narayanan-Telecommuting.pdf

Nashwan, A. J. (2025). Data endowment as a digital waqf: An Islamic ethical framework for AI development. *Philosophy & Technology*, *38*(2), 74. Advance online publication. DOI: 10.1007/s13347-025-00905-5

National Institute of Standards and Technology. (2023). *AI risk management framework (AI RMF 1.0).* U.S. Department of Commerce., DOI: 10.6028/NIST.AI.100-1

Nay, J., & Daily, J. (2022). Aligning Artificial Intelligence with Humans through Public Policy. *arXiv preprint arXiv:2207.01497.*

Necula, S. C., Fotache, D., & Rieder, E. (2024). Assessing the impact of artificial intelligence tools on employee productivity: Insights from a comprehensive survey analysis. *Electronics (Basel), 13*(18), 3758. DOI: 10.3390/electronics13183758

Neiroukh, S., Emeagwali, O. L., & Aljuhmani, H. Y. (2024). Artificial intelligence capability and organizational performance: Unraveling the mediating mechanisms of decision-making processes. *Management Decision*. Advance online publication. DOI: 10.1108/MD-10-2023-1547

Nerobkova, N., Park, Y. S., Park, E.-C., & Jang, S.-Y. (2022, July 11). The Association between Working Hours Flexibility and Well-Being Prior to and during COVID-19 in South Korea. *International Journal of Environmental Research and Public Health, 19*(14), 1–11. DOI: 10.3390/ijerph19148438

Nguyen, D., Pathirana, P., Ding, M., & Seneviratne, A. (2020). Blockchain for 5G and beyond networks: A state of the art survey. *Journal of Network and Computer Applications, 166*, 1–38. DOI: 10.1016/j.jnca.2020.102693

Novelli, C., & Sandri, G. (2024). Digital democracy in the age of artificial intelligence. *arXiv preprint arXiv:2412.07791.*

OECD. (2020, September 20). *Productivity gains from teleworking in the post COVID-19 era: How can public policies make it happen?* Retrieved October 31, 2022 from OECD Policy Responses to Coronavirus (COVID-19): https://www.oecd.org/coronavirus/policy-responses/productivity-gains-from- teleworking-in-the-post-covid-19-era-a5d52e99/

OECD. (2021). *Regulatory sandboxes and innovation in agriculture*. Organisation for Economic Co-operation and Development.

Okeke, N. I., Alabi, O. A., Igwe, A. N., Ofodile, O. C., & Ewim, C. P.-M.Nnenna Ijeoma OkekeOlufunke Anne AlabiAbbey Ngochindo IgweOnyeka Chrisanctus OfodileChikezie Paul-Mikki Ewim. (2024). AI-driven personalization framework for SMES: Revolutionizing customer engagement and retention. *World Journal of Advanced Research and Reviews, 24*(1), 2019–2035. DOI: 10.30574/wjarr.2024.24.1.3208

Olan, F., Arakpogun, E. O., Suklan, J., Nakpodia, F., Damij, N., & Jayawickrama, U. (2022). Artificial intelligence and knowledge sharing: Contributing factors to organizational performance. *Journal of Business Research, 145*, 605–615. DOI: 10.1016/j.jbusres.2022.03.008

Olatoye, F. O., Awonuga, K. F., Mhlongo, N. Z., Ibeh, C. V., Elufioye, O. A., & Ndubuisi, N. L.Funmilola Olatundun OlatoyeKehinde Feranmi AwonugaNoluthando Zamanjomane MhlongoChidera Victoria IbehOluwafunmi Adijat ElufioyeNdubuisi Leonard Ndubuisi. (2024). AI and ethics in business: A comprehensive review of responsible AI practices and corporate responsibility. *Int. J. Sci. Res. Arch.*, *11*(1), 1433–1443. DOI: 10.30574/ijsra.2024.11.1.0235

Omowole, B. M., Olufemi-Philips, A., Ofadile, O., Eyo-Udo, N. L., & Ewim, S. E. (2024). Barriers and drivers of digital transformation in SMEs: A conceptual analysis. *International Journal of Frontline Research in Multidisciplinary Studies, 5*(2), 019-036. DOI: 10.56781/ijsrst.2024.5.2.0037

Oosterbaan, R. (1994). Frequency and regression analysis. In *Drainage Principles and Applications* (3rd revised Edition ed., pp. 175-223).

Oreg, S., Vakola, M., & Armenakis, A. (2011). Change recipients' reactions to organizational change: A 60-year review of quantitative studies. *The Journal of Applied Behavioral Science*, *47*(4), 461–524. DOI: 10.1177/0021886310396550

Organisation for Economic Co-operation and Development. (2019). *OECD principles on artificial intelligence.* OECD Publishing. https://oecd.ai/en/ai-principles

Ostern, N. K., Holotiuk, F., & Moormann, J. (2022). Organizations' approaches to blockchain: A critical realist perspective. *Information & Management*, *59*(7), 1–14. DOI: 10.1016/j.im.2021.103552

Oyekunle, D., & Boohene, D. (2024). Digital transformation potential: The role of Artificial Intelligence in business. *Int. J. Prof. Bus. Rev.*, *9*(3), e04499. DOI: 10.26668/businessreview/2024.v9i3.4499

Pallant, J. (2010). *SPSS survival manual: a step by step guide to data analysis using SPSS* (7th Edition ed.). Routledge.

Patanjali, S., & Bhatta, N. (2022). Work from Home During the Pandemic: The Impact of Organizational Factors on the Productivity of Employees in the IT Industry. *Vision*, •••, 1-13. https://doi.org/10.1177/09722629221074137

Patil, D. (2024). Artificial Intelligence-Driven Customer Service: Enhancing Personalization, Loyalty, And Customer Satisfaction. *Loyalty. Customer Satisfaction, 5057432*. Advance online publication. DOI: 10.2139/ssrn.5057432

Păuceanu, A. M., Văduva, S., & Nedelcu , A. C. (2023). Social Commerce in Europe: A Literature Review and Implications for Researchers, Practitioners, and Policymakers. *Journal of Theoretical and Applied Electronic Commerce Research, 18*(3), 1283–1300. DOI: 10.3390/jtaer18030065

Pedersen, S. M., Fountas, S., Have, H., & Blackmore, S. (2020). Agricultural robots—System analysis and economic feasibility. *Precision Agriculture*, *21*, 1473–1491. DOI: 10.1007/s11119-020-09736-0

Perez, J. R., & de Pablos, P. O. (2003). Knowledge management and organizational competitiveness: A framework for human capital analysis. *Journal of Knowledge Management*, *7*(3), 82–91. DOI: 10.1108/13673270310485640

Philip, A., Afolabi, B., Adeniran, O., Oluwatolani, O., & Ishaya, G. (2010). Towards an Efficient Information Systems Development Process and Management: A Review of Challenges and Proposed Strategies. *Journal of Software Engineering and Applications*, *3*(10), 983–989. DOI: 10.4236/jsea.2010.310115

Pingali, P. (2007). Agricultural mechanization: Adoption patterns and economic impact. *Handbook of Agricultural Economics*, 3, 2779–2805. https://doi.org/DOI: 10.1016/S1574-0072(06)03054-2

Pivoto, D., Waquil, P. D., Talamini, E., Finocchio, C. P. S., Dalla Corte, V. F., & de Vargas Mores, G. (2019). Scientific development of smart farming technologies and their application in Brazil. *Information Processing in Agriculture*, *6*(1), 15–34. DOI: 10.1016/j.inpa.2018.08.002

Prager, F., Rhoads, M., & Martínez, J. (2022). The COVID-19 economic shutdown and the future of flexible workplace practices in the South Bay region of Los Angeles County. *Transport Policy*, *125*, 241–255. DOI: 10.1016/j.tranpol.2022.06.004

Prasanna, R., Jayasundara, J., Naradda Gamage, S. K., Ekanayake, E. M. S., Rajapakshe, P. S. K., & Abeyrathne, G. (2019). Sustainability of SMEs in the Competition: A Systemic Review on Technological Challenges and SME Performance. *Journal of Open Innovation*, *5*(4), 100. DOI: 10.3390/joitmc5040100

Prasetyaningtyas, S. W., Heryanto, C., Nurfauzi, N. F., & Tanjung, S. B. (2021). The effect of work from home on employee productivity in banking industry. *Journal of Applied Management (JAM), 19*(3), 507-521. http://dx.doi.org/10.21776/ub.jam.2021.019.03.05

Prime Minister Office. Brunei Darussalam. (2021, October 26). *National Covid-19 Recovery Plan.* Retrieved Decemebr 21, 2022 from Prime Minister Office, Brunei Darussalam: https://www.pmo.gov.bn/SiteCollectionDocuments/covid19/National-COVID-19- Recovery-Framework.pdf

Priyatharsini, G. S., Bhimaavarapu, K., Charaan, R. D., Konakalla, J. P., & Chandralekha, E. (2025, March). Design and Analysis of Smart Health Care Predictions Using Machine Learning. In *2025 International Conference on Machine Learning and Autonomous Systems (ICMLAS)* (pp. 389-395). IEEE.

Quantum Workplace. (n.d.). *What is Employee Engagement? What, Why, and How to Improve It*. Retrieved October 16, 2022 from Quantum Workplace: https://www.quantumworkplace.com/future-of-work/what-is-employee-engagement-definition

Qu, C., & Kim, E. (2024). Reviewing the roles of AI-integrated technologies in sustainable supply chain man-agement: Research propositions and a framework for future directions. *Sustainability (Basel)*, *16*(14), 6186. DOI: 10.3390/su16146186

Radhakrishnan, J., & Gupta, S. (2020). Artificial intelligence in practice – real-world examples and emerging business models. In *IFIP Advances in Information and Communication Technology* (pp. 77–88). Springer International Publishing.

Rahmadika, S., Firdaus, M., Jang, S., & Rhee, K.-H. (2021). Blockchain-Enabled 5G Edge Networks and Beyond: An Intelligent Cross-Silo Federated Learning Approach. *Security and Communication Networks*, *2021*, 1–14. DOI: 10.1155/2021/5550153

Rahman, M., Kistyanto, A., & Surjanti, J. (2020). Flexible Work Arrangements in Covid-19 Pandemic Era, Influence Employee Peformance: The Mediating Role of Innovative Work Behaviour. *International Journal of Management Innovation & Entrepreneurial Research*, *6*(2), 10–22. DOI: 10.18510/ijmier.2020.622

Raju, P. V. M., & Sumallika, T. (2023). The impact of AI in the global economy and its implications in Industry 4.0 era. *Information Technology, Education and Society*, *18*(2), 53–62. DOI: 10.7459/ites/18.2.05

Ramadhan, K. R., & Wijaya, C. (2022). The Challenges of Personal Data Protection Policy in Indonesia: Lesson learned from the European Union, Singapore, and Malaysia. *Technium Social Sciences Journal*, *36*(1), 18–28. DOI: 10.47577/tssj.v36i1.7442

Rane, N. (2023). Enhancing customer loyalty through Artificial Intelligence (AI), Internet of Things (IoT), and Big Data technologies: improving customer satisfaction, engagement, relationship, and experience. *SSRN*, 4616051. DOI: 10.2139/ssrn.4616051

Rantala, T., Ukko, J., Nasiri, M., & Saunila, M. (2023). Shifting focus of value creation through industrial digital twins—From internal application to ecosystem-level utilization. *Technovation*, *125*, 102795. DOI: 10.1016/j.technovation.2023.102795

Ray, T., & Pana-Cryan, R. (2021, March). Work Flexibility and Work-Related Well-Being. *International Journal of Environmental Research and Public Health, 18*(6), 1–17. DOI: 10.3390/ijerph18063254

Rialti, R., & Zollo, L. (2023). *Digital Transformation of SME Marketing Strategies*. Palgrave Macmillan Cham., DOI: 10.1007/978-3-031-33646-1

RM., D. C., Chithambaramani, R., & Marichamy, D. (2024, September). Historical Strategies Flow Detection for Organizations using Machine Learning. In *2024 International Conference on Integration of Emerging Technologies for the Digital World (ICIETDW)* (pp. 1-6). IEEE.

Roberts, H., Cowls, J., Hine, E., Mazzi, F., Tsamados, A., Taddeo, M., & Floridi, L. (2021). Achieving a "Good AI Society": Comparing the aims and progress of the EU and the US. *Science and Engineering Ethics, 27*(6), 68. DOI: 10.1007/s11948-021-00340-7

Roldán, J. J., Peña-Tapia, E., de León, J., & García-Aunon, P. (2018). Autonomous robotics in precision agriculture: A review. *Robotics (Basel, Switzerland), 7*(4), 48. DOI: 10.3390/robotics7040048

Rose, D. C., Wheeler, R., Winter, M., Lobley, M., & Chivers, C. A. (2021). Farming and agri-tech: Developing a responsible innovation agenda for smart agriculture. *Frontiers in Sustainable Food Systems, 5*, 671276. DOI: 10.3389/fsufs.2021.671276

Rotz, S., Gravely, E., Mosby, I., Duncan, E., Finnis, E., Horgan, M., LeBlanc, J., Martin, R., Neufeld, H. T., Nixon, A., Pant, L., Shalla, V., & Fraser, E. D. G. (2019). Automated pastures and the digital divide: How agricultural technologies are shaping labour and rural communities. *Journal of Rural Studies, 68*, 112–122. DOI: 10.1016/j.jrurstud.2019.01.023

Ruggeri, F., Lagioia, F., Lippi, M., & Torroni, P. (2022). Detecting and explaining unfairness in consumer contracts through memory networks. *Artificial Intelligence and Law, 30*(1), 59–92. DOI: 10.1007/s10506-021-09288-2

Rulandari, N., & Silalahi, A. D. K. (2025). *Human-AI collaboration for efficiency and employee job satisfaction in public administration: insights from a resource-based perspective. Transforming Government: People*. Process and Policy., DOI: 10.1108/TG-09-2024-0149

Russell, S. J., & Norvig, P. (2003). Artificial Intelligence A Modern Approach; Pearson Education [1] S.J. Russell and P. Norvig, Artificial Intelligence A Modern Approach; Pearson Education. 2003.on. In Pearson.

Sarangi, S., Chatterjee, A., & Balasubramanian, V. (2023). Edge computing for smart agriculture: Architecture, applications, and challenges. *Computers and Electronics in Agriculture, 209*, 107880. DOI: 10.1016/j.compag.2023.107880

Schein, E. H. (2010). *Organizational culture and leadership* (Vol. 2). John Wiley & Sons.

Schut, M., Klerkx, L., Sartas, M., Lamers, D., Mc Campbell, M., Ogbonna, I., Kaushik, P., Atta-Krah, K., & Leeuwis, C. (2016). Innovation platforms: Experiences with their institutional embedding in agricultural research for development. *Experimental Agriculture, 52*(4), 537–561. DOI: 10.1017/S001447971500023X

Schwaeke, J., Peters, A., Kanbach, D. K., Kraus, S., & Jones, P. (2024). The new normal: The status quo of AI adoption in SMEs. *Journal of Small Business Management.*

Scroggins, R. (2014). SDLC and Development Methodologies. *Global Journal of Computer Science and Technology: C Software & Data Engineering, 14*(7). Retrieved from https://computerresearch.org/index.php/computer/article/view/148

Setyadi, M. H. (2024). Melayu Islam Beraja: Identitas nasional Brunei Darussalam. *CARITA: Jurnal Sejarah dan Budaya,* 2(2), 109–118. DOI: 10.35905/carita.v2i2.7406

Shagvaliyeva, S., & Yazdanifard, R. (2014). Impact of Flexible Working Hours on Work-Life Balance. *American Journal of Industrial and Business Management, 4*(1), 20–23. DOI: 10.4236/ajibm.2014.41004

Shaikh, F., Afshan, G., Anwar, R. S., Abbas, Z., & Chana, K. A. (2023). Analyzing the impact of artificial intelligence on employee productivity: The mediating effect of knowledge sharing and well-being. *Asia Pacific Journal of Human Resources, 61*(4), 794–820. DOI: 10.1111/1744-7941.12385

Shamrat, F., Tasnim, Z., Rahman, A., Nobel, N. I., & Hossain, S. A. (2020, January). An effective implementation of web crawling technology to retrieve data from the world wide web (WWW). *International Journal of Scientific & Technology, 9*(1), 1252–1256. http://www.ijstr.org/final-print/jan2020/An-Effective-Implementation-Of-Web-Crawling-Technology-To-Retrieve-Data-From-The-World-Wide-Web-www.pdf

Shamshiri, R. R., Kalantari, F., & Ting, K. C.. (2018). Advances in greenhouse automation and controlled environment agriculture: A transition to plant factories and urban agriculture. *International Journal of Agricultural and Biological Engineering, 11*(1), 1–22. DOI: 10.25165/j.ijabe.20181101.3210

Sheffi, Y. (2024). Technology is not enough: Potential job displacement in an AI-driven future. *Journal of Supply Chain Management. Logistics and Procurement*, *6*(4), 338–351. DOI: 10.69554/FAVX7910

Shrestha, Y. R., Ben-Menahem, S. M., & von Krogh, G. (2019). Organizational decision-making structures in the age of artificial intelligence. *California Management Review*, *61*(4), 66–83. DOI: 10.1177/0008125619862257

Sieber, R., Brandusescu, A., Sangiambut, S., & Adu-Daako, A. (2025). What is civic participation in artificial intelligence? *Environment and Planning. B, Urban Analytics and City Science*, *52*(6), 1388–1406. DOI: 10.1177/23998083241296200

Sifah, E. B., Xia, H., Cobblah, C. N., Xia, Q., Gao, J., & Du, X. (2020). BEMPAS: A Decentralized Employee Performance Assessment System Based on Blockchain for Smart City Governance. *IEEE Access, 8*, 99528-99539. doi: 10.1109/ACCESS.2020.2997650

Sigfrids, A., Leikas, J., Salo-Pöntinen, H., & Koskimies, E. (2023). Human-centricity in AI governance: A systemic approach. *Frontiers in Artificial Intelligence*, *6*, 976887. DOI: 10.3389/frai.2023.976887 PMID: 36872934

Singh, E., & Bakshi, E. (2018). Human Resource Management System(HRMS)- The Effects and Organizational Performance. *International Journal of Advance Research in Science and Engineering*, *7*(3), 137–145. http://www.ijarse.com/images/fullpdf/1521196206_Vedant634ijarse.pdf

Singla, B., Shalender, K., & Singh, N. (Eds.). (2025). Navigating Data Science: Unleashing the Creative Potential of Artificial Intelligence.

Siuly, S., Huang, R., & Daneshmand, M. (2018). Guest editorial: Special issue on "Artificial Intelligence in Health and Medicine". *Health Information Science and Systems*, *6*(1), 2. DOI: 10.1007/s13755-017-0040-y

Šmite, D., Moe, N. B., Klotins, E., & Gonzalez-Huerta, J. (2023). From forced Working-From-Home to voluntary working-from-anywhere: Two revolutions in telework. *Journal of Systems and Software*, *195*, 1–10. DOI: 10.1016/j.jss.2022.111509

Smith, A., & Stirling, A. (2010). The politics of social-ecological resilience and sustainable socio-technical transitions. *Ecology and Society*, *15*(1), 11. DOI: 10.5751/ES-03218-150111

Starke, C., & Lünich, M. (2020). Artificial intelligence for political decision-making in the European Union: Effects on citizens' perceptions of input, throughput, and output legitimacy. *Data & Policy*, *2*, e16. DOI: 10.1017/dap.2020.19

Stiles, J., & Smart, M. (2021). Working at home and elsewhere: Daily work location, telework, and travel among United States knowledge workers. *Transportation, 48*(5), 2461–2491. DOI: 10.1007/s11116-020-10136-6

Stone, M., Aravopoulou, E., Ekinci, Y., Evans, G., Hobbs, M., Labib, A., Laughlin, P., Machtynger, J., & Machtynger, L. (2020). Artificial intelligence (AI) in strategic marketing decision-making: A research agenda. *The Bottom Line (New York, N.Y.), 33*(2), 183–200. DOI: 10.1108/BL-03-2020-0022

Sull, D., Sull, C., & Zweig, B. (2022). Toxic culture is driving the great resignation. *MIT Sloan Management Review.*

Sun, L., & Bunchapattanasakda, C. (2019). Employee Engagement: A Literature Review. *International Journal of Human Resource Studies, 9*(1), 63–80. DOI: 10.5296/ijhrs.v9i1.14167

Sun, T. Q., & Medaglia, R. (2019). Mapping the challenges of Artificial Intelligence in the public sector: Evidence from public healthcare. *Government Information Quarterly, 36*(2), 368–383. DOI: 10.1016/j.giq.2018.09.008

Taherdoost, H. (2021). Data Collection Methods and Tools for Research; A Step-by-Step Guide to Choose Data Collection Technique for Academic and Business Research Projects. *International Journal of Academic Research in Management, 10*(1), 10–38. https://www.researchgate.net/publication/359596426_Data_Collection_Methods_and_Tools_for_Research_A_Step-by-Step_Guide_to_Choose_Data_Collection_Technique_for_Academic_and_Business_Research_Projects

Tambe, P., Cappelli, P., & Yakubovich, V. (2019). Artificial intelligence in human resources management: Challenges and a path forward. *California Management Review, 61*(4), 15–42. DOI: 10.1177/0008125619867910

Tasrin, K., Wahyuadianto, A., Pratiwi, & Masrully. (2021). Evaluation Study of the Implementation of Flexible Working Arrangement in Public Sector Organization during Covid-19 Pandemic. *BISNIS & BIROKRASI: Jurnal Ilmu Administrasi dan Organisasi, 28*(3), 143-157. DOI: 10.20476/jbb.v28i3.1274

Tavakol, M., & Wetzel, A. (2020). Factor Analysis: A means for theory and instrument development in support of construct validity. *International Journal of Medical Education, 11*, 245–247. DOI: 10.5116/ijme.5f96.0f4a

Techbehemoths. (2025). *How SMEs Use Artificial Intelligence in 2024 - Survey Results.* Tech Behemoths. Retrieved July from https://techbehemoths.com/blog/how-smes-use-ai

Telukdarie, A., Dube, T., Munsamy, M., Murulane, K., & Mongwe, R. (2024). Navigating Digital Challenges for SMEs: A Two-Tier Approach to Risks Mitigation and Sustainability. *Sustainability (Basel), 16*(14), 5857. DOI: 10.3390/su16145857

Thompson, B. Y. (2019). The Digital Nomad Lifestyle: (Remote) Work/Leisure Balance, Privilege, and Constructed Community. *International Journal of the Sociology of Leisure*, *2*(1-2), 27–42. DOI: 10.1007/s41978-018-00030-y

Timely. (2018, April 18). *KPIs for measuring employee performance*. Retrieved November 1, 2022 from Timely blog: https://timelyapp.com/blog/kpis-for-measuring-employee-performance

Torelli, R., Balluchi, F., & Furlotti, K. (2020). The materiality assessment and stakeholder engagement: A content analysis of sustainability reports. *Corporate Social Responsibility and Environmental Management*, *27*(2), 470–484. DOI: 10.1002/csr.1813

Treviño, L. K., Hartman, L. P., & Brown, M. (2000). Moral person and moral manager: How executives develop a reputation for ethical leadership. *California Management Review*, *42*(4), 128–142. DOI: 10.2307/41166057

Trigos, F., & Doria, M. (2021, June 22). *The Benefits of Flexible Work in the Post-Covid-19 Era: The Transdisciplinary Flextime Hiring Method (TFHM) considers both employee and company needs*. Retrieved November 5, 2022 from Egade Ideas - Thought Leadership in Action: https://egade.tec.mx/en/egade-ideas/research/benefits-flexible- work-post-covid-19-era

Tripoli, M., & Schmidhuber, J. (2018). *Emerging opportunities for the application of blockchain in the agri-food industry*. FAO and ITC.

Tummalapalli, H. K., Rao, A. N., Kamal, G., Kumari, N., & Kumar, J. R. S. (2024). Exploring AI-Driven Management: Impact on Organizational Performance, Decision Making, Efficiency, and Employee Engagement. *Journal of Management Research and Analysis*. (Dalam proses publikasi).

UCLA. (n.d.). *What does Cronbach's alpha mean? | SPSS FAQ*. Retrieved October 26, 2022 from UCLA Advanced Research Computing Statistical Methods and Data Analytics: https://stats.oarc.ucla.edu/spss/faq/what-does-cronbachs-alpha-mean/

Underwood, J., Wendel, A., McCool, C., & Walsh, D. (2017). The future of autonomous farming. *IEEE Potentials*, *36*(6), 19–24. DOI: 10.1109/MPOT.2017.2704158

United Nations Educational, Scientific and Cultural Organization. (2021). *Recommendation on the ethics of artificial intelligence.* UNESCO. https://unesdoc.un.org/ark:/48223/pf0000380455

United Nations Office on Drugs and Crime. (2018). *International standards on drug use prevention*. UNODC.

United Nations Office on Drugs and Crime. (2022). [UNODC.]. *World Drug Report*, •••, 2022.

United Nations. (2015). *Transforming our world: The 2030 Agenda for Sustainable Development*. https://sdgs.un.org/2030agenda

van der Burg, S., Bogaardt, M. J., & Wolfert, S. (2021). Ethics of smart farming: Current questions and directions for responsible innovation towards the future. *NJAS Wageningen Journal of Life Sciences*, *90-91*, 100289. DOI: 10.1016/j.njas.2019.100289

Vasudevan, I., Nasurudeen, M. M., Kumar, M. S., Charaan, R. D., Kumar, S. A., & Jenefa, L. (2024, November). Hierarchical Model for Email Fraud Detection Using Naïve Bayes and SVM. In *2024 First International Conference for Women in Computing (InCoWoCo)* (pp. 1-6). IEEE. DOI: 10.1109/InCoWoCo64194.2024.10863458

Vatamanu, A. F., & Tofan, M. (2025). Integrating artificial intelligence into public administration: Challenges and vulnerabilities. *Administrative Sciences*, *15*(4), 149. DOI: 10.3390/admsci15040149

Velimirović, D., Velimirović, M., & Stanković, R. (2011, March). Role and importance of key performance indicators measurement. *Serbian Journal of Management, 6*, 63-72. DOI:10.5937/sjm1101063V

Visave, J. (2025). Transparency in AI for emergency management: Building trust and accountability. *AI and Ethics*, *5*(4), 1–14. DOI: 10.1007/s43681-025-00692-x

Vrontis, D., Christofi, M., Pereira, V., Tarba, S., Makrides, A., & Trichina, E. (2023). Artificial intelligence, robotics, advanced technologies and human resource management: A systematic review. *Artificial Intelligence and International HRM*, 172–201.

Vyas, L. (2022). "New normal" at work in a post-COVID world: Work–life balance and labor markets. *Policy and Society*, *41*(1), 155–167. DOI: 10.1093/polsoc/puab011

Vyas, L., & Butakhieo, N. (2021, December 23). The impact of working from home during COVID-19 on work and life domains: An exploratory study on Hong Kong. *Policy Design and Practice*, *4*(1), 59–76. DOI: 10.1080/25741292.2020.1863560

Wang, T., Li, N., & Li, H. (2021). Design and development of human resource management computer system for enterprise employees. *PLoS One*, *16*(12), 1–21. DOI: 10.1371/journal.pone.0261594

Weideman, M., & Hofmeyr, K. (2021). Corrigendum: The influence of flexible work arrangements on employee engagement: An exploratory study. *SA Journal of Human Resource Management, 19*(0), 1–18. DOI: 10.4102/sajhrm.v19i0.1522

Westerman, G., Soule, D. L., & Eswaran, A. (2019). Building digital-ready culture in traditional organizations. *MIT Sloan Management Review, 60*(4).

WHO. (2020, March 13). Clinical management of severe acute respiratory infection (SARI) when COVID-19 disease is suspected. 2.

Wiseman, L., Sanderson, J., Zhang, A., & Jakku, E. (2019). Farmers and their data: An examination of farmers' reluctance to share their data through the lens of the laws impacting smart farming. *NJAS Wageningen Journal of Life Sciences, 90-91*(1), 100301. DOI: 10.1016/j.njas.2019.04.007

Wishart, J. (2022, August 25). *Why are KPIs Important? The Importance of KPIs.* Retrieved November 1, 2022 from Rhythm Systems: https://www.rhythmsystems.com/blog/5-reasons-why-you-need-kpis-infographic

Wolfert, S., Ge, L., Verdouw, C., & Bogaardt, M.-J. (2017). Big Data in Smart Farming – A review. *Agricultural Systems, 153*, 69–80. DOI: 10.1016/j.agsy.2017.01.023

Wolniak, R., & Stecuła, K. (2024). Artificial intelligence in smart cities—applications, barriers, and future directions: a review. *Smart cities, 7*(3), 1346-1389.

Wong, A. (2021, August 10). *Brunei tightens control measures amid new surge of COVID-19 cases.* Retrieved December 21, 2022 from Biz Brunei: https://www.bizbrunei.com/2021/08/brunei-tightens-control-measures-amid-new- surge-of-covid-19-cases/

World Health Organization. (2021). *Ethics and governance of artificial intelligence for health: WHO guidance.* World Health Organization.

World Health Organization. (2022). Strategic *Preparedness, Readiness and Response Plan to End the Global Covid-19 EMeergency in 2022.* Geneva: World Health Organization. Retrieved from https://www.who.int/publications/i/item/WHO-WHE-SPP-2022.1

Wu, Y.-C., Chen, C.-S., & Chan, Y.-J. (2020, March). The outbreak of COVID-19: An overview. *Journal of the Chinese Medical Association, 83*(3), 217–220. DOI: 10.1097/JCMA.0000000000000270

Wu, Y.-C., Liu, Y.-C., Tsao, C., & Huang, R.-Y. (2023, March). Micro expression recognition robot. *IAES International Journal of Robotics and Automation, 12*(1), 20–28.

Xiao, Y., Becerik-Gerber, B., Lucas, G., & Roll, S. (2021, March). Impacts of Working From Home During COVID-19 Pandemic on Physical and Mental Well-Being of Office Workstation Users. *Journal of Occupational and Environmental Medicine*, *63*(3), 181–190. DOI: 10.1097/JOM.0000000000002097

Xu, H., Omitaomu, F., Sabri, S., Li, X., & Song, Y. (2024). Leveraging generative ai for smart city digital twins: A survey on the autonomous generation of data, scenarios, 3d city models, and urban designs. *arXiv e-prints*, arXiv: 2405.19464.

Yahya, R., Jailani, R., Hanapiah, F. A., & Zakaria, N. K. (2024). A scoping review of artificial intelligence-based robot therapy forchildren with disabilities. *Indonesian Journal of Electrical Engineering and Computer Science*, *33*(3), 1855–1865. DOI: 10.11591/ijeecs.v33.i3.pp1855-1865

Yin, Z., Kong, H., Baruch, Y., Decosta, P. L. E., & Yuan, Y. (2024). Interactive effects of AI awareness and change-oriented leadership on employee-AI collaboration: The role of approach and avoidance motivation. *Tourism Management, 105*, 104966. DOI: 10.1016/j.tourman.2024.104966

Yuan, Q., & Chen, T. (2025). Holding AI-based systems accountable in the public sector: A systematic review. *Public Performance & Management Review*, *48*(6), 1–34. DOI: 10.1080/15309576.2025.2469784

Yugendran, V., Jenefa, L., Jayakumar, M., & Sakthivel, M. (2025, March). Ethics of AI Technology Interruption and Discomfort on Employee Turnover. In *2025 International Conference on Data Science, Agents & Artificial Intelligence (ICD-SAAI)* (pp. 1-6). IEEE.

Yukl, G. (2013). *Leadership in organizations* (8th ed.). Pearson.

Yu, P.-H., Susanto, H., Liu, L.-X., Wu, S.-J., & Leu, F.-Y. (2022). The Implementation of Dynamical Shortest Path and Resource Management for Network Slicing in 5G Networks. *In Advances on Broad-Band Wireless Computing, Communication and Applications: Proceedings of the 16th International Conference on Broad-Band Wireless Computing, Communication and Applications (BWCCA-2021)* (pp. 206-215). Springer International Publishing.

Zainal Abiddin, N., Ibrahim, I., & Abdul Aziz, S. A. (2022). A Literature Review of Work From Home Phenomenon During COVID-19 Toward Employees' Performance and Quality of Life in Malaysia and Indonesia. *Frontiers in Psychology, 13*, 1–8. DOI: 10.3389/fpsyg.2022.819860

Zhang, L., & Erturk, E. (2022). Potential lessons from Chinese businesses and platforms for online networking and marketing: An exploratory study. *Social Sciences & Humanities Open*, *6*(1), 100274. DOI: 10.1016/j.ssaho.2022.100274

Zhang, Q., Reid, J. F., & Noguchi, N. (2020). *Agricultural automation: Fundamentals and practices*. CRC Press.

Zhang, Y., Geng, L., Tang, Y., & Zhao, Y. (2022). Development of autonomous agricultural machinery and intelligent equipment: A review. *Computers and Electronics in Agriculture*, *199*, 107128. DOI: 10.1016/j.compag.2022.107128

Zhang, Y., Wang, H., Wang, J., & Cao, Z. (2020). Smart agriculture based on cloud computing and IOT. *Journal of Sensors*, *2020*, 1–10. DOI: 10.1155/2020/2970143

Zhang, Y., Xie, H., Liu, T., & Chen, D. (2021). A review of digital agricultural technologies and their applications. *Intelligent Agriculture*, *1*(1), 18–25. DOI: 10.1016/j.inag.2021.08.002

Zuiderwijk, A., Chen, Y.-C., & Salem, F. (2021). Implications of the use of artificial intelligence in public governance: A systematic literature review and a research agenda. *Government Information Quarterly*, *38*(3), 101577. DOI: 10.1016/j.giq.2021.101577

About the Contributors

Muhammad Anshari is an Associate Professor in Business Information Systems at the Universiti Brunei Darussalam School of Business and Economics (UBDSBE), and currently serves as Director for the Institute of Policy Studies. He has been named on the Stanford University List of Top 2% World Researchers since 2021 for the categories of ICT, Business & Management. Together with colleagues from UBDSBE and IPS, winning Outstanding Paper awards at the Emerald Literati Awards 2023. Patent Impact: His research has also been referenced in two patents, US Patent 10,999,416, 2021, and US Patent 11,489,906, 2022. Following the completion of his PhD at FBEPS UBD, Dr. Anshari worked as a research fellow at National Taiwan University. Before that, he was a research fellow at King Saud University, Saudi Arabia. He has also completed eight research grant projects and three research industry consultancies. His research focuses on Business Information Systems, Knowledge Management Systems, Digital Business, Digital Humanities, and Digital Health, contributing primarily to SDG No. 9 on Industry, Innovation, and Infrastructure.

Patricia Ordóñez de Pablos is a professor in the Department of Business Administration in the Faculty of Business and Economics at The University of Oviedo, Spain. She completed her education in The London School of Economics, UK. Her teaching and research interests focus on the areas of strategic management, knowledge management, organizational learning, intellectual capital and information technologies, with special interest in Asia (Bhutan, China, Myanmar). She is Editor-in-Chief of the International Journal of Learning and Intellectual Capital (IJLIC) and International Journal of Asian Business and Information Management (IJABIM), respectively. She has edited books for IGI Global, Elsevier, Routledge, and Springer. In 2021, 2022 and 2023, she earned placement on Stanford University's "Ranking of the World Scientists: World's Top 2% Scientists" list. Additionally she is listed in

World Top Scientists of Research.com in the Areas of Social Science and Humanities in Spain and Engineering and Technology in Spain.

Mohammad Nabil Almunawar is currently a professor at School of Business and Economics, Universiti of Brunei Darussalam (UBDSBE), Brunei Darussalam. He was the former dean of UBDSBE. He received his bachelor degree in 1983 from Bogor Agricultural University, Indonesia, master Degree (MSc Computer Science) from the Department of Computer Science, University of Western Ontario, London, Canada in 1991 and Ph.D. from the University of New South Wales (School of Computer Science and Engineering, UNSW) in 1998. Dr Almunawar has published more than 250 papers in refereed journals, book chapters and international conferences. He has more than 30 years teaching experiences in the area computer and information systems. His overall research interests include applications of IT in Management, Electronic Business/Commerce, Health Informatics, information security, cloud computing, Big Data and Internet of Things. He is also interested in object-oriented technology, databases and multimedia retrieval.

***

D. Amutha presently is working as Associate Professor of Economics, St.Mary's College (Autonomous), Tuticorin, Tamilnadu. She has over twenty years of experience in teaching and research. Her main research areas are agricultural economics, development economics, socio economic analysis, women studies, rural development, micro credit and micro enterprises. She has guided number of projects in the area of Economics. She has published more than 250 research papers in refereed national and international journals. Nine of her papers make SSRN (Social Science Research Network) top ten list. She has received ICSSR sponsored research project. Moreover, she has received 'Best Teacher Award' for 2015 from the GRABS Educational Charitable Trust, Chennai, 'Best Social Scientist Award' from Indian Academic Researchers Association at Bharathidasan University, Tiruchirappalli on 21st May 2016, 'Dr. APJ Abdul Kalam Award for Teaching Excellence – 2016' from Marina Labs Research and Development, Chennai, on 22nd October 2016 and received Bright Educator Award 2017 in Economics from International Institute of Organized Research (I2OR), India and received International Academic Excellence Award 2018 from International Association of Research and Development Organisation (IARDO) in association with Gurukul Institute of Engineering &Technology, Kota (India), at The International Centre Goa, Panjim, Goa (India) on 28th October 2018 and received MTC Global Award for Distinguished Teacher Award in Economics 2019 at the 9th World Edu Summit, on 7th Sep 2019, Bangalore. She is serving as resource person for various institutions and serving as Executive Editor, Editor in Chief, International Editorial Board Member and reviewer of 18 International and National Research Journals. She is also Published 18 books. She is a Life Member of a number of journals. She has been acting as a speaker in All India Radio. She also served as NSS Programme Officer over 5 years.

Saad Haj Bakry Full Professor of Information Networks at King Saud University since 1989 PhD from Aston University, England, UK, 1980 CEng and FIET, UK Consultant to King Abdulaziz Establishment for the Gifted (Mawhiba) Organization, Member of a Technical Committee at the Saudi Arabia Standard Organization (SASO), Saudi Arabia, Past Consultant to: Ministry of Higher Education; Communication and Information Technology Commission; King Abdulaziz City for Science and Technology; Advanced Electronic Company and other organizations, Saudi Arabia

George F is a student in the Department of Management Studies at St. Joseph's College of Engineering, Sriperumbudur, Chennai. He is known for his dedication to academic excellence and active participation in college activities. With a keen interest in management and leadership, he strives to apply theoretical knowledge to practical situations. Fr. George demonstrates strong communication and teamwork skills, contributing positively to group projects and discussions. His commitment to learning and holistic development reflects his passion for personal and professional growth.

Leena Jenefa, working as an Associate Professor in Hindustan Institute of Technology and Science, Chennai India, Prior that she worked in Vel Tech Rangarajan Dr Sagunthala R&D Institute of Science and Technology, Avadi, Chennai. She is having 24 years of experience in the teaching field. Prior to joining to Vel Tech -Chennai, she worked in Tecnia Institute of Advanced Studies Delhi, DMI- St. Eugene University-Zambia, Linton University affiliated to University of East London-Malaysia

Jayakumar M. working as a Assistant Professor in Vel Tech Rangarajan Dr. Sagunthala R&D Institute of Science and Technology - (India).Having 15 years of experience in teaching and in Administrative experiences. Publications

Zokir Mamadiyarov is a professor working in the Department of Finance and Tourism at Termez University of Economics and Service, Termez, Uzbekistan.

Sakshi Mann is an Assistant Professor of Human Resource Management at Indira Institute of Management, Pune. With a Ph.D. in HR and over 11 years of combined industry and academic experience, she brings a practical edge to her teaching. Her expertise spans Organizational Behavior, Recruitment & Selection, Employee Engagement, and Leadership. Having managed HR operations across various organizations, she seamlessly integrates real-world insights into academia. Passionate about research, she explores contemporary HR challenges to contribute valuable insights to the field. Committed to bridging academia and industry, Dr. Mann fosters critical thinking and practical application, equipping students for the evolving HR landscape.

Muafi, S.E., M.Si., is a Professor at the Faculty of Business and Economics, Universitas Islam Indonesia (UII). His expertise lies in Strategic Human Resource Management, dan Strategic Organization,. Actively engaged in research and academic publications, He has authored numerous works on service performance and the implementation of a circular economy for business sustainability

Sofyan Ashari Nur is a Lecturer and researcher at the Management Study Program of Universitas Tidar, Magelang. Born on August 21, 1994, in Magelang, he completed his undergraduate studies in 2017 and earned his master's degree in 2019 at Universitas Islam Indonesia, Yogyakarta. As an educator and researcher, his academic interests center on strategic management, marketing strategies, and human resource development strategies, particularly within the context of business and public organizations.

Ananya Pandey is a Research Scholar in School of Law at Christ University, Bangalore. She has her research interests in the field of Constitutional Law, Environment Law, Human Rights, Food Security, Intellectual Property Law and Jurisprudence.

Ravikumar R. Natarajan is an experienced academician with over 12+ years of teaching and research expertise across institutions in India, the UAE, and the Maldives. He currently serves as an Assistant Professor at Marwadi University, Rajkot, specializing in Machine Learning, Recommender Systems, and AI-driven applications in healthcare and security. He holds a Ph.D. in Machine Learning and Recommender Systems from Amity University, Jaipur, a Master of Engineering in CSE from VMRF University, Salem, and a Bachelor of Engineering in CSE from Anna University. He also has a MiniMBA from the Swiss eLearning Institute. Dr. Ravikumar has authored more than 8+ multiple SCIE/Scopus-indexed journal articles, 25+ IEEE/Springer conference papers, and co-authored a book on Artificial Intelligence. He has also published 9 patents and contributed 10+ book chapters in emerging domains such as Federated Learning, Blockchain, and Digital Twins for IGI Global, Wiley and Springer publisher. He actively mentors students through initiatives like the Research Activities Club (RAC) and Student Research Internship Training (SRIT), promoting innovation and research culture.

Yussi Ramawati is a lecturer with a research focus on marketing management. She has expertise in various aspects of marketing strategies, consumer behavior, and digital marketing. Throughout her academic career, she has been actively involved in research, publishing studies related to market dynamics, brand management, and customer engagement. Her contributions aim to bridge theoretical insights with practical applications, supporting businesses in adapting to evolving market trends. In addition to her research, she is dedicated to teaching and mentoring students in the field of marketing, equipping them with analytical and strategic skills essential for success in the competitive business landscape.

Yoga Religia is a lecturer and researcher specializing in marketing management, marketing strategy, and digital marketing. His research focuses on consumer behavior, digital transformation in marketing, and the adoption of technology in small and medium enterprises (SMEs). He has published various studies exploring the impact of digital marketing strategies, e-commerce adoption, and AI-driven personalization on business performance. In addition to his research contributions, he is actively involved in teaching and mentoring students, equipping them with critical analytical skills and strategic insights to navigate the evolving marketing landscape. His work bridges academic research with practical business applications, helping SMEs leverage technology for sustainable growth.

Aarthi S is a dedicated Assistant Professor in Computer Science with over six years of teaching experience. She is currently pursuing her Ph.D. at Marwadi University, Gujarat, and holds an M.Phil. and MCA from Bharathiar University, Tamil Nadu. Throughout her academic career, Aarthi has specialized in programming languages such as C++, Java, and C, and contributed to research in recommender systems and AI-related data privacy. She has published journal articles, contributed to book chapters, and actively participated in technical workshops. Known for her student mentorship and engagement in academic events, Aarthi remains committed to fostering innovation and excellence in computer science education.

Heru Susanto is a researcher and academic with extensive experience in the fields of information systems, cybersecurity, and mobile health technologies. He is currently affiliated with KAKS-BRIN and UTB-SB, also THU, where he focuses on the development of mobile physiological sensor systems, cloud computing for healthcare, and data analytics for long-term patient care. His research interests also include Internet of Things (IoT) in health applications, big data management, and digital transformation in modern management. Dr. Susanto has published numerous scientific papers and actively participates in international conferences as a speaker and reviewer.

Index

A

C

D

E

F

H

I

K

www.ingramcontent.com/pod-product-compliance
Lightning Source LLC
LaVergne TN
LVHW080905300926
849162LV00003B/556
* 9 7 9 8 3 3 7 3 8 6 0 7 2 *